Praise for *Globalization and Self-Regulation*

"An unusually valuable contribution to business decision-making and responses to the powerful impacts of business on the larger society. This book presents the comprehensive work on the foremost pioneer in developing corporate codes of conduct."

—Murray Weidenbaum, Founder and Honorary Chairman,
Murray Weidenbaum Center on the Economy, Government,
and Public Policy, Washington University in St. Louis

"This seminal volume represents an authoritative contribution to the literature on corporate codes. It addresses corporate codes at various levels (company, industry, universal) and offers a rich source of insights on corporate codes of conduct for both academics and practitioners. I strongly recommend this book to anyone with an interest in the topic."

—Adam Lindgreen, Professor, Cardiff Business School,
UK, and co-section editor of the *Journal of Business Ethics'*
section on corporate social responsibility

"*Globalization and Self-Regulation* deals with a critically important topic in an intelligent, comprehensive and accessible manner. Few companies will escape pressures for self-regulation, for participation in voluntary codes of conduct, whether at the company, industry, or more general level. Essential reading for both practitioners who need to deal with self-regulation and academics who study the phenomenon."

—Stephen J. Kobrin, William Wurster Professor of Multinational
Management, The Wharton School, University of Pennsylvania

"This book is an excellent collection of field-based case studies to show the effectiveness and failures of voluntary codes of conduct in global business. It demonstrates that multinational companies should go beyond their—often opportunistic and arbitrary—CSR initiatives and live up to their duties of serving the common good."

—Laszlo Zsolnai, Professor and Director, Business Ethics Center,
Corvinus University of Budapest, and Chairman, Business Ethics
Faculty Group, CEMS–Global Alliance for Management Education

"This volume makes an important contribution to the research on corporate codes of conduct. Among the growing body of literature it stands out because of the contributors' enormous field experience, which covers a whole range of different types of corporate self-regulation. This book is required reading for business people, activists, and academics interested in what corporations can contribute to global governance."

—Klaus Dieter Wolf, Professor of International Relations,
Darmstadt University of Technology, and Deputy Director of
Peace Research Institute Frankfurt (PRIF)

Globalization and Self-Regulation

The Crucial Role That Corporate Codes of Conduct Play in Global Business

Edited by
S. Prakash Sethi

palgrave
macmillan

GLOBALIZATION AND SELF-REGULATION
Copyright © S. Prakash Sethi, 2011.

First published in 2011 by
PALGRAVE MACMILLAN®
in the United States—a division of St. Martin's Press LLC,
175 Fifth Avenue, New York, NY 10010.

Where this book is distributed in the UK, Europe and the rest of the world,
this is by Palgrave Macmillan, a division of Macmillan Publishers Limited,
registered in England, company number 785998, of Houndmills,
Basingstoke, Hampshire RG21 6XS.

Palgrave Macmillan is the global academic imprint of the above companies
and has companies and representatives throughout the world.

Palgrave® and Macmillan® are registered trademarks in the United States,
the United Kingdom, Europe and other countries.

ISBN: 978–0–230–61155–9

Library of Congress Cataloging-in-Publication Data
    Globalization and self-regulation : the crucial role that corporate codes
of conduct play in global business / edited by S. Prakash Sethi.
        p. cm.
    ISBN 978–0–230–61155–9
    1. Business ethics. 2. Corporate governance. 3. Industrial
management—Moral and ethical aspects. 4. Social responsibility of
business. I. Sethi, S. Prakash.

HF5387.G587 2011
174'.4—dc22   2010050075

A catalogue record of the book is available from the British Library.

Design by Newgen Imaging Systems (P) Ltd., Chennai, India.

First edition: July 2011

10 9 8 7 6 5 4 3 2 1

Printed in the United States of America.

To
those "haves" and "have-nots" among us
who still have hope
that when people of reason and conscience get together,
they will plan the survival and not the extinction of the
human race and of humanity,
this book is affectionately dedicated

Contents

Exhibits and Tables

Exhibits

Tables

Preface

In one sense, this book has been in the making for almost ten years. While the subject of voluntary codes of conduct has developed a large body of research and academic scholarship, this literature has largely focused on constructing theoretical frameworks and analyzing their relevance and effectiveness under various political and economic environments. When it came to field testing, research efforts have been particularly lagging because companies and industries have been extremely reluctant both to create such information and share it with researchers. Where possible, researchers have been limited to the use of case studies generated either under the close supervision of the companies involved or through secondary data, which lacked details as to the internal workings of the corporate persona.

The principal reason for this reluctance lies in the very nature of issues that are now the raison d'être for the need of voluntary codes of conduct. To wit, in the past, corporate social responsibility was mostly associated with corporate philanthropy and corporate citizenship wherein companies provided extra financial resources, management acumen, and leadership to the communities where their headquarters were located and where they had primary operating facilities.

The advent of globalization has radically altered this paradigm, where traditional notions of corporate social responsibility play a marginal role at best. Instead, companies are expected to account for the adverse consequences of their core business activities, that is, negative externalities that are inextricably related to the way a company or an industry conducts its business. Under these circumstances, self-disclosure is seen as contrary to the company's or industry's best interests, and even worse, provides otherwise confidential information to their adversaries and thus invites further pressure, increased costs, and regulatory oversight.

At the same time, national governments—from both the industrially advanced countries and the emerging economies—have been unable or unwilling to extend their oversight function for fear of losing badly needed foreign capital, technological resources, and management competence. Therefore, the only viable option for the time being has been for all parties to work around the notion of voluntary codes whose scope and effectiveness vary widely based on the resources and leverage that different parties bring to the code-creation and implementation process.

A unique strength of this book lies in the fact that all the contributors have had considerable field experience in every facet of individual company, industry, and multisector codes of conduct. They were able to bring their personal insights in field operations, internal company management processes, issues of corporate culture, and importance of corporate governance, to name a few.

The case studies included in this volume cover individual company codes, industry codes where governance is internally controlled, and those where civil society organizations have played major roles in the governance, accountability, and transparency of company/industry operations. Finally, we provide an in-depth study and analysis of one of the more popular universal codes of conduct, the UN Global Compact, and one of the most controversial universal codes, the Kimberley Process Certification System, commonly known as the code that deals with "conflict" or "blood" diamonds.

We also acknowledge the superb work of Ms. Olinda Anderson of the Sethi International Center for Corporate Accountability, Inc., in tackling the difficult task of preparing the manuscript for publication. One cannot overestimate, but admire, the complexity of dealing with the sensitivity and writing style of different authors, the particular love they develop for their own writing, and the extreme reluctance they display when some of their work is deleted in the cause of efficient writing.

New York, March 31, 2011

I

Current State of Voluntary Codes of Conduct

Self-Regulation through Voluntary Codes of Conduct

S. Prakash Sethi

The current wave of globalization has brought about a radical transformation in geopolitical arrangements. It has shifted the locus of economic power and bargaining leverage between private economic institutions, national governments, and regulatory authorities. National governments in developing countries have had to compete among themselves to attract and maintain MNC investments. They have been forced to make concessions to the MNCs in terms of taxes and other "giveaways," and thereby limit their ability to fashion domestic policies with better focus on national interest (Johnston and Yufan, 1995; Sethi, 2002). At the same time, governments of industrially advanced countries have been reluctant to exert political pressure because of domestic strategic and economic interests, and from a reluctance to interfere in the internal affairs of other sovereign nations. Nor have international organizations such as the United Nations and multilateral and regional entities organizations such as the World Bank, International Monetary Fund, and Asian Development Bank shown a willingness to cooperate and create effective and enforceable oversight mechanisms.

In the midst of all this stands the institution of the multinational corporation (MNC), which has become an engine of change through its access to capital, technology, organizational skills, and control of markets through brand recognition and dominant market share. In their current form and scope of activities, MNCs can and do exert tremendous influence by creating a new equilibrium in economic power and political leverage. Unfortunately, they have been unwilling to react to these situations in a proactive manner that would provide a balanced arrangement between private economic interest and societal needs (Sethi, 2003a).

Voluntary Codes of Conduct

Nature abhors a vacuum, and the current situation is no exception. A lack of effective legal responses from the national governments and other international, regional, and multilateral institutions to restrain MNC conduct considered socially undesirable has given rise to other organizations, mostly nongovernmental civil society organizations (NGOs), to challenge MNC hegemony in the international economic and sociopolitical arena. These NGOs have been quite effective in pressuring MNCs to be accountable for their business activities and their negative side effects in such areas as environmental protection, fair treatment of workers, human rights abuses, and bribery and corruption, to name a few. Even more important, an increasing number of civil society organizations have acquired enough financial and technological expertise to confront MNCs on equal terms in various legal and regulatory forums as to the MNCs' compliance with prevailing laws and regulations. Furthermore, where appropriate, they have also formed alliances—both among themselves and also with national governments—to seek greater accountability from MNCs for their conduct and modus operandi with regard to their core business activities.

A recognition of increasingly hostile sociopolitical environments on the part of individual MNCs and industry groups has led these organizations to take action in the form of voluntary codes of conduct that would outline corporate and industry responses to societal concerns. The primary focus of these codes of conduct is to: (a) assuage public concerns and build further trust in MNC assertions; and (b) take actions that would ameliorate these actions without unduly restricting corporate managements in the conduct of their business or imposing onerous regulatory oversight and heavy financial burdens.

Companies and industry groups have always had codes of conduct that are intended to provide a framework that defines a company's relationship with its employees, suppliers, and other stakeholders directly related to their business and financial operations. Industry-wide codes are intended to allow member companies to coordinate their activities in the public policy and regulatory arenas to protect the member companies' vital interests. The most common form of these initiatives are to be found in (a) companies' codes of ethics, and (b) industry trade associations (Paton, 2000; Howard, Nash and Bhrenfeld, 1999; Tapper, 1997; Sethi, 2003b; Sethi, 1979).

In a similar vein, a new class of voluntary codes of conduct has also emerged. These codes primarily focus on issues that cross both industry-specific concerns and national and regional boundaries. Broadly defined as universal codes of conduct, they are invariably initiated by a combination of stakeholders that may include national, regional, and international bodies; civil society organizations; and, private-sector institutions (Sethi and Schepers, 2011).

The economic case for voluntary cooperation among business enterprises is clear and compelling. Business organizations develop voluntary arrangements to standardize technical and quality standards for products, contracts, and other arrangements that create economies of scale and reduce transaction costs (Sethi, 2006). Companies may also cooperate among themselves to advance their economic interests in the political arena (Harris and Carmen, 1983; Wolf

1979; Clark, 1998). A third dimension of the benefit of industry coalitions is to protect companies from paying the cost of negative externalities (Murty and Russll, 2005; Afraro and Rodriguez-Clare, 2004; Herve, 1990; Dybvig and Spatt, 1983). Examples of such externalities may be air pollution, untreated wastewater, et cetera. Individual companies and industries mobilize their combined efforts to minimize their cost burden for such externalities by pushing them onto the community.

Voluntary Codes of Conduct in the Sociopolitical Arena

The business case or the economic justification for the corporate social responsibility (CSR) principles or codes of conduct is infinitely more complex than those of the conventional business groups. In direct contrast to conventional principles or codes, CSR-related codes of conduct call for companies and industry groups to voluntarily assume some of the costs associated with the industry's negative externalities. The notion of voluntariness, however, creates a number of philosophical, operational, and accountability problems. Consequently, voluntary codes of conduct in the sociopolitical arena have a different rationale that includes both economic and noneconomic considerations, and raises difficult issues toward implementation.

a. Many companies are philosophically opposed to creating voluntary codes, which they view as giving in to their critics.

b. When it comes to an entire industry, there is the inherent difficulty of finding common ground among member companies that otherwise compete vigorously against each other.

c. Another set of difficulties emanates from individual companies' operational constraints, financial concerns, and, above all, corporate culture and management orientation toward responding to social and environmental challenges (Sethi, 2005; Hermann, 2004; Sethi, 1994). For example, when individual company codes significantly diverge from the overall industry position, the company risks alienating the rest of the industry and thus creating a hostile environment for itself in other aspects of industry activities where it must seek the cooperation of other industry members.

d. The long-term benefits of industry-wide cooperative effort, nevertheless, carry short-term costs that must be compensated for via improved productivity. This takes time and requires structural and organizational changes that are not always easy to accomplish.

e. The prevailing nature of competitive markets, shareholder expectations, incentives of the financial middlemen, and management reward system (i.e., agency costs) overwhelmingly emphasize the short-term character of earnings (Eisenhardt, 1989; Cho, 1992; Marrewijk, 2003). There is a strong incentive to underestimate long-term risks since recognition of these risks would lower the expected earnings of a company when compared with competitors that choose to ignore them.

f. When it comes to universal codes of conduct, the challenges of code creation, governance structure, performance monitoring, and accountability become almost insurmountable and raise potentially serious issues as to their viability. The major drive for the creation and implementation of universal codes invariably arises from sources that are outside the control of the corporate sector. And yet it is the corporate sector that is expected to bear the burden of code compliance.

Essential Characteristics of Corporate Social Responsibility–Related Codes of Conduct

A voluntary code of conduct consists of a set of activities that the sponsoring organization (SO) commits to undertake. The effectiveness of an SO's responses to society's concerns depends on a number of factors: the sociopolitical environment, public awareness, the emotional intensity generated by the issue, the dynamics of competition and industry structure in which the company operates, and the institutional character, corporate resources, and management style of a particular corporation.

To be effective, such a code must have a large measure of acceptability from all relevant stakeholders and must fit within the competitive realities of the marketplace. It must be dynamic and flexible to respond to evolving conditions. A specific action can be socially responsible only if it takes account of time, environment, and the interests of the parties involved. The same activity may be considered socially responsible at one time, under one set of circumstances, and in one culture. It may be considered socially irresponsible when any of these factors change.

A voluntary code of conduct is in the nature of a "private law" or a "promise voluntarily made," whereby an institution makes a public commitment to certain standards of conduct. The nature of voluntariness and, by implication, the flexibility afforded to companies depends on the basic premise that the sponsoring organizations and their critics share a common interest in improving the underlying conditions of the affected groups and regions, and a common understanding that it is in the interest of all parties to resolve the underlying issues within the realistic constraints of the available financial resources and competitive conditions (Sethi, 2003b; Melrose, 2004).

The private-law character of voluntary codes of conduct gives the sponsoring organization a large measure of discretionary action. It also imposes a heavy burden on the organization to create independent systems of performance evaluation, monitoring and verification, and public disclosure. This is a proactive stance, and perhaps the best of all possible worlds. It provides scope for experimentation and building consensus, and facilitates the enactment of public law. The success of this system, however, depends on the industry's ability to create and sustain a high level of public credibility. The private-law character of the code does not reduce the obligations of the companies or industry groups, it increases their burden to ensure that its skeptical critics and the public at large believe in the industry's responses and performance claims.

Companies, industry groups, and cross-industry (universal) alliances, therefore, must not only create a set of laws—a code of conduct—they must also provide a system by which their performance will be measured, evaluated, and verified. The private-law character of the code does not reduce the obligations of the companies or industries. It increases their burden to ensure that skeptical critics and the public at large are persuaded that the sponsoring organizations' performance standards are adequate and that their claims of performance are true. The organization will be expected to implement a system of policing, monitoring, and judging its performance while ensuring that the system is completely independent of the company—both in perception and in reality.

From the public's perspective, voluntary codes also serve an important purpose. They avoid the need of further governmental regulation with the prospect of imposing onerous regulatory conditions. They also allow the moderate elements among the affected groups to seek reasonable solutions to the issues involved (O'Rourke, 2003).

Individual Company-Based Voluntary Code of Conduct

A company-based code of conduct is the most likely initial corporate response to social pressures, especially when the issues involved emanate directly from the company's core business operations. A company-based code provides its sponsor considerable flexibility in defining the parameter of the social issue in contention—especially in its earlier stages of public awareness. It also allows the company to offer solutions that build on its strengths. There are also no problems of free riders and adverse selecton. Therefore, a meaningful company-sponsored code, when thoughtfully implemented and providing measurable results, can return enormous dividends in terms of first mover's advantage, enhancement in corporate reputation, and public trust.

However, the success of such an effort creates tensions with other industry members that are pressured by external stakeholders to follow the first company's example. Additionally, when there is not enough external pressure on other industry members, the company is likely to face pressure from its own shareholders for fear of lower profits, and from managers of operating units chafing under increased security and higher costs (Sethi, Veral, Shapiro, and Emelianova, 2011; Sethi, Lowry, Veral, Shapiro, and Emelianova, 2011). Therefore, it takes a determined top management that can resist short-term considerations in favor of long-term sustainability of the enterprise, lower risk, enhanced corporate reputation, and a more trusting regulatory environment. In the following chapters, we present two case studies—Mattel, Inc., and Freeport-McMoRan Copper & Gold, Inc.—that amplify both the strengths and weaknesses of individual corporate codes of conduct and the pressures they face from a company's external and internal stakeholders.

Industry-Based Voluntary Codes of Conduct

Industry-based voluntary codes of conduct dealing with societal issues serve an important business and social purpose. From the business viewpoint, such a code provides industry members with a mechanism to develop solutions that are focused, take cognizance of the industry's special needs and public concerns, and are economically efficient. They engender public trust through the "reputation effect" while avoiding being tainted by the actions of other companies (Sethi, 2003; Kapstein, 2001).

Voluntary business groupings, however, must contend with two problems, such as free riders and adverse selection, the magnitude and severity of which would adversely affect their collective operation. The free-rider problem accrues from the situation where some type of pressure and coercion is necessary to ensure that member organizations, which benefit from the collective effort, also share the cost of maintaining such effort in proportion to the benefits derived from them (Andreoni and McGuire, 1993; Conlon and Pecorino, 2004). Adverse selection occurs where companies joining the group are likely to exploit the benefits accruing from their participation in the group without any consideration of the harm that their actions might cause other members of the group (Inderst, 2005; Fabel and Lehmann, 2000; Wilson, 1980). The success and the longevity of an industry-based group depends on its ability to find a common ground wherein most members benefit in joining and adhering to the goals of the group and the methods employed in implementing them. Finally, industry-based groups also face major challenges in transforming this need to "do something" into actionable strategies. The difficulties faced by these groups arise from conflicts among member companies within the industry and a lack of trust by external constituencies in the industry's external sociopolitical environment.

Universal Codes of Corporate Social Responsibility

Universal codes of corporate conduct confront the same set of problems as industry-wide codes of conduct. However, in this instance, universal codes have fewer advantages of common ground, which prevail in the case of industry-wide codes of conduct. For universal codes, the issues of free riders and adverse selection are further amplified since in their desire to entice and encompass the largest number of corporate participants, code sponsors invariably yield ground in terms of meaningful adherence to the code's principles. Unfortunately, this relaxation or weakening of compliance standards—when accompanied with a relative lack of transparency—diminishes the reputational value of group membership and takes away what little incentive there remains to comply beyond empty rhetoric (Sethi and Schepers, 2011).

Growth in the Use of Voluntary Codes of Conduct

The previous decade has been a period of extraordinary growth in the number of companies and industries that have adopted some form of voluntary code of conduct. There has also been sharp growth in the number of universal codes initiated by collaborative partnerships among various stakeholders, notably NGOs; national, regional, and international bodies' quasi-governmental organizations; and private-sector institutions.

One indication of this growth can be found in a recent study of corporate social responsibility–sustainability reports (CSR-S).[1] This study included CSR-S reports by all 514 companies that had published such reports from a worldwide database of more than 1,300 corporations.

Of the 514 companies, 452 (88 percent) indicated that they had created a company-based code of conduct. Among these companies, 177 (39 percent) indicated that in addition to their corporate code of conduct, they had also participated in at least one industry-wide code of conduct, while another 144 companies (32 percent) also acknowledged participating in a universal code of conduct.

A review of the titles of individual corporate codes of conduct suggests some interesting insights as to the underlying purpose envisaged by the corporations creating these codes (table 1.1). It is interesting to note that a very small number of companies used terms such as "corporate social responsibility" or "sustainability" in their code titles.

Corporations also specified participating in a number of industry-wide codes of conduct. A fairly large number of companies acknowledged participating in more than one industry code. Table 1.2 describes some of the major industry-wide codes of conduct and the number of companies participating in them. To an extent, the large number of code participants reflected the size of an industry or the diverse nature of industry.

Among the universal codes of conduct, the study identified six universal codes with the largest number of corporate signatories (table 1.3). The other universal codes had fewer than eight signatories each.

Unfortunately, this large number of participants is not indicative of improved corporate adherence either to higher standards of corporate social responsibility or even compliance with the company's or industry's own principles and standards espoused in their codes of conduct. The reason for this lack of progress is twofold.

1. There are structural and market-based considerations that create negative incentives for companies and industry groups to go beyond superficial claims of code compliance.
2. Company and industry codes, and even universal codes, have built-in conditions that allow participants tremendous leeway to minimize meaningful compliance.

As things currently stand, most codes of conduct promise a great deal while delivering very little. This situation is untenable for the future survival of the private-sector institutions whose existence depends on a large reservoir of

Table 1.1   Variation in the Titles of Individual Corporate Codes of Conduct

Title Designation	Number of Companies
General code of conduct	78
Mentions "ethics" in the title	36
Mentions "principles" in the title	18
Mentions "best practices" in the title	11
All others	34
	177

Table 1.2   Industry-Wide Codes of Conduct (Select Industry Groups)

Code Title	Number of Signatory Companies
Forest Stewardship Council and the Criteria Forest Management	54
Equator Principles	31
Extractive Industry Transparency Initiative (EITI)	23
UN Principles for Responsible Investment (PRI)	23
Voluntary Principles on Security and Human Rights	19
Electronics Industry Code of Conduct (EICC)	17
United Nations Environmental Programme Financial Institutions	14
ICMM Sustainable Development Framework	11
Fair Labor Association	10
Marine Stewardship Council	8
Social Accountability International Association	7
Chemical Industry Association	5
IFAC Code of Ethics for Professional Accountants	4
Fair Trade Labeling Organization	4
PhRMA Guiding Principles on Direct Consumer Advertising	4

Table 1.3   Corporate Participation in Universal Codes of Conduct

Code Name	Number of Participating Companies
United Nations Global Compact	211
Carbon Disclosure Project	168
UN Declaration of Human Rights	115
International Labor Organization	113
World Business Council for Sustainable Development	37
Ethical Trading Initiative	8

public trust in capitalism and the working of competitive markets to create economic growth and social well-being in an environment that enhances quality of life and fair distribution of the benefits of economic growth among all groups. In this context, it serves no useful purpose to argue that government-directed economic activities are necessarily less effective and prone to greater inequalities. In the final analysis, people's judgment as to who are the best custodians of society's well-being will depend not on abstract claims of rational choice, but on what people at large will come believe based on their own experiences.

Current Approaches in CSR-Related Industry-Wide and Universal Codes of Conduct

Both industry-based and universal codes of conduct fall along a spectrum where one end of the spectrum is composed of codes, which are broad principles or statements of good intent. They lack specificity in terms of performance expectations and thus require a low level of commitment on the part of the member companies. The other end of the spectrum is similarly devoid of meaningful and measurable performance reporting in code implementation.

The performance reporting is seldom, if ever, supported by independent external verification of information and integrity assurance.

An overwhelmingly large number of current industry-based CSR-related codes fall in or lean heavily toward the category of broad principles. Industry groups feel that to be successful, an industry-wide or group-based approach must include the largest possible number of companies in the collective effort. The consensus approach is intended to create solutions that are amenable to most members and thus facilitate industry-wide effort in bringing about desired changes.

It may seem counterintuitive, but this approach yields exactly the opposite result from the one publicly claimed by the code's sponsors. Industry-wide CSR-related codes that depend on voluntary compliance and rarely incorporate enforcement measures greatly suffer from the problems of free riders and adverse selection. This problem is more acute in the case of universal codes of conduct.

The need to keep the largest number of companies in the group pushes performance standards to the lowest common denominator. This situation admirably suits the poorly performing and recalcitrant companies, that is, adverse selection, that stand to gain from enhanced public approval—at no cost to themselves—as a result of the time and resources expended by the best-performing companies. At the same time, the best-performing companies suffer from the taint caused by the actions of recalcitrant companies. This situation creates disincentives for the companies that are willing to offer greater compliance to the code's broader principles because they cannot get improved believability from the public. Another perverse outcome of this approach is that it may lead the code effort to be captured by the companies with the least amount of commitment to code compliance. This situation is akin to the capture theory of regulation, where the regulators are co-opted by the regulated and thus lose their legitimacy as regulators (Thompson, 2003).

Another problem confronting industry-wide and universal codes of conduct is that of inward-looking and insular governance structure. To an extent, this problem also confronts individual company codes. However, in the case of individual companies, the burden of proof as to meaningful and substantive compliance rests solely with the company. Therefore, an independent governance structure can provide an avenue for integrity assurance, but would not reduce corporate responsibility for performance accountability.

In the following chapters, we provide a variety of case studies dealing with industry-wide and universal codes of conduct that suggest the importance of a governance structure that is not controlled by the industry members or signatories of the universal code. An insular and self-selecting governance structure has strong incentives to protect the industry or the groups' self-interest and thereby minimize transparency and external accountability. And yet these are the very conditions that would ensure and enhance the credibility and legitimacy of the group-based codes to their external constituencies.

The proof of this logic is obvious. Despite years of consultation and negotiation, this author knows of no single industry group or multi-industry, multisectoral institutions that have developed or implemented a meaningful code that includes the essential elements of specificity of goals, outcome-oriented performance measures, independent external monitoring for compliance verification, and full transparency in public disclosure. In the following chapters, we present detailed case studies of both effective and ineffective code initiatives, where external credibility and stakeholder trust have been strongly influenced by the governance structure of a particular code of conduct and the manner in which it has monitored code performance by the member companies and industry groups.

Preconditions for Creating and Implementing a Successful Industry-Wide or Multi-Industry Universal Voluntary Code of Conduct

The aforementioned discussion is not intended to suggest that industry-wide or universal codes of conduct are unlikely to be viable under any set of circumstances. Analyses by the contributing authors in this book of a number of currently operating industry-based and universal codes point to a set of necessary preconditions that must be met if industry-based codes are to succeed in narrowing the performance-expectations gap between the industry and large segments of society. Furthermore, these standards can serve as guideposts to determine the potential weaknesses in a company, industry-wide, or universal code of conduct and to take corrective action before putting it in practice.

1. The code must be *substantive* in addressing broad areas of public concern pertaining to industry's conduct. It must cover issues that are of concern to the community and not merely those preferred by the industry. The broad principles must be amplified into objective, quantifiable, and outcome-oriented standards. These would allow for uniformity in performance evaluation and compliance assurance.
2. Code principles or standards must be *specific* in addressing issues embodied in those principles.
3. Code performance standards must be *realistic* in the context of the industry's financial strength and competitive environment. The industry should not make exaggerated promises or claim implausible achievements.
4. Member companies must create an effective *internal implementation system* to ensure effective code compliance.
5. Code compliance must be an integral part of a *management performance evaluation and reward system*. For example, at the individual company level, code compliance must be integrated into the firm's normal decision-making structure and systems. It should also have the oversight for compliance assurance at the level of corporate general counsel, and preferably with a reporting obligation to a committee of the board of directors, such as an audit committee or public policy committee. In the final analysis, the top management of the company must be held accountable for ensuring the company's compliance with code standards.
6. The industry or universal group must create an *independent governance structure* that is not controlled by the executives of the member companies or dominated by private-sector organizations to the exclusion of other important stakeholders whose lives and livelihoods are affected by the conduct of

the member companies and industry groups. An effective governance structure should

a. allow for a balanced representation of various industry segments and thus minimize the prospect of any industry segment to dominate decision-making in code implementation;

b. have independent, external input to ensure that performance monitoring is not controlled by the same group of people whose performance is being monitored at the company level. The external input in the governance structure does not have to be from the industry's critics, but from independent experts who have the respect and confidence of all parties involved; and

c. have a fee structure to defray the cost of code implementation that allows for funding sufficient to manage the operations and that also takes into account individual members' ability to pay. The fee should not be used to allocate decision-making power in the governance structure.

A weak or internally controlled governance structure often yields to members' pressures to do the minimum by way of code implementation and compliance verification. Lacking internal control and external trust, the system is reduced to an exercise in superficial changes that are unlikely to carry any weight with the stakeholders, whose trust in the code's sponsors must be one of the systems primary goals. It would also result in the erosion in public credibility in the reported outcomes.[2] This phenomenon is also apparent in many other group-based efforts sponsored by multilateral and international organizations, such as the UN Code of Global Compact, the Equator Principles jointly developed by banks and the International Fincance Corporation (IFC), and the code sponsored by the Organization for Economic Cooperation and Development (OECD), and the Kimberley Process Certification System (KPCS) jointly sponsored by the United Nations, members states, diamond mining and retailing industries, and nongovernmental organizations, to name a few (see also CorpWatch/Tides Center, 2002; BankTrack, 2004; Sethi, 2003; Tesner and Kell, 2000; Jackson, 1999).[3]

7. There must be an *independent external monitoring and compliance verification system* to engender public trust and credibility in the industry's claims of performance. Performance with code compliance on the part of member companies or groups must be subjected to independent external monitoring and compliance verification. It is in this area that companies and industries offer the most resistance. It is argued that external monitoring would create an environment of distrust and policing. Companies also fear diluting their reputation with related negative consequences to their business and financial operations. Unfortunately, mere assertions of compliance—in the absence of credible evidence—are unlikely to carry much weight with external constituencies.

8. There should be maximum *transparency and verifiable disclosure* of industry performance to the public. Standards of performance disclosure should be the sole province of the code's governing board. The code sponsors must be willing to make the findings of independent external audits available to the public without prior censorship. This condition has also faced considerable resistance on the part of companies and industry groups. It is argued

that releasing such reports would expose those companies to further assaults by their critics, who would not have access to similar information from other companies whose performance may be far worse.

Several authors whose work is presented this book have been responsible for conducting independent external audits with guarantees of full disclosure. Their experience has effectively demonstrated that responsible social critics and the news media fully understand that no company is perfect and that there is always room for improvement. Full disclosure inevitably leads to greater trust in the company's performance claims and thereby shifts the benefit of doubt in the company's favor.

Notes

1. SICCA, "Making Sense of CSR-S Reports 2010," www.sicca-ca.org.
2. See, for example, FLA Code, www.fairlabor.org; and World Business Council on Sustainable Development Chemical Industry Code, www.wbcsd.org. See also Pieschek; Holms Reports, 2002. A halfway approach to shared governance can be found in some industries where industry-NGO joint councils have developed certification programs. However, the quality of these programs and the public's trust in their credibility depend largely on the nature of power sharing between the industry and NGO representation, and the reputation of the NGOs that are participants in such arrangements; Rugmark Foundation, www.rugmark.org; Rainforest Alliance, www.rainforest-alliance.org; GoodCorporation, www.goodcorporation.com. See also Forsyth, 1999; Townsend, 1999; Zaidi, 1999.
3. For details, visit www.unglobalcompact.org, www.equator-principles.com, and www.oecd.org.

II

Individual Company-Based Voluntary Codes of Conduct

2

Mattel, Inc., Global Manufacturing Principles (GMP): A Life-Cycle Analysis of a Company's Voluntary Code of Conduct

S. Prakash Sethi, Emre A. Veral, H. Jack Shapiro, and Olga Emelianova

In November 1997, Mattel announced the creation of a global code of conduct for its production facilities and contract manufacturers. Called the Global Manufacturing Principles (GMP), the code covered such issues as wages and hours, child labor, forced labor, discrimination, freedom of association, legal and ethical business practices, product safety and product quality, protection of the environment, and respect for local cultures, values, and traditions.

At the time of the GMP announcement, Mattel was the world's largest producer of toys. With $4.5 billion in annual revenue, the company was the worldwide leader in design, manufacture, and marketing of children's toys. Headquartered in El Segundo, California, Mattel has offices in thirty-six countries and markets its products in more than 150 nations.

This case study offers a detailed account of how a company's voluntary code of conduct was created, implemented, and ultimately abandoned over a period of approximately nine years.[1] It started out as a highly innovative response to societal concerns, and challenged the toy industry's routine pledges of code compliance, which were rarely, if ever, independently verified and publicly reported. Moreover, this situation was not confined to the toy industry, but was endemic to other industries where large multinational corporations were establishing long supply chains and outsourcing operations in the emerging economies to take advantage of cheap labor and lax enforcement of health and safety conditions, pollution, and other environmental protection standards.

In one sense, Mattel's code was not terribly different than a host of other codes of conduct that were sponsored by individual companies and industry groups from industrially advanced countries with large manufacturing and procurement operations in low-wage countries with an abundant supply of young workers. In large part, these codes appeared to have been created to assuage public opinion that these businesses were exploiting workers by forcing them to work under sweatshop-like conditions. There was, however, little effort to implement these codes or show demonstrable improvement in the alleged abuses. Mattel, however, took a major step to move beyond the "me too" type of code of conduct. Mattel's GMP was quite different in one important aspect: Mattel committed itself, its strategic partners, and primary suppliers to comply with all of the provisions of the GMP.

The second aspect of this case study is an evaluative analysis of both the achievements and shortfalls in the company's code compliance during its short life of nine years. The life cycle of the code, from its inception to abandonment, suggests a bell-shaped curve, where early efforts were taken with considerable commitment on the part of top management, but with significant pockets of resistance from operational groups who were concerned about their own performance on GMP compliance and how it would be balanced with their performance on conventional business criteria of cost efficiencies and profitability.

A detailed analysis of the monitoring activities by the authors of this chapter over the entire period of code compliance under study would indicate that field managers responded to GMP compliance standards in terms of direct and indirect signals they received from top management. In the initial phase of compliance, early activities were slow and deliberate since most actions were new and ad hoc. However, once the policies and procedures were established, they resulted in a steep learning curve. The initial phase also had strong oversight interest from top management, including a representative of Mattel's board of directors, and called for frequent reporting. The response from top management was also quick and was supported with additional physical and human resources. The process was accelerated and became increasingly robust and effective. The success of code compliance and increased transparency in public disclosure energized field managers with a sense of professional satisfaction as they noted market recognition of their efforts, increased public trust, and enhanced corporate reputation.

Unfortunately, the decline in the company's commitment to code compliance and transparency was equally steep. By the middle of the code's life cycle, it became apparent that all of the easily attainable goals had been accomplished and that further progress would be incremental and accommodated in normal business operations. Moreover, some of the initial stage expenditures that were designed to bring the company-owned and -controlled plants to GMP standards had resulted in significant overall improvement in code compliance.

The next phase, starting at the peak of the code life cycle of the bell-shaped curve, presented a new set of challenges. It would require additional resources and top management commitment to encourage vendor plants to improve their compliance efforts.

Two other factors had a strong bearing on Mattel's decision to discard public disclosure of its code compliance activities.

1. The company's top management did not see any economic benefit from its proactive response to code compliance, and other companies in the industry did not seem to suffer adverse consequences for not pursuing a robust and transparent form of code compliance. Thus the company had to justify its GMP-related actions as "the right thing to do," a position that required a sustained value-based ethical commitment.

2. Mattel's top management was distracted with other issues pertaining to its manufacturing and marketing activities, which had strong and potentially negative effects on its corporate reputation. Mattel was engulfed in a product recall of 17.4 million toys because of loose magnets that could be swallowed by children. The company also recalled another 2.2 million toys because of impermissible levels of lead. It was the biggest recall in the company's history. As if all this adverse publicity were not enough, one of Mattel's senior executives made a widely publicized public apology to Chinese authorities for inadvertently blaming China's weak regulation of that country's toy factories (Story, 2007; Story and Barboza, 2007; Press Trust of India, 2007).

Antecedents to the Creation of Global Manufacturing Principles

Public concerns about worker exploitation and environmental degradation arose in line with the expansion of outsourcing and production in emerging economies where poverty, abundant labor, and need for job creation provided unprecedented opportunities for large multinational corporations to shift production from high-wage countries to low-wage countries, while at the same time controlling the high-value customers in economically advanced countries.

Starting with isolated complaints from civil society organizations, human rights groups, and organized labor in the mid-1980s, the anti-sweatshop movement became a major force by the early 1990s in the United States, Canada, Europe, and other industrially advanced countries. Global companies were under fire for operating factories with working conditions that violated basic human rights and labor laws in terms of wages and working conditions. Instances of worker exploitation and employment of underage workers were widespread.

For example, in the South Pacific island of Saipan, the first assault was on companies that were characterized as labor intensive and required relatively simple and mature technologies and relatively smaller capital outlays. However, the protest movement soon engulfed high-technology industries where environmental contamination was a primary concern. Levi Strauss and Co. was accused of practicing "slave labor" (Schoenberger, (2000). In Indonesia, Nike was being paraded against for its poor treatment of workers. Asian American Free Labor Institute–Indonesia (AAFLI) was appointed by the U.S. Agency for International Development (USAID) to conduct a study related to worker treatment in East and Southeast Asia. The study found that Nike paid the lowest wages to its factory workers. This led to international campaigns against sweatshop conditions in Nike factories (NBOER, 2004). Levi Strauss established a code of conduct in 1991 after being reproached by media scandals. This was followed by Nike, which also established a voluntary code of conduct in 1992. Similar concerns were expressed and became objects of public reprobation. Another group discovered that Kathy Lee Gifford, a celebrity talk-show host, owned a clothing line made by sweatshops. Big names in the apparel industry like Walmart, Kmart, Gap, and others were implicated in profiting from sweatshop-like manufacturing operations. Given the highly recognizable nature of these brands, international labor and human rights organizations launched campaigns against these and other companies. President Clinton formed the White House Apparel Industry Partnership in August 1996 to end sweatshops (United States Department of Labor, 1997). Organizations like the National Labor Committee (NLC), Fair Labor Association (FLA), United Students Against Sweatshops (USAS), and Campaign for Labor Rights (CLR) were highly involved in castigating labor abuses (Botz, 2007).

Crisis at Mattel

In line with apparel and footwear industries, the toy industry had also taken steps to respond to public concerns with regard to sweatshop-like conditions and worker exploitation in toy manufacturing factories in China and other developing countries. These efforts were quite similar to those of other industries in that codes of conduct were created with tremendous fanfare, but with insufficient effort to improve and monitor actual working conditions in those factories.

The crisis at Mattel occurred on December 17, 1996 (Barboza and Story, 2007; *New York Times*, 1997). The company was caught off guard by an investigative report aired by NBC's news program *Dateline* on December 17, 1996. An Indonesian factory that manufactured toys for Mattel was found to have employed underage workers who were also working long hours and excessive overtime. Although Mattel disputed some of the findings of the investigative report, it also realized that it must provide a more meaningful response in terms of corrective action.

Companies are more likely to respond forcefully, and even take radical action, when they are confronted with an external crisis that has the potential of adversely affecting their core business operations and a diminution of corporate reputation. In that sense, Mattel was no exception. The result was the creation of Mattel's Global Manufacturing Principles (exhibit 2.1).

Exhibit 2.1   Global Manufacturing Principles, Mattel, Inc., 1997

These Manufacturing Principles sets standards for every facility manufacturing our products in every location in which they are produced. Compromise is not an option.

Wages and Hours: All Mattel factories and vendors must set working hours, wages, and overtime pay that are in compliance with governing laws. Workers must be paid at least the minimum legal wage or a wage that meets local industry standards, whichever is greater.

While overtime is often necessary, in consumer product production, Mattel factories and vendors must operate in a manner that limits overtime to a level that ensures humane, safe and productive working conditions. Overtime, if necessary must be paid in accordance with local laws.

Child Labor: No one under the age of 16 or under the legal age limit (whichever is higher) may be allowed to work in a facility that produces products for Mattel. Simply stated, Mattel creates products for children around the world—not jobs.

We encourage the creation of apprenticeship programs tied to formal education for young people as long as students will in no way be exploited or placed in situations that endanger their health or safety.

Forced Labor: Under no circumstances will Mattel, Inc. use forced or prison labor of any kind nor will we work with any manufacturer or supplier who does.

Discrimination: Discrimination of any kind is not tolerated by Mattel, Inc. It is our belief that individuals should be employed on the basis of their ability to do a job—not on the basis of individual characteristics or beliefs. We refuse to conduct business with any manufacturer or supplier who discriminates either in hiring or in employment practices.

Freedom of Association: Mattel is committed to abiding by all the laws and regulations of every country in which we operate. We recognize all employees' rights to choose (or not) to affiliate with legally sanctioned organizations or associations without unlawful interference.

Working Conditions: All Mattel, Inc. facilities and those of its business partners must provide a safe working environment for their employees. Facilities must engage in efforts including:

- Complying with or exceeding all applicable local laws regarding sanitization and risk protection and meeting or exceeding Mattel' s own stringent standards.
- Maintaining proper lighting or ventilation.
- Keeping aisles and exits accessible at all times.
- Properly maintaining and servicing all machinery.
- Sensibly storing and responsibly disposing of hazardous materials.
- Having an appropriate emergency medical and evacuation response plan for its employees.
- Never using corporal punishment or any other form of physical or psychological coercion on any employee.

Facilities that provide housing to their employees as a benefit of employment must ensure that housing be kept clean and safe.

Legal and Ethical Business Practices: Mattel will favor business partners who are committed to ethical standards that are compatible with our own. At a minimum, all Mattel business partners must comply with the local and national laws of the countries in which they operate.

In addition, all of our business partners must respect the significance of all patents, trademarks, copyrights of our and other's products and support us in the protection of these valuable assets.

In the case of Mattel, two distinguishing elements influenced its design of the new code of conduct. The company's products are aimed at children and the company emphasizes children and family values. Therefore, it could not be seen to be undermining these values by employing children and young adults to make toys under sweatshop conditions. The company also had a strong CEO who favored entrepreneurial approaches to business strategy and operations. Mattel's board included a number of directors who were imbued with the ethics of corporate social responsibility and were fully supportive of the GMP. And finally, the company's employees generally took pride in being part of the company.

Putting Thoughts into Action

Establishment of the Mattel Independent Monitoring Council (MIMCO)

Mattel's GMP called for the creation of an independent and externally based monitoring system that would verify Mattel's compliance with its code of conduct in a manner that would be credible to the public and engender trust in Mattel's GMP-related performance claims. The exploratory process within Mattel led the company to identify S. Prakash Sethi, professor at Baruch College, as someone who could help the company in creating a credible process of code implementation that would be trusted by the public. Sethi had long been identified as a strong advocate of voluntary codes of conduct provided they could be implemented in an effective and transparent manner, and where companies could be held accountable for compliance with their codes of conduct (Sethi, 2003).

Sean Fitzgerald, Mattel's vice president of external communications, established the initial contact between Sethi and Mattel. In an interview with the *New York Times*, Sethi recalled: "They asked me if I could work with them, and I said, 'What do you mean, work with you?' They said, 'We have a problem: we want to make sure that we are doing the right thing, and that the public believes we are doing the right thing" (Dee, 2007).

After some serious soul searching, Sethi conveyed his willingness to work with Mattel. The company would commit itself to three initiatives in implementing the code.

1. The GMP-related compliance efforts by Mattel, its strategic partners, and primary suppliers would be audited by an independent group of respected and knowledgeable experts. This group would have complete access to all facilities, workers and supervisors, and payroll and financial records pertaining to the plants owned and operated by Mattel, its strategic partners, and primary suppliers.
2. The external monitoring group would have complete discretion in making its findings public, as to both their content and frequency.
3. GMP audits would not be a onetime phenomenon. Instead, they would be undertaken on a regular basis as an integral part of the company's operational philosophy.

Sean Fitzgerald was sold on what he called "the concept of Prakash." According to Fitzgerald, "You've got to have a strong sense of self in order to be successful in an endeavor like that. And Prakash has got that going on." Fitzgerald briefed Mattel's executives at the corporate headquarters in El Segundo, California, on his discussions with Sethi and received their concurrence to proceed with the project (Dee, 2007).

Sethi was invited to visit Mattel's headquarters and meet with top management. The resultant discussions led to the establishment of the Mattel Independent Monitoring Council (MIMCO), the precursor to the International Center for Corporate Accountability (ICCA). The council was composed of three members, with S. Prakash Sethi as its chairperson, and the other two members were L. Murray Weidenbaum and Paul F. McCleary.

In a press release following the creation of MIMCO, Mattel also commented on the positive aspects of the monitoring process. Mattel CEO Jill Barad stated, "Mattel is committed to improving the skill level of the workers in our facilities so that they, in turn, will experience increased opportunities and productivity." According to Joseph Gandolfo, then president of Mattel's worldwide manufacturing operations, "These principles are intended to create and encourage responsible manufacturing business practices around the world—not serve as a guideline for punishment. However, manufacturers that do not meet our standards, or refuse to take swift, corrective action to do so, will no longer work for Mattel" (*PR Newswire*, 1997).

As part of its overall strategy of code compliance, Mattel's top management also undertook to

a. make compliance with the principles an integral part of management evaluation and compensation;
b. develop training procedures and information systems by which all levels of the company's managers and employees would be familiarized with these instructions and implementation procedures;
c. constantly revise and improve these instructions and operational procedures in light of experience gained from its own operations and those of other companies facing similar operational challenges in countries where Mattel has its operations; and
d. verify that all of the company's operations and those of its major suppliers and strategic partners remain in full compliance at all times with the GMP and the company's implementation procedures and instructions.

Putting Principles into Practice

Transforming a two-page document that consisted of broad ethical declarations into detailed operational standards that would not only specify process, but even more important, require measurable outcomes, was quite complex. By any measure, it was not an easy task. Nevertheless, the endeavor was an enormous learning exercise. According to Sethi, "It was totally unprecedented. Really intoxicating, I was inventing everything as I went along. There just weren't any systems of its kind. Nobody could say, 'It can't be done'" (Dee, 2007).

The process required that a company must engage its various operational divisions, which would be differently affected by costs and benefits from complying with the code. Similarly, there were considerable differences of opinion among senior managers in the corporate headquarters and those in the field as to the potential benefits and risks of breaking the prevailing industry mold, and whether in the end the company would even gain anything by way of public trust in the implementation of this program.

Mattel set up two task forces, one in El Segundo and the other in Hong Kong, to work with Sethi's group to create operational standards. The two task forces were composed of more than fifty managers and technical experts. This group, along with MIMCO and its own team of academic experts, worked extensively over a twelve-month period to create detailed operational standards and performance measures, and to secure agreement with Mattel's top management and field managers as to those standards.

The newly devised standards had to meet four criteria:

1. *The standards must be quantifiable and objective in measuring and evaluating performance.* In other words, two different people observing compliance with a given criterion must draw similar conclusions.
2. *They must be outcome oriented.* It is not enough to indicate that moneys are being spent or that policies and procedures exist. Rather, the plant management is required to show that there are so many bathrooms per one hundred workers, so many square feet of living space per worker in a dormitory, and that the injury rate per 1,000 worker hours meets industry standards.
3. *At a minimum, these standards must meet the legal criteria mandated by the labor and environmental laws of the country where a plant is located.* Where country-specific standards do not exist or are lower than Mattel standards, local plants must meet Mattel's own standards. As a long-term proposition, Mattel must endeavor to have its plants meet or exceed the best industry practices prevailing in their specific regions or localities.
4. *The standard-setting process is dynamic and interactive.* Standards of performance must continue to evolve in light of experience gained from existing operations, competitor conduct, and the company's desire to continue building on its leadership position. In addition, standards must evolve to meet changing societal expectations because of new data and conduct of major players in the industry, NGO community, public opinion, and behavior of host country governments.

The end product was the creation of an audit protocol, including a detailed seventy-five-page checklist for quantifying conditions inside every one of Mattel's factories and vendor plants. To exemplify, field audits addressed questions such as "Are eyewash stations and safety showers installed in areas of corrosive material use (e.g., battery servicing areas, cooling towers, storage of corrosive material, electroplating) and in high-volume solvent usage areas (e.g., paint mixing, chemical storage and dispensing, solvent distillation)?"; "Do dormitory facilities provide private lockers?"; or "How many people share a room?".

By all accounts, both Mattel and Sethi's group fought energetically for their positions. But in the end, in return for the promise of restored public trust, Mattel was willing to let Sethi be Sethi. It would be wrong to say he is abrasive—on the contrary, he is chatty and hospitable in person—but he is most certainly unafraid to be abrasive when the situation calls for it. He has no interest in ingratiating himself with those in power. Jim Walter, senior vice president for global product integrity at Mattel, who has been in constant contact with Sethi and his staff for the past seven years, calls him "an appropriately positioned thorn in our side" (Dee, 2007).

This process led to the development of more than 200 specific standards. They define the compliance parameters for each principle and cover all aspects of manufacturing operations; environment health and safety standards; worker hiring and training; working conditions; working hours, performance bonuses, wages, and overtime; conditions in dormitories and recreational facilities; and non-job-related skill-enhancement programs. The China document alone is sixty pages long. Similar compliance documents were prepared for twenty other countries where Mattel had operations. These documents are continuously revised in light of changes in local labor and environmental laws.

Changes in Mattel's Top Management

No sooner had the field audit process gotten underway than Mattel was rocked by a major financial crisis that led to a wholesale change in the company's top management. Early in 1999, Mattel CEO Jill Elikann Barad made an ill-timed acquisition of the Learning Company, a maker of educational software, for US$3.8 billion (Miller, 2000). It was a controversial acquisition both for its price and its potential fit with Mattel's existing business model. The acquisition soon turned out to be a financial disaster, risking the future of the company as a going concern. Mattel was losing about a million dollars in cash daily. Mattel's CEO was forced to resign, and in an effort to turn the company around, Mattel's board of directors brought in a new CEO, Robert A. Eckert, then president of Kraft Foods.

The new CEO faced major challenges in restoring the company's financial health, and could easily have relegated the GMP to lower priority. Eckert, however, chose a different course. In his first meeting with MIMCO and his senior managers, Eckert declared, "I am a libertarian by conviction. I also believe that the corporation's freedom to manage its operations cannot be sustained without our assuming our social responsibility to the community" (Sethi, 2003). He indicated that Mattel would behave in all its actions with "unwavering integrity,"[2] and that the company's commitment to the GMP remained unequivocal and undiminished. In an interview with a *New York Times* reporter, Eckert admitted that it would have been tempting to eliminate the program as a cost-cutting measure when none of Mattel's competitors even bothered with it. " 'We had a pretty frank discussion about it,' Eckert admits, but in the end he chose to keep it going. 'We want to be contributing to the development of these societies,' he told me, 'not merely taking advantage of the fact that they're not as developed as we are' " (Dee, 2007).

Modification of the GMP: Explicit and Implicit Exclusions

The new top management team refocused the company's attention to its core business operations, including better oversight and control of its global supply chain. Among the changes, the company issued four policy initiatives to further enhance internal GMP compliance. These included a revised GMP (exhibit 2.2); documents outlining the roles and responsibilities of Mattel's corporate responsibility worldwide; Disney sourcing policies and procedures, which apply to all Mattel facilities and contractors that source Disney products worldwide; and policies and procedures that apply to all Mattel facilities and operations that license Mattel-branded products.

Exhibit 2.2   Mattel Corporate Responsibility

Policy: Global Manufacturing Principles   Date: January 1, 2001
GMP-01

Scope: Mattel's Global Manufacturing Principles (GMP) policy applies to all parties that manufacture, assemble, or distribute any product, or package bearing the Mattel logo.

Purpose: GMP is the cornerstone of Mattel's ongoing commitment to responsible worldwide manufacturing practices. The establishment and implementation of GMP provides a framework within which all of Mattel's manufacturing must be conducted.

GMP provides guidance and minimum standards for all manufacturing plants, assembly operations, and distribution centers that manufacture, assemble or distribute Mattel products. GMP requires safe and fair treatment of employees and that all locations protect the environment while respecting the cultural, ethnic, and philosophical differences of the countries where Mattel operates.

Introduction: As "The World's Premier Toy Brands -Today and Tomorrow," Mattel takes pride in the quality of its products, its customer relationships, its employees, its communities and its global reputation, as well as the value built for its shareholders.

Mattel is committed to executing GMP in all areas of its business and will only engage business partners who share its commitment to GMP. Mattel expects all its business partners to enforce GMP, and will assist them in meeting GMP requirements. However, Mattel is prepared to end partnerships with those who do not comply. Compromise is not an option.

Our Values The foundation for the successful implementation of GMP lies within the Mattel core values. It is essential that the company's business partners share these values.

We Value:

1. Our Consumers
   The well being of children is an inherent part of the reason that Mattel exists and this is reflected in all aspects of our business. A child's well-being is our primary concern in considering the quality and type of toys produced, and in the way Mattel toys are manufactured. At Mattel, we want to inspire children's imaginations and enrich their

lives with our products. Accordingly, Mattel is committed to creating safe and quality products for children around the world. Mattel products will be manufactured in a manner which will meet its GMP stringent standards.

2. Our Work

We strive for excellence and creativity in every aspect of our business. Mattel understands that the implementation of GMP is an on-going process, and is committed to making continuous improvements to its GMP performance as the company strives for full compliance.

We are dedicated to a creative approach in addressing areas of particular concern and resolving compliance issues. We will protect the environment and continue to reduce our use of resources and materials. In every aspect of our business, we will conduct ourselves with unwavering integrity.

3. Our Partners

We will share success with our customers, our suppliers, our shareholders and the communities where we operate.

Our shareholders and customers demand that Mattel products are manufactured and assembled under ethical working and living conditions. Enforcement of the company's GMP policy illustrates to customers and shareholders that Mattel shares their concern and is committed to ensuring that Mattel products are manufactured under conditions that meet GMP standards.

We are also committed to supporting and working closely with our individual vendors in complying with GMP.

4. Ourselves

We operate with unwavering integrity and take ownership of all issues that pass in front of us. We are accountable for the results of our business and the development of our fellow employees. We are dedicated and committed to implementing GMP with honesty and have incorporated measures to ensure continual improvement in our performance.

While the development of GMP is essential to success, enforcement of the code is equally as important. Mattel has initiated an extensive three-stage auditing process - that is overseen by an independent monitoring council - to thoroughly inspect both the company's owned-and-operated facilities around the world, as well as those of our contractors.

We will continue to refine GMP to ensure that all employees are treated fairly, with respect, and work under safe and healthy conditions that encourage dignity and pride for themselves and their workplace.

Our Commitments

Mattel will operate its facilities in compliance with applicable laws and regulations of every country where the company operates. In countries where the laws are not well defined, Mattel has developed country-specific standards that govern our operations and those of the companies that manufacture, assemble or distribute our products.

Mattel has defined the following basic standards of conduct to guide Mattel and each of its business partners' operations in implementing GMP. These standards are dynamic and evolving to ensure ongoing protection of employees and the environment.

1. Hiring, Wages and Working Hours
   a. Work Hours: Mattel will comply with country laws. Overtime work must be voluntary.
   b. Work Week: We will comply with country laws but require at least one rest day per week.
   c. Wages: Wages must meet or exceed legally mandated minimum wage. Wage rates for overtime work must also meet legally mandated rates.
   d. Benefits: All benefits provided to employees must comply with country laws.
   e. Payment of wages: Employees must be paid at least monthly. Accurate records for each employee's regular and overtime hours must be maintained either through time cards punched by each employee or through other similar systems. Pay records must include employee work hours; and every employee must be provided a pay stub with pay calculations and deductions clearly listed.
   f. Deductions: Deductions must comply with local laws. Deductions for company provided food and living must be reasonable, affordable and if employees choose to live and eat outside of the company facilities they will not be charged.
   g. Hiring: Every employee must be provided a written document which outlines their work hours, wages and wage calculations, benefits, costs for food and living and length of employment contract. Mattel and its partners will not charge employment fees and we will monitor our hiring agencies to ensure that fees are reasonable.

2. Age Requirements
   a. No one under the age of 16 will be employed. If the local law requires a higher minimum age, we will comply with the local law.
   b. In cases where employees are hired between 16 and 18 special considerations must include annual physicals and will exclude hazardous duties.
   c. A system must be in place to detect forged and false identity documents.

3. Forced Labor
   a. Under no circumstances will forced or prison labor be used to manufacture, assemble or distribute Mattel products. Each employee must be provided with a document stating that employment and overtime is voluntary.

    b. Mattel will not allow or condone physical or verbal abuse, or any form of physical or psychological coercion of employees.

    c. There must be a written grievance procedure in place.

    d. Every employee must be provided with general orientation on GMP as well as the local company code that includes: wages, working hours, dormitory rules, canteen procedures, grievance procedures, disciplinary procedures, safety training, evacuation, fire prevention, self improvement opportunities and a plant tour.

4. Discrimination

    a. The location must have a procedure on hiring, promotion and disciplinary practices that addresses discrimination. Discrimination or harassment on the basis of age, religion, sex, or ethnicity will not be tolerated.

    b. Mattel will make every attempt to further employee job skills through training. The company will give strong preference to promotion from within the ranks of the current employees. No employee will be denied promotion opportunities for reasons of age, sex, ethnicity, or religion.

5. Freedom of Expression and Association

    a. Each employee has the right to associate, or not to associate, with any legally sanctioned organization.

    b. Management must create formal channels to encourage communications among all levels of supervisors and employees – without fear of reprisal –on issues that impact their working and living conditions.

    c. Senior managers must hold quarterly meetings with all levels of employees to share information and discuss plant-wide issues.

6. Living Conditions

    a. Dormitories (if provided)

        i. Every employee must be provided with adequate living space.

        ii. Ventilation must be provided.

        iii. Showers and bathrooms must be convenient, centrally located or in the room.

        iv. Lockable storage space for each employee must be provided.

        v. Hot water must be provided.

        vi. Dormitories must be maintained, clean and safe.

        vii. Safety hazards must be eliminated.

    b. Canteens (if provided)

        i. Canteen staff must have annual physical examinations.

        ii. Canteen staff must wear clean clothing with proper protective equipment when serving food.

        iii. Canteens must be clean, well lit, and free of food scraps.

        iv. Refrigeration must be available if perishable food is stored.

        v. Tables and chairs must be provided.

        vi. Meals provided must meet nutritional requirements.

7. Workplace Safety

   a. There must be trained or certified safety professionals and a written safety program must be developed.

   b. Combustible materials must be properly handled with special precautions taken in spraying and mixing areas.

   c. Machines with revolving or moving parts must be guarded and employees will receive special training on the use of this machinery.

   d. Hazards must be eliminated where possible. Employees must be provided and trained on the use of Personal Protective Equipment where hazards cannot be fully eliminated.

   e. Mattel will identify all hazardous materials and properly train employees on the appropriate procedures for handling these materials.

   f. Safety training must be conducted for special work categories (industrial trucks, electricians, maintenance, painters, molding operators, etc).

   g. Employee exposure to chemicals and vapors must be below legal requirements or Mattel Standards whichever is the most stringent. In special cases where ventilation cannot eliminate the exposure, respiratory protection will be used and employees trained.

   h. All accidents must be investigated and corrective actions documented.

   i. All locations must continuously reduce accident rates and have specific targets on reductions.

8. Health

   a. In locations where there are more than 1000 employees, there must be an on site medical facility for routine medical treatment and work-related injuries. In locations where there are less than 1000 employees treatment must be available to employees within 15 minutes if there is not a clinic on site.

   b. The facility must have lighting which meets Mattel's standards or local requirements, whichever are higher.

   c. Temperatures must be measured during hot and cold seasons and if they exceed local or Mattel standards corrective actions must be taken.

   d. Noise must not exceed 85dBA. Hearing protection must be used in any areas that exceed this limit. If the local limit is lower, the lower limit will be used.

9. Emergency Planning

   a. Emergency plans for evacuation, spills and natural disasters must be current and identify key responsibilities.

   b. Emergency evacuation signals must be understood and audible in all locations of the facilities.

   c. Emergency exits must meet local or Mattel standards.

   d. Emergency lighting must provide immediate (within 5 seconds) and sufficient lighting to allow evacuation.

    e. Fire extinguishers must be provided and employees designated to use fire extinguishers must be trained.

    f. Employees must be trained on reporting emergencies and evacuation procedures.

    g. Emergency equipment and respective documentation must be maintained.

    h. Special protective and prevention systems like "hot work" must be used when open flames are present.

10. Environmental Protection

    a. Trained environmental personnel must be assigned to manage the areas of air and water emissions and waste management.

    b. Hazardous wastes must be properly contained, stored and only disposed of at approved facilities.

    c. Water discharges must meet local requirements or Mattel's standards.

    d. Mattel will quantify its wastes and continually reduce them.

    e. Air emissions must meet local requirements or Mattel's standards.

    f. Any and all spills or releases must be immediately cleaned.

    g. Odors and noise that cause undue disruption to the community must be eliminated.

    h. Plans to handle environmental emergencies must be current and identify key responsibilities.

11. Evaluation, Corrective Action & Monitoring:

    a. Mattel and its business partners will undergo an audit process to assess compliance with GMP. This process must include a corrective action plan to ensure that audit findings are corrected and GMP compliance achieved. Mattel will work closely with all business partners to ensure that corrective actions are completed in a timely manner.

    b. In cases where corrective actions are not taken in a timely manner, Mattel will identify alternative suppliers. However, Mattel is prepared to terminate any operation or partnership where compliance is not achieved within the time frame agreed upon. Mattel will not engage potential business partners unless they meet the company's stringent requirements or are committed to achieving full compliance.

    c. Mattel's commitment to the public includes verification audits by an independent monitoring organization to assess the GMP performance of Mattel and its business partners. An independent monitor will conduct periodic evaluations of a select number of locations of its choosing to verify compliance with GMP standards. They will be provided with complete access to all information and facilities in order to make an evaluation of Mattel's performance in ensuring that Mattel locations and those of its partners meet GMP standards. The independent monitor has the discretion to periodically issue reports to the public on our progress.

Explicit Exclusions

The original GMP (exhibit 2.1) included product safety as an integral part of the GMP provisions. In practice, however, both Mattel and MIMCO agreed that MIMCO's initial focus would be on worker employment and health and safety issues, as well as monitoring emissions from factories. MIMCO felt that this was a good arrangement since it was in Mattel's own interest to ensure that its toys were safe and met all regulatory requirements applicable in the United States and other toy-importing countries.

As things turned out, MIMCO's assumptions were not borne out by realities. The culture of product safety is not so thoroughly embedded in developing countries, where expectations toward adherence to product safety standards are generally lower than those prevailing in industrially advanced countries. Given the fact that factories in China need constant monitoring to ensure compliance with local employment laws, neither the company nor MIMCO should have assumed that factory owners would not be tempted to cut corners and save money through the use of substandard materials and lower safety standards in the manufacturing process.

As the world's largest toy manufacturer, Mattel has had more than its share of safety-related product defects. Mattel also has had a long history of contentious relations with regulators, notably the Consumer Product Safety Commission (CPSC), which has repeatedly charged the company with violating its rules for timely notification pertaining to safety-related product defects. This contention is consistently denied by the company, which sticks to its own interpretation of the regulatory requirements for timely disclosure (*CNN Money*, 2007). Nevertheless the company has paid numerous fines for alleged violations, and in a number of cases settled with individual consumers (Casey, 2007). The latest in this sequence of events was a civil penalty of $2.3 million paid by Mattel in 2009 for violating the federal lead paint ban. "In retrospect," Murray Weidenbaum, a former ICCA board member, told Jonathan Dee of the *New York Times*, "the mission we were assigned was narrower than perhaps it should have been. We focused on the working conditions, because that was our task, and because critics at the time were focusing on it—child labor, prison labor, all that. It turns out we missed the big picture, which is the nature of the product" (Dee, 2007).

Implicit Exclusions

The preamble to Mattel's revised GMP states:

Scope: Mattel's Global Manufacturing Principles (GMP) applies to all parties that manufacture, assemble or distribute any products or package bearing the Mattel logo. Similarly, Section II of revised GMP states: "Mattel and its business partners will undergo an audit process to assess compliance with GMP...Mattel's commitment to the public includes verification audits by an independent monitoring organization to assess the GMP performance of Mattel *and its business partners* [emphasis added]." (See exhibit 2.2.)

In practice, however, this did not turn out to be the case. From the very start of the independent monitoring process, Mattel resisted every effort by MIMCO to provide information about its licensing partners—companies that make products using the Mattel logo, such as Barbie sleepwear and children's furniture. The company initially argued that given the enormity of the task at hand, MIMCO should focus on auditing those plants, that is, Mattel-owned and -controlled plants and vendors that make products for Mattel. It was also suggested that Mattel was setting up its own internal organization to monitor all of its licensees, and thus any audits by MIMCO should be postponed until such time that Mattel had completed its in-house organization and implemented initial audits.

However, despite repeated requests, Mattel never provided MIMCO and ICCA with any information about the scope of its licensee operations, the extent to which they have been audited by Mattel's in-house auditing organization, and the overall state of licensed compliance with the GMP. During the period 1999 to 2008, when MIMCO and ICCA were responsible for GMP external audits, there were numerous incidents and news reports of worker abuse and poor factory conditions in Mattel's licensee factories. All of these were handled by Mattel without any involvement by MIMCO-ICCA. It should also be noted that Mattel does not separately disclose revenues from licensee operations in its financial statements. They are consolidated in the company's total sales. However, the general consensus is that these operations account for almost 50 percent of Mattel's total sales.

Framework for a Viable External Audit Regimen

A basic premise of MIMCO's audit regimen was that Mattel would create an in-house auditing organization that would be responsible for conducting GMP compliance audits of its own plants and those of its vendors and licensees. MIMCO would in fact be verifying the quality and veracity of audits conducted by Mattel's own people. This is a critical distinction, because any shortfalls in factory compliance discovered by MIMCO would also imply a failure on Mattel's part in carrying out its own auditing and monitoring responsibilities.

MIMCO established a systematic three-year cycle to meet its obligations for external audits. The first year of the cycle would concentrate on Mattel facilities. These would include all of the company-owned plants and other plants in which Mattel controlled 100 percent of the output. The second year would focus on a statistically selected sample of the plants that are owned and operated by Mattel's strategic partners and primary suppliers, and from which Mattel buys 70 percent or more of the plant's output. The third year of the audit cycle would focus on a statistically selected sample of second-tier plants from which Mattel buys between 40 percent and 70 percent of the plant's output. This audit cycle would be repeated on a three-year basis. This approach ensures that every plant in a group has an equal chance of being selected for a verification audit, and no plant has prior knowledge of being selected. Vendor plants with less than 40 percent of output dedicated to Mattel products were excluded from MIMCO audits. Plants in each group would be subjected to MIMCO audits once every three years. In addition, MIMCO had complete discretion to include additional plants in its audit sample to arrive at a more accurate picture of how well Mattel's strategic partners and primary suppliers were complying with GMP requirements.

MIMCO's Audit Protocols

MIMCO had to create its own audit protocols and audit instruments. The objective was to ensure that MIMCO audit reports were comprehensive and provided the public at large a fair, objective, and unbiased picture of conditions in the audited plants. These were composed of four elements: management compliance reports, payroll and personnel file desk audits, systematic walk-through examinations of the plant and dormitories, and one-on-one worker interviews (exhibit 2.3).

Exhibit 2.3   MIMCO (ICCA) Audit Protocols

The implementation of Mattel's GMP is carried out according to detailed standards of performance as prescribed by detailed checklists tailored to meet the specific legal requirements of each country as well and/or Mattel's GMP, whichever is more stringent.

PRE-AUDIT PREPARATION

Prior to the on-site audit, ICCA formally requests information from the plant management regarding its operational and human resource management practices. The Management Compliance Report (MCR) is a standard document that contains detailed information on all aspects of the plant's operations, the extent of management's compliance with various GMP provisions, details of any shortfalls, and management's plans for corrective action.

THE FIELD AUDIT

The intent of the field audit is to ensure that all workers receive wages for regular and overtime work as mandated by law; the factory operates within legal and GMP standards as to regular and overtime hours; and provides benefits as mandated by law and GMP standards. The field audit is composed of four parallel activities. The first one is an audit of a randomly selected sample of workers' personnel files and payroll records. Contracted professional auditors who have extensive knowledge of local labor laws and accounting practices conduct this audit under ICCA supervision. Where complex issues of interpretation of local labor laws and regulations are required, ICCA relies on advice from its local legal counsel.

The second element of the audit involves interviews with the same group of workers who were selected for the payroll and personnel file audit. Each worker is interviewed individually in a private, secured space to ensure complete confidentiality. A typical interview lasts around forty-five minutes. The interview questionnaire was developed by ICCA and is designed to elicit information on all aspects of the worker's working and living conditions at the plant. This process allows for a comparison of the information contained in the plant's payroll records and personnel files, and the information elicited from the workers through the interviews. Professional interviewers, retained independently by ICCA and generally meeting the age and gender profile of the workers, conduct these interviews in the workers' native language.

The third element of the audit is a thorough examination of the plant's policies, procedures, and practices with regard to environment, health, and safety issues. The EHS audit entails

- An evaluation of the MCR completed by plant management, indicating the extent of compliance with Mattel's applicable checklist;
- A walk-through of the plant; and
- An examination and verification of site history, permits, monitoring, surveillances, and compliance documentation as required by law.

Locally-based independent environmental engineers who are trained in the country's laws and regulations in manufacturing operations conduct this phase of the audit under ICCA engineers' supervision. Inspection includes an examination of the general maintenance of the manufacturing facilities; storage, treatment, and disposal of hazardous waste materials; and hygiene in bathrooms, kitchen, and eating facilities, with particular emphasis on safety and health. The walk-through also includes a thorough inspection of the dormitories and recreational facilities in terms of hygiene, adequacy of space, worker comfort, privacy, security, and other related matters as deemed appropriate in specific situations.

The final element of the ICCA audit is a series of meetings with various functional managers, which serves to confirm and clarify issues in the MCR and elaborate on the plant management's practices regarding issues that emerge during the field audit.

POST-AUDIT ACTIVITIES

All audit documents are hand-carried to the New York offices of ICCA for analysis and report preparation. Initial findings are reported to Mattel to ensure factual accuracy. In case of a material error, ICCA revises the draft report before making it public. In other cases, Mattel responds with corrective action commitments. ICCA assesses this response and indicates the extent of follow-up to be undertaken by ICCA to ensure full and timely compliance. The audit report indicates the findings of the audit as well as Mattel's responses and commitments. In the event of a disagreement between ICCA and Mattel as to the nature of findings or the adequacy and timeliness of corrective measures, both perspectives are made public without any editing by ICCA or Mattel.

Summary of Audit Findings

The first round of audits was initiated in the second half of 1998, and was in the nature of a dry run. Their intended purpose was to familiarize both plant managers and factory owners with the expectations of GMP audits and how they would be conducted. At the same time, they would provide MIMCO members with an understanding and appreciation of the field conditions they would face while conducting GMP audits.

The full-fledged formal audits started in earnest in the latter half of 1998 and continued through 2008, when they were unilaterally discontinued by Mattel.[3]

To facilitate better understanding and comprehension of the audit findings, we have grouped them into four categories:

1. Mexico: all plants owned and operated by Mattel
2. China: all plants owned and/or operated by Mattel
3. China: all plants owned and operated by suppliers
4. All plants owned and operated by Mattel in Indonesia, Malaysia, and Thailand

MEXICO

The first round of formal audits took place between August 2 and 6, 1999, and involved two plants: Montoi S.A. de V.C. in Monterrey, and Mabamex S.A. de V.C. in Tijuana. Both plants were dedicated to the production of Barbie dolls and other Mattel-branded toys. The Tijuana plant was moved to its current location in April 1998, and was still undergoing the process of settling in. The Monterrey factory had peak employment of approximately 2,300 workers, and the Tijuana plant around 2,150 workers. These numbers were considerably reduced during the off-peak season.

MIMCO's audit found the Monterrey plant to be a well-managed facility, and commended its management for its commitment to GMP standards. Montoi, while being an old plant with a non-air-conditioned work space, was well maintained and in general provided a clean, safe environment. Montoi met all of the important GMP standards with regard to the workplace environment, and maintains detailed records on various aspects of manufacturing operations and employee status. Analysis of the plant's payroll records and worker interviews confirmed that the Montoi plant met all regulations of the Mexican government as well as GMP standards with regard to the determination of normal and overtime hours, and payment of wages for regular and overtime work. MIMCO's one-on-one confidential interviews with a randomly selected group of workers confirmed a high level of satisfaction with all aspects of their work at the plant and covered under the GMP.

The formal audit of the Tijuana plant (Mabamex) also revealed a satisfactory picture. The Mabamex plant also met all regulations of the Mexican government as well as GMP standards with regard to the determination of normal and overtime hours and payment of wages for regular and overtime work.

Mabamex is a well-maintained, clean, and completely air-conditioned facility. A small group of workers, however, expressed concerns about excessive noise and poor ventilation. MIMCO's own inspection attributed these deficiencies to the plant's recent relocation. These deficiencies were soon rectified and confirmed by MIMCO.

Second Round of Audits, Mattel Manufacturas de Monterrey, S.A. DE C.V. (MX3)

During the MIMCO visit to Monterrey, the audit team was shown the location and partial construction of a very large new Mattel plant called MX3. The new plant incorporated all of the activities from the old Monterrey plant. The first formal audit of MX3 was conducted on November 7–8, 2000. At the time of the audit, MX3 was a brand-new facility in the start-up phase, with approximately 1,500 workers during the peak period. It was a very modern facility designed to be completely air-conditioned, with programmable controls. The factory manufactures large toys using primarily injection- and blow-molded parts. The workforce is predominantly female. It is also relatively young, with a low level of education and little prior work experience. The plant has high levels of worker turnover, 235 percent per year, which may go even higher during certain months.

The field visit turned out to be an unpleasant surprise, especially given the fact that it was a brand-new facility. The new plant was already showing signs of severe neglect in both routine and preventive maintenance. Furthermore, the flow of materials, processing, waste handling, storage, and disposal suggested a disregard of normal safe handling procedures. The molding area of the plant was unkempt, with oil spills on the floor. Part of the oil spills from the molding machines drained into an open channel and then ran down the wall into the regrinding area. There were large amounts of makeshift electrical wiring and bare electrical connections. In several places, live electrical cords were lying across employee pathways. These conditions created an unacceptable level of hazard for workers and increased danger of fire in the plant.

Worker Safety

There appeared to be little emphasis on the use of personal protection equipment (PPE). Most employees working in high-noise-contaminated areas did not wear earplugs. MIMCO also noticed a red metal cabinet standing in the middle of the assembly area. It was filled with open containers of volatile flammable liquids. One employee, who was not wearing protective clothing, stood in a puddle of dried paint and debris, spraying plastic parts under insufficient light. Employees using forklifts on the factory floor were driving them at excessive speeds and did not appear to be properly trained in their safe operation. In two instances MIMCO observed that a live-electrical injection-molding machine was being repaired by a mechanic working on the interior of the machine without using the proper maintenance lockout/lock-in procedure. This is an unsafe and highly dangerous work practice.

Treatment of Workers

The plant was in full compliance with regard to working hours and payment of regular and overtime hours. In other areas of worker treatment, the MIMCO team found the factory's practices questionable. All MX3 workers, whether in molding or assembly areas, were required to stand on their feet through their entire work shifts, which can be either seven or eight hours long, depending on the shift. This was an unprecedented situation. In all MIMCO audits of Mattel-owned and -operated facilities in Asia and Mexico, it did not find a single plant where workers were not provided with some type of stool or chair and were instead required to stand through their entire work shifts. An examination of the workers' interview data showed that a vast majority (87 percent) of interviewed workers complained about the lack of stools and chairs at their workstations and about being asked to work while standing for seven to eight hours.

Kitchen and Bathroom Facilities

The kitchen area was unclean and below GMP standards. Several pieces of kitchen equipment were grease encrusted, as were places on the tile walls and floor. Workers' hygiene and sanitation conditions as reflected in the toilet facilities were extremely poor. The lavatory facilities on the production floor were mostly nonoperational and unclean. Wash bowls, soap containers, toilet seats, automatic flushing devices, and faucets were missing and were nonoperable. In one of the men's lavatories, there was no running water in any of the sinks tested. Employees were not able to wash their hands after relieving themselves. Soiled toilet paper was on the floor adjacent to the toilet bowls because it could not be flushed down the inoperable drains.

Routine housekeeping was nonexistent or deficient, as indicated by severely discolored sinks, toilets, and urinals. Most toilet stall doors were covered in graffiti and were, for the most part, inoperative. Half of one of the two men's toilet areas was blocked off with a makeshift partition, reducing the availability of the facilities by 25 percent. Our inspection revealed that the toilets in the blocked-off area were broken and unusable.

Management's Response to MIMCO's Draft Audit Report

Overall, MIMCO found that MX3 raised significant issues of potential risk to workers' health and safety and safe environmental practices. MIMCO provided a report to Mattel's management. This was in accordance with established practice wherein the plant management or general managers have an opportunity to respond to MIMCO's findings.

In response, for the first time, MIMCO experienced considerable pressure from the operational-level managers to modify its draft report, suggesting we had overreacted to isolated instances and that management had already identified many of these issues and was taking corrective action. MIMCO was also provided with a list of "changes in language," and was urged to insert them in the draft report.

It also turned out that midlevel managers had not as yet apprised Mattel's top management of MIMCO's draft report. MIMCO flatly refused to modify its findings and insisted that its draft report was sent to Mattel's headquarters in El Segundo, California.

The response from Mattel's top management was short and swift. It did not argue with MIMCO's findings. Instead, it asked for a ninety-day period to fix the problems and invited the MIMCO team for a full-fledged follow-up audit. In a written response to MIMCO, Mattel stated:

We recognize that this report does not reflect favorably on the performance of our MX3 facility. There are a number of reasons that led to these conditions but none justify MIMCO's findings in November 2000. We will not accept this performance and will not make excuses. As evidenced by the follow-up audit in February 2001, we did take immediate action to correct the discrepancies found. Our senior management team at Mattel is new and committed to full implementation of GMP. MX3 is a valuable part of our manufacturing strategy and will fully comply with GMP. We also welcome MIMCO's intent to conduct an unannounced visit of the MX3 facility.

Follow-Up Audit, February 5, 2001

The follow-up audit revealed a radically transformed factory. It would seem that plant management had paid careful attention to MIMCO's audit findings and addressed them in a systematic manner. MIMCO's overall observation was that in all essential areas, MX3 was in compliance with the GMP.

MIMCO found the assembly area to be clean and layouts improved significantly. All electrical outlets had been secured and cords removed from employee walkways. All kitchen appliances had been cleaned and grease removed. All plumbing was repaired and proper drains were operating. Leaks were sealed and all electrical connections were repaired and in compliance with GMP standards. MIMCO found that lavatories and hygiene facilities had been repaired and were properly operating. All new fixtures were stainless steel, which would allow for proper cleaning and ease of repair. Additional maintenance and service personnel had been added to ensure that all repair work is completed in a timely manner and that lavatories are kept clean at all times.

With regard to workers being forced to stand in all assembly-line positions, the follow-up found that currently 50 percent of the assembly and molding positions had been designated as positions where sitting is permitted. The remaining positions required standing due to frequent movements or heavy lifting of the product. Further evaluation of the work positions would be an ongoing process as the product mix changes. New roller-type assembly lines were being installed that would allow more orderly, efficient movement of product and flexibility of production operations. Interviews with workers also revealed that plant management had made additional efforts to ensure that employees have a forum to voice concerns about working conditions. Training programs with supervisors and employees will focus on communicating effectively.

Mexico Plant Audits During 2001–2007

During the six-year period of 2001–2007, MIMCO/ICCA conducted two rounds of audits covering all Mattel plants in Mexico. In general, these plants were found to be in compliance with GMP standards. Where minor short-falls were found, they were considered normal in any factory and were easily corrected.

Indonesia

Mattel's Indonesian operations have undergone a series of changes during the period 1999–2008. These transformations involved both changes in product mix and plant restructuring. Mattel-owned and-operated plants in Indonesia were audited by MIMCO/ICCA in February 1999, May 2002, and April 2008.

Initially, these plants were called Mattel Indonesia Cikarang Plant (MJS) and Mattel Indonesia Cikarang Baru Plant (MJD). By 2008, the two plants were operating as PTMI East and PTMI West. The East plant is PTMI's major facility. Most of the West plant's employees and equipment were relocated to the East plant. Approximately one-third of the West plant was still operative. The ongoing production operations in the West plant primarily consist of injection molding, spray painting, and preassembly. The primary production processes at the East plant were molding, spray painting, final assembly, and packaging. At the time of the third audit in April 2008, PTMI employed 7,000 people. However, the workforce might increase to 10,000 employees during production peak season. The workforce consists of 65 percent permanent employees and 35 percent temporary contract workers. Female workers constitute 91 percent of the direct labor workforce. The average age is thirty-one years and no employee is under the age of eighteen.

Outsourcing

While in Indonesia, during the second round of audits in May 2002, Mattel informed ICCA that it had outsourced some sewing operations to a privately owned factory located about a 1.5-hour flight from Jakarta. The ICCA team was invited to visit the factory on an informal basis with the understanding that a formal audit would be conducted during the next audit round of the Indonesian plants. The visit indicated that the factory appeared to be well managed, with more than 500 workers dedicated to manufacturing Mattel products. The team, however, did not conduct any worker interviews. Nor did it examine payroll records to ascertain employee wages and working hours and the extent to which they were in compliance with Mattel's GMP. Mattel did not include this factory in the third and final round of audits of the Indonesian plants and no further information was made available.

General Findings

Throughout the three audits, ICCA found the two plants to be in general compliance with GMP standards for physical work environment and health and safety standards. The plants were also in general compliance with GMP's requirements and Indonesian laws with regard to wages for regular and over-time work and the total number of work hours per week. There were some deviations from GMP compliance as applied to workers. These are noted in the sections below.

Principal Areas of Concern and Disagreement

ICCA's concerns with regard to compliance with GMP were twofold. In some cases, the shortfalls and deficiencies identified by the audit team were rectified. However, in certain other areas where GMP noncompliance was considered to be serious, satisfactory corrective action was not taken.

1. Environmental Protection, Worker Health and Safety Issues

In the 1999 audit, it was noted that there was the presence of chemical odors and high noise levels. The 2002 audit showed that the noise levels, especially in the roto-casting area, to be 90 decibels, which was above the acceptable 85-decibel level. All employees in the area wore protective earplugs. The 2008 audit confirmed that the EHS problems noted in the previous audits were satis-factorily addressed, except for the noise levels, which exceeded the Indonesian and Mattel standard of 85 decibels in five separate locations. The 1999 audit found that although PPE was available, its usage was not being enforced. The 2002 audit showed no improvement. Finger protection, safety shoes, earplugs, and facemasks were not being used by some employees where required. PPE problems were addressed and corrected, as observed in the 2008 audit.

2. Dormitories

The management and operation of dormitories presented a major area of disagreement between Mattel and ICCA, and remained unresolved during the entire cycle of three audits over a nine-year period. The principal areas of noncompliance pertained to: (a) the maximum number of workers per room, and (b) a mandatory requirement that certain workers must stay in the dor-mitories as a condition of their employment. Mattel's GMP requires that the number of workers per room be limited to a maximum of twelve. This was intended to provide the workers with a minimum level of privacy and to minimize noise levels, since the shift changes inevitably cause disturbances to the workers who are sleeping. It was found during all three audits that both dormitories were built to accommodate thirty workers per room. Although the dormitory space allocated per employee met the GMP guidelines, the number of workers per room was far in excess of the twelve permitted in individual rooms.

In response to the first audit, Mattel indicated that suitable changes would be made in the reconfiguration of the larger rooms. The second round of audits revealed that this change had not been made. It was also found that since they were given the choice, fewer workers were willing to live in the dormitories. By the time of the third audit round in April 2008, and despite its earlier promise, Mattel had failed to undertake changes in the dormitory configuration. At the conclusion of the third and last round of audits, Mattel again assured ICCA that the necessary changes in the dormitories would be made.

The second issue, which ICCA considered to be an even more serious violation of the GMP, had to do with requiring workers to stay in the dormitory as a condition of their employment. When this issue was raised with the plant management during the first post-audit meeting, the management offered the following defense of their policy:

a. Most of the workers, who are both young and female, come from villages and are not used to independent urban living. Their parents expect plant managers to provide these workers with secure and safe living conditions. This rationale, however, fails to offer a justification for universal residency mandatory requirements where workers are from the nearby areas, are old enough to be responsible for their actions, and are married.
b. Plant management also argued that since workers accept the mandatory dormitory living as a condition of their employment, there was no violation *per se* of GMP standards.
c. MIMCO/ICCA disagreed with these contentions and formally noted its disagreement in the formal audit report. In response, Mattel agreed to find a mutually acceptable solution prior to the scheduled second round of audits.

The second round of audits noted some changes in the company's policies. Married and permanent workers were no longer required to stay in the dormitories. However, all temporary workers were still required to stay in the dormitories. The relaxation of mandatory residency standard for married and permanent workers resulted in the departing of a large number of workers to private housing, leaving the plant with unfilled dormitory space and a heavy cost burden of maintaining these dormitories while generating even lower rental income.

By the third round of audits, the situation had not changed. Moreover, the justification for requiring workers to stay in the dormitories was no longer tenable. ICCA's interviews with workers revealed that many workers chose to pay the dormitory rent to meet the mandatory residency requirement, but still opted to rent private housing in the surrounding neighborhoods. This situation was also recognized and confirmed by the plant management in post-audit meetings with MIMCO/ICCA.

ICCA's experience with regard to the dormitory situation strongly suggested that while the nature of noncompliance with the GMP was unambiguous, local managers continually found ways to avoid making necessary changes, and Mattel's top management was reluctant to enforce GMP standards. In ICCA's view, the primary consideration was money. Given the changing demographics, workers were no longer willing to stay voluntarily in the dormitories. Consequently, the carrying cost of maintaining empty dormitories was a burden that the company wished to avoid. However, the issue of Mattel's compliance with GMP standards—after eight years of persistent reporting by ICCA—has since become moot because Mattel canceled its program of independent external audits by ICCA and thus avoided the embarrassment of publicly disclosing its corrective action or lack thereof.

3. Employee Relations

The 2008 audit showed that 10 percent of the interviewed workers were pressured to work overtime even when they were unwilling to do so. Mattel has assured ICCA that corrective actions will be instituted and communicated so as to prevent unwilling overtime. Involuntary overtime and verbal abuse by floor-level supervisors was not fully addressed by the time the 2008 audit was completed.

4. Checkout Time

Another major discrepancy in compliance with GMP standards that has persisted over the entire audit cycle of nine years had to do with electronic checkout time. Both plants have an electronic system whereby workers swipe magnetic cards to log the time they enter the factory. However, their checkout time was not recorded by the computer system. This situation was identified by MIMCO/ICCA during the first round of audits in 1999. Plant management has consistently resisted making changes although it involved no additional costs. Instead, it argued that since all workers left at the same time at the end of their respective shifts, it is easier for the supervisors to log in the time for all workers and that individual clockout was not necessary. Finally, in the post-audit meeting in April 2008, Mattel agreed that the plants would change their clockout policies, and that all clocked employees would have their checkout times recorded in the computerized records. However, ICCA has no further information since Mattel has canceled its program of independent external audits.

Malaysia

At the time of the first audit round on February 8–10, 1999, Mattel had four plants in Malaysia. Since then, Mattel has closed two plants due to changes in demand for its products and resultant downsizing of its worldwide production facilities. The remaining plants were Mattel (Malaysia) Sdn. Bhd. (MMSB) and Mattel Tools Sdn. Bhd. (MTSB). In addition to the first-round audit, the two plants also underwent full-fledged formal audits in May 2002, April 2005, and April 2008.

MMSB

This plant is a dedicated facility for the production of Hot Wheels toy cars. It employs approximately 3,500 workers on a year-round basis, with additional workers added during peak production periods. MMSB's workforce is unusual among Mattel's plants in that it tends to be somewhat older, more mature, and with longer tenure of employment. The average age of workers is twenty-eight and the average length of employment is thirteen years. For 40 percent of the interviewed employees, this was their first job.

MMSB also participates in Malaysia's guest worker program, which is supervised by the Malaysian government. The plant hires guest workers exclusively from Indonesia via recruitment agencies. At the time of 2008 audit, there were more than 800 such workers, comprising 29 percent of the direct labor workforce.

Physical Environment and Working Conditions

The MMSB plant has a well-maintained physical facility and provides a safe and comfortable working environment for its workers. Overall, workers have indicated a high level of satisfaction with the safety and quality of their work environment. The plant safety and maintenance conditions were also confirmed by the MIMCO/ICCA audit team of experts through an extensive walk-through of the plant facilities and review of the company's records with regard to environment and health and safety requirements stipulated in the GMP in all three audit rounds in 2002, 2005, and 2008.

With regard to maintaining electronic time record, MMSB follows a similar practice that was criticized by MIMCO/ICCA in the case of Indonesian plants: workers swipe their magnetic card while coming into the factory, but do not clock out upon completing their shift. And just as in the case of Indonesian plants, the plant management's arguments in support of this practice were equally untenable and spurious.

Treatment of Workers

Malaysia has no minimum wage requirements. MMSB pays market-based competitive wages that are also in full compliance with Mattel's GMP standards. An overwhelming number of workers interviewed by MIMCO/ICCA during its four audit rounds expressed satisfaction in regard to wages and benefits, working hours, and in the way they were treated by the management. There were, however, some complaints expressed by the workers during one-on-one confidential interviews (2008 audit) about pressure from supervisors to work overtime when an employee was unwilling to do so.

Medical Facilities, Food, and Canteen Services

MMSB contains a very good clinic with four beds, which is staffed with three nurses (one state enrolled nurse and two state registered nurses) (RNs), with one RN per shift. There is no charge for medical services or medicines provided to workers. The plant operates two canteens accommodating approximately 1,800 workers per day. The plant pays the workers a food allowance of RM3.2 per day. Cost of food at the factory's canteens is approximately RM2 to RM2.5. Workers who bring their food from home are entitled to the biweekly paid meal allowance.

Dormitories

At MMSB, the dormitories and living conditions are perhaps the best—homelike and on a more human scale than any other facility visited by MIMCO/ICCA among the Mattel-owned and -operated plants. Moreover, these employee quarters are far superior to any dormitory facilities operated by Mattel's vendors and audited by MIMCO/ICCA. In terms of the density in living space and in relative level of comfort, these facilities provide a good benchmark to be emulated by other plants.

At MMSB, all single female workers live in the dormitories. MMSB management considers it necessary for the safety and security of workers. Among the interviewed workers, employee satisfaction with various elements of dormitories and living accommodation ranged between 91 percent and 100 percent. In informal discussions with workers during MIMCO/ICCA's visit to the dormitories, workers expressed tremendous pride in their living accommodations. Each unit was decorated with personal items and gave the impression of a private homelike atmosphere. These dormitories generally meet and exceed all pertinent GMP standards.

Other Notable Points

MMSB has a handicapped-worker program that deserves special mention. Under this program, MMSB hires and trains blind workers and places them in regular assembly line jobs. During the walk-through of the plant, MIMCO/ICCA members had the opportunity to observe these workers at their workstations and talk to them about their work experience. Without exception, these workers appeared happy and proud of their work. We also noted that there was no difference in the production efficiency and safety levels of these and other plant workers.

MDT

This audit report covers two plant sites used by Mattel's development and tooling operations in Malaysia. The first facility, Mattel Tools Sbn. Bhd. (MTSB), was audited in February 1999, May 2002, and April 2005, when it was renamed Mattel Development Tooling Sbn. Bhd (MDT). The plant is located in the Prai Free Trade Zone outside Penang, Malaysia. It is a tool and die manufacturer that supports Mattel plants worldwide. The last audit was conducted on April 23, 2008, at a new site, which was also located in the Prai Free Trade Zone.

The plant employs around 180 workers. Of these, approximately 75 percent are direct labor (manufacturing) and the remaining 25 percent are non-manufacturing labor (professional administrative and clerical personnel). The workforce consists of highly skilled technicians and professionally trained tool and die makers. Most workers have eleven years of basic schooling. Turnover among regular workers is quite low, with an average tenure at the plant of thirteen years. The gender composition of the workforce is 93 percent male.

Plant Facilities, Environment, Worker Health and Safety

MTSB is an efficiently laid-out and well-managed plant facility. It is completely air-conditioned. The factory maintains detailed and up-to-date records on plant maintenance, air filtration systems, noise control, fire prevention, and safe storage and handling of hazardous materials. The facility has satisfactory compliance with GMP requirements.

Employee Relations, Wages, Work Hours, and Amenities

Workers at MDT are highly skilled and technically qualified employees. They receive wages far exceeding market rates for hourly workers. MDT workers' monthly base salaries exceed wage rates for comparable jobs in the area.

There is an extensive and formalized communication system in place at MDT, which facilitates two-way communication between the employees and different levels of management. Workers were almost unanimous (94 percent) in stating that they would seek advice on personal problems from the line leaders or supervisors.

MDT shares a clinic with MMSB, and all MDT workers have full access to these facilities. MDT keeps first-aid boxes on its premises for immediate first-aid treatment. There is no charge for medical services or medicines provided to workers. Food in the factory canteen is provided by a contracted caterer. Costs are subsidized by the factory and average RM1.5–3.5, (US$0.39–0.92) per meal, paid in cash. The canteen serves four meals a day throughout all shifts.

Overall Observations and Areas of Concern

The last audit of the MDT was conducted at the factory's new site. ICCA's overall observations with regard to MDT's practices at the new site were quite satisfactory. MDT has clearly established policies and rules with regard to verbal or physical abuse, including sexual harassment. These rules apply to all employees, staff personnel, and management. However, in practice, these rules did not appear to be effectively implemented. During ICCA's confidential one-on-one interviews with workers, almost 40 percent of the interviewed workers felt that there was favoritism and unfair treatment in employee appraisal for promotion and assignment for overtime work. In response, plant management provided a detailed plan of action. Follow-up inquiries by MIMCO/ICCA indicated that the issues were largely resolved.

A major point of contention in the case of MDT is the factory's practice with regard to maintaining time records; this problem is similar to the one described in the case of other plants in Indonesia and Malaysia. Unfortunately, the responses by the plant management are similarly untenable.

Thailand

Mattel Bangkok Ltd (MBK)

MIMCO/ICCA has conducted four formal audits of this plant. These were in April 1999, May 2002, April 2005, and April 2008. The plant is located in the Bangpoo Industrial Estate Export Zone in Samutprakam outside Bangkok. It is a wholly owned Mattel facility and is dedicated to the exclusive production of Hot Wheels toy cars. The factory is capable of producing 100 million Hot Wheels cars a year.

Worker Profile

Employment at MBK has ranged between 1,350 and 1,400 workers. Of these, 80 percent are direct labor and the remaining 20 percent are clerical, administrative, and supervisory staff. Almost 98 percent of the workforce is female. The entire workforce is over eighteen years old, and the average age is twenty-nine. The level of education of the workers employed by the plant is relatively low, averaging between six and seven years of formal education, which is equivalent to slightly above primary school.

Physical Environment and Working Conditions

Throughout the four audit cycles, MIMCO/ICCA found the plant facilities maintenance and upkeep to be excellent and in full compliance with the Thailand government regulations and Mattel's GMP standards. MBK maintains up-to-date records with all aspects of plant operations and management. The walk-through inspection of the plant showed the factory to be in good operating condition. All work areas were clean and free of oil spills and litter. ICCA also noted, where applicable, employees were using the proper personal protective equipment (PPE) in all areas of the operation. The usage of PPE appeared to be strictly enforced by floor supervisors.

A recurring theme of discord among the workers has been excessive heat in the factory, as the plant is not air-conditioned. The factory has launched a major effort to reduce plant temperatures and increase air circulation. The plant was being modified by changing the configuration of ceilings, walls, and location of plant functions, and other heat-reduction technologies such as air curtains at certain workstations. It is expected that when all construction work is completed, WBGT temperatures should decrease by three to five degrees centigrade.

Treatment of Workers

MBK's wages and benefits policies as well as regular and overtime hours are in compliance with Thailand laws and GMP standards. ICCA's examination of factory payroll records confirmed the accuracy of appropriate payments for the workers.

MBK employees are represented by a union, and membership is voluntary. There is a standing union committee that is responsible for facilitating daily communication between workers and plant management. Union leadership is elected annually by the plant's workers. Employees have unhindered access to top management. MBK senior management organizes regular plant-wide meetings.

MBK has installed computerized management systems to ensure that each employee's work hours conform to Mattel's GMP. This system checks the work schedule every day to make sure it is in compliance with GMP provisions. MBK also practices not swiping cards for time-out record keeping, which is similar to other Mattel-owned plants in Indonesia and Malaysia. ICCA has already noted its objections. The situation defies rational explanation and remains a mystery to ICCA.

Medical Facilities and Health Care

The plant contains a good clinic with five beds, staffed by a doctor and a state enrolled nurse (RN). The majority of injuries and sicknesses are burns, cuts, and respiratory problems. There is no charge for the medical services or medicines provided to workers. Employees are given annual health examinations free of charge.

Dormitories and Food Services

MBK has no on-site residential facilities. All workers live at home or make their own living arrangements. MBK subsidizes 47 percent of the cost of meals. The kitchen and canteen are well lit and clean. The factory kitchen and canteen can serve three meals a day to all workers. All food handlers are required to have an annual physical checkup. In addition, workers may purchase other food items from any of the five shops selling a variety of food products.

Overall Observations

MBK is been one of the best Mattel-owned and -operated plants audited by MIMCO/ICCA. The plant has a stable cadre of senior managers who appear committed to operating a well-maintained and smoothly functioning plant. The management has also demonstrated a strong commitment to creating a worker-friendly environment.

China

Mattel-Owned and -Operated Plants

ICCA conducted three rounds of formal audits of Mattel-owned and -operated plants in China. Mattel has four plants in China. The first two plants are Chang An (CA), also known as Meitai, and Guan Yao (GY), also known as Zhongmei. These two plants are dedicated to the manufacture of Barbie dolls and related toys. The third plant is Mattel Die Cast (MDC). It became operational in 2000 and is dedicated to the manufacture of die-cast toys. In 2006, it was retooled to include plastic toys in its manufacturing portfolio. The fourth plant is Mattel Engineering China (MEC), which is dedicated to the manufacturing and repairing of the tools and dies used in other Mattel plants worldwide.

Mattel's manufacturing arrangement in China is based on a processing fee agreement with its local partners, which are government-controlled entities. In this business model, the local partner owns the facilities and employs the workforce, and Mattel provides raw materials, equipment, and manufacturing engineering advice. The local partner is compensated by Mattel based on production volume. While the final authority and responsibility lies with the local partner[4] in matters concerning worker rights, safety, and treatment, it should be noted that the sole purpose of these facilities' founding and existence is to build Mattel toys for export.

Both CA and GY are large factories, with each employing between 8,000 and 9,000 workers during peak production periods. MDC is a medium-sized facility that employs between 1,000 and 2,500 workers, and is located in the vicinity of the GY plant. Workers in all three facilities are mostly young and female. MEC is the smallest of the four plants, employing about 350 to 400 workers. These are mostly male workers who are trained, professional technicians and engineers.

Audit Findings

ICCA conducted three rounds of formal audits of Mattel's China plants. The first round of formal audits took place in 1999[5] and was repeated in 2003 and 2007. They also involved several follow-up visits to all four facilities through mid-2008. The purpose of the follow-up visits was to evaluate the effectiveness of corrective action plans submitted by Mattel to ICCA. All of these reports were made public and are available on the Mattel and ICCA websites.

Workforce Management

Guan Yao and Chang An—the two plants accounting for a majority of the workers—turned out to be the Achilles' heel of the entire duration of ICCA's audit life cycle. From the very start, ICCA had serious questions about the practices in these plants with regard to proper compensation of workers as mandated in China labor laws and stipulated in GMP standards. There were similar questions with regard to legally mandated benefits, such as maternity leave and annual leave, deductions for dormitory rent, charges for food, et cetera. These issues continued to be challenging through the entire duration of ICCA's involvement.

In the early stages of the audit process, Mattel's internal group followed through on ICCA's findings with continued inspections and advice to the plant's management for improved compliance efforts. The process, however, turned out to be that of a wave effect showing ebbs and flows, but in the end nothing much changed.

From the very start, MIMCO/ICCA audits reported serious violations of GMP standards and Chinese law. However, in the early phases, Mattel's response to ICCA's findings was quite proactive even when it involved significant cost in the form of capital improvements.

For example, during the initial audit round, ICCA found a dormitory in such poor condition that it was almost uninhabitable. However, the plant's China partner argued that since the dormitory was built long before the introduction of the GMP, it should be exempted from GMP standards. This was an untenable argument and was rejected by ICCA. For Mattel's top management, this situation was equally unacceptable. Consequently, Mattel took the responsibility of paying for the dormitory's rehabilitation and to bring it up to GMP standards. The improvements, mostly in the female workers' living conditions, were so significant that it moved the Asia regional manager for Mattel to comment as to the tremendous difference this audit had made in the lives of current and future workers at the plant.

Unfortunately, ICCA's experience with other issues identified in the audit was not so encouraging. As details in the following sections indicate, a majority of other GMP noncompliance issues—both substantial and routine—remained unsolved. In every formal audit or its follow-up, either new or equally blatant practices were observed or old ones had resurfaced.

Shortly after ICCA's last audit, in 2008, Mattel indicated that it would pay for some of the important changes in the plants' accounting and record-keeping systems that were at the core of opaque reporting of workers' wages, working hours, and working conditions. However, before these changes could be monitored and confirmed, Mattel decided to discontinue its independent external monitoring program.

While Mattel's responses toward mediation were well intentioned and earnest, they were quite often unsuccessful. It was apparent that Mattel's China partners were unwilling to make changes in their record-keeping practices that would result in greater transparency. There was also strong resistance to making any changes that would incur additional costs, which China partners were unwilling to undertake. From ICCA's perspective, the China partners at the two plants viewed the GMP as something that belonged solely to Mattel and that Mattel should pay to implement. However, it was not clear that even if Mattel had agreed to pay for the necessary changes that China partners would be willing go along.

Hiring Practices and Worker Relations

A serious issue of concern at the start of the monitoring program was workers' awareness of Mattel's GMP initiative. Without proper awareness of the underlying principles, it would not be meaningful to expect or monitor compliance. ICCA interviews revealed that orientation programs and periodic communication protocols did not succeed in this area, with the exception of MDC, which showed that 87 percent of workers were aware of the GMP. Management concurred with ICCA's findings and promised to take appropriate steps to ensure all workers' GMP awareness. Follow-up audits of CA and GY revealed that a good-faith effort was in place, and ICCA was convinced that the situation would be remedied in a sustainable manner in the future.

The second round of audits noted that while the smaller MDC and MEC plants sustained their workers' GMP awareness, GY and CA, the two plants with the largest number of workers, had not made noticeable progress. By the time of the third round of audits, only 30 percent of GY and CA plant workers were aware of the GMP.

Working Hours

The extent of maximum allowable work hours had been the most vexing problem that ICCA encountered in its monitoring program in China. The initial audit of CA and GY plants in 1999 encountered problems in the transparency and clarity of payroll records. As a result, it was not possible to make a determination as to the accuracy of working hours and wage payments because of the opaqueness of the factories' record-keeping practices. The situation was also exacerbated by the confusion among workers with regard to their understanding of the pay stubs and their inability to verify their wages. Following the audit, Mattel and ICCA reached an understanding that the payroll systems would be redesigned for transparency, and that ICCA would revisit these plants within one year to verify compliance with the new systems. There were no payroll-related problems encountered in the MDC and MEC plants during the first round of audits.

ICCA's second round of audits in 2003 found all Mattel plants to have circumvented the spirit of the GMP via the use of several local variances that allowed them to exceed China's nationally mandated working hours limits. These included *consolidated hours,* which allowed a plant to schedule the total permissible yearly overtime hours (thirty-six hours per month for twelve months) during a shorter time span; *extended hours permits,* which allow plants to schedule sixty-hour workweeks throughout the year; and *peak-season extended hours permits,* which allow plants to schedule custom-tailored work schedules based on their stated needs. All four Mattel plants had secured these three permits, albeit without the locally required stipulations about their duration and specific daily and weekly limits. ICCA expressed concern over these practices, recognizing them to be carte blanche for unfettered management liberties at the expense of the workforce. This observation was also accompanied by a formal request from Mattel to take a clear stand on this issue and establish standards to which these plants would adhere.

In 2006, Mattel responded by allowing for a maximum of twelve-hour workdays and sixty- to seventy-two-hour workweeks, where such weeks would be limited to seventeen per year. Furthermore, no worker would work in excess of thirteen consecutive workdays, ensuring at least one rest day per week. Even though similar practices were the norm in the region, this policy was in violation of the Chinese labor law, as acknowledged by Mattel.

ICCA's 2007 audit found all four plants to exceed the twelve-hour workday and seventy-two-hour workweek standards, as well as the seventeen-week limit on sixty- to seventy-two-hour workweeks. ICCA concluded that all applicable laws, permits, and standards, self-imposed or otherwise, had been entirely meaningless throughout nine years of the monitoring program.

CA and GY had also created an arbitrary set of rules denying workers overtime pay when they had exceeded their regular hours work schedule rates while workers were required to be on premises in CA and GY plants. CA did not pay overtime wages to line leaders for a maximum of two hours per day even though their workday may extend beyond ten hours per day. MDC did not pay overtime wages if it totaled less than thirty minutes per day or if daily overtime exceeded 3.67 hours per day; workers were given time off on other days, but were compensated at regular wage rates. ICCA requested that Mattel pay back wages to those who were not paid at their entitled rates. Somewhat similar, although less severe problems were identified in MDC's record-keeping system, which resulted in workers being compensated based on established production schedules rather than their time card records.

Benefits and Deductions

Contrary to the provisions of the Chinese labor law, which allows for ninety days paid leave, the GY, CA, and MEC plants were not extending any maternity leave benefits to their workers at the time of the first round of audits. Upon ICCA's observations of this issue, the second round of audits noted some policy revisions: GY allowed one month paid leave with three-year tenure; CA allowed forty-five days paid leave to staff, and was planning to extend ninety days paid leave to all workers in 2001. MEC and MDC complied with the law and Mattel's GMP regarding this issue. The second round of 2003 revealed that GY and CA had implemented their stated plans, and that MDC was paying the benefit upon the workers' return, thus denying those who resign their entitled benefits. The third round of audits conducted in 2007 found no changes in the plants' respective policies. With regard to annual leave policies, three of the four plants had been compliant with GMP standards starting with the first round of audits; CA had no annual leave benefits in 1999, and had planned to offer one week paid leave to staff in 2001, extending it to all workers in 2002. The 2003 audit observed that the annual leave was offered only in December, and any worker who resigned before then would forego their benefits even if they were entitled. This policy was changed to conform to GMP standards by 2007.

ICCA recognized that all plants made considerable progress in meeting their obligations through the third round of audits in 2007. Nevertheless, it noted its disappointment that such apparent violations with the resultant loss of income for the workers should take so long to remedy in Mattel's China plants.

Most workers in Southeast China come from other provinces as guest workers. They also tend to stay in the dormitories and eat in the cafeterias provided by the factories. Chinese labor law allows these charges to be deducted from the workers' paychecks provided that these expenses do not exceed 50 percent of the monthly minimum wage for the district.

ICCA's first round of audits found no irregularities with respect to deductions applied to workers' earnings. MDC had a noteworthy policy of providing free food to all workers during their employment. However, during the second round in 2003, the CA and GY plants were found to be charging in excess of the 50 percent of minimum wage, which was the standard established by Mattel under the GMP. The third round of audits also noted a predatory policy on the part of CA management, which required workers to opt in or out of the dorm and meal plans for the duration of their contract. For guest workers in the province, and mostly first-time employees, the practical impact of this policy was to have 100 percent of the workforce on mandatory meal plans regardless of whether they ate at the company canteens.

Environment Protection and Worker Health and Safety Issues

Mattel's China plants, and notably the Chang An and Guan Yao plants, were equally lagging in their compliance efforts and reticent about providing information with regard to these activities. Looking back, the emerging theme through ICCA's monitoring span of nine years is that the Chinese plants had not followed through with the environmental or health and safety measures they had initially undertaken to comply with Mattel's GMP. Although the plants had started monitoring programs with commendable efforts in terms of ensuring worker safety and environmental consciousness, over the years these efforts had given way to a managerial attitude of "getting away with investing as little as possible, while maintaining compliance with the bare minimum standards." Predictably, and unfortunately, instead of the "continuous improvement" culture that ICCA had signed on to facilitate, this approach resulted in a continued deterioration of plants, facilities, equipment, and ultimately, worker safety.

Mattel's China Vendor Plants

Mattel outsources approximately one-half of its production needs to about forty major vendors in China. During the period of 2000–2008, over the entire audit life cycle, ICCA audited twenty top vendor plants from single to multiple audits.

These factories represented approximately 75 percent of the total procurement of Mattel's third-party manufacturing in terms of dollar value. These are top-tier Mattel suppliers, and in a number of cases, these vendor plants are solely dedicated to the production of Mattel-branded toys. All of the production facilities are located in Guangdong Province in South China, and offer employment to between 70,000 and 100,000 workers, depending on the production cycle.

The compliance requirements for the vendor plants are set up at a somewhat lower level compared to the company's owned and operated plants. Nevertheless, they stipulate compliance with legal requirements as a minimum for acceptable performance.

Overall Observations

ICCA's work with Mattel's China vendor plants started in 2000–2002 with a series of initial vendor consultation visits. These consultations were aimed toward developing a better understanding of the prevailing operating conditions in the supplier plants and their impact on employees' working and living conditions. The findings provided a mixed picture of the vendors' performance (Sethi et al., 2000). In one sense, this was to be expected considering the overall low level of environmental and social performance in locally owned and managed plants. Both Mattel and ICCA anticipated that moving forward, these plants would demonstrate significant improvement in their GMP compliance. There was also the implied expectation that all things being equal, Mattel would reward these plants with additional business.

First Round of China Vendor Audits, 2002–2003

The first round of formal audits of China vendors was conducted in August 2002 and January 2003. It covered twelve plants that comprised approximately 50 percent of Mattel's procurement from China vendors in U.S. dollars. As a matter of commercial nondisclosure agreement, all audited plants have been assigned a number (e.g., Plant 1, Plant 2, etc.) and are referred to by the corresponding number in all of Mattel's and ICCA's documentation (exhibit 2.4).

The findings of the audit revealed a number of areas where substantial improvements had been achieved. They also indicated that more work needed to be done in general maintenance of the facilities and in treatment of workers. The audit established that there were no underage workers employed in any of

Exhibit 2.4   Characteristics of Plants

China Vendor Plant #	Number of Employees, Regular Peak	Capacity Dedicated to Mattel Products
Plant 1	3,700	60%
Plant 2	1,100	100%
Plant 3	1,700	85%
Plant 4	1,250	70%
Plant 5	9,200	60%
Plant 6	8,100	60%
Plant 7	7,800	20%
Plant 8	6,200	40%
Plant 9	3,500	40%
Plant 10	5,800	60%
Plant 11	1,400	80%
Plant 12	4,500	100%
Plant 18	4,200	Not Available
Plant 17	4,200	Not Available
Plant 21	2,200	Not Available
Plant 15	2,400	Not Available
Plant 14	8,500	45%
Smile	Not Available	Not Available
Plant 13	4,000	50%
Plant 16	4,600	Not Available
Plant 19	2,500	Not Available
Plant 20	1,900	Not Available

the audited vendor plants. Vendor plants were paying appropriate wages for regular and overtime working hours. There were also noticeable improvements in health and safety standards, although from a very low starting point.

Dormitories and canteen facilities were a mixed bag. In part, it reflected the unusual situation wherein a unit of the local government built and operated dormitories to meet the needs of a cluster of factories. The situation created a conflict of incentives and split responsibility. The dormitory owner sought to maximize its profit margin by building poor-quality dormitories and skimping on maintenance and upkeep. Factory owners did not have enough influence over the dormitory providers to improve cleanliness and maintenance. Instead, some unscrupulous factory owners sought to earn extra revenue by expanding the difference in the rent they charged the workers and the factory's cost of rental and canteen facilities.

Record keeping for workers' normal hours also showed improvement from the conditions observed by ICCA during the initial round of informal fact-finding visits. A major area of persistent noncompliance pertained to the maximum numbers of hours worked, which invariably exceeded the legally mandated standards and even somewhat relaxed standards in the GMP.

The problem of excessive work hours had four dimensions, which made it all but impossible to comply with any of the legal or other standards, such as the GMP.

1. Factory owners were strongly motivated to get contracts from foreign buyers with promises of on-time delivery that would be impossible without resorting to work weeks of sixty-eight to seventy-two or more hours.
2. While foreign buyers made public displays of their anguish over excessive working hours, there was no planning to create timely order flow, keeping in mind the plant capacity and total manpower available. This was equally true in the factories that were completely dedicated to manufacturing goods for a single buyer, in which case the buyer (a) had to be fully aware of the number of work hours/workers that would be needed to fill the order, and (b) had total control over the production process to restrict excessive hours.
3. In a majority of cases, workers themselves were interested in working long hours to earn more money from a meager base, both to support themselves while working and to save money for their families left behind in their home town and villages. Therefore, they would leave factories that did not provide work with lots of overtime hours.
4. To avoid problems with foreign buyers, factory owners often resorted to a variety of accounting and bookkeeping tricks to create superficial compliance with laws or voluntary code standards with regard to regular and overtime working hours, and payment of appropriate wages for those hours.

From this step, it was not too difficult for some unscrupulous factory owners to use similar tactics and thus underpay their workers for the amount of work done. Some vendors also manipulated wage calculations by creating a parallel system of piece rates (which were hard to calculate and poorly understood by the workers) and hourly rates (as required by the law) and thereby making the system complex and opaque, which invariably benefited the factory owner at the expense of the workers.

During the various audits, it was observed that Mattel had to deal with the reality of the marketplace and allow for working hours that exceeded legal limits of maximum hours. Nevertheless, Mattel succeeded in (a) maintaining a transparent and fully verifiable system of time records and, even more important, (b) ensuring that workers received appropriate wages for the number of regular and overtime hours worked. Furthermore, Mattel's auditors were substantially successful in keeping to minimum, and within reasonable limits, the deductions from workers' wages for such items as dormitory rent, cost of food, uniforms, medical charges, cash fines for various work-related infractions, et cetera. Needless to say, it was a continuing source of concern to Mattel and ICCA since local factory owners were quite inventive in finding new deductions that could be imposed on the workers. It should also be noted that Mattel was quite reluctant to use its strongest weapon, or even threaten to do so, namely, to drop a factory from its supplier pool.

The situation with regard to plant maintenance and prevention of contamination of air, ground, and water resources has improved over the audit life cycle, although there was considerable divergence among different plants. In general, most of the factories were responsive to changes that would improve the overall routine maintenance of plant and physical facilities, which were also conducive to improving working conditions for the workers. However, when it came to major equipment purchases such as water treatment for paint removal, air-circulation systems, et cetera, there was considerable resistance because the equipment required capital expenditures that could not be directly related to increased production. There was also the issue of lax regulatory oversight, which further reduced any pressure toward making needed improvements. A third element had to do with lack of trained and experienced personnel. In a number of cases, ICCA observed that the factory had excellent equipment, but it was inoperable because of improper installation and poor upkeep. Notwithstanding, ICCA observed one factory that would be top rated for the quality and upkeep of its plant and equipment even though the factory was also the subject of repeated multiple violations of GMP standards with regard to workers' hours, wages, and other related conditions.

Areas showing significant improvement included safety of workplace; dormitories and canteens; workers' access to all levels of management; lack of discrimination or promotion based on sex, race, or ethnic origins; and a significant reduction in poor treatment of workers.

Most plants demonstrated increased attention and concern for environmental issues, both as they affected the workers inside the plants' facilities and as the plants' air emissions, water discharge, and waste treatment affected the surrounding areas. However, overall upkeep as well as certain EHS aspects needed further improvements.

Audit Findings on Specific Issues from Different Vendor Plants' Working Hours

At the time of the first formal audit of vendor plants, Mattel's GMP did not have any adjustments in its requirement for overtime hours that would address variations in seasonal production. Instead it restricted the workweek to a maximum of sixty hours, including overtime. ICCA's audit of the twelve vendors visited during the first formal visit showed that all of the vendors were routinely scheduling work hours that were in excess of the sixty-hour-per-week limit stipulated in the GMP, generally scheduling workweeks of sixty-six to seventy-two hours based on a six-day workweek.

Furthermore, in a number of cases, the consolidated work hours permits provided by local labor bureaus were so outside the prevailing norms as to question their authenticity. For example, the local authorization permits received by Plants 10 and 11 included an authorization to exceed the maximum annual overtime hours provided under the Chinese labor law. ICCA had found no other instance of similar extension in its audit work in China. The permits for Plants 11 and 12 allowed them to work a total of 1,040 overtime hours during 2002, extending the national China labor law limit of 432 overtime hours by almost 250 percent.

Mattel's GMP requirements obliged factories to provide workers with a compensatory day off within thirty days for work scheduled beyond seven days. Where a compensatory time-off day is not provided within thirty days, workers must be compensated at twice the normal wage rates. Of the twelve plants audited, five plants (3, 6, 7, 9, and 11), representing 23,000 workers or 43.4 percent of the total workers covered in the audit, were unable to provide any records to ICCA to show that they either provided an alternate rest day within thirty days or compensated their workers with double wages as required by the GMP standards.

Mandatory Overtime

Both China labor law and Mattel's GMP require that all overtime work must be voluntary and that workers have the right to decline overtime work. In reality, a large part of overtime is mandatory and built into the workers' employment expectations. This is a common practice and is accepted by workers. Therefore, from the perspective of the workers, the issue of involuntary overtime arises where (a) the implied consent as discussed above does not apply, and (b) a worker's request to be excused from overtime work because of tiredness, illness, or other personal reasons has been denied. For example, in the case of Plant 1, management required that a worker must find a substitute replacement before he or she is allowed to decline overtime work. Similarly, some plants limited the number of workers who could refuse mandatory overtime (Plants 5 and 6). A particularly serious noncompliance of voluntary overtime policy was discovered by ICCA at Plant 12, where the entire workforce of 4,600 workers was asked to work on a national holiday.

Appropriate Payment of Wages

While the payment of minimum wages and compensation for overtime hours improved since initial informal assessment, many plants were found to be involved in questionable practices involving monetary deductions from workers' wages. One such area included imposition of cash fines as a disciplinary measure. Cash fines were found to be imposed by five factories (Plants 1, 5, 6, 11, and 12), representing 50 percent of the workers covered in the audit. It should be noted here that the imposition of cash fines is permissible under Mattel's GMP, which restricts cash fines to no more than 20 percent of the legal minimum monthly wage. Although individual fines imposed by the plants did not exceed the maximum limit provided in GMP, the frequency with which these fines were imposed, the total amount of funds raised by the plants' management through fines, and the disposition of these funds raised questions as to their effectiveness and utility. Vendors generally indicated that funds collected through cash fines were used for employee welfare activities, including holiday celebrations and other entertainment programs. The factory managers' assertions in all these plants, however, could not be verified because the plants failed to provide any information or financial records to show how these funds were expended.

Questionable Deductions from Workers' Paychecks

Another area pertaining to monetary deductions involved charges for dormitory accommodations and food served at the factories' canteens. Plants 8 and 9 required workers to make an upfront, nonrefundable payment of RMB80 as the cost of initial supplies for dormitory living, such as bed sheets, towels, et cetera. Plants 1 and 11 also imposed a mandatory monthly fee regardless of where a worker lived. Plants 7 and 11 imposed mandatory deduction for food from workers' paychecks, regardless of whether they ate in the canteen. In Plant 1, eating in the canteen was mandatory. In Plant 8, although eating in the canteen was voluntary, many workers were not aware of it and ended up paying for it through mandatory deductions.

Improper Record Keeping

Other areas needing improvement included nonavailability of records to verify that workers who performed overtime work on rest days received either double the normal rate of wages or a compensatory day off; inconsistent application of regulations with regard to fringe benefits, such as maternity leave, annual leave, and ineffective use of cash fines; worker training with regard to safety; and inadequate use of personal protective equipment.

Environmental Protection Issues

Among other negative findings was inadequate attention to macro environmental issues, such as treatment and disposal of wastewater, air and water quality, and ventilation, and a culture of inadequate attention to general plant maintenance and operations. Most factories were in noncompliance in varying degrees with GMP standards pertaining to environmental issues.

Mattel's Response

In response to the ICCA findings, Mattel provided details of its remedial action. The company's internal auditors analyzed more than 300 specific findings from

ICCA reports pertaining to the twelve plants. They worked with individual vendors to develop plans for corrective action to address the initial audit findings. The company provided ICCA with a detailed report showing how each and every change was organized and implemented, with a record of verification, and, where appropriate, provided for ICCA's review copies of proper certification from appropriate government agencies and professional bodies. The company also provided photographic evidence of new and repaired installations indicating the extent and scope of corrective measures taken by the vendors in cooperation with Mattel. As a result, of the twelve plants in the original audit, ICCA undertook a follow-up audit of the seven plants (Plants 1, 2, 3, 6, 9, 10, and 12) to verify the adequacy of compliance efforts. The follow-up audit indicated that with the exception of two plants (Plants 1 and 12), all were in full compliance with the GMP standards. The improvement of vendor plants' performance since the initial visits, and Mattel's robust corrective action in response to ICCA findings, marked substantial progress in China vendor plants' management and oversight.

Follow-Up Inspections of Vendor Plants

Over the period of 2004–2007, ICCA undertook formal field audits of nine additional plants as well as follow-up visits to the vendor plants that were found to be at various levels of violation of Mattel's GMP. The audits revealed that the plants were generally in compliance with the main provisions of Mattel's GMP that were considered to be "zero tolerance" issues, such as child labor, forced labor, minimum wage, and discrimination in hiring.

Nevertheless, a number of questionable practices were discovered in relation to plant upkeep, use of personal protection equipment, workers' access to bathroom facilities and drinking water, and monetary deductions. Most common practices included charging workers for a medical examination required upon hiring, additional sets of uniforms, and factory IDs, and offering maternity payment for workers only if they returned to the factory after ninety days of leave. The issue of extended overtime continued to be a general practice at most of the plants. However, management had improved its compliance with securing consolidated work hours permits, and violations in the overtime scheduling, although occurring in some instances, were no longer found to be a routine issue.

Another disturbing practice found in China vendor plants had to do with the plant management coaching production workers in order to "pass" the inspection. In ICCA's audit practice, such incidents happened twice: in Plant 18 during the initial formal audit in 2005, and in Plant 1 during the second formal audit in 2008.

Although Mattel management and its internal audit department continued to cooperate with the ICCA audit team in examining areas of compliance concerns and assuring ICCA in taking remediation, the changes in vendor plants' operations did not address all key findings, and in many cases included only policy and documentation improvements. ICCA's follow-up visits found numerous instances of continuous violation of maternity leave policies, as well as persistent workers' complaints of inadequate access to bathrooms and drinking water during production hours. This situation is particularly troublesome, as improvement of workstation leave permits or payment of benefits should not pose any capital or operational burden on the plant management.

Environment, Health, and Safety Issues

ICCA's first round of audits and follow-ups noted that both the vendors and Mattel internal audits had emphasized worker-related issues, that is, employment of underage workers, excessive work hours, poor record keeping, and payment of improper wages for regular and overtime work. This was to be expected since these issues were closely identified with allegations of sweatshops. ICCA's audit team strongly indicated that worker health and safety issues and macro-environmental concerns dealing with air, water, and ground pollution were an integral part of the GMP and China labor laws.

In this case, vendor responses and Mattel's efforts were mixed and uneven. In fairness, it should be noted that Mattel's China vendor plants did not represent a homogeneous picture. Some of the vendor facilities showed substantial progress in improving the physical work environment at the factories. For instance, Plants 19 and 20 had air-conditioning systems installed in all production floors—a practice seldom seen among supplier plants. Moreover, these plants offered worker accommodations that were better than the typical worker dormitories, both in terms of individual space and general upkeep.

At the same time, other factories continued to use obsolete and poorly maintained equipment for water treatment, sludge removal, and air ventilation, since corrective action in these areas required capital expenditures and additional staff for maintenance and monitoring. The plants consider these expenses as nonessential given the low profit margins and highly competitive markets. Mattel's internal audit group was invariably in agreement with ICCA's findings and made efforts to improve the situation. However, Mattel was unwilling or unable to insist that these plants make the necessary improvement as required by China's laws and Mattel's GMP standards.

Mattel's Reluctance to Discipline Recalcitrant Vendor Factories

Unfortunately, toward the end of the second round of audits, it became apparent to ICCA that Mattel's enforcement of its GMP standards was losing momentum despite clear-cut violations and repeated promises of change. Several factories stood out in their below-average level of management of social issues and their inability to adequately respond to Mattel's requirements for independent audit.

The Case of Plant #7

One of these factories was Plant 7, which was inspected during the first round of China vendor plant audit. During the initial audit, Plant 7 was found to have significant noncompliance issues in the areas of payment of regular and overtime wages, excessive overtime hours, and poor record keeping with regard to working hours and wage payments to workers. Mattel informed ICCA that the company had decided to discontinue its business relationship with this vendor. However, Mattel subsequently informed ICCA that, for business reasons, it had continued its contractual relationship with this vendor.

As a result, ICCA continued to observe the plant's operations with regard to meeting Mattel's GMP standards. This factory was revisited three more times over the period of 2005–2007. During these visits, ICCA identified a number of noncompliance issues involving mandatory deductions for medical checkups, recruitment fees, charges for uniforms and factory IDs, discrimination in hiring for pregnant workers. One of the most persistent issues that ICCA brought to the attention of Mattel's internal audit department was the unavailability of a consistent computerized record-keeping system. The factory was found to have two sets of books to meet the recording standards of two clients. Moreover, workers' hours were recorded by line leaders. The lack of transparency with regard to double bookkeeping and manual record keeping was repeatedly brought to the plant management's attention by ICCA, and was also noted by Mattel internal audit reports over the years of the factory's inspection, but to no avail.

Another persistent practice in Plant 7's operations related to routine work on Sundays, creating a work schedule of one rest day for every thirteen days (instead of every seventh day). It also became apparent during ICCA's discussions that Plant 7's management had no plans to change its practices with regard to scheduling work hours that were in excess of the maximum permissible limit or other practices, such as work on Sundays.

In its latest response to ICCA's findings on Plant 7's practices, Mattel noted that it would not "continue a relationship with a vendor that does not demonstrate a commitment to comply with GMP." However, ICCA does not have any information as to whether Mattel's business with Plant 7 has been terminated.

The Case of Plant #18

The most unprecedented situation occurred in Plant 18. The first audit of this facility was intended to take place in December 2005, following informal plant consultation. However, the audit was terminated by ICCA after it became apparent that a large number of workers were told not to come to work on the day of the audit. Other workers were found to have been coached by the management to provide predetermined answers, which compromised the integrity of the audit process. Both Mattel and ICCA agreed that Plant 18 would be given an opportunity to undertake the necessary corrective action, following which the plant would be formally audited by ICCA.

The second formal audit took place on July 10–11, 2006. The audit found a number of noncompliance issues with regard to workers' treatment and general plant upkeep. However, during confidential one-on-one interviews with workers, it became apparent that the management had again resorted to coaching the entire plant workforce to give similar answers to questions that might be asked by ICCA's audit team. The inconsistency between management's claims and workers' responses posed serious concerns about the integrity of the already quite negative audit findings. The widespread violation of extended overtime permit and the deteriorating physical conditions of the plant facilities and workers' amenities left little faith in management's ability and intent to make the necessary improvements in management style and operational policies.

Mattel was disappointed with Plant 18's lack of improvement and indicated that it would not provide any new business to the plant until the management adequately addressed the compliance issues outlined by ICCA. Unfortunately, the third audit visit of Plant 18 in 2008 did not indicate any improvements in the plant's management of labor and environmental issues. The plant was found to be one of the biggest offenders of Mattel's GMP standards as well as of China's labor laws. However, ICCA did not receive a formal confirmation from Mattel as to its action with regard to Plant 18.

The third audit of Plant 18 coincided with ICCA's third visit of Plant 1. The audit of this plant was terminated due to similar findings of workers' being coached and cutting the workforce more than twice on the day of the audit. Moreover, worker surveys conducted at another facility (Plant 11) visited during the same round of audits revealed that coaching of workers prior to audits was a regular practice. Workers at Plant 11 stated that they usually received cash awards for responding to the auditors' questionnaires with the predetermined answers. While the workers at Plant 11 refrained from giving ICCA's team preset responses due to the confidential nature of the survey, their acknowledgement of such practices raises serious concerns about the integrity of independent audits conducted by various groups in China vendor plants.

Overall, the second and third round of vendor plant audits suggested a widening gap between instances of noncompliance with GMP standards and Mattel's promises and performance to improve compliance by the vendor plants. Finally, as a follow-up to ICCA's third round of audits, Mattel provided ICCA in late 2008 with details of its proposed corrective action pertaining to the vendor plants. The actual implementation of these actions remains unknown to ICCA as Mattel has terminated its independent third-party external audits.

Concluding Remarks: Lessons Learned and Unlearned

In this chapter, we have presented a detailed description and discussion of Mattel's voluntary code of conduct, the circumstances that led to its creation, and the process by which it was implemented and ultimately abandoned by the company. The authors were intimately involved in almost every aspect of code creation and implementation throughout its entire life cycle of approximately nine years.

This case study offers an invaluable opportunity to examine the dynamic nature of changes within the company and how they affect and are affected by the changes in the company's external competitive and sociopolitical environment. Mattel's GMP was a highly innovative and one-of-its-kind initiative. In this sense, it became a live laboratory, however imperfect, to examine various aspects of the viability of a voluntary code of conduct by companies and industry groups. To the extent that it provides a meaningful mechanism toward self-regulation that would be flexible and adaptable enough to changing economic and sociopolitical circumstances, it could also help to narrow, if not completely eliminate, the gap between societal expectations and corporate performance.

Ideally, it would have been desirable to examine similar cases of voluntary codes of conduct and follow them through the process of code creation and implementation over a certain length of time. Unfortunately, this has proved to be impossible. An extensive search of literature has failed to discover any instances of publicly reported voluntary codes of conduct. Notwithstanding the paucity of other comparable case studies, we believe our observations may suggest potential pathways that companies and industries could put to good use in creating and implementing voluntary codes of conduct.

Our analysis in this section has been divided into four categories:

1. Corporate responses to external crisis.
2. Importance of ethical norms, corporate culture, and institutional memory.
3. Operational aspects of implementing global manufacturing principles (GMP).
4. Corporate response to external forces of competition, regulatory environments, and reputational risk.

1. Corporate Response to External Crisis

Why is it that companies in a given industry, when confronted with an external crisis, respond differently to similar situations? Our analysis in this instance, and in a number of others examined by this author (Sethi and Williams, 2000), indicates that a large part of the differences can be traced first to the character and vision of the company's CEO and top management. The innovative and potentially risky challenge of launching Mattel's GMP was the responsibility of Mattel's then CEO, Jill Barad. From all accounts, she was a highly focused and determined executive who would force the organization in a preferred direction by sheer force of personality. She had also spent a major part of her career as a marketing executive and was thus very sensitive to public perception and risk to corporate reputation. In addition, she had the confidence and support of Mattel's board, which included a member of Mattel's founding family.

Barad saw the crisis in terms of public perception and reputational risk that would need a bold response to gain public confidence. In this assessment, she was quite right. Despite some skepticism, the GMP initiative received positive coverage in the news media and supportive comments from Mattel's critics and the NGO community concerned about sweatshops and human rights abuses. Therefore, from the very start, the top management was committed to the creation of the GMP. While there were extensive discussions and differences of opinion, they focused on making the code work.

No sooner had the code been put into practice than there was a change in the top management. Barad's successor at Mattel was Robert A. Eckert, who also came with a background in marketing, having previously served as the CEO of Kraft Foods, Inc. (Hays, 2000). The new CEO and his top management team found good reasons to be supportive of the new initiative. He offered strong endorsement based on his belief that companies must demonstrate responsible social conduct to legitimize the right of self-regulation. As we stated in an earlier part of this paper, he further reiterated his belief in a speech at a United Nations conference (ICCA, 2007) and in comments to a reporter with the *New York Times* (Dee, 2007).

2. Corporate Culture and Ethical Norms

Corporate culture—a company's institutional values and traditions—provides the glue that binds a company's various internal constituencies into a cohesive community. It also serves as a filtering mechanism through which the company views its external environment. Without a supportive corporate culture (internal) and corporate reputation (external), the CEO and top management team are likely to meet strong resistance from within and without when trying to impose discrete and substantive changes in corporate strategy and conduct. Similarly, a CEO who is not in sync with corporate culture and prevailing societal expectations is unlikely to maximize the value of these resources. It will be difficult to create a viable strategy that the company's managers and employees will enthusiastically implement and that the company's stakeholders will accept.[6]

From our observations and from working with executives at various levels of the Mattel organization, we could not ascertain a discernible corporate culture that was unique and distinct from the corporate culture prevailing in most large corporations and, more notably, large multinational corporations. In part, this may have been due to Mattel's turbulent corporate history where the company went through severe financial and strategic missteps that brought it to the brink of financial collapse. The latest change in corporate leadership at Mattel appears to be symptomatic of this trend. This culture can best be described as insular, focused on internal efficiencies, and where most other constituencies are viewed in transactional terms and bargaining leverage determines their relative value to the corporation.

From our perspective, the contemporary Mattel, Inc., is a company driven by economic and market considerations. Its business practices, apart from the GMP, are no different than most other companies in the toy industry. When it comes to corporate social responsibility and good corporate citizenship, the company uses it as a thin patina to wrap around its "business as usual" modus operandi. The primary intent of the GMP was to embed corporate social responsibility (CSR) and make it an integral part of corporate strategy and operations. This would transform the notion of corporate social responsibility to corporate social accountability. It would imply that GMP-related activities would not be viewed as a reflection of good corporate citizenship, but as an integral part of managing reputational risk and maintaining a sustainable business model.

3. Operational Aspects of Implementing
Global Manufacturing Principles

The initial response of Mattel's management to ICCA's audit findings was prompt and unambiguous. ICCA was encouraged to communicate directly with Mattel's top management. The president of ICCA was invited to speak at Mattel's annual shareholders' meeting. At the operational level, Mattel's social audit department provided timely and systematic response to ICCA's findings, and supervised corrective action at Mattel-owned and -operated plants as well as vendor plants. Even more important, Mattel's top management supported ICCA by requiring major changes in its factories in Mexico and China.

Field operations received two types of signals as to top management's expectations with regard to GMP compliance. The first set consisted of formal communications that outlined lines of authority and responsibility for GMP compliance. These were reinforced through regular meetings between top management and senior managers from the field. Equally important were the signals that were sent by top management's actions, such as the rehabilitation of factories in Mexico and China.

The progress in GMP compliance during the first four years was impressive and system-wide. Under the circumstances, it would be logical to assume that top management expectations with regard to the GMP would be integrated in business operations, management performance, and compensation. Unfortunately, in reality this expectation was not fully realized, and it set in motion a gradual erosion in Mattel's commitment to GMP principles and practices.

a. From the outset, Mattel had excluded its licensee operations from ICCA audits. The company does not publicly disclose its revenue from licensing fees. However, financial analysts estimate that Mattel derives almost 50 percent of its total revenue from licensing operations. The exclusion of this activity would thereby significantly impact the company's overall attitude toward GMP. It will make licensing operations more profitable and less subject to public scrutiny when compared with revenues from Mattel's own manufacturing and procurement operations.

b. A similar situation existed between the company-owned and -operated plants and the vendor-owned plants. Managers of Mattel-owned plants often complained about Mattel's double standard whereby vendor plants were held to a lower standard of GMP compliance, which put Mattel's own plants at a competitive disadvantage when making similar products.

c. Among the vendor plants, ICCA also received comments that Mattel does not necessarily reward vendors having a higher level of GMP compliance with either bigger orders or higher prices to compensate for their GMP compliance costs.

d. As we have noted in earlier parts of this chapter, notwithstanding Mattel's formal commitments and assertions, the company was extremely reluctant to discontinue its business relationships with vendors that were charged with repeated violations of GMP standards.

e. With regard to social audits and Mattel's GMP compliance efforts, the company's organizational structure and operational procedures created conflicting goals. The field-level auditors, especially in China, had a direct line of reporting to the area-level managers, who were also responsible for timely and cost-effective procurement of toys.

f. ICCA's continuous interaction with Mattel's field operators suggested that area managers were happy to ensure GMP compliance where such compliance was easily accomplished, did not elicit resistance from the vendors, and would not disrupt the flow of products. This had the effect of many vendor plant managers and even Mattel's own plant manger to downgrade, if not ignore, recommendations of Mattel's own social compliance auditors.

g. ICCA found Mattel's social compliance auditors in the field to be quite experienced and dedicated to the task of improving GMP compliance, and where appropriate, helping vendor plant managers with advice and training. This was especially true in the case of China, where conditions for improving GMP compliance were difficult and challenging. Nevertheless, Mattel's China-based social audit group frequently lost its most experienced people because of the less rewarding work environment at Mattel and more remunerative career opportunities elsewhere.

h. The situation with regard to the social audit group at Mattel's headquarters was equally uncertain. Over the nine-year time span, ICCA noticed a high rate of turnover among its professional technical staff. The reasons for such turnover were also apparent and predictable. From ICCA's perspective, these professionals appeared not to be confident in the company's total commitment to GMP and thus found their work somewhat marginalized, leading to poor job satisfaction, lower financial rewards, and fewer opportunities for upward mobility.

4. Corporate Response to External Forces

Mattel's initial response to external challenges was bold and unequivocal, and it achieved its desired result. However, maintaining that response required that Mattel make a long-term commitment to GMP with its conditions of complete transparency, third-party external monitoring, and compliance verification. It was hoped that this approach would engender strong public support and pressure the rest of the toy industry to follow suit.

Unfortunately, this did not happen. Public and NGO campaigns against sweatshops were short-lived and could not be sustained without consumer support in the marketplace. While at the corporate level, the cost of GMP compliance—improving conditions in the factories to comply with Mattel's standards—was not materially significant when measured as a proportion of total production costs or sales prices, these costs were significant at the procurement level compared to the company's competitors. Consequently, Mattel's field managers felt pressured to minimize and delay compliance to contain costs. From ICCA's perspective, this widened the gap between Mattel's GMP promise and actual compliance and brought further pressure on Mattel. Under the circumstances, Mattel chose to discard its GMP compliance based on cost-benefit analysis. It did not see any material or reputational benefit by adhering to its GMP. Instead, it opted for the industry-wide voluntary code of conduct called ICTI Care, which provided no independent third-party external monitoring. Nor did it call for public disclosure of audit findings.

Notes

1. Mattel could legitimately argue that it had not abandoned its code of conduct, Global Manufacturing Principles (GMP), and continues to implement it. However, as we shall discuss in this chapter, Mattel terminated two of the main principals that made its code unique from other individual company or industry-wide codes. These were an independent third-party external monitoring of Mattel's compliance with its code, and full public disclosure of audit findings (including deficiencies found by the auditors and corrective action taken by the company). These principals were also the prime reason that impelled Mattel to stay and for the industry-wide voluntary code called ICTI Care. At the time, Mattel discontinued its external monitoring system and joined the toy industry's ICTI

Care program. This program professes to carry out independent audits. However, it does not provide any details as to how these audits are carried out so that one might assess their quality and independent character. Secondly, the findings of these audits are not publicly disclosed.

2. Comments made by Robert A. Eckert, chairman and CEO, Mattel, Inc., to MIMCO members at a meeting at Mattel headquarters in El Segundo, California, on October 4, 2000.

3. All audit reports cited in this paper are available on Mattel and ICCA's website, http:// www.sicca-ca.org/reports.php.

4. MDC has been an exception to this separation of responsibility and authority; Mattel has exercised full control over the entire plant regardless of the legal partnership structure.

5. For the purposes of this discussion, even though the first formal audit of the MDC facility took place following its opening in 2000, its findings are reported as a part of the first round of audits in 1999.

6. This situation was dramatically stated in the case of Nestlé and the infant formula boycott controversy. During the early stages of the controversy, the decentralized organization proved ineffective in responding to public pressure, because the source of the problem was in one region while the source of public pressure was in another part of the world. Thus the problems of turf, budgetary constraints, and differing management style and operational tactics in the two regions contributed to an exacerbation of the problem. Consequently, the top management of Nestle in Switzerland took control of the problems and installed a separate management team in Washington, D.C., which would report directly to Nestlé's top management and bypass the authority of the area manager in the United States as well as the managers responsible for the worldwide marketing of infant formula products. This turned out to be a most innovative and effective approach. Within four years, the new organization not only resolved the issues, but also caused a 180-degree turnaround in Nestlé's reputation, from a highly negative to a substantively positive level.

   The ad-hoc organization, however, could not be integrated into the Nestlé's existing global organization and decision-making structures. Soon after the issue was resolved, the new organization was dissolved and all authority to manage infant formula marketing reverted to the regular managers. Once in power, these managers undertook to erase all credit for resolving the issue from the new ad-hoc organization. Instead, Nestlé commissioned a journalist to write a book for general public distribution at Nestlé's expense. This book rewrote the history of the infant formula controversy as Nestlé's executives wanted the world to see it. It placed all the blame for the controversy on Nestlé's critics and projected Nestlé as the hapless victim of NGOs' less-than-ethical conduct and spreading of inaccurate and misleading information. It also largely credited Nestlé's seasoned managers for successfully handling the issue with only a minor role assigned to the ad-hoc organization. See S. Prakash Sethi, *Multinational Corporations and the Impact of Public Advocacy on Corporate Strategy: Nestle and the Infant Formula Controversy* (Boston: Kluwer Academic Publishers, 1994); S. Prakash Sethi and Bharat B. Bhalla, "A New Perspective on International Social Regulation of Business: An Evaluation of the Compliance Status of the International Code of Marketing of Breast-Milk Substitutes," *Journal of Socio-Economics* 22, no. 2 (1993): 141–158.

3

Freeport-McMoRan Copper & Gold, Inc.
An Innovative Voluntary Code of Conduct to Protect Human Rights, Create Employment Opportunities, and Create Economic Development of the Indigenous People

S. Prakash Sethi, David B. Lowry, Emre A. Veral,
H. Jack Shapiro, and Olga Emelianova

In December 2003, Freeport-McMoRan Copper & Gold, Inc. (hereinafter referred to as Freeport) announced the creation of a voluntary code of conduct, called "Guiding Principles for Indonesian Operations—People and the Community." The code outlined a set of principles that would guide the company's activities at its mine site in Papua, Indonesia.

This code was indeed a *sui generis* and unprecedented for a company in the mining industry. It incorporated elements of compliance on issues that have never been fully recognized by any company in the extractive industry. These pertain to, among others, protection of human rights of the mine workers and people in the surrounding community; creation of job opportunities and training programs for the local population who would have been deprived of their land and traditional means of income; treatment of the indigenous people and their rights to land and resources; and contributions to their economic development.

Furthermore, in another first for the industry, the company also undertook two additional measures: it would make regular reports as to its compliance efforts, and would engage the services of an independent outside monitoring group to audit its activities and claims of compliance. The report of the auditing group would be made public without any prior censorship by the company, and the company would also make public its response as to corrective actions.

It should be apparent that in creating its code of conduct, Freeport was not entirely motivated by altruistic considerations. Instead, it was a response to public outcry and criticism—both in Indonesia and around the world—for its actions in the preceding five-year period. In one sense, public criticism of mining companies was not limited to Freeport, but was pervasive in most other companies in the industry and included issues of environmental degradation, human rights violations, collusion with local police and military to suppress dissent among the indigenous people, and bribery and corruption involving various government agencies that would help mining companies circumvent local laws. These situations were particularly egregious in poor and less developed countries in Asia and Africa that were resource rich but suffered from oppressive and otherwise weak governments that were unable or unwilling to protect the legitimate interests of their people.[1]

This chapter has a twofold objective. First, to examine the conditions—physical, resource-based, and organizational (i.e., orientation of the company's top management and corporate culture)—that would propel a company to take a particular approach in response to external challenges. And second, to examine how the management commitment was translated into action over a sustained period of time and in response to external challenges and internal stresses among various segments of the corporate management.

Freeport-McMoRan: The Company

Freeport-McMoRan Copper & Gold, Inc., was formed in the late 1980s as a spin-off from the parent company, Freeport-McMoRan, Inc., whose roots go back to the early 1900s. Freeport-McMoRan Copper and Gold Company, Inc. (Freeport) is an international mining company with its primary reserves in copper, gold, and molybdenum. In March 2007, the company merged with Phelps Dodge Corporation and moved its headquarters from New Orleans, Louisiana, to Tucson, Arizona.

In 2009, Freeport ranked 140th on the Fortune 500 list of the largest companies in the United States. It ranked 258th prior to its merger with Phelps Dodge. As of December 31, 2009, Freeport's revenues totaled to $15.04 billion. The company has approximately one-third of its copper reserves in Indonesia, another third in South America, 26 percent in North America, and 8 percent in Africa. It conducts its operations primarily through its operating subsidiaries, PT Freeport Indonesia (PTFI), Freeport-McMoRan Corporation (formerly Phelps Dodge), and Atlantic Copper.

The company's portfolio of assets includes the Grasberg mining complex in West Papua, Indonesia, the world's largest copper and gold mine in terms of recoverable reserves; the Morenci and Safford minerals districts in North America; the Cerro Verde and El Abra operations in South America; and the Tenke Fungurume minerals district in the Democratic Republic of Congo. Freeport's consolidated recoverable proven and probable reserves totaled 104.2 billion pounds of copper, 37.2 million ounces of gold, 2.59 billion pounds of molybdenum, 270.4 million ounces of silver, and 0.78 billion pounds of cobalt.

Freeport's mining subsidiary PTFI presented enormous operational, managerial, and sociopolitical challenges for the parent company. For many years,

Freeport's Ertsberg and Grasberg mines were mostly operated by expatriate engineers and managers. With the expansion of the mine in the early 1990s, the government of Indonesia put enormous pressure on the company to have more Indonesian managers. This pressure came at the very time that the operation was becoming more difficult to manage. In addition, the new Indonesian managers largely came from the western Indonesian islands and were mostly Muslims. The Papuans, who were not always well disposed to expatriates, were far less well disposed to non-Papuan Indonesians.

Corporate Culture and Top Management

From its early days, the company was guided by the mercurial and strong-willed board chairman and CEO James Robert (Jim Bob) Moffett. He was a geologist by training and a risk taker who would most likely bet the house when it came to finding the next big thing. It was, therefore, not surprising that when it came to digging for copper and gold, Moffett would trust his instinct and operate at the edge of risk taking to increase output. He was an authoritarian leader who would not hesitate to contact his executives directly without going through channels when he felt the need to do so, and he demanded unfiltered responses to his inquiries. As with managers who have strong charismatic characteristics, Moffett was both admired and feared.[2] At the same time, he was a spiritual person, a regular churchgoer, who often revealed an ethical streak where normative values would influence his business decisions. Although the audit was not Moffett's idea, he openly supported it when it was presented to him.

Freeport's mining operations in Papua, Indonesia, are influenced by an expatriate corporate culture that is typical of highly developed Western societies and their multinational corporations in the mining industry. Some of these cultural traits are:

- Top-down, unilateral decision making.
- Driven by getting things done as quickly, efficiently, and completely as possible, with the goal of providing the greatest shareholder value.
- Distrust of outsiders and their opinions of what Freeport does.

Freeport also has an Indonesian culture that needs to be considered, since many of Freeport's Indonesian managers are non-Papuan Indonesians (mostly Javans). The culture of Freeport's Indonesian employees is similar, if not the same as the culture and attitudes of the non-Papuan Indonesian migrants to Freeport's operations area, including Indonesian security forces and governmental officials. Although there are many Indonesian cultures, a few cultural traits can be readily identified:

- A belief that Javan culture is superior to all other Indonesian cultures, *especially* Papuan cultures.
- Information is shared in a limited manner.
- Conflicts are resolved indirectly and, hence, often remain intentionally unresolved.

Freeport-McMoRan Copper & Gold, Inc., Operations in Indonesia

The Grasberg mine in Papua, Indonesia, started in 1972. It is Freeport's largest mining venture. By any measure, the Grasberg mine is massive. It is the single largest producer of gold in the world and the second-largest producer of copper. It also produces silver as a by-product. The amount of material that goes through Freeport milling operations each day is approximately 250,000 tons of rock, most of which becomes tailings (ground waste) that is transported by river to a disposal area.[3] In 2009, PTFI operations accounted for approximately 40 percent of Freeport's revenues. PTFI is also a 25 percent owner of PT Smelting, which operates a copper smelter and refinery in Gresik, Indonesia. The Grasberg mine is one of the few remaining mines that use rivers to help deal with mine wastes. This is one of the most controversial aspects of Freeport's operation.

Freeport's mining operations and the accompanying challenges in Papua, Indonesia, are a microcosm of similar scenarios that are being played out at other mining and oil and gas production sites around the world. Freeport, like most other mining and oil companies, had to deal with issues of environmental degradation. Additionally, these companies must also deal with the human aspects of mining operations, which invariably involve conflicts between the company's interests and those of the indigenous people whose traditional rights to land, water, and air resources have been abrogated by the country's national government with less than adequate regard for their legitimate economic concerns, traditional culture, and values.[4] The corporate responses, and those of the national governments of the countries involved, have differed widely because of the unique character of the tribes, economic value of potential mineral resources, the character of national governments, and the ability of local tribes to seek redress through legal channels.

Antecedents to the Creation of Guiding Principles for Indonesian Operations

History of Violence

For the first twenty years, Freeport's mining operations were engulfed in a series of skirmishes involving the indigenous people who were antagonistic toward the Indonesian government in Jakarta. They sought independence, or at the very least substantial autonomy, both of which were strongly opposed by the Indonesian government in Jakarta. Popular unrest and resentment against Freeport was also fueled by the Papuans' greater exposure—with the advent of telephone, television, and most notably the Internet—to events in other parts of the world involving extractive industries where incidents of pollution, land degradation, and severe mistreatment and oppression of the local people occurred, and that were often blamed on the mining companies involved, who were seen as equally involved with corrupt national governments and police.

Through Indonesia's transmigration policy, local tribal communities' indigenous land was seized to give place for migrants' farms. However, the largest impact on the tribal community came from the U.S. mining giant Freeport, whose land rights are still the subject of large debate. The company portrayed itself as a source of social and economic development for the local tribal population. According to James Moffett, chairman of Freeport in the early 1990s, the company was "thrusting a spear of development into the heart of West Papua."[5]

In the eyes of the Papuans, the mine became a cornerstone in the battle for freedom and land rights. Freeport moved the local population from the historic land, cut down the forest, and polluted the land, rivers, and costal area with tailing depositions. Freeport employed company security forces to protect its property and safeguard the continuity of its operations. At the same time, the Indonesian military increased its presence in the area to deter Papuans' campaign for independence. More guns inevitably called for stronger resistance, creating a self-feeding conflict. Clashes between armed forces and the local population became an everyday reality.

In the early years of the mine operation, members of the opposition group Free Papua Movement (OPM) stole explosives and blew up a slurry pipeline at mine site. The resultant military crackdown killed as many as 900 local villagers.[6]

In late 1994 and through the middle of 1996, Freeport's Grasberg mine became the focus of NGO attacks on the extractive industries. OPM claimed that since the beginning of the mining operations, the company was complicit with the Indonesian army. Army personnel were accused of large-scale torture, detention without trial, and acts of intimidation, which led to the disappearance of nearly 43,000 indigenous people.[7]

Over the period of 1994–1995, witnesses reported five incidents of clashes between protesters and military forces, which resulted in the killing of thirty-seven civilians.[8] In November 1994, one of Freeport's employees was shot and killed and several others wounded in an attack on Freeport's main road. Although separatists were suspected, none were found. Freeport requested additional security from the Indonesian government, which dispatched 600 police and army troops to Freeport's operations area. In the ensuing months, harsh actions by the Indonesian army and local police followed. The army and police were accused of the disappearances and presumed deaths of five local Papuans and the beatings of several other Papuans.[9]

One of the most cataclysmic confrontations occurred on Christmas Day, when the Papuan (Morning Star) independence flag was raised in Freeport's administrative center of Tembagapura. The flag raiser was shot and killed by the police. This event began a "bloody Christmas" in Tembagapura and Timika. Freeport's vehicles (cars, trucks, and buses) were commandeered by the police and army. Several Papuans died; others were wounded. The events were widely reported in the Indonesian and international news media; some reporters assigned partial responsibility to Freeport and its role in managing the conflict on the mine site.

Freeport's subsequent challenges included violence in the region of the mine. In January 1996, a team of twelve biological researchers from the World Wide Fund for Nature (WWF) was kidnapped eighty kilometers east of Freeport's mine. Although the kidnapping was not directly connected to Freeport's mining operations, the rescue operation was headquartered in

Timika (which is within Freeport's mining concession area), and the local population believed Freeport was a supplier of logistical support for the operations. In early April, the kidnapping episode came to a violent end with the Indonesian army killing three kidnappers and two hostages. Following the end of the kidnapping episode, the army carried out sweeps in several villages where villagers accused the army of violence and human rights' violations. Near the end of the kidnapping saga, two days of severe violence broke out in Tembagapura and Timika.[10]

Socioeconomic Impact of Mining Operations

Freeport's operations in the mountains of southwestern Papua have attracted Papuan migration and multiple claims of traditional ownership of the land on which Freeport undertakes mining activities. Six highland tribes make some claim on Freeport's mining area, and one coastal tribe is substantially affected by Freeport's presence. The cultures of the six highland tribes are relatively similar; the coastal people have strikingly different cultural traits.[11]

West Papua has had a volatile political history. The tribal people have a culture and ethnicity that is distinct from the rest of Indonesia. The political unrest has led to increased military presence in the area, with concomitant human rights abuses. Given the mine's presence and its importance to all sides, Freeport's Indonesian operations could not escape accusations of involvement and complicity in some of the human rights abuses that occurred in the mine's area of operations. Equally important, the company was accused of not doing enough to prevent the use of excessive force by the military and of acquiescing to military demands for cooperation through provision of transportation and other support services. There was also widespread belief that Freeport's CEO, James Moffett, had built strong friendly ties with the then Indonesian president Suharto, which helped the company to secure military presence and assistance in the mine area. PTFI was also accused of providing funding and other support to the military forces stationed in the mine area.[12]

Conflicts between the Papuan community and Freeport's Grasberg mine operation can be grouped into three broad categories:

- Security for the mining operations and in the area around the mine.
- Environmental impacts of the mining operations.
- Economic development in the area surrounding Freeport's mining operations.

In dealing with these issues, Freeport had to contend with certain cultural traits of the Papuan people that would affect all aspects of its mining operations as well as the company's responses to their aspirations and expectations. Papuans see the land as a crucial part of their being. Land is not so much a commodity to be exploited as it is a spiritual and physical treasure to be enjoyed and protected. Extractive industries see land very differently. Land is a resource that is exploited in a manner that results in permanent changes in its quality and suitability for traditional uses. Although mining companies promise to restore the land to its original condition, these promises are seldom kept, and in any case are not believed by the local people who are most affected by this change, which was instituted against their best wishes and without their consent.

Freeport's massive mine and its use of the land that is part of Freeport's contract of work is an area where the local indigenous community has substantial differences with the company.[13] Although environmental issues are generally the uppermost public concern, including those at PTFI, the cultural issues are just as important because they influence the community's attitude toward environmental issues. However, these issues are generally ignored by the mining companies, which have been suffering the consequences of their ignorance and neglect in this area.[14]

Papuan cultural values and beliefs raise environmental concerns that could not be easily addressed in economic and technical terms. Papuans consider the land to be alive and spiritual. The very act of mining, transportation of mine waste, and impounding tailings is an act of violence against the spirit of the land.[15] Papuans' community structure is essentially informal, and leadership is temporary rather than long-term elected or appointed, with decisions made on a consensus basis whenever possible. Overall and coordinated governance within Papua has not existed. Individual families and tribes govern their own areas. Papuans define themselves by ethno-linguistic groups and families, although for some purposes (such as the desire for independence) they transcend family and tribal loyalties.[16]

Freeport's Response to the Concerns of the Papuan Community

Freeport's earlier dealings with the Papuans were largely framed within the concept of legally obtained rights by the company from the Indonesian government. These rights would carefully prescribe the conditions of work. The company officials felt that beyond some voluntary initiatives to help the local population, the company had no specific mandate. The expatriate managers at the mine site appeared to be insensitive to the needs and expectations of the Papuan people, and often resorted to seeking help from the Indonesian military forces, which were prone to violent suppression and human rights abuses. The military and police forces were also heavily involved in corruption and extortion, and the victims were invariably the local Papuans.

The company was also accused of discrimination against the Papuan people in job training and employment, disregard of Papuan people's traditional rights, and neglect of the Papuan people's social and economic development.[17] PTFI has denied these charges and has pointed to many instances of abuse from all sides against the company's employees and facilities.[18]

Freeport's initial response to the Papuan community's concerns was not atypical and followed the pattern that most mining companies, including Freeport, have followed in the past: focus on the problems that are at the forefront of conflict and dissent (perceived as urgent and critical) and throw money at them—that is, promise more money and "consultation" to the most vocal and supposedly influential groups. If jobs are the issue, promise more jobs. If the community's quality of life is an issue, promise to open another school, a clinic, or a daycare center. If the concern is about economic development, launch an entrepreneurship program and set up small businesses to sell highly subsidized products.

The process is seldom carefully thought through. To wit, what types of jobs are being created and are they jobs that are likely to last and lead to something, or are they make-work, dead-end jobs? How do the Papuans look at their future in terms of work at the mine site and mine-related jobs, or other types of productive and self-sustaining jobs that are not dependent on the mine's revenues? Do the Papuan's believe that mine management is really interested in building a skill base among the Papuan employees through professional training, and how Papuans are moving up in the technical and professional cadres of the mine's operations?

Notwithstanding, PTFI and its U.S. parent, Freeport, undertook a series of positive actions to ameliorate the situation and put emphasis where it belonged: on providing greater training and job opportunities to the Papuan people. The company injected significant financial resources and professional expertise into the community with a view to building greater capacity for self-governance and economic development among the local Papuan tribes. PTFI's new community relations plan focused on some of the demands of the local community: (1) more jobs; (2) a more active participation in the economic and social development programs provided by Freeport; and (3) a more active program to protect the human rights of the people living in proximity to the mining operation.[19]

Change in Strategy at Freeport: Drive toward the Creation of a New Code of Conduct

The Papuan community's response to PTFI's efforts ranged from neutral to negative. It appeared that no amount of job creation or support for community well-being was considered satisfactory. Expanded services by PTFI further raised expectations on the part of the Papuan community, which demanded an even broader scope and a higher level of services. PTFI felt that many of the community's demands were beyond the control of the company. These included protection from harassment by the provincial police and Indonesian military, and company support for Papuan interests to the Indonesian government.

The turnaround in Freeport's strategy in dealing with the Papuan people at the mine site was sharp and substantial. Once again, it reflected the decisive nature of Freeport's CEO and his predisposition to risk taking when he is convinced that it will enhance the economic and social well-being of the Papuan people. Along with his strong commitment to expanding Freeport's operations (and profits), Moffett was a visionary in matters of corporate social responsibility. Moffett directed his senior executives to come up with new ideas to address the problems at the mine site.

David Lowry, Freeport's vice president for human resources, strongly felt that the company had to explore other opportunities, that is, take a different path to address the socioeconomic concerns of the Papuan community. It was apparent that simply throwing more money at the problem was not yielding positive results. Among the actions the company took as part of its new strategy:

1. PTFI undertook to double the employment of Papuan people at PTFI during a five-year period, that is, by 2001. This commitment was fulfilled.
2. In 2001, PTFI again committed to double the employment of the Papuan people by 2006, which was met.
3. PTFI made further commitments toward giving preference in training and hiring to the Papuan people.
4. PTFI had also been devoting significant resources in terms of money and professional expertise to improve the health, education, and entrepreneurial opportunities of the Papuan people.
5. In 1996, PTFI made a radical commitment to support Papuan economic development. This commitment was unprecedented in the mining industry. It was not very popular among the company's mine-site executives and especially the Indonesian executives. The company would henceforth devote 1 percent of its annual gross revenues from the mining operations toward the economic and social uplifting of the Papuan people. This fund, originally called the Freeport Fund for Irian Jaya Development, is now named the Freeport Partnership Fund. By the end of 2010, the Fund had received over $250 million from PTFI.. Equally important, the company instituted a plan of action whereby Papuan leaders would assume increasing responsibility toward self-governance in the management and spending of these funds.
6. It should also be noted that PTFI provided these funds with the full approval of its parent, Freeport, in New Orleans. As such, the funds reflected a corporate commitment to the Papuan people. Furthermore, these funds were in addition to the funds PTFI was already spending as a part of its community outreach efforts.
7. Toward the end of 1999, Freeport released a board-approved social, employment, and human rights policy, and PTFI's board of governors gave their assent to that policy for the Papuan operations. This was, however, a broad document enunciating a set of aspirational principles that would henceforth guide the company's conduct in dealing with the Papuan people at the Grasberg mine site and surrounding communities.

Partnership between Freeport and ICCA

The partnership between ICCA and Freeport came by happenstance and by design. Early in 2002, Lowry met with Sethi at a seminar at the University of Notre Dame, where Sethi presented a paper on voluntary codes of conduct and described his experience in creating and implementing such a code for Mattel, Inc., the world's largest toy company, and applying it to toy manufacturers for Mattel in China, other countries in Asia, and Mexico. Lowry wondered whether a somewhat similar code could be created that would be suitable for more complex operations of a mining company in Indonesia. Sethi suggested that such a code was indeed possible, because while the issues may be different, the code would need to meet five criteria to be effective and credible:

1. The goals to be achieved by the code must be specific and objectively measurable.
2. At a minimum, the standards enunciated in the code must meet the legal criteria mandated by the country's laws and regulations. Where country-specific standards do not exist, the company must incorporate best industry practices.
3. They must be outcome oriented. It is not enough to indicate that money is being spent or that policies and procedures exist. Instead they should describe the actual level of accomplishments or goal achievement.
4. All claims of performance and compliance with code standards must be independently verified.
5. The findings of the compliance verifications should be transparent and made public.

Discussions between Lowry and Sethi continued over the next few months. Lowry also explored these ideas with other Freeport executives in New Orleans. The reaction among corporate executives was mixed. There was considerable apprehension as to how such a code might affect the company. Nevertheless, Lowry decided to present his ideas to Freeport's CEO for his approval. Once again, Moffett's ethical streak would manifest itself. Although the code and its audit requirements were not his idea, he immediately supported them. Thus, he broke all the rules of the mining industry, and against the advice of some of his senior executives, initiated Freeport's code of conduct.

Sethi was invited to New Orleans to meet with Moffett and other senior Freeport executives. These were followed by a period of intense activity over the ensuing six months, when Lowry and Sethi carried out extensive consultations with all levels of executives at PTFI's headquarters in Jakarta and at the mine site. The objective was to seek their buy-in and to ensure that the specific requirements of the proposed code and its implementation procedures were reasonable and practical. Lowry and Sethi also met with leaders of the Papuan community to make them aware of Freeport's new initiative and to seek their views regarding its contents and benefits for the community.

The final outcome of these efforts and extensive consultation process was the public announcement, in December 2003, of Freeport's code of conduct, called "Guiding Principles for Indonesian Operations—People and the Community" (GPIO-1), which codified Freeport's commitments to the Papuan people in the area of its mining operations (appendix 3.1). GPIO-1 was also accompanied by a guidance document articulating Freeport's social, employment, and human rights policies (SEHR).

The most important defining characteristics of the GPIO-1 are as follows:

1. It creates detailed, objective, quantifiable, and outcome-oriented measures of performance in each of the five areas covered by the principles. These include: people and community, including workers employed by PTFI and its affiliated companies, contractors, and suppliers; business-government relations, including proscription of bribery and corruption; protection of human rights; special status of Papuan workers; and economic and social development of the local tribes.

2. It makes a commitment to the effect that Freeport and its affiliated organizations will undergo regular audits of all activities covered under the guiding principles. The organization's respective internal audit departments will perform the audits to assess their compliance with the guiding principles. The internal audit process will include performance evaluations, plans for corrective action, and a follow-up mechanism to ensure compliance in a timely fashion.

3. Freeport also agreed to undergo an external audit by an independent monitoring agency to assess the extent of compliance with the guiding principles by PTFI and its affiliated organizations on a regular basis, and to give these audits maximum transparency and thus engender greater public credibility.

4. As part of its commitment to independent external monitoring, Freeport agreed to provide the independent monitoring organization with complete access to all information and facilities to make an evaluation of Freeport's performance on the guiding principles and their implementation standards. The independent monitor have complete discretion in issuing its reports without any censorship from Freeport, provided that Freeport is afforded a suitable opportunity to respond to any findings of fact and conclusion by the independent monitor. The International Center for Corporate Accountability (ICCA) has acted as the independent external auditor under an agreement with Freeport, and has been responsible for conducting all field audits, the findings of which are summarized in the following sections.

Scope of the Audits, Audit Protocols, and Terms of Public Disclosure

The scope of the audits is fully delineated in the company's document describing its guiding principles (GPIO-1). The implications of the audit findings and their public disclosure should also be apparent.

- The audit report should provide an objective and unbiased picture of the efforts made and achievements, in compliance with the standards of Freeport's social, employment, and human rights policy and the guiding principles for the company's Indonesian operations.
- It should evaluate Freeport's success in implementing policies and programs to create a work environment that protects the human rights of all people in the area of PTFI's operations.
- The findings of the report should engender public trust in Freeport's efforts toward creating employment and economic growth opportunities for the Papuan people in general and those of the seven Papuan tribal communities in particular that have been affected by Freeport's mining operations.

Findings of the Independent Monitor's Field Audits

ICCA's field audits were conducted in three parts and were carried out during the periods November–December 2004, August 2006, and November–December 2006. Prior to initiating the actual field audits, ICCA created a set of documents that would be completed by mine site managers providing details of their activities in meeting the requirements of (GPIO-1). These documents would be submitted to ICCA in advance of the field audits and would be integrated in the field audits. ICCA also created a set of audit protocols outlining how various facets of field audits would be actually carried out. These protocols were made available to the mine site executives to assist them in preparing for the field audits (appendix 3.2).

In 2004, at start of the Phase I audit, PTFI's total operations and those of its contractors and privatized companies involved approximately 18,500 employees. The Phase I audit covered all PTFI employees (more than 7,850 people). It also included all activities pertaining to public health and welfare, as well as management of the Freeport Partnership Fund. The Phase II audit covered similar activities and pertained to all workers employed by PTFI's contractors (approximately 7,500 people) who were dedicated exclusively to providing services to PTFI.

The Phase I audit was conducted between November 23 and December 1, 2004. The final report, consisting of 136 single-spaced pages, was released to the general public in July 2005. It found certain shortfalls in PTFI's implementation of its social and human rights commitments. In response, PTFI made a commitment to take all necessary corrective actions within six to nine months, and invited ICCA to do a follow-up audit. The follow-up audit was conducted in August 2006.

The Phase II audit was devoted to an examination of the activities of PTFI's contractors. It was conducted in November and December 2006. The full audit report consisted of eighty-seven single-spaced pages. This audit raised a number of contentious issues that were subject to differing interpretations on the part of PTFI and one or more of its contractors and ICCA. Some of these differences pertained to the applicability of Indonesian employment laws to various categories of employees and independent contractors. Consequently, publication of the final report was considerably delayed, and was finally published in December 2007.

Findings of the Phase I Audit[20]

The Phase I audit focused on various elements of PTFI's compliance with its GPIO-1 and its social, employment, and human rights policy. Among the interviewed 353 workers in Phase I audit, 44 percent identified themselves as Papuans and the remaining as non-Papuans. One-third of those who identified themselves as Papuans indicated belonging to one of the seven *sukus* (tribes) that lived in Freeport's area of operations. The sample of interviewed workers reflected the proportionality of Papuans, seven-*suku* Papuans, and contract workers on the Freeport payroll. The average length of employment for the entire sample was 4.8 years, and the average length of employment among contractor-supplied workers was 2.4 years.

Promotion of Human Rights Policies and Prevention of Human Rights Abuses

The ICCA audit confirms that all potential human rights violations have been reported to the appropriate authorities and dealt with in accordance with

PTFI's human rights policy. None of the reported human rights violations involved activities of PTFI's security personnel or security personnel of the government of Indonesia charged with protection of PTFI's operations or property. The reported incidents fell within the definition of criminal acts, and were treated as such.[21]

The ICCA audit also addressed the issue of perceived incidents of human rights violations as experienced by PTFI workers under different work situations and involving both PTFI's internal security organization and external security organizations, that is, the local police and the Indonesian army. Beyond any "official" definition of human rights, individuals have personal perceptions of their human rights and of instances where their rights and those of others have been violated and/or abused. Among the interviewed workers, a little over 80 percent indicated that they did not personally experience any human rights violations. Similarly, a majority of the interviewed workers denied knowing someone else who had suffered from human rights violations.

Of those who indicated having suffered from human rights violations, it would appear that PTFI workers had an overarching view of human rights violations, including work-related complaints. Interview data suggested that approximately one-half (48 percent) of the instances cited by the interviewed workers fall in the category of conventional human rights abuses. Although small in absolute numbers (thirty-one), this figure was nevertheless a cause of concern since the abuses mostly comprise allegations of army abuse, security abuse, police interrogation, sexual harassment, and religious persecution. ICCA also held discussions with human rights compliance officers, who reported that twenty-six potential human rights violations were formally reported to PTFI. ICCA was also informed that all of those formal reports were investigated and appropriate actions were taken. However, based on the information gathered by ICCA, it is probable that employees perceived that there were many more suspected violations than were reported to the human rights compliance officers.

Analysis also suggested that a majority of workers' perceived and reported human rights violations fell into the two categories of verbal and physical abuse (28 percent) and misbehavior and violence among employees (28 percent). In the absence of more specific details, which interviewed workers were reluctant to provide, it appears that a large proportion of these complaints did not involve human rights abuses as the term is generally understood and applied.

Workers' experiences in dealing with the security department should also be a cause for concern for PTFI's management and reason to seek further explanation. Of the interviewed workers, 60 percent indicated that they did not have any contact with Security Department personnel. However, slightly less than half (48 percent) agreed with the statement that the Security Department respects employees' human rights.

Human Rights Training Program

In 2002, PTFI launched a human rights training program to make certain that PTFI personnel were sufficiently knowledgeable in human rights and human rights violations. This action was directed to ensure that all PTFI personnel would be able to avoid violating the rights of employees and members of the local community, and would be able to accurately report on human rights violations if they saw them being committed.

ICCA's assessment of the training program confirmed that the program had been carefully articulated and well suited for PTFI's operating environment. PTFI's senior management was committed to the human rights portion of the SEHR, and had provided resources for training for employees in human rights. In 2004, 5,400 employees (including contractors and privatized employees) attended this training. Among the employees interviewed by ICCA, over 78 percent had received human rights training. However, among those who had acknowledged to receiving this training, only a little over 40 percent could demonstrate their full understanding. The greatest awareness and learning from the training program appears to have occurred among the workers who were at the lowest level of the employment hierarchy and the temporary workers supplied by contractors. These workers also had the lowest level of education. Furthermore, workers expressing greater concern with possible human rights abuses and discrimination were also the workers who demonstrated the best understanding of the human rights training program.

Two departments at PTFI had the most interaction with the local community: the Security Department (SD) and the Social and Local Development Department (SLD). Although over 90 percent of SD personnel attended the human rights training, and the average length of the training period was approximately twelve hours compared to an average of four hrs, interviews indicated that 59 percent of SD personnel did not have sufficient understanding of the company's human rights policies and programs.

Security Department Personnel Working with Indonesian Army Personnel

PTFI has made a public commitment to make transparent their logistical and financial support to Indonesian security forces (police and army). The audit revealed that eight PTFI SD personnel were assigned to government security forces to drive personnel from the lowlands to the highlands. The use of PTFI vehicles by government security forces and the provision of PTFI personnel to provide transportation for the police and army was a major issue, as mentioned before. The use of PTFI drivers for government security forces blurs those distinctions for the local and international communities. ICCA considered this practice to be contrary to the spirit of the company's human rights policies. A majority of the security department employees interviewed by ICCA stated that they "almost never" or "only occasionally" met the local police (72 percent) and the army personnel (57 percent).

It would seem that, relatively speaking, there were greater occasions in that part of security department employees to encounter army personnel than local police. Finally, when asked about their experience in dealing with the local police and army personnel, a majority (61%) described their experience as "somewhat or very pleasant" with regard to the police and 44% with regard to army personnel.

ICCA recommended that PTFI's SD should establish a policy of keeping PTFI personnel separated from operations of government security forces. PTFI should find ways by which trust could be enhanced among employees and the local community. Increased transparency about security and safety issues would be a good way to start. Regular reports about security and "town meetings" would be good ways to make transparency more personal and friendly.

Enhancements in Training and Employment of the Papuans at PTFI

Over the past eight-plus years, the company had made certain specific commitments and adopted general principles with a view to increase Papuan employment and promotion opportunities at the mine site. In 1996, PTFI committed itself to doubling the employment of the Papuan people at the mine site by 2000, and doubling it again by 2006. The cumulative effect of these two initiatives would place 2,580 Papuan nonstaff and 100 Papuan staff into PTFI's workforce by 2006.

In 2002, the company initiated a highly focused and technically oriented training program that would prepare people for jobs at the mine site. The program gives first preference to the Papuan candidates, especially those from the seven local tribes. PTFI also undertook creation of a work environment that would prevent discrimination against the Papuan people in all aspects of their employment at PTFI.

The audit indicated that the company had met its obligation of doubling the Papuan employment by 2001, and that it was on track for doubling this number again by 2006. Among the staff, PTFI had already exceeded the target of 100 by 100 percent (200 Papuan staff). However, the issue about Papuan employment cannot end with reaching an employment goal alone. It must also deal with ongoing issues of Papuan employee satisfaction, fair treatment for Papuans in the workforce, and enhanced advancement opportunities in the future.

After PTFI made its Papuan employment commitment in 1996, it refined its targets to give special preference to Papuans from the seven tribal groups lived closest to the mine. However, no numerical target was made for seven-sukus employment over employment of non-seven-suku Papuans. The interviews showed that Papuan nonstaff are being promoted at a rate equal to those of non-Papuans, and that Papuans from the seven sukus are being promoted among staff at a higher percentage than other Indonesians. ICCA recommended that these programs should be supported and enhanced. PTFI also must continue to enhance the employment climate for Papuans.

It appeared likely that PTFI would fulfill its commitments with regard to Papuan employment by 2006. Therefore, no corrective action was called for with regard to commitments made in SEHR or GPOI-1. However, significant challenges remained for PTFI and the Papuan community with regard to training and development. As the pool of educated people in the seven sukus was depleted, effective remedial education and training became essential. PTFI has established a training institute that shows promise of success. ICCA has provided recommendations to the management of PTFI on ways to enhance the employment and advancement opportunities for Papuans.

Social Development of the Papuan People

In late 1960s, Papuan communities in Southeastern Indonesia were primarily characterized as traditional economic systems with dominant hunting-and-gathering and agricultural lifestyles. Freeport's mining development brought along social and economic challenges and opportunities to the local tribal communities. To gain communities' support, prevent violence and social unrest, and help enhance the opportunities available to the local communities, Freeport, in the early stage of its Indonesian operations, applied a strategy of infrastructure development and direct monetary subsidies to the communities.

More recently, this approach has been modified through a long-term social and business development plan to enhance relationships between PTFI and local communities. One area of importance to the well-being of the Papuan community was the need for developing a more diversified base of economic activity. Freeport and PTFI recognized this challenge and its efforts have taken two forms.

1. The company created the department of Social and Local Development (SLD), which is entirely funded and supervised by PTFI. SLD's mandate is to implement programs to which PTFI has made public commitments.
2. Freeport and PTFI also created the Freeport Partnership Fund for Community Development, and committed to allocate annually 1 percent of PTFI's gross operating revenues to the fund. An important feature of the fund is that it is entirely managed by the Papuan community through its organizational entity, Lembaga Pengembangan Masyarakat Amungme dan Kamoro (LPMAK), subject to Freeport-established donor guidelines to ensure financial integrity and performance accountability.

Social and Local Development Department (SLD)

SLD works closely with LPMAK in implementing community development programs focused on education, health, and local business development. SLD's primary focus is on three groups of activities.

1. Community Business Development (CBD) is the largest group, and is responsible for about 45 percent of SLD's operations. It focuses on specific projects aimed at facilitating entrepreneurship among local communities, agricultural development, farms, and fishing. One of its major activities is to provide consultation and training to the local communities in the areas of social and business development.
2. The Business Incubator Program aims to take people who are inclined to start new businesses and help them with a basic understanding of business start-up processes, financial plans, and elementary aspects of sales, purchasing,

customer service, inventory management, bookkeeping, etc. Between 2002 and 2004, forty small and medium business enterprises were supported or assisted by CBD, and of these, 77 percent are generating positive cash flow. In addition, PTFI-assisted businesses have provided work opportunities for more than 1,200 local people.

3. Information Support and Liaison Office (ISLO). The primary role of this organization is to serve as a liaison with the local communities. ICCA's investigations indicated that ISLO was providing a needed service to the community. ISLO officers are well respected in the community, especially in the far-flung villages, where their liaison activities and support services among the villages are particularly helpful.

4. ICCA's audit determined that PTFI had fulfilled its commitments to the local community through the programs it had developed for and with the local community. In this context, ICCA has made a number of recommendations with the goal of achieving long-term operating efficiencies and orienting SLD toward "deliverables achieved" rather than activities performed.

Freeport Partnership Fund and LPMAK

The Lembaga Pengembangan Masyarakat Amungme dan Kamoro (LPMAK) was established in 2002 to manage the Freeport Partnership Fund. The fund and its predecessor organization were established in the early part of 1996 and had received US$132 million over a nine-year period.

As presently constituted, LPMAK has a dual governance structure. The management of LPMAK is composed of a board of commissioners (Badan Musyawarah or BM), consisting of representatives from the local government, Papuan regional leaders, leaders from the Amungme and Kamoro tribal groups, and representatives from PTFI. The board of commissioners establishes annual budgets for three main development areas: education, health, and village development. The second board is the board of directors (Badan Pengurus or BP), which is responsible for approving overall budgets for various programs, oversight of plan implementation, and managing external financial audits.

To support the LPMAK, PTFI established Community Management Services (CMS), which provides technical and professional advisory services to LPMAK in planning, managing, and monitoring social programs sponsored by the CMS personnel are employed by PTFI, but work directly with the executive secretary of LPMAK and the various bureaus set up by LPMAK to administer the Freeport Partnership Fund. CMS also acts as the implementers of PTFI's donor guidance.

ICCA's audit found that PTFI has made the required payments to the Freeport Partnership Fund, and that the fund transferred those monies to the LPMAK as stipulated in the donor guidance. LPMAK's programs covered a wide variety of activities, ranging from health education, public health and malaria control, community development, and infrastructure development to education and training. By mutual agreement between ICCA and PTFI, Phase I of this audit was limited to the activities of LPMAK's education bureau, with other activities to be covered in Phase II of the audit.

The Education Bureau oversees planning and implementation of six major programs: scholarship programs; dormitories; out of school and adult education/skills training; cooperation with the government; infrastructure; and cooperation with third parties (bank, foundation, and church). Two of the six programs—educational assistance/scholarships and dormitories—have accounted for 96 percent of LPMAK's spending on educational programs. Therefore, these programs were subjected to careful analysis by ICCA during this audit.

I.   Educational assistance/scholarships: In 1996, the program began giving educational aid to more than 5,000 students per year at an annual cost that ranged between $3 million and $5.9 million. The data show that approximately 80 percent of those receiving educational subsidies were preschool through high school students, and 20 percent were attending universities.

II. Exact expenditures for the program were not available for the period 1996–2000, nor was it possible to ascertain how many recipients were involved, their educational progress, graduation/completion, or LPMAK's own payroll. While the Education Bureau must deal with cultural sensitivities, its inability to manage the program effectively was symptomatic of management, which did not have the capacity to administer such a program.

III. Dormitories: The Education Bureau of LPMAK built, maintained, and operated a number of dormitories, not only in the Timika area (mostly for high school students), but also in other parts of Papua (for high school and college students) and in areas within Indonesia where Papuan students, especially those from the seven-sukus area, were attending a university. In terms of spending, dormitories were the second major project of the Education Bureau after the scholarship program. From 2001 through June 2004, almost US$2.5 million had been spent on the dormitories.

IV. ICCA visited a girls' dormitory located in the Timika area, within thirty minutes' driving distance from the Education Bureau's offices. The condition of the dormitory and the conditions in which the girls lived were unacceptable with regard to safety, hygiene, and conditions that would be conducive to effective learning. The ICCA team noted a lack of electricity, ventilation, running water, transportation to and from school, and security personnel, as well as restrooms without doors.

V.   Out-of-school and adult education programs: Approximately 1 percent of the total funds of LPMAK are devoted to remedial and adult education. Remedial education programs are intended for young adults who are currently enrolled in school. This program also gets support from the local government. The Education Bureau could not adequately explain its involvement in remedial education programs other than indicating that public schools were failing in their responsibility of educating the youth. These programs were aimed at enhancing students' skill sets and helping them attain basic knowledge, which make them better qualified to seek jobs.

VI. ICCA's overall finding with regard to LPMAK's management of the educational program was unsatisfactory. LPMAK's top leadership had allowed this situation to deteriorate to an unacceptable level, given the importance of this program to the Papuan community and the fact that it had consumed a large part of LPMAK's annual funding. The program must be considered an unequivocal failure both from operational and fiscal management perspective. Giving so much control to a local community that is not yet experienced in management has its inherent challenges.

VII. Equally, this situation had caused consternation for ICCA as an auditor. ICCA's advisers were aware of cultural sensitivities and local community perceptions. However, in an area of such importance as education, ICCA recommended that the entire relationship between PTFI, the Freeport Partnership Fund, and the LPMAK must continue to be rethought and redeveloped.

VIII. ICCA strongly urged that PTFI through LPMAK take immediate and decisive action to correct the situation at the dormitories. Although some might argue that the conditions in the dormitory were not that different from the conditions found in the villages from which the students had come, the dormitories must be maintained to the standard at which they were intended.

Contract Labor Providers

The issue of workers provided by contract labor suppliers was one of persistent complaints raised by the workers interviewed by ICCA. Historically, contractor-supplied workers were used where work was of a project nature, such as expansions, construction, et cetera. However, for reasons unclear to ICCA, PTFI had developed a policy whereby different business units, and even administrative support service units, such as human resource management, industrial relations, SLD, and the security department, would allocate a fixed percentage of their manpower needs to be filled through contractor-supplied workers.

Contract labor companies providing labor to PTFI were required to pay wages and benefits to workers, which were fixed by PTFI's contract department. Wages paid to contractor-supplied workers generally were 15 percent to 20 percent below the wages paid to PTFI's own employees who did the same or similar work. PTFI's contract department also paid contract labor providers between 35 percent and 40 percent of the workers' wages to cover their overhead. As such, these contractors were independent in name only, and for all intents and purposes were under the direct supervision and control of PTFI's contract department. The fact that these practices violated Indonesian labor laws and fair and equal treatment of workers must be placed solely with PTFI's contracting department and, by implication, PTFI's management.

Among the interviewed contract workers, 93 percent indicated that they had worked for the contract labor providers for more than one year, with 20 percent having worked more than four years before being transferred to the PTFI payroll. In general, fewer Papuans workers (26 percent) have been with the contractors for less than twelve months compared to 37 percent of non-Papuans. In all, 94 percent of all current PTFI employees spent more than twelve months with a contract labor provider; 34 percent spent between two and four years; and 22 percent spent four or more years.

Among the administrative services and support units, the gap between current contractors and PTFI employees with regard to average length of time spent with the contractors ranges from one year to four or more years (92 percent). However, it would seem that the Papuans, on average, are spending more time with the contractors (71 percent) than non-Papuans (51 percent). Based on these findings, ICCA recommended to PTFI that:

1. It should immediately abandon the use of contract labor providers for other than temporary labor, probationary employment, and training new employees.
2. When contractor-supplied workers are considered on probation or in training prior to their employment at PTFI, the relevant conditions of probation and training must be specified a priori and made known to the workers. Furthermore, these terms must conform to the Indonesian Labor Law and meet the notions of fairness and equal treatment.

Freeport's Response to Phase I Audit Findings

Freeport provided a formal response to ICCA's first audit report in October 2005. The following excerpts outline the commitments made by PTFI toward improving the shortcomings noted by ICCA's Phase I audit (appendix 3.3).[22]

Promotion of Human Rights Policies and Prevention of Human Rights Abuses

FCX and PTFI will work through its SEHR education program to ensure that employees know how to identify and report human rights concerns, and to create an atmosphere in which employees feel comfortable in submitting such reports.

Human Rights Training Program

FCX/PTFI will undertake to create new mechanisms to improve the effectiveness of its training programs. To this end, PTFI has already begun revising the human rights training curriculum to focus on "effective learning," especially in the Security and Social and Local Development Departments. As part of this process, PTFI has appointed a Senior Human Rights Compliance Officer, a distinguished Papuan, whose role is to ensure that our training and communications efforts are effective, appropriate, and ongoing.

Security Department Personnel Working with Indonesian Army Personnel

Because of safety considerations—driving conditions in the mining area are among the most challenging in the world—PTFI has provided competent drivers for military personnel using PTFI roads. We acknowledge ICCA's findings that this practice may have led to confusion between the company and government security. Consequently, PTFI has arranged to discontinue this practice and to provide training to enable government security to drive safely in PTFI's area of operations.

Enhancement in Training and Employment of the Papuans at PTFI

PTFI will continue to develop and implement programs with the goal to: (a) establish employee development plans for all workers, including Papuan employees; (b) hold supervisors responsible for the evaluation of work performance of all their subordinates and the implementation of all employee development plans; and (c) make regular reports on the development of all employees to the PTFI Manpower Planning and Review Board.

In 2003, PTFI established the Nemangkawi Mining Institute (NMI), which currently has more than 700 students, more than 90 percent of whom were Papuans. NMI focuses on technical training in various trades. PTFI expects that those who successfully complete the program will obtain meaningful skilled employment with PTFI or another enterprise, and that at least 10 percent of NMI graduates will have the capacity to advance to supervisory and managerial levels. PTFI is specifically targeting talented Papuans for this program, and is recruiting at least ten new Papuan graduates this year.

Social Development of the Papuan People

PTFI and LPMAK recognize that the LPMAK Education Program is a beneficial program, but acknowledge that certain areas need to be addressed and improved. LPMAK has decided to reduce the emphasis on scholarships and educational subsidies in favor of enhanced local education. Toward this end, LPMAK and PTFI have been working with the local education authorities to improve the quality of basic education. LPMAK has developed and is implementing a five-year plan that includes specific initiatives to improve the structure and effectiveness of the Education Bureau, refocus educational resources, and bring the overall results achieved in line with expectations.

PTFI believes that working with LPMAK to improve programs, rather than having PTFI take over direct administration of them as suggested in the audit report, will produce a more sustainable result for the future. We also acknowledge that emphasis should be placed on "results achieved," not "activities," and we are working to develop measurable objectives in all SLD areas.

Contract Labor Providers

PTFI acknowledges that a number of the contract employees have been engaged as contract workers for periods that may extend longer than specified by Indonesian labor law. However, certain aspects of this law are unclear, and other provisions of the law, which are applicable to certain workers provided by licensed manpower providers, permit such employees to be contracted for an indefinite period of time.

Since 2004, we have been systematically and objectively evaluating each worker to determine whether he or she meets our current standards for hiring him or her as employees. If a contract worker achieves these standards, the individual is hired as an employee by PTFI. Otherwise, the individual is offered enrollment in a development program to gain the skills required for direct employment. PTFI has developed plans to reduce its use of contract labor and to recruit all hourly employees from students who graduate from the Nemangkawi Mining Institute.

The audit noted that PTFI should "create a set of guidelines clearly specifying the conditions under which contract workers can be hired by PTFI." PTFI has established guidelines, which are set forth in the policy on the *Secondment of Managed Contractors' Indonesian Employees to PTFI*. This policy has been recently revised to incorporate new practices and changes in the labor law. We will further assess existing guidelines in response to the audit's recommendations. PTFI also invited ICCA to return to its Indonesian operations in early 2006 to review and assess the actions that PTFI has taken in response to issues in its audit report.

ICCA'S Follow-Up of the Phase I Audit

ICCA's follow-up field audit took place in August 2006. It was intended to assess the progress and effectiveness of PTFI's initiatives in five areas.

- Use of PTFI security department drivers to transport Indonesian military personnel in the areas of PTFI mining operations.
- Employees' and contractor's inadequate knowledge of PTFI's Social, Employment, and Human Rights Policy (SEHR).
- Enhancement in the employment opportunities and corporate upward mobility for Papuan workers.
- Improvement in the management and oversight of education programs of Freeport's sponsored community fund.
- Changes in the employment practices in regard to contract workers.

The follow-up visit generally confirmed that Freeport had taken adequate actions to address human rights policies training and the issue of military personnel's transportation. ICCA also noted progress in improving Papuan workers' professional training to ensure better employment and promotion within the company. The visit found that the Lembaga Pengembangan Masyarakat Amungme dan Kamoro (LPMAK) had positively responded to the ICCA's recommendations and substantially improved management of the Education Bureau. However, in the area of contract workers' employment practices, ICCA remained largely unsatisfied with the level of PTFI's actions.[23]

Transportation of Military Personnel

The PTFI security department had discontinued the practice of providing transportation to military personnel, as confirmed by the follow-up visit, and instead set up a dedicated training program for government drivers to prevent injuries and disruptions to the mine operations. Considering the safety risk of driving in the mining area, ICCA finds this approach necessary and adequate.

Human Rights Training

By the time of the follow-up audit, PTFI had revised its human rights training program to focus on continued education and enhancement of human rights compliance. To oversee the human rights training and compliance program, PTFI had appointed a native Papuan employee to be a senior human rights compliance officer. The company also initiated a training program for several employees to become associate compliance officers.

Information about the six key human rights provisions is posted in English and Indonesian Bahasa in public areas, offices, and mess halls. The human rights principles are also printed on the employees' identification cards. All newly hired workers are required to attend a workshop on the PTFI's human rights policy along with other job-related orientation programs. For the security department, the training is held twice a year. Security personnel are no longer allowed to carry weapons and are prohibited from using physical force.

Papuan Employment

To facilitate Papuan workers' professional development, PTFI has continued its efforts in providing professional training and on-site education programs. At the time of the follow-up audit, NMI had more than 1,000 students, mostly Papuan, with nearly half of the students from the local tribal communities. One hundred seventy-five apprentices had been hired as employees of PTFI or one of the PTFI's partner companies. In addition to NMI, PTFI worked with a number of Indonesian universities to set up a graduate development program. The program offers one to three years of business skills development programs to some of the best-performing students at Indonesian universities. The training was offered to about one hundred students, twenty of whom were Papuan.

PTFI continued to offer on-site professional training to its employees, and created an additional incentive program to fifty Papuan employees. The program allows indigenous employees to take up to one year off work to participate in skills enhancement courses and potentially be reemployed at higher positions.

Following ICCA's recommendations, PTFI included a Papuan development component into every department's succession plan. Performance appraisals for department managers as well as other staff include criteria for advancing department's efforts in meeting five-year plans for Papuan employment. As a result, the proportion of Papuan staff has gone from 7.7 percent at the end of 2005 to 12.4 percent as of August 2006, and nonstaff from 19.8 percent to nearly 31 percent. Promotion rates for Papuan workers were at the same level as for non-Papuan employees. Despite these high achievements, the turnover rate among Papuan workers is extremely high. While 331 new Papuan employees were hired between November 2004 and July 2006, 309 Papuans left the company during the same period.

The LPMAK Education Bureau (EB)

The ICCA team was pleasantly surprised by the scope of remediation activities taken by LPMAK to resolve the situation. Sufficient financial and manpower resources had been directed to addressing the deficiencies of the EB, and resulted in tangible improvements in the activities of the EB. The structure of LPMAK's EB was completely revamped to streamline the supervision and execution capabilities. All employees of the bureau received proper job training and were subject to annual performance evaluations.

The EB student scholarship program was restructured to offer financial support only to qualified Papuan students who were pursuing degrees at accredited local universities. The new scholarship policy manual further strengthened application procedures, assigning approval responsibility to the universities rather than LPMAK. Working together, PTFI and EB have identified future employment needs in the Mimika region, including mine operations as well as other new business developments, and provided sponsorship assistance only in the relevant fields of study.

The policy manual has imposed stricter education performance requirements for the scholarships recipients. Students failing to complete their course work on time or at satisfactory levels will now be dropped from the program and their scholarships will be rescinded. All participating students in the program are now required to return to the Mimika region upon completion of their degree programs. This data is shared with PTFI's human resources department and other potential employers to create a better match between the students' qualifications and the employers' job requirements.

In response to ICCA's recommendations to improve living conditions for children's dormitories, EB had to close five facilities that were beyond repair, and started construction of six new housing facilities. The new dormitories were expected to meet enhanced LPMAK requirements, such as light, running water, adequate living space per student, safety, and security.

EB had also made some progress in addressing the need for basic education in the Mimika regency. Unfortunately, the problem of basic schooling could not be resolved simply through the assistance of PTFI, because all elementary schools as well as teachers and supporting personnel are obliged to receive government certification and approval.

Treatment of Contract Workers

In its response to ICCA's findings, Freeport revised its policies concerning contract workers and made a commitment to reduce contract labor through training programs and transferring temporary employees to full-time status upon completion of a work performance evaluation. The follow-up audit noted some progress in this regard; however, PTFI's efforts to that date had not resolved the problem completely, and the practice remained in violation of the local laws.

PTFI indicated that contract workers' wages were initially raised to 63 percent of the full-time employee levels, and then increased again to 73 percent. Although the increase was notable progress in resolving the issue of the pay inequality, it did not eliminate the problem—the contract workers' salaries were higher than before but still not equal to salaries paid to the full-time employees. Freeport claimed that wages of contract workers were determined based on the initial competency assessment, and were adjusted annually due to skill enhancements. However, this explanation begged the question, "If the temporary workers lacked necessary skills, why are they not hired at less demanding positions instead of jeopardizing the safety and quality of operations?" Similarly, if PTFI kept contract workers for three or more years at jobs that have certain professional requirements, the company had to be satisfied with the level of skills provided by such workers, otherwise their contracts would not be extended. PTFI reported that the number of contract workers with tenures of three or more years was reduced from 700 to almost 300. In ICCA's opinion, the number of contract workers with such a long tenure should be zero.

Other actions reported by PTFI to remedy unfair employment terms for contract workers included reduction of the number of contract worker suppliers and outsourcing some of the jobs to the local service providers. It was, however, not clear to ICCA how such activities could rectify existing problems of the temporary workers with tenures of three or more years.

Overall, ICCA's follow-up audit found that actions taken by PTFI in regard to treatment of temporary workers had neither improved the company's compliance with legal and company-wide requirements, nor resolved the situation with contract workers employed for three or more years. As a result, ICCA outlined several recommendations, including creation of a separate committee supervised by a senior human resources executive and external legal experts, which would examine all cases of temporary contract workers individually. ICCA further recommended that PTFI

1. should suspend any new hiring of temporary workers, and transfer all contract employees with three or more years of service at PTFI or privatized companies to full-time employment positions foregoing any proficiency tests.
2. should compensate all temporary nonstaff for the "loss of pay" based on the salary levels of the full-time employees, with additional interest paid for lost income.

Phase II Audit

The second phase of the audit took place in November and December 2006. The audit protocols used for the Phase II audit were similar to those applied to Phase I audit. Phase II focused on two areas: (a) medical care that PTFI provides for the local population who does not work for PTFI or its contractors; and (b) major contractors that provide essential services to PTFI's mining operations. As major contractors provide their services exclusively to Freeport, all of these contractors are covered by PTFI's SEHR.

In general, these contractors can be grouped into two categories based on their need for relatively skilled or unskilled workers, and their willingness and ability to train lower-skilled Papuans for higher-skilled and better-paying jobs. Among the contractors requiring highly skilled workers are mining equipment and repair services for equipment (PT Trakindo); specialized mine drilling (PT Sandvik); and port services, road maintenance, and truck and bus operations/maintenance (PT KPI). Among the contractors requiring relatively low-skilled workers are catering, housing, and hospitality services (PT Pangansari Utama); and a labor supplier owned and operated by Papuans (PT SAS).

Medical Services to the Papuan Community[24]

It should be noted that PTFI has no contractual obligation to provide medical care to people who are not employed by the company. However, PTFI has supplied medical care to local Papuans since the inception of mining and milling activities in Irian Jaya in the early 1970s. As the number of Papuans who did not work for the company increased in the area surrounding PTFI's operations, PTFI made a commitment to expand the public health and medical care programs available to the local Papuan communities.

From 1996 to 2006, the Freeport Partnership Fund provided $100 million to support medical activities for the local Papuan communities in and around PTFI's operations. The local community now has direct management responsibility for the hospital in the lowland city of Timika (RSMM) through the Amungme Kamoro Community Development Institute (LPMAK) and the public health programs for the local community (Public Health and Malaria Control, or PHMC). International Security Overseas Services/AEA (ISOS/AEA) and LPMAK share the management of the highland hospital (Rumah Sakit Waa-Banti) in Timbagapura.

ICCA audited the three major community-based health programs for their effectiveness in improving the health of the Papuans in the local community and the management structure of the LPMAK and PTFI's Social and Local Development Department (SLD) for the efficiency of the operation. The audit concluded that PTFI has fulfilled all of its financial and human resources support that the company made in its *Social, Employment, and Human Rights Policy* and the *Guiding Principles for Indonesian Operations*. ICCA also found that the medical care providers, the Yayasan Caritas Timika (YST), which operates the RSMM, and International ISOS/AEA, which operates the Banti hospital PTFI's Public Health and Malaria Control (PHMC), are deeply committed to the health of the local population. The audit also indicated that, by and large, the local community shares this assessment.

ICCA's audit team made certain recommendations that would further improve the effectiveness and efficiency of PTFI's community health-care programs. In particular, that LPMAK should employ a health-care professional to help evaluate the distribution of money to the three entities that LPMAK supports, and to allocate funds based on community medical needs and targets. Units receiving funding must deliver on targets based on verifiable outcomes.

The Public Health, Malaria Control, and Community Clinics program has provided effective programs within the community to alleviate malaria, tuberculosis, and, of late, HIV/AIDS. ICCA recommends that PHMC should expand its programs in health education within local communities.

Privatized Companies

In the early years of its mining operations in Indonesia, PTFI secured all its services internally. However, starting in the 1980s, the company experienced tremendous growth in its core mining operations. The company decided that it would be more efficient to outsource its ancillary support services to independent contractors with expertise in specific areas. As the size of the mining operations increased in the early 1990s, PTFI decided to concentrate on its core business and to have specialized contractor companies to take over major portions of support activities and some very specific, technical mining operations. These contractors were required to take over the management of PTFI's existing facilities. Quite often these contractors were major companies in their own right and thus would bring advanced technologies and economic efficiencies through economies of scale. PTFI called this process "privatization," and the companies that managed the operations and personnel came to be called "privatized companies." All privatized companies were required to adhere to two conditions: (1) their operations in the PTFI mining area would be exclusively devoted to PTFI; and (2) all privatized companies were expected to adhere to PTFI's SEHR as applied to PTFI's own operations and covered in ICCA's Phase I audit.

PT KPI

PT KPI operates PTFI's Portsite and truck and bus transportation. It also provides light vehicle maintenance and the upkeep of PTFI's roads. Most of PT KPI's workers are skilled. In general, worker satisfaction at KPI was good, and KPI had made a good-faith effort to implement PTFI's SEHR. The two major issues raised in the audit were the employment of Papuans among the staff employees of KPI (KPI had done an acceptable job in employing Papuans in nonstaff positions) and the use of temporary contract workers with salaries lower than those of regular KPI employees and for periods in excess of those permitted by Indonesian labor law.

PT Sandvik

Sandvik provides specialized mining services for PTFI. Because of the nature of its work, Sandvik has a number of highly skilled professionals, many of whom are expatriates, a greater number of skilled assistants who provide services to the specialized mining professionals, and a number of semiskilled workers. Relatively few Papuans (8.6 percent of the workforce) are employed by Sandvik, most of whom fall in the last category. Although Sandvik's management states that the company has active on-the-job and developmental training programs, nearly half of the employees state that they have had little or no training geared toward advancement in the workforce. Similarly, a divergence of opinion existed among employees of Sandvik about the company's commitment to human rights: the staff believes the commitment is real and vital; nonstaff employees are less certain.

However, the major issue that ICCA has focused on with Sandvik (as with PTFI and some of the other contractors) is the use of temporary contract workers. For Sandvik the issue is one group of workers doing a single task for more than three years, but still deemed "temporary."

PT Trakindo

Trakindo, which sells and services the mining equipment used by PTFI, has worked at PTFI's operations site for twenty-seven years. Over the past five years, its presence and the scope of activities at PTFI have substantially expanded. Given the long period of time that Trakindo has been providing services for PTFI, one would expect that Trakindo would be further advanced in its compliance efforts pertaining to PTFI's SEHR. Unfortunately, this turned out not to be the case. Trakindo's performance has lagged behind other contractors in its employment of Papuans, both in the staff and the nonstaff areas. In addition, Trakindo had no robust implementation of human rights training and monitoring. Finally, Trakindo, like PTFI and other privatized companies, has been using temporary contract workers in ways that ICCA considered contrary to Indonesian labor law. On the positive side, most of Trakindo's staff employees expressed satisfaction with Trakindo as an employer and stated that they believed Trakindo treated Papuans well.

PT Pangansari Utama

Pangansari's primary areas of work include providing meals to all workers (both PTFI and privatized companies) at the mine site and managing housing and other related services. This company is, therefore, expected to be at the forefront of hiring and training lower-skilled workers—and thus have a substantially large proportion of its employees from the Papuan community.

ICCA's audit finding, however, revealed that Pangansari's employment of Papuans was proportionately far less compared to PTFI as a whole. Furthermore, Papuans at Pangansari had not advanced or been promoted at the same rate as non-Papuan employees.

ICCA's findings also showed that Pangansari was not making sufficient efforts in helping the economic development of the local Papuan community by directing its purchases of basic commodities needed for its catering services, such as fruits, vegetables, and fish. Pangansari had argued that as far as local purchases were concerned, it must abide by PTFI regulations to buy at the lowest prices available, which the local suppliers were not able to meet.

From ICCA's perspective, the nature of Pangansari's activities lend themselves to providing greater employment and economic development opportunities for the Papuans. Therefore, PTFI would need to examine its procurement policies to encourage local purchases. PTFI should also become more actively involved in Pangansari's hiring policies, especially as they pertain to the hiring of Papuan workers.

1. Pangansari should be required to double its Papuan workforce during the next five years. Moreover, PTFI and Pangansari should institute training programs to ensure that Papuan workers are promoted at the same rate as their non-Papuan counterparts in Pangansari's workforce.
2. PTFI and Pangansari should develop a joint plan to evaluate the potential of increased local purchases and take the necessary step to implement these plans.

PT SAS

PT SAS manages a small set of activities for PTFI, including a cattle ranch and some general maintenance functions. However, its primary role is that of hiring temporary workers for PTFI and privatized companies. Another notable fact about PT SAS is that it is owned and operated by local Papuans. In this sense, PT SAS is a great success story for the joint efforts of PTFI and the local community to establish locally owned and operated businesses. It is, therefore, disappointing that PT SAS employed relatively few Papuans for its own operations.

Freeport's Response to Phase II Audit

Freeport provided its response to ICCA's Phase II audit on November 30, 2007.[25] In general, there was broad agreement as to the objectivity and comprehensiveness of ICCA's audit findings and recommendations. There were some disagreements with regard to the scope of the audit's coverage, which went beyond ICCA's mandate, such as PTFI's medical programs as contrasted with LPMAK's medical and health-care facilities. The main source of disagreement, however, pertained to employment and differences in the interpretation of legal requirements in the hiring of contract workers; PTFI's responsibility in monitoring the activities of privatized companies with regard to hiring, length of employment, and promotion of contract workers; and employment and promotion of Papuans on the part of privatized companies.

Given below are extracts of relevant portions of Freeport's response document dated November 30, 2007.[26]

Medical Audit

The management of FCX and PTFI wishes to express appreciation to ICCA for having conducted the medical care audit. The audit has enabled FCX and PTFI to prove their success in a number of areas and to identify others that need to be addressed. FCX and PTFI management agree with ICCA's recommendation to expand the role of professionals in advising the LPMAK on program objectives, budgeting, and spending on medical care and public health initiatives. We further agree that operating units must be held accountable and that data-based decision-making is an area for improvement. At the same time, the LPMAK is a community-owned and -led organization, and funding allocations must be based on community input and the assessment of their own health needs. We would also like to point out that both PTFI and LPMAK are very aware of the connection between increasing public health activities to make people healthier and thereby decreasing hospital costs.

Freeport Public Health and Malaria Control (PTFI PHMC) program and the LPMAK Public Health and Malaria Control (LPMAK PHMC) program in both the general medical audit and the executive summary.

To clarify:

- ICCA was hired to do an audit of LPMAK's medical programs, not PTFI's. It seems that the ICCA has looked at PTFI's programs and compared them to the LPMAK programs but has confused them in the audit report.
- The PTFI PHMC program has functioned in an exemplary fashion, providing services to PTFI and also extending their operations outside PTFI's contract of work area in order to assist the Papuan community.
- The LPMAK PHMC program is very rudimentary and has yet to develop into an identifiable and sustainable program. PTFI agrees with the recommendations of the auditors that the LPMAK PHMC program needs to be better organized, structured and more focused in its functions.

Privatized Companies

As part of PTFI's commitments to its Social, Employment, and Human Rights (SEHR) policy, PTFI requested that the ICCA undertake audits on each company contracted by PTFI. It is important to point out that a number of these entities have operations in other parts of Indonesia and their business practices are independently set for their entire operations, not just the Papuan subsidiary.

PTFI would like to point out that some of the audit findings are generated from interviews conducted by ICCA of employees of each company. While these interview responses are important, they represent the views of that particular interviewee and we believe that it would be beneficial to obtain further information to confirm that all appropriate sources are considered. It is evident in the audits of these companies that further information is needed in order to draw supportable conclusions and to be able to make recommendations.

In response to a number of issues raised in the audits, PTFI, under the direction of its chief financial officer, will work with its contract companies to take appropriate steps to ensure the following:

- PTFI will provide assistance to all contracted companies in order to help them improve compliance with PTFI's SEHR policy or to establish a similar policy.
- All contracted companies will be required to certify their compliance with Indonesian labor laws.
- The contracted companies will be encouraged to work with the PTFI QMS department to develop training programs for unskilled persons who, with training, could become suitable permanent employees.
- The contracted companies will be encouraged to support the local community through the purchase of local products and other forms of contributions.

Employment of Contract Workers

PTFI expressed its disagreement with ICCA's interpretation of Indonesian law with regard to contract workers, and the law's application to the "terms and conditions" under which contract workers were employed by PTFI and privatized companies. Given below are relevant extracts from PTFI's response document.

PTFI would like to clarify that:

- The employment agreements for contract workers are between the labor supply company and their workers—not PTFI. There is no employment relationship between these contract workers and PTFI. This is noted in the legal memorandum appended to ICCA's report: "There is no employment relationship between the Outsourced Workers and the Principal Company."
- PTFI has a written agreement with the labor supply company to supply workers for noncore/support type functions.
- The issue of temporary employment status is determined by the employment agreement between the labor supply company and the worker. PTFI will take steps to ensure that the labor supply companies do not engage workers as temporary employees for periods longer than permitted by law.

Remedial Actions

In response to the concerns raised by ICCA, PTFI has developed and begun implementing a policy for the contract worker program that will clearly establish the scope of the program and ensure that it is in compliance with Indonesian labor standards.

Further actions will be undertaken under the direction of the executive vice president having responsibility for human resources within the company, with the assistance of outside labor law counsel. As of November 2007, a number of the following actions have been put into place and are making good progress.

- Establish categories of workers delineated between core and noncore work.
- In the case of labor supply companies that supply contract workers to PTFI who have been under contract for more than the maximum permissible period and are employed by the labor supply company as temporary employees, PTFI will work with the labor supply company to evaluate each of these workers on a case-by-case basis to determine their future status. If these contract workers meet PTFI's basic competency and occupational standards, PTFI will immediately offer the worker a job as a permanent employee of PTFI, provided that the worker terminates his/her employment status with the labor supply company.
- In those cases where evaluations show that the contract workers do not meet basic competency and occupational standards, PTFI will undertake additional training to raise the performance of these contract workers to the required competency standards. PTFI expects this process to be completed no later than March of 2008. At the end of this process, the contract workers will be evaluated and if they are eligible for PTFI employment, they will be offered a permanent position with PTFI.
- All contract workers who have been under contract for less than the maximum period allowed by Indonesian law will be evaluated to ascertain whether their roles are considered to be core or noncore/support work. If the PTFI contract worker is performing tasks that are considered core, the worker will be, based on evaluation, offered permanent employee status in the same manner

as set forth above, or placed into one of PTFI's apprentice programs. If the contract worker is performing tasks that are considered noncore, the contract worker will be evaluated every six months to one year for competency and occupational skills. PTFI will also evaluate its on-the-job training program for noncore workers to ensure that the training is achieving desired results. PTFI will ensure that no contract worker will be engaged for more than the legally allowed period of time.

- All contracts and contract renewals between PTFI and labor supply companies as well as other contractors must conform to the Indonesian labor law standards and the principles and policies of PTFI with regard to the employment and work opportunities of the Papuan people. PTFI will periodically evaluate these companies for compliance with these standards.
- These objectives will be implemented and completed by March 2008.
- All actions described above regarding contract workers will be independently verified by year end 2008.

Epilogue

ICCA's audit contract was fulfilled with the completion of Phase II audit and Freeport's response. Although ICCA has no formal information with regard to PTFI's activities pertaining to the issues covered in its Guiding Principles for Indonesian Operations, we presume that PTFI has continued to implement its programs and corrective actions outlined in the company's response to Phase II audit.

Unfortunately, publicly available information from the news media indicates that sociopolitical conditions and unrest in the Papuan community have not subsided, as can be seen from the brief summary of events that have occurred around the mine site during the period 2007–2010. In many ways, these incidents echo the continuation of issues that were observed during the 2003–2007 audit period covered by ICCA.

In mid-July 2009, gunshots killed three people, including an Australian PTFI employee. The next day, another Australian, a security guard for PTFI, was killed at the same location.[27] Only few days later, eleven buses en route from Timika to Tembagapura were attacked, leaving five police officers with gunshot injuries.[28]

The Indonesian army again blamed Papuan separatists for the attacks and the killings. Six people from nearby Papuan villages were arrested and allegedly threatened and beaten.[29] Nevertheless, police reported that there was no reason to suspect members of the Papuan freedom movement, and that the ammunition used in the guns was standard for military and police forces.[30]

Some of the local-affairs experts suggested that the shootings could be a result of rivalry between the Indonesian army and the local police over the job of providing security for the mine. According to George Junus Aditjondro, the author of *Rebellions in Indonesia*, military forces were eager to demonstrate police incompetence in guarding foreign businesses.[31]

Some other mysteries were involved in the incidents. For instance, the doctor who conducted the autopsy on the Australian PTFI technician reported that the bullets were removed from the body before the examination.[32]

Shortly after the string of attacks, police reported that one of the most prominent leaders of OPM, Kelly Kwalik, was shot to death after allegedly threatening a police officer. Although OPM denied any involvement in the recent attacks, Indonesian police blamed Kwalik for the ambush and killing of three people.[33]

As the investigation carried on, gunshots continued to be heard in the area of the Grasberg mine. In January 2010, gunmen attacked another convoy, wounding six people,[34] while Indonesian army considered sending thousands of additional troops into the area.[35]

In March 2010, the much-respected International Crisis Group issued a white paper on Papua, "Radicalization and Dialogue in Papua." A section of the paper dealt with the events in the Timika area from 2007 to 2010.[36] The report notes the restraint of the Indonesian army and police as well as Freeport during a time of danger and stress. The conclusion of the report is that the actions seen in Papua over the past few years have been driven by a new generation of Papuans who are more radicalized than previous leaders. However, it also notes that the enhanced education of the leaders gives hope that more concerted and comprehensive discussions on issues of importance to all parties may lead to more peaceful resolutions in the future.

Appendix 3.1

Guiding Principles of Operations in Indonesia (GPOI-1) Guiding Principles for Indonesian Operations—People and the Community

Part I

1.1. Mission Statement

Freeport has always been cognizant of its multiple responsibilities toward the economic and social development of the local people, respect for their culture, human rights and civil liberties and protection of the environment. The Company has conducted its Indonesian operations with concern for the environment and a sense of responsibility toward its Papuan employees and the indigenous people who live around its operations area.

To this end, Freeport has voluntarily devoted resources, and will continue to do so in the future, which go beyond its legal and contractual commitments to the Government of Indonesia and the Papuan people of the region. The Corporate mission for the future is to conduct its mining operations in Papua in a manner that is economically efficient, protects the environment, and nurtures the economic growth and development of the Papuan people with respect for their tribal culture and value system and their human rights.

1.2. Corporate Commitment

The Guiding Principles enunciated here are intended to codify Freeport's Social, Employment, and Human Rights Policy by enumerating practices and operational standards in Papua in the areas of social and economic development of the indigenous people of Papua, protection of human rights and respect for their culture and dignities. These Principles address how Freeport's polices and operational practices are intended to impact employment, business-government relations, protection of human rights, and economic and social development of the local tribes in the area of operations. They also set forth Freeport's commitment for the welfare of the people of Papua and their unique culture and value set.

Furthermore, to ensure compliance with these Principles, Freeport has already undertaken a series of measures:

1. Created detailed, objective, quantifiable, and outcome-oriented measures of performance in each of the five areas covered in the Principles.
2. Initiated policies and procedures whose implementation and enforcement will be required of all levels of supervisors and managers.
3. Undertaken an extensive training program to familiarize managers and workers with these policies. This training program has also been offered to local community leaders as well as police and military units to sensitize them to these issues.
4. Developed internal monitoring programs to evaluate compliance with the Principles and their Standards of Implementation.

5. Made compliance with the Principles and Standards an integral part of every manager's performance evaluation, promotion, and compensation.
6. Implemented an internal communication program whereby all employees and managers are made aware of their responsibilities under the Principles and are encouraged to participate in the implementation and enhancement of these Principles.

Part II

II.1. People and the Community

The Guiding Principles address how Freeport's policies and operational practices are intended to impact employment, protection of human rights, and economic and social development of the local tribes in the area of operations. In particular, they pertain to the Seven Papuan Tribal Communities (7-PTC), which encompass the area of Freeport's mining operations.

These Principles are a public expression of Freeport's commitment and how the Company intends to meet the self-imposed obligations that Freeport has voluntarily assumed. The Principles further demonstrate the Company's resolve to conduct its operations in Papua in a highly professional, economically efficient, and socially responsible manner.

The Principles described here cover five areas:

1. Treatment of Workers employed by Freeport and its affiliated organizations.
2. Special Status workers from the Seven Papuan Tribal Communities (7-PTC) with regard to Employment, Training, and Promotion at Freeport.
3. Protection of Human Rights.
4. Business-Government Relations.
5. Economic and Social Development of the Seven Papuan Tribal Communities (7-PTC).

II.2. Treatment of Workers

1. Freeport will comply with all national and local labor laws with regard to employment practices. This will also apply to all independent contractors, privatized companies, and major suppliers and service providers doing business with Freeport. There can be no exception to this rule.
2. Where economically feasible, Freeport will act affirmatively to create policies and programs that go beyond the national and local labor laws and regulations to demonstrate the Company's commitment to be a responsible corporate citizen.
3. The treatment of workers includes such issues as: Hiring, wages, and working hours; training and skill enhancement; protection from discrimination based on religion, ethnicity, gender, and political affiliation; protection from physical abuse, sexual harassment, and unfair treatment; workplace safety; provision of adequate living space and eating facilities; workers' health; and safety. Freeport is also committed to the protection of freedom of speech, religion, and association.

Freeport's implementation of its policies with regard to worker treatment will necessarily differ according to the extent of the Company's control over the workers in affiliated organizations and service providers as described below. However, Freeport will assume overall responsibility to ensure that these units comply with Indonesia's national and local labor laws, do not practice discrimination among different classes of workers, and that differences as to wages and working conditions are reasonable, non-exploitative, and non-discriminatory.

These policies cover four classes of workers and include both permanent and temporary workers.

1. All workers employed directly by Freeport in its mining operations and related facilities. These are called Category 1 workers.
2. All workers employed by independent entities who perform specialized services connected with Freeport's mining operations are called Category 2 workers.[1]
3. All workers employed by independent companies with significant business relationship with Freeport, but not connected specifically with Freeport mining operations. These are called Category 3 workers.[2]
4. All workers employed by companies that supply labor at Freeport's operations for temporary work at Freeport's various facilities. These are called Category 4 workers.[3]

Category 1 Workers. Freeport has developed detailed policies covering workers directly employed by Freeport at the mine and its affiliated facilities. Salient elements of these polices are briefly described here.

Category 2 Workers. Independent entities ("privatized companies," specifically referring to privatization contracts developed during 1994–1995) that perform specialized services connected with Freeport's mining operations hire these workers. A company employing Category 2 workers must meet all the conditions applicable to Category 1 workers subject to the following exception:

Category 2 workers may receive wages and benefits that are significantly different than those paid to Category 1 workers provided that the nature of work performed by Category 2 workers is not comparable to any work performed by Category 1 workers.

Category 3 Workers. Companies employing Category 3 workers have a significant business relationship with Freeport, but are not directly connected with Freeport's mining operations. These companies have their own policies and programs covering wages and working conditions of their employees. Freeport has no control over the employment practices of these companies. Notwithstanding, these companies must abide by Freeport's policies with regard to compliance with local and national laws, non-discrimination, and human rights policies.

Category 4 workers. Category 4 workers perform temporary jobs. If their work is required for a period of less than three years, their wages and

---

[1]   Privatized companies: PT Alas Emas Abadi (AEA/ISOS), Sheraton Timika, PT Kuala Pelabuhan Indonesia (KPI), PT Tata Disantara (TDS), PT Mahaka Industri Perdana, PT Pangansari Utama, PT AVCO, PT Puncak Jaya Power (PJP).

[2]   For example, PT Trakindo Utama, PT United Tractors, PT Petrosea, PT Redpath Indonesia, PT Hero, etc.

[3]   PT Inamco Varia Jasa, PT Buma Kumawa, PT Jasti Pravita, PT Tomi Irja, PT Srikandi Mitra Karya, PT Nurul Amaliyah.

benefits will gradually achieve parity with those of workers employed in similar positions at Freeport. Upon the completion of three years of service, if the work is still needed, all qualified Category 4 employees will become Category 1 employees.

- Where work performed by Category 4 workers is similar to the work performed by Category 1 workers, wages and benefits paid to Category 4 workers must be substantially similar to those of Category 1 workers.
- Where Category 4 workers terminate employment with their employer and become Category 1 workers, the criteria for transfer must be non-arbitrary, clearly established, and made known to all Category 4 workers. There can be no discrimination among Category 4 workers seeking status of Category 1 workers with the exception noted in the case of workers belonging to the 7-PTC.

II.3. Hiring Practices

1. At the time of hiring, each worker must be provided with a document that provides complete details of the terms and conditions of his or her employment, method of wage calculation, and the regularly scheduled dates of payment of wages.
2. Each worker must also receive appropriate training with regard to plant safety, fire drills, safe handling of hazardous materials, and job-specific training.
3. Workers may be required to undergo a reasonable probationary period. However, workers must be paid no less than the prevailing minimum wage during the probationary period.

II.4. Wages, Working Hours, Benefits

1. Freeport must comply with all national, provincial, and local laws pertaining to payment for overtime work, mandatory deductions, holidays, vacations, medical benefits, and other provisions of the country's labor laws. Where Freeport has obtained specific dispensation from the Department of Manpower for additional overtime required for certain jobs, Freeport will comply fully with these guidelines.
2. All Company provided benefits, e.g., healthcare benefits, housing, meals, and other incentive bonuses must be paid to all employees within similar job categories. Where differences exist as to specific benefits between various job categories, these must be based on clearly defined criteria such as specialized skills, job characteristics, and seniority, to name a few.
3. All overtime work must be voluntary except where it is integral to the type of work performed and scheduling of work shifts at the work location. The employees must have agreed to "standard overtime" as part of the employment contract. The Company must also comply with all applicable laws with regard to the maximum number of overtime hours permitted during a given day, week, or month.

II.5. Discrimination at the Workplace

Freeport must ensure that its human resource management policies are free of any form of discrimination against workers on the basis of age, gender, ethnicity, sexual preference, religion, or tribal affiliation. The only exception to this rule applies to workers from 7-PTC areas. This is discussed in a latter part of the document. Furthermore, any form of harassment based on similar considerations is prohibited.

II.6. Disciplinary Actions and Grievance Handling Procedure

1. Freeport has created written procedures, rules, and regulations to maintain discipline and safe working conditions in the operations areas and other related facilities, dormitories, canteens, and recreational areas. These include, among others, implementing a formal program of handling grievances and resolving disciplinary issues and awareness on the part of all workers about these rules and procedures.
2. Freeport will also ensure that its grievance handling and conflict resolution procedures are free from any pro-management bias and are transparent as to their findings and implementation. This attribute is necessary if the Company is to engender trust among the workers, enhance workplace harmony, and achieve greater worker loyalty.

II.7. Worker Access to Management

1. Freeport's policies require that mine management should provide and encourage access by workers to all levels of management on issues that impact their wages, benefits, working, and living conditions. All levels of management must also hold regular meetings with workers on issues of concern to them.
2. Freeport will also create an effective mechanism that allows and encourages workers to communicate anonymously with the management on issues of concern to them and also make suggestions toward improvement of the vendor's operations and human resource management practices.

II.8. Dormitory and Living Space

Allocation of dormitory space in different job categories will be based on work-related criteria. These criteria will be explained to the workers. Where enough dormitory space is not available to all eligible workers, comparable financial compensation will be provided to workers who cannot be accommodated in the dormitories.

II.9. Food Services and Canteen Privileges

These services will be available to all workers under rules that are clearly defined and applied to all workers in a fair and equitable manner.

Part III

Business-Governmental Relations

III. 1. Compliance with Host Country Laws

Freeport will obey and support the laws of the Republic of Indonesia and will support the development of civil government in the area of its operations.

III. 2. Bribery and Corruption

1. In its dealings with the representatives of the Indonesian government, provincial and local officials, and other functionaries performing government work, Freeport employees and representatives of its affiliates, contractors, and privatized corporations are prohibited from using bribes or other unethical practices toward seeking favorable treatment from government agencies in furtherance of their business.

2. Under certain circumstances, where it is considered normal and customary to make small payments (defined as "facilitating payments" under the Foreign Corrupt Practices Act, 1977) to minor officials, Freeport accepts the reality of this situation, but expresses aversion to this practice. In all such cases, business practices must meet the standards specified in the U.S. Foreign Corrupt Practices Act of 1977. Any violation of this Act on the part of Freeport employees or anyone representing Freeport will be considered a serious breach of Company policy and the offending employee or representative will be subjected to severe penalties including termination from employment.

3. All such payments, whether in kind or cash, must also meet the reporting requirements of the Foreign Corrupt Practices Act, 1977 and those of the U.S. Securities and Exchange Commission.

Part IV

IV.1. Protection of Human Rights

1. Freeport is one of the few multinational companies in the extractive industries with a well-defined human rights policy and implementation program. This includes the appointment, at the corporate level, of a Vice President with direct responsibility for Human Rights.

2. In developing this policy, Freeport is guided by the United Nations Universal Declaration of Human Rights and the Voluntary Principles on Security and Human Rights as its standard for upholding the human rights of the employees, dependents, and those who live in the area of the Company's operations.

3. Freeport considers that each worker has the right of freedom of association, freedom of speech, and freedom of religion without fear of intimidation or punishment on the part of the employer.

4. In implementing this policy, Freeport will train its management employees—and all members of its Security and Community Relations Departments—to ensure their respect of human rights of the workers and the community. Freeport will also put in place a systematic program whereby all managers will be held accountable to ensure that everyone under their supervision has knowledge of Freeport's Human Rights policies and to ensure that their conduct conforms with the standards and procedures laid out in the Company's policy and policy manuals.

5. Freeport will also conduct internal monitoring programs to assure compliance with its policies with regard to human rights by all those who are responsible for implementing these policies. Where necessary, the company will take appropriate disciplinary measures against those who violate these

policies and will also report all suspected human rights violations in its area of operations to appropriate governmental officials.

Part V

V.1. Special Status of Papuan Workers

The Principles recognize the special status of 7-PTC Papuans and that Freeport will have a proactive bias to support increased employment of 7-PTC workers in all of the Company's operations and those of its affiliates, contractors, and privatized corporations.

Freeport has made a commitment that—at a minimum—it will quadruple the number of Papuan employees between the years 1996 and 2006. In addition the number of Papuan staff employees will double during the same period of time.

To make increased employment of Papuans a reality, Freeport will initiate training programs that will increase the supply of skilled and qualified Papuans. Freeport will also recruit aggressively for qualified Papuans to work at Freeport.

Freeport will work closely with its affiliates, contractors, and privatized corporations to ensure increased levels of employment and promotion of Papuan workers in their operations commensurate with Freeport's commitment enunciated in this document.

Freeport will develop a viable plan of action, including in-house training and aggressive recruiting, to ensure that it can meet its 2006 goals for 7-PTC workers at all levels of the organization. It will also establish annual targets for evaluating progress toward meeting the 2006 goal. This plan will be prepared in consultation with 7-PTC representatives, 7-PTC members currently in the employment of Freeport and its affiliated agencies. The plan will also have the approval of senior management in Indonesia and in Freeport's headquarters in New Orleans.

V.2. Economic and Social Development of the Local Tribes

Freeport is committed to the economic development and cultural protection of the local tribes. The Company has already taken important steps to engage the local 7-PTC in developing programs and policies designed to improve their economic conditions while respecting their traditions in terms of communal organization and leadership.

The Company has devoted substantial financial resources to this effort. Between 1996 and 2002 the Company has allocated or spent over $100 million on the development activities in support of the 7-PTC communities. These funds have been spent on healthcare, education, infrastructure development, and small business development. From these funds two hospitals have been built and are operating, scholarships and educational aid has been provided for more than 5,000 students, houses, community buildings, roads, bridges, and drainage facilities have been constructed, and more than a dozen small business have been developed and nurtured in the local indigenous community.

V.3. Freeport Fund for Community Development
(One Percent Fund)

In an initiative that is unprecedented in the mining industry and in other industries with significant direct foreign investments anywhere in the world, Freeport has agreed to devote one percent of its net revenue from the mining operations to the economic and social development of the 7-PTC. This commitment is strictly voluntary and is undertaken by Freeport to extend its support to the development and transformation of the seven Papuan Tribal Communities to adapt to the exigencies of the modern world while protecting their unique culture and value set.

Legal and governance infrastructure to assure proper usage of these funds has already been developed. The LPMAK provides a community-based management structure so that the community can use these funds in accordance with the overall donor guidance. These funds will be spent under the guidance and supervision of the local tribes and will be primarily devoted to four areas: Education, Public Health, Housing and Infrastructure, and Economic Development.

As a first step, the Company has agreed to make these contributions through the year 2006. Freeport has made a commitment to extend the program through 2011. It will be re-evaluated at that time.

Part VI

Evaluation, Corrective Action and Monitoring

Freeport is determined to ensure that all of its activities under the Principles have the full support of senior management and employees. Freeport also wishes to engender public confidence and trust in the Company's compliance with the Principles. To achieve these twin goals:

1. Freeport and its affiliated organizations will undergo regular audits of all activities covered under GPIO-1. The organizations' respective internal audit departments will perform the audits to assess their compliance with the Principles. The internal audit process will include performance evaluations, plans for corrective action, and a follow-up mechanism to ensure compliance in a timely fashion.
2. Freeport's commitment to the public includes verification audits by the International Center for Corporate Accountability (an independent monitoring organization) to assess the extent of compliance with the Principles by Freeport and its affiliated organizations on a regular basis and to afford these audits maximum transparency and public credibility. Freeport will provide the independent monitoring organization with complete access to all information and facilities in order to make an evaluation of Freeport's performance on the Principles and their implementation standards. The independent monitor will have complete discretion in issuing its reports without any censorship from Freeport provided that Freeport is afforded a suitable opportunity to respond to any findings of fact and conclusion by the Independent Monitor.

Appendix 3.2

Field Audit Design and Protocols

ICCA's field audit design consisted of three main instruments. The first is the **management compliance report (MCR)**, which is prepared by the management in charge of each business unit and provides details of that unit's compliance with GPOI-1. This document is submitted to ICCA at least two to four weeks prior to the start of field audit. The second element consists of **worker interview questionnaires**. ICCA used four questionnaires that varied in length and complexity based on the needs of individual business units. All questionnaires are prepared in local languages and local interviewers conduct the interview in the language of the interviewee. These interviewers are trained by ICCA and generally reflect the age, education, ethnic orientation, and other factors pertinent to each group of interviewees. All interviews are conducted in strict privacy on a one-on-one basis, and ICCA representatives bring all data back directly to New York for analysis. The fourth element of the audit protocol pertains to **site visits and consultations** with professional staff members of various business units. These interviews are also conducted in private by ICCA representatives. However, the questionnaire design remains somewhat open-ended and respondents are given broader latitude to respond within specified parameters.

The ICCA team consisted of four senior members and two junior members, whose combined portfolio of experience included production systems management, field audits of manufacturing systems, questionnaire design and administration, database management, statistical analysis, empirical and analytical research, and global manufacturing operations. In addition, the team brought ten years of experience in designing and field monitoring global code of conducts of multinational corporations.

Procedures for Public Disclosure of Audit Findings

An important part of the Freeport-ICCA agreement was to set forth clear procedures by which the findings of the audits would be made public. This was a two-step process. The preliminary findings in the draft report would be first submitted to the company. The review process would normally take thirty days. Any factual errors—agreed to both by Freeport and ICCA—would be deleted from the draft report. For all other findings, Freeport and ICCA would discuss and mutually agree to a plan for corrective action. In such cases, both the original findings and corrective action plans would be made public as part of ICCA's final report. Finally, in the event of a disagreement between Freeport and ICCA as to the substantive nature of ICCA's findings or the adequacy of Freeport's remedial plans, the entire matter would be made part of ICCA's formal report to be released to the public. Under no circumstances would Freeport have the right to demand any changes in the final text of the report except as described above. Moreover, ICCA would have the right to undertake a follow-up audit in case it were necessary to verify that remedial actions had been successfully carried out.

Appendix 3.3

PT Freeport Indonesia and Freeport-McMoRan Copper & Gold Inc.
Response to the Audit of Indonesian Operations by the International Center for Corporate Accountability
October 4, 2005

Introduction

In 1999, the Board of Directors of Freeport-McMoRan Copper & Gold Inc. (FCX) and the Board of Commissioners of PT Freeport Indonesia (PT-FI) adopted a wide-ranging Social, Employment, and Human Rights Policy for all operations, with particular emphasis on its Indonesian operations. In 2004, these Boards adopted an enhanced version of the policy. The policy recognizes that protection of human rights begins with the cessation of violence against individuals and groups, but also extends to economic and social development and the opportunity for people to lead healthy and productive lives.

FCX and PT-FI have created programs to foster human rights; to provide education, health care, and economic development opportunities; to develop education and training programs; and to aid in the social development of the indigenous people living in PT-FI's operations area. The main engine of these programs was and continues to be the Freeport Partnership Fund, which was created in 1996 to provide one percent of the revenues from the operations in Papua managed by PT-FI for the benefit of the local communities. By the end of 2004, total contributions from this "One Percent Fund" since inception were $152 million.

In 1996, PT-FI also made commitments to quadruple total Papuan employment at the Grasberg mine and to double the number of Papuans in staff positions. These commitments have been exceeded.

Fulfilling these commitments relating to social employment and human rights matters involves significant challenges. For that reason, FCX and PT-FI have established a number of initiatives to enable achievement of its commitments and to ensure that the results of these initiatives are measurable.

In 1999, FCX named Judge Gabrielle Kirk McDonald, former President of the International Criminal Tribunal for the former Yugoslavia and former U.S. federal judge and civil rights attorney, as Special Counsel for Human Rights to the Office of the Chairman. Judge McDonald has had a strong influence on the implementation of the FCX and PT-FI human rights programs, and she has championed the social and developmental rights of women in the PT-FI operations area.

Also in 2000, FCX agreed to be a participant in the U.S. State Department/ British Foreign Office Voluntary Principles for Security and Human Rights. The Voluntary Principles establish standards for extractive companies working in developing countries with regard to providing for necessary security within an operating framework that ensures respect for human rights.

FCX and PT-FI have committed to assess their social development, employment, and human rights programs periodically through use of an independent and respected organization. To that end, FCX and PT-FI engaged the International Center for Corporate Accountability (ICCA) to perform an independent audit of its commitments and results.

PT-FI's Grasberg operation is one of the most complex in the world. PT-FI and ICCA undertook extensive preparation in order to conduct an audit taking into account these complexities. In consideration of the size and diversity of PT-FI's operations, ICCA and PT-FI agreed that the scope of the audit would focus on the key components of the Social, Employment, and Human Rights Policy.

The management of PT-FI and FCX wishes to express appreciation to ICCA for having

conducted the audit. An important benefit of the audit has been that this process has provided a framework for PT-FI to evaluate its activities from the perspective of its intended performance goals and actual achievements. FCX and PT-FI have designed and implemented new operational procedures, management systems, performance evaluation, and accountability measures to improve their performance in these areas. These modifications are expected to yield significant enhancement in performance, not only in the areas covered by this audit, but also in PT-FI's business operations. FCX and PT-FI have and will continue to assess the matters ICCA identified in the audit requiring corrective actions, having already embarked upon remediation in a number of areas and striving for continual improvement in all aspects of these programs.

The audit report will be publicly distributed. The company, its workforce and the local community will derive important benefits from this process as the audit has provided a mechanism to highlight those areas in which improvement is necessary to enable PT-FI to achieve its goals and commitments in human rights, the employment and advancement of Papuans in all areas of our operation, and the social development of the local community.

FCX and PT-FI are establishing a team headed by Judge McDonald to ensure the continued implementation of PT-FI's Social, Employment, and Human Rights Policy, including addressing the recommendations made in the ICCA audit report.

Response to ICCA Audit

Human Rights

ICCA confirms that all potential human rights violations noted in its audit have been reported to the appropriate authorities and addressed in accordance with PT-FI's human rights policy. None of the reported human rights violations involved activities of PT-FI's security personnel, its other employees or the security personnel of the government of Indonesia involved in the protection of PT-FI's operations and property. The reported incidents fell within the realm of criminal acts and were dealt with accordingly. In the audit, PT-FI employees were also asked about their perceptions of possible human rights violations. While 80% of those involved in the random sample said they knew of nothing that could be construed to be a violation suffered either by them or anyone they knew, 20% said they knew of events that they considered might involve a possible violation, even though few of these instances of potential inappropriate conduct were reported. FCX and PT-FI will work through its SEHR education program to ensure that all 3 employees know how to identify and report human rights concerns and to create an atmosphere in which employees feel comfortable in submitting such reports.

Human Rights Training

The audit commends PT-FI's human rights training programs as being "carefully articulated and well suited to PT-FI's operating environment." However, even with this training program, ICCA reported that some employees did not adequately comprehend concepts of human rights and how they were applicable to PT-FI's operations. FCX/PT-FI will undertake to create new mechanisms to improve the effectiveness of its training programs. To this end, PT-FI has already begun revising the human rights training curriculum to focus on "effective learning," especially in the Security and Social and Local Development Departments. As part of this process, PT-FI has appointed a Senior Human Rights Compliance Officer, a distinguished Papuan, whose role is to ensure that our training and communications efforts are effective, appropriate, and ongoing.

Although not included in the audit report, FCX/PT-FI's Annual Human Rights Certification achieved 100% compliance, and all issues identified from the certification process were addressed and resolved.

Security Department Drivers for Police and Military

The Government of Indonesia mandates that government security institutions serve to protect the area of PT-FI operations, which has been designated as one of Indonesia's "National Vital Objects." PT-FI strives to separate activities undertaken by its employees and contractors from Government security personnel. However because of safety considerations -- driving conditions in the mining area are among the most challenging in the world -- PT-FI has provided competent drivers for military personnel using PT-FI roads. We acknowledge ICCA's findings that this practice may have led to confusion between the Company and government security. Consequently, PT-FI has made arrangements to discontinue this practice and to provide training to enable government security to drive safely in PT-FI's area of operations.

Papuan Employment

The audit noted that PT-FI has fulfilled or exceeded its commitments to increase the number of Papuan employees in the workforce. The audit also noted the challenges that PT-FI faces with continuing to provide employment opportunities for Papuans in the future. While PT-FI agrees with the audit assessment about these challenges, PT-FI has and will continue to take steps to meet them. After successfully quadrupling the total number of Papuan employees and more than doubling the number of Papuans among the management and technical staff, the management of PT-FI believes its next important milestone is the complete integration of Papuan employees into the workforce through employee development programs, including mentoring and training.

PT-FI will continue to identify qualified Papuans for positions required in the work force. PT-FI will also continue to develop and implement programs that will accomplish the following:

1. Establish employee development plans for all workers, including Papuan employees
2. Hold supervisors responsible for the evaluation of work performance of all their subordinates and the implementation of all employee development plans
3. Make regular reports on the development of all employees to the PT-FI Manpower Planning and Review Board.

Early in 2004, PT-FI established a Graduate Development Program to attract top graduates from the best Indonesian universities. Candidates are assessed using a variety of tools, and those selected to participate are placed in a special development program. The program, now in its second year, has been highly successful, with 75 participants in September 2005. PT-FI is specifically targeting talented Papuans for this program and is recruiting at least 10 new Papuan graduates this year. In 2003, PT-FI established the Nemangkawi Mining Institute, (NMI) which currently has more than 700 students, more than 90% of whom are Papuan. NMI focuses on technical training in various trades. We expect that those who successfully complete the program will obtain meaningful skilled employment with PT-FI or another enterprise and that at least 10% of NMI graduates will have the capacity to advance to supervisory and managerial levels.

Contract Labor Providers

The ICCA audit notes that a number of workers at PT-FI are employed through contract labor providers. The audit notes that such employment is permissible under Indonesian labor law so long as certain conditions are met. PT-FI acknowledges that a number of the contract employees have been engaged as contract workers for periods that may extend longer than specified by Indonesian labor law. However, certain aspects of this law are unclear, and other provisions of the law, which are applicable to certain workers provided by licensed manpower providers, permit such employees to be contracted for an indefinite period of time.

Since 2004, we have been systematically and objectively evaluating each worker to determine whether he or she meets our current standards for hiring them as employees. If a contract worker achieves these standards, the individual is hired as an employee by PT-FI. In cases where the contract workers do not meet hiring standards, the individual is offered enrollment in a development program to gain the skills required for direct employment. Individual skill development and performance are reviewed every six months. PT-FI has developed plans to reduce its use of contract labor and to recruit all hourly employees from students that graduate from the Nemangkawi Mining Institute. Although contract workers earn less than PT-FI employees, in most cases they lack the full competency to meet the work requirements of employees. PT-FI offers contract workers the opportunity to develop competencies and, as their competency increases, so does their pay rate. When a contract worker has reached full competency—assuming all other conditions are met—he or she can be hired by PT-FI.

The audit noted that PT-FI should "create a set of guidelines clearly specifying the conditions under which contract workers can be hired by PT-FI." PT-FI has established guidelines, which are set forth in the Policy on the Secondment of Managed Contractors' Indonesian Employees to PT-FI. This policy has been recently revised to incorporate new practices and changes in the labor law. We will further assess existing guidelines in response to the audit's recommendations.

Industrial Relations

The audit recommended changes to the Industrial Relations (IR) Department to enhance the employees' perceptions regarding its fairness and objectivity from the perspective of the workforce. PT-FI management will consider these recommendations. The report also recommended that the IR Department publish an annual report for senior management on the number of cases handled, their nature, timing, and resolution. Currently, the IR department publishes such a report and it is furnished monthly to the PT-FI Manpower Planning and Review Board.

Social and Local Development Department (SLD)

The audit report states that "from ICCA's perspective, SLD is a remarkable success story ..." and that "PT-FI clearly fulfilled its commitments to the local community through programs developed for and with the local community." The PT-FI personnel working in the SLD Department are genuinely involved and committed to helping Papuans. PT-FI is pleased that the audit recognized the benefits to the local community from its programs.

PT-FI recognizes its responsibility to foster the efficient and effective use of its donated funds by the local community. PT-FI has committed that the local community will have a significant role in the administration of the Freeport Partnership Fund. The formation of the LPMAK in 2002 was designed to address this objective.

PT-FI and LPMAK recognize that the LPMAK Education Program is a beneficial program, but acknowledge that certain areas need to be addressed and improved. LPMAK has decided to reduce the emphasis on scholarships and educational subsidies in favor of enhanced local education. Toward this end, LPMAK and PT-FI have been working with the local education authorities to improve the quality of basic education. LPMAK has developed and is implementing a five-year plan that includes specific initiatives to improve the structure and effectiveness of the Education Bureau, refocus educational resources, and bring the overall results achieved in line with expectations. In the future:

1. The number of scholarships will be reduced and refocused to provide support for performing students
2. University scholarships will be linked with employment opportunities within Papua
3. Scholarships will be provided in fields of study that match these links to employment opportunities
4. Teacher training programs will be implemented to focus on improving the quality of instruction at elementary and secondary levels
5. LPMAK will work with partner institutions to provide programs to improve the quality of basic education to create a stronger education foundation within the Mimika area
6. A quality dormitory program with high standards and accountability will be created and linked with selected quality schools. Performance standards for students living in dormitories will be enhanced. The situation with the dormitory identified in the audit has been addressed.
7. The Education Bureau will be restructured to make it a more effective body for implementing and monitoring programs.

PT-FI and LPMAK have already begun to address the problems identified in the LPMAK education program. PT-FI believes that working with LPMAK to improve programs, rather than having PT_FI take over direct administration of them as suggested in the audit report, will produce a more sustainable result for the future. We also acknowledge that emphasis should be placed on "results achieved," not "activities," and we are working to develop measurable objectives in all SLD areas.

Employee Perceptions

ICCA reported a number of findings that suggest negative employee perceptions of PT-FI, in particular its Industrial Relations Department (IRD). PT-FI will develop a communication program in which employees and management can engage in an ongoing dialogue about issues and perceptions. Overall, the audit found that PT-FI employees generally hold a positive opinion the company as a good employer and that most respondents feel that PT-FI contributes to the welfare of the Papuan people.

Audit Follow Up

PT-FI would like to invite ICCA to return to its Indonesian operations early in 2006 to review and assess the actions that PT-FI has taken in response to issues in its audit report.

ICCA Recommendations to PT-FI Management

ICCA has made recommendations to PT-FI for ways in which to improve performance in certain areas adjunct to, but not directly part of, the audit. PT-FI appreciates these recommendations and will take these into consideration as we move forward with our programs.

Notes

1. Freeport actively defended itself from numerous accusations of human rights violations and environmental degradation. The accusations against Freeport became more numerous after Freeport discovered the Grasberg deposit in 1989 and began rapidly developing its mining operations. In November 1994, suspected members of the *Organisasi Papua Merdeka* attacked Freeport employees along the Freeport road, killing one and wounding several others. This led to increased military presence at the mine and heightened attention to Freeport and its mining activities by critics of mining operations and the local communities. In December 1994, there were many protests in the area of Freeport's operations that were linked not only to Freeport and its mine, but also to independence for Papua. On Christmas morning, the Papuan independence flag was raised in Tembagapura, the Freeport administrative center. That event led to several days of violence, during which at least six Papuans died. Although the army was accused of the killings, the military used Freeport's vehicles and other facilities. Accusations of complicity by Freeport in the detentions, disappearances, and deaths of Papuans led to a firestorm of accusations against and denials by Freeport. Serious unrest continued in and around Freeport's mining area through 1996. This included kidnappings of biologists who were surveying flora in early 1996, and later that year, rioting in Tembagapura and Timika. The Internet became a venue for the global debate about Freeport and its operations in West Papua (Irian Jaya), Indonesia. The first Internet-published report of troubles at Freeport was written by the Roman Catholic Bishop of Jayapura. This report was edited by the Australian Council for Overseas Aid (ACFOA) and published online in April 2005 (*Trouble at Freeport*, http://utwatch.org/corporations/freeportfiles/acfoa). Freeport immediately attacked the report by taking out full-page ads in the *New York Times, the Washington Post*, and *the Wall Street Journal*. Freeport also posted letters and articles in mining-oriented periodicals and Southeast Asian publications, including the *South East Asian Mining Letter* (13.04.95 and 30.11.95). Eventually, Freeport began to publish an additional part of its annual report concerning social, human rights, and environmental issues. *Working Toward Sustainability* became Freeport's most important tool in sharing its side of these pressing issues. In November 1999, Freeport released a press statement that the company had hired Judge Gabrielle Kirk McDonald as human rights adviser. The press release noted support for the appointment by the U.S. ambassador to Indonesia, Robert Gelbard.

2. These comments are based on the personal observations by two of the book's authors. Sethi worked and interacted with Freeport's managers both in the company's headquarters in New Orleans and PTFI's offices in Jakarta and the mine site in Papua. He also had formal meetings with Moffett. Lowry worked for Freeport for fourteen years and was the primary force within the company toward creating and implementing its code of conduct. Lowry is an ordained Episcopal priest and was the dean of the Episcopal Church in New Orleans. He resigned his position with Freeport in 2004 and has since resumed his duties with the Episcopal Church in New York; Institute for Human Rights Study and Advocacy, Summary Report, "What's Wrong with Freeport's Security Policy?" October 21, 2002, http://wpaction.buz.org/Elsham-Freeport-Report-Oct-2002.htm (accessed July 13, 2010).

3. Forbes Wilson, *The Conquest of Copper Mountain* (New York: Atheneum, 1981); George Mealey, *rasberg* (New Orleans: Freeport-McMoRan Copper & Gold, 1996). In addition to the size of the operation, the Grasberg mine is an unbelievably complex engineering venture. The Grasberg deposit is located 13,000 feet above sea level in an area that receives approximately 300 inches of rain per year. Building the mine was a remarkable achievement; keeping it running is nearly as daunting.

4. Lex Rieffel, "Indonesia's Quiet Revolution," *Foreign Affairs* 83, no. 5 (2004): 98–110.

5. Aidan Rankin, "Mind Who You Call Primitive: The West Papuans Holding a Group of Europeans Are Fighting Against Extermination," *Independent* (London), January 17, 2006.

6. Ibid.

7. Ibid; Robert Bryce, "Struck by a Golden Spear." *Guardian* (London), January 17, 1996.

8. Stewart Yerton, "And Then the Solders Came: Mine Distances Itself from Army, Abuse," (Series: "A Rock and a Hard Place: Trouble in the Jungle for Freeport's Mountain Mine), *Times-Picayune*, January 28, 1996, Section A21.

9. Dan Murphy, "Violence, a U.S. Mining Giant, and Papua Politics," *Christian Science Monitor* 94, no 196, (2002): 1.

10. Ali Kotarumalos, "Timika and Freeport Calm, but Tension Still High After Riotings." Associated Press, March 16, 1996.

11. S. Prakash Sethi, David B. Lowry. *"Coping with Cultural Conflicts in International Operation," Europe-Asia Dialogue on Business Spirituality*, 67–88. Antwerpen-Apeldoom: Garant, 2008.

12. Anonymous, "Millions Paid for Mine," *Herald Sun*, March 14, 2003, http://www.lexisnexis.com/us/ (accessed July 13, 2010).

13. Matt Richards, "Freeport in Indonesia: Reconciling Development and Indigenous Rights," Report on a Public Forum at the Gorman House Arts Centre. Edited by Pat Walsh and Sharmini Sherrard. Canberra: Australian Council for Overseas Aid, 1996.

14. The land issue is very complex. On the one hand, there is a great interest among many to keep traditional land for the common use of the tribal communities. On the other hand, many economists argue that such land use without full individual ownership is a barrier to economic and social development. See de Soto (2000) for the view that capitalist development in traditional societies is thwarted by common land ownership without the ability to "unlock" the inherent value of the land through sale or lease.

15. Freeport's mine is located high in the mountains (above 13,000 feet) in southern New Guinea. No people live at the altitude of the mine, and few people wonder through the area of the mine. Using Western cultural understandings, one would believe that there would be little if any objection to Freeport's mining activities, because its direct impact on the local communities would be minimal. However, in the minds of the Amungme, the fact that they could not see the mine and its activities was unimportant because, from their perspective, their sacred mountain was being violated by mining activities.

16. The issue of governance among Papuan groups is most complex. The sparse population of the island of New Guinea and the difficult terrain has lead to linguistic, social, and cultural differences. For millennia, Papuans who have been separated only by a single river valley have had little or no commerce with each other. It has been only since the end of the Second World War that outsiders have had access to Papuans and vice versa. Equally, the intersection of Papuans with other Papuans was rare prior to the mid-twentieth century. The unit of governance in Papua has been called "pre-tribal." Small family units, connected by geography and language, have informally governed through coastal and interior (highland) Papua. For a generalist's view of Papua and Papuan governance, see Jared Diamond, *Guns, Germs, and Steel: The Fates of Human Societies*, (New York: W.W. Norton, 2005). The division of Papuans into very small units of informal governance has been problematic for Papuans when dealing with larger units of governance (such as the government of the Republic of Indonesia and large multinational companies (such as Freeport-McMoRan). It has also caused difficulties for the larger and more formal entities as they try to make there way through the maze of families and informal ethno-linguistic groups when decisions need to be made and problems on a larger scale solved. See Bruce Knauft, *From Primitive to Postcolonial in Melanesia and Anthropology* (Ann Arbor: University of Michigan Press, 1999). For a specific view of governance and communities in coastal Papua, see Knauft, *South Coast New Guinea Cultures: History, Dialectic, Culture* (Cambridge: Cambridge University Press, 1993).

17. BBC Monitoring Asia Pacific, "Indonesia: Protesters End Blockade of U.S. Mine," *Jakarta Post*, February 26, 2006 (accessed July 13, 2010). (Excerpt from article by Tb. Arie Rukmantara, "Stone Fire Ends Freeport Standoff," published online in English by Indonesian newspaper the *Jakarta Post*).

18. For the anti-Freeport perspective, see "Scraping the Bottom: Freeport-McMoRan in Irian Jaya," http://www.isforum.org/tobi/reports/minding/freeportmcmoran; "Endgame File of Freeport-McMoRan," (Freeport in Indonesia), http:www.endgame. org/freepprt.html; "Indonesian Misadventure: A U.S. Mining Giant's Clash," http:/ www.asiapacific.fj/PJR/issues/next/962indon.html; "The Mining Menace of Freeport-McMoRan," http:/www.etan/.news/Kissinger/themine.html.

19. Benedict Y. Imbun, "Cannot Manage Without the 'Significant Other,' " *Journal of Business Ethics* 73, no. 2 (2007): 177–192.

20. The entire text of this section has been extracted from ICCA's audit report, "Human Rights, Employment, and Social Development of Papuan People in Indonesia on the Part of Freeport-McMoRan Copper and Gold, Inc., New Orleans, LA, and PT Freeport Indonesia," Jakarta and Papua, July 7, 2005. The complete audit report is available at www.sicca-ca.org.

21. The Phase I audit focused on various elements of PTFI's compliance with its Guiding Principles of Operations in Indonesia, and its Social, Employment, and Human Rights Policy were audited. Among the sampled 353 workers in Phase I, 44 percent identified themselves as Papuans and the remaining as non-Papuans. One-third of those who identified themselves as Papuans indicated belonging to one of the seven sukus (tribes). The sample of interviewed workers reflected the proportionality of Papuans, seven-suku Papuans, and contract workers on the Freeport payroll. The average length of employment for the entire sample was 4.8 years, while the average length of employment among contractor-supplied workers was 2.4 years.

22. PT Freeport Indonesia and Freeport-McMoRan Copper and Gold, Inc., "Response to the Audit of Indonesia Operations by the International Center for Corporate Accountability, Inc., October 4, 2005," http://icca-corporateaccountability.org/PDFs/PTFIResponse05.pdf.

23. All information provided in this section has been extracted from "Audit Report: Human Rights, Employment, and Social Development of Papuan People in Indonesia on the Part of Freeport-McMoRan Copper and Gold, Inc., New Orleans, LA, and PT Freeport Indonesia, Jakarta and Papua, July 7, 2005." The complete audit report is available at www.sicca-ca.org.

24. For the purpose of the medical care audit, two outside additions were made to the ICCA audit team. The first was Dr. Emon Winardi Danudirgo, an Indonesian physician who is chief of internal medicine at a large at a Jakarta hospital and who had formerly worked with the ministry of health in Irian Jaya. Dr. Danudirgo provided context for the auditors with regard to Indonesian medical standards and the delivery of medical care in Papua. The second addition to the medical auditing team was Dr. David Lowry, formerly an executive at Freeport in Indonesia and Papua, who advised on access to Papuan villages and people and had an understanding of Papuan communities and their needs

25. The entire text of this section has been extracted from "PT Freeport Indonesia and Freeport-McMoRan Copper & Gold Inc.: Response to the Phase I Follow-Up Audit of Indonesian Operations and Phase II Audit of Medical Facilities and Contract Companies by ICCA, November 30, 2007." The complete audit report is available at www.sicca-ca. org.

26. The entire text of this section has been extracted from "PT Freeport Indonesia and Freeport-McMoRan Copper & Gold Inc.: Response to the Phase I Follow-Up Audit of Indonesian Operations and Phase II Audit of Medical Facilities and Contract Companies by ICCA, November 30, 2007." The complete audit report is available at www.sicca-ca. org.

27. Geoff Thompson, "Military, Police 'Among Suspects' in Freeport Killings," *Australian Broadcast Corporation*, July 13, 2009, http://www.abc.net.au/news/

stories/2009/07/13/2623717.htm?section=world; Jonathan Pearlman, "Death in Papua: Political Intrigue Clouds Miner's Murder," *Sydney Morning Herald*, November 21, 2009.

28. Kristina Kazmi, "Gunmen Attack Bus at Mine in Indonesian Province of Papua," *IHS Global Insight Daily Analysis*, August 17, 2009, http://global.factiva.com; Niniek Karmini, "Indonesia to Deploy Special Police Force After Wave of Shootings at Freeport Mine in Papua," *Canadian Press*, July 16, 2009.

29. Jonathan Pearlman, "Death in Papua: Political Intrigue Clouds Miner's Murder," *Sydney Morning Herald*, November 21, 2009.

30. Ninek Karmini, "Indonesia to Deploy Special Police Force After Wave of Shootings at Freeport Mine in Papua," *Canadian Press*, July 16, 2009.

31. Anonymous, " 'Foreign Countries' Could Be Behind Indonesia Mine Attacks: Minister," *Agence France Presse*, July 16, 2009; Tom Allard, "Nine Slain in 'Inside Job' Attacks on Jakarta Hotels," July 18, 2009.

32. Anonymous, "Missing Bullets Mystery," *Herald Sun*, July 14, 2009.

33. Staff reporter, "Papuans Demand Closure of U.S. Mine in Indonesia," *Daily the Pak Banker*, December 22, 2009.

34. Anonymous, "Six Hurt in Latest Attack on Papua Mine," *Hobart Mercury* (Australia), January 25, 2010.

35. Anonymous, "Indonesia Sees Need for More Troops in Papua," *Agence France Presse*, March 23, 2010.

36. International Crisis Group, "Radicalization and Dialogue in Papua," *Asia Report* No. 188–11, March 2010, pp. 18–24.

III

Industry-Wide Voluntary Code of Conduct with Industry-Controlled Governance Structure

The Defense Industry Initiative: From Business Conduct Program Innovator to Industry Standard?

By Andrea Bonime-Blanc[1]

"The defense industry companies who sign this document have, or commit to adopt and implement, a set of principles of business ethics and conduct that acknowledge and address their corporate responsibilities under federal procurement laws and to the public. Further they accept the responsibility to create an environment in which compliance with federal procurement laws and free, open and timely reporting of violations become the felt responsibility of every employee in the defense industry."[2]

Thus opens the document entitled "Defense Industry Initiatives on Business Ethics and Conduct," dated June 9, 1986; it is the beginning of what has come to be widely known as the Defense Industry Initiative (DII). A narrow and not completely incorrect reading of this paragraph might lead one to conclude that the sole purpose of the initiative was to address procurement fraud and provide parameters around mitigating and eliminating such fraud. A broader interpretation that reflects the actual eventual evolution of the DII, however, would suggest that even if the original intent of the drafters of this initiative may have been to address only defense industry procurement issues, the DII in many ways represented the beginnings of a revolution in how corporations, especially in the United States but increasingly elsewhere, create and implement internal business conduct and ethics programs.

The largely U.S.-centric DII[3] was perhaps the first of its kind—a more or less voluntary industry-wide code of conduct or set of business principles adopted by an entire industrial sector (or at least by those who voluntarily signed it at the time and over time) and focused on one compliance objective: not getting into trouble with the U.S. government (and, more specifically, the U.S. Department of Defense) for procurement fraud. Did the defense industry adopt this voluntary code of conduct for altruistic reasons, business reasons, or legal reasons? Probably all of the above, with an emphasis on avoiding the legal consequences of noncompliance.

A key differentiator of the DII was that it was not created to deal with the quality, provenance, or other characteristics of the products or services provided by the industry, as was the case with some other industry-wide codes of conduct, such as the Kimberly Process regarding diamonds. The DII emerged as a result of government, media, and public pressure about procurement fraud or the widespread perception thereof. While the DII was not directly about the actual products and services provided by the defense industry (which ranged from fighter jets and intercontinental ballistic missiles to auditing services by accounting firms and health-care services from health-care providers), it was about the sometimes exorbitant pricing of such products and services (reflecting potential or actual fraud, waste, and abuse). What brought the defense industry together to create the DII was the fear of financial, legal, and reputational consequences from procurement fraud—such as debarment from further contracts with the U.S. Department of Defense (DOD), the imposition of severe fines, or even the incarceration of guilty individuals. In particular, it was the work of a government commission appointed by President Ronald Reagan, which came to be known as the Packard Commission, that became the catalyst for the birth of the DII.[4]

As one reviews and analyzes the DII, it is important to keep in mind that it was a voluntarily created organization borne from public circumstances and focused almost exclusively on eliminating or mitigating procurement fraud. Over time, however, the DII became both a harbinger and major contributor to the larger debate about and the development of a paradigm for how companies can create and develop an internal business conduct program.[5] As will be seen later in this chapter, the DII was the principal precursor to the single most important legislative development in the United States regarding the encouragement of effective compliance and ethics programs: the U.S. Sentencing Guidelines. The U.S. Sentencing Guidelines, first enacted in 1991 and amended twice since then (in 2004 and 2010), have, in turn, had a major effect on the global debate about internal organizational code of conduct programs (U.S. Sentencing Guidelines).[6]

It should be noted that the DII started as and remains a voluntary code and program that only applies to DOD contractors that have agreed to join the program and abide by its parameters, and does not apply to any other companies. Clearly, defense industry contractors—like some that have achieved headline notoriety for scandal and legal troubles over the years, as will be examined later in this chapter—have not or did not at the time of their scandals subscribe to the tenets of the DII. An important issue that this chapter raises, but is not able to answer completely, is whether belonging to the DII has had a positive direct or indirect effect on the defense contractor companies that are members. In other words, have the standards required by the DII of the companies that voluntarily subscribe to its tenets had the effect of improving the behaviors that such defense contractor members would have engaged in but for their DII membership? While difficult or perhaps even impossible to answer, this is a question that is important to keep in mind as one attempts to understand the contour, content, and impact of the DII on the defense contractor industry overall since its inception.

This chapter provides an overview of the DII—its origins, antecedents, and development; that is, the historical and political context into which it was borne and through which it has developed. The chapter also details and analyzes the main components of the DII, and reviews how its various parts may relate to the track record of the defense industry. The chapter closes with a discussion of challenges and possible future trends regarding this initiative, plus some suggestions on how the DII fits into the reality of global business today.

I. Overview: Historical and Political Context

Whether one is critical, neutral, or admiring of the defense industry, the historical record provides support for the notion that the defense industry was indeed the trendsetter among industrial sectors in creating a set of standards for business behaviors around ethical and business conduct. The defense industry was one of the first, if not the first, industries to create a paradigm for the conduct of business ethics within a business sector. Although the record shows that the defense industry did not take these steps solely voluntarily, there was certainly a to and fro between the industry and the U.S. government, with each side nudging the other. Eventually, this tension yielded something quite valuable and, at the time, unique: a voluntary code of internal governance and business conduct applicable to an entire industry. Whether such a voluntary program was or continues to be effective at achieving its strategic objective is something that this chapter will attempt to address and provide context for.

Before examining what happened in the mid-1980s that led to the creation of the DII, certain developments from the 1970s and early 1980s need to be understood as they provided the seeds for the later emergence of the DII. These seeds were sown in the form of a series of corruption and bribery scandals in the 1970s (defense contractor Lockheed had the most notable cases) and the procurement scandals of the 1980s (of which the infamous $600 toilet seat scandal provided the most notorious fodder) that had direct consequences on the emergence of the DII.

A. The Foreign Corrupt Practices Act of 1977

In the early 1970s, a series of foreign official corruption and bribery cases involving U.S. companies making such alleged payments captured the attention of the media and eventually the U.S. Congress. One of the more notorious cases involved defense contractor Lockheed and its sale of fighter jets and other military equipment to numerous foreign governments. The emerging bribery allegations covered a vast swath of geography, from Europe (Germany, Italy, and the Netherlands) to the Middle East (Saudi Arabia) and Asia (Japan), and involved accusations of extensive bribery of foreign government officials in each country in exchange for the placement of orders for fighter jets and other military equipment. However, Lockheed was not alone; the foreign bribery scandals exemplified by the Lockheed allegations ultimately involved admissions by more than 400 U.S.-based companies to the U.S. government that they had paid approximately $300 million in bribes over a period of several years for similar purposes.[7]

These bribery scandals, coupled with the heightened sensitivities occasioned by the other unprecedented scandal suffusing the United States in the early 1970s (Watergate and President Richard Nixon's resignation from the presidency), led Congress and the Senate to hold hearings in the mid-1970s. These hearings delved into the various allegations of foreign corrupt practices by defense contractors and eventually yielded a groundbreaking new law: the Foreign Corrupt Practices Act of 1977 (FCPA).[8]

In essence, the FCPA forbade bribery by U.S.-based businesses of foreign officials to obtain or retain business in other countries. The extraterritorial implications of this law were unprecedented and unparalleled at the time. No other country imposed serious criminal liability on companies or individuals for bribing foreign officials outside of their national jurisdiction. In fact, until the early 2000s, no other country, including the leading industrial nation members of the Organization for Economic Cooperation and Development (OECD), had anything like this law. To add insult to injury, government policies in some of these advanced industrial countries, most notably France (until 1997) and Germany (until 1999), not only allowed corporations to bribe foreign officials to obtain or retain business, but also permitted them to claim corporate tax deductions for their bribery-related expenses.[9]

Because it was a rare and unique law that seemed to single out U.S. companies for punishment, the FCPA was widely unpopular both inside and outside of the United States. It was unpopular within the country because U.S. companies complained that it put them at a serious competitive disadvantage vis-à-vis their German and French competitors, for example. But it was also unpopular outside of the United States because it was viewed as a heavy-handed attempt by the United States to impose its laws on other national jurisdictions, and mettlesome and preachy in its attempt to dictate legal morality, as it were, to other cultures with different business practices.

President Carter signed the FCPA into law in December 1977. Beyond the fact that it was generally unpopular, the new law had two major long-term effects on the world of compliance and the eventual emergence of DII over the following two decades. First of all, the FCPA had a strong, albeit indirect, effect on the eventual emergence of the DII in that it created a stark precedent for the U.S. government to hone in on the defense industry for issues of non-compliance. However, as will be seen later in this chapter, the DII effort arose more directly from another set of scandals that were uncovered in the early 1980s involving instances of procurement fraud. Because both the bribery scandals of the 1970s and the procurement scandals of the early 1980s were perpetrated primarily by defense contractors, both sets of scandals and their legal, regulatory, and reputational consequences acted as strong incentives to the defense industry to create a more systematic approach to internal compliance and ethical business conduct.

The FCPA had another, perhaps even more dramatic, long-term effect on the field of compliance and business conduct and thus indirectly on the emergence of DII. Over a lengthy period of time, stretching for several decades, the FCPA became the instigator and precursor of a much broader set of similar laws, culminating with the passage in 1997 of the OECD's Convention on Anti-Bribery and Anti-Corruption, which by 2010 had been adopted in almost forty countries.[10] This major historical development, together with other important developments in the field of compliance and governance, have contributed in the past few years to the increasing recognition of the value of internal compliance and ethics programs by companies both within and outside of the United States, including, significantly, non-U.S.-based defense contractors such as BAE and EADS, two leading European-based defense contractors with major U.S. subsidiaries that not only are members of DII, but also have global compliance and ethics programs headquartered outside of the United States.[11]

B. The Defense Industry Procurement Scandals of the Early 1980s

The defense industry found itself squarely in the line of sight of the U.S. government during the 1970s bribery scandals that led to the creation of the FCPA in 1977. Only a few years later, the defense industry found itself again the object of media attention and eventually government investigation, this time regarding procurement fraud. Thus, the more immediate cause of the eventual emergence of the DII took place in the early 1980s, when Ronald Reagan was president, and during a period when the U.S. national defense budget was growing dramatically in the context of the increasingly competitive Cold War between the United States and the Soviet Union, when such budgets accelerated and achieved new heights.

It was in this environment of exponentially increasing defense budgets that another major domestic scandal began to brew involving $400 hammers and $600 toilet seats, which, if media and watchdog reports were to be trusted, seemed to signal widespread abuse and waste by defense contractors and the widespread defrauding of the U.S. government and thus U.S. taxpayers.

It was in this context that the Project on Government Oversight, an investigative nonprofit organization created in 1981 under the name Project on Military Procurement, conducted investigative journalistic work that exposed the $640 toilet seats and $436 hammers.[12] These revelations, subsequent media inquiries, and further investigations of what appeared to be widespread fraud became notorious fodder that fed into President Reagan's somewhat reluctant creation a few years later of a blue-ribbon commission to be known as the Packard Commission. This commission was entrusted to look into how widespread the alleged fraud and abuse was and suggest more systemic solutions to what appeared to be blatantly illegal activity on both sides of the equation— the private sector that got away with charging astronomical prices for simple products, and the governmental agencies and officials that appeared to tolerate such practices at best or engage in blatant conflicts of interest or even fraud themselves at worst.[13]

C. The Establishment of the Packard Commission in 1985

On July 15, 1985, under increasing pressure to investigate whether defense contractors and the DOD were indeed mismanaging the defense procurement process or, worse, engaging in fraud and abuse, President Reagan issued Executive Order 12526 and established the President's Blue Ribbon Commission on Defense Management, which became known as the Packard Commission (the "Packard Commission"), named after multimillionaire computer magnate David Packard, cofounder of Hewlett Packard, who became head of the commission. The Packard Commission was entrusted with examining the extent, depth, breadth, and shape of what appeared to be widespread defense industry fraud and/or mismanagement, and was charged with coming up with recommendations to minimize or eliminate such practices and create systemic solutions to any widespread bad practices on both sides of the equation, within the DOD and the private-sector defense industry.[14]

In 1985, at the time the Packard Commission studied the defense industry and its relationship to the U.S. government, the DOD had 60,000 prime contractors as well as hundreds of thousands of other suppliers and subcontractors.[15] In that same year, the DOD entered into contracts valued at $164 billion, the vast majority of which were with the top one hundred contractors. As stated in the Packard Commission's final report dated June 1986 (the "Packard Commission Final Report"), "twenty-five contractors did business of $1 billion or more, 147 did $100 million or more, and almost 6,000 did $1 million or more."[16]

The members of the Packard Commission consisted of former, existing, or future military and governmental luminaries and experts associated with the military-industrial complex at the time. Among them were Robert H. Barrow, then recently retired 27th Commandant of the United States Marine Corps; Nicholas Brady, the future secretary of the treasury under President Reagan and the first President Bush; Frank Carlucci, the future secretary of defense under President Reagan; Brent Scowcroft, the past and future national security adviser under Presidents Ford and Bush, Sr.; R. James Woolsey, Jr., President Clinton's director of central intelligence; and William J. Perry, the future secretary of defense under President Clinton. Other members of the Packard Commission included Ernest C. Arbuckle, Louis W. Cabot, William P. Clark, Jr., Barber Conable, Paul Gorman, Carla Anderson Hills, James Holloway III, Charles J. Pilliod, Jr., and Herbert Stein.[17]

For its work, which lasted a little over one year, the Packard Commission itself commissioned several expert services firms or nonprofits to assist in gathering survey data and expert analysis. Among the experts hired and the data contributed were Market Opinion Research, which conducted the survey of public opinion entitled "U.S. National Survey: Public Attitudes on Defense Management"; the Ethics Resource Centre (ERC), which provided a study encapsulated in a final report entitled "Final Report and Recommendations on Voluntary Corporate Policies, Practices, and Procedures Relating to Ethical Business Conduct"; and Arthur Andersen & Co., which wrote the "Study of Government Audit and Other Oversight Activities Relating to Defense Contractors." These studies provided critical contributions to the two reports that the Packard Commission would issue in early and mid-1986, the interim report and the Packard Commission final report, examined below.

The Packard Commission in the end issued an interim report (the "Packard Commission Interim Report") on February 28, 1986, and the Packard Commission Final Report in June 1986. In the Packard Commission Interim Report, the commission issued six broad recommendations regarding the defense industry procurement process, touching all aspects of the procurement process on both sides of the equation: on the DOD side with recommendations to improve internal procedures and controls for the acquisition process, and on the defense industry/contractor side with recommendations focused on improvements in companies' internal governance and procurement processes.

III. The Packard Commission and the Rise of DII: Rationale, Worldview, Substance

A. The Packard Commission: Rationale and Worldview

The Packard Commission Final Report consisted of four chapters, one of which—chapter four, "Government-Industry Accountability"—delved directly into the issue that occupies the attention of this chapter, private industry codes of conduct and accountability. The chapter thus begins with the following admonition:

> *Our study of defense management compels us to conclude that nothing merits greater concern than the increasingly troubled relationship between the defense industry and the government.*[18]

The Packard Commission further noted: "The depth of public mistrust of defense contracting is deeply disquieting," but not necessarily because there was so much fraud, according to the Packard Commission Final Report, but because of the public perception that there was widespread fraud. To wit: "[T]he current popular impression of runaway fraud and waste undermines crucial support for implementing precisely those management reforms that would increase efficiency."[19] To that point, the Packard Commission Final Report cited the market opinion research survey commissioned by the Packard Commission in January 1986, which was designed to provide feedback on a variety of defense industry issues from the American public's standpoint.[20]

The Packard Commission Final Report outlined several key, disturbing trends that they were aiming to eliminate through their work:

1. *Eliminate public misperceptions.* Eliminating what they considered to be a vast misperception by the American public of the extent and depth of corruption in the defense industry contracting process. As stated in the Packard Commission Final Report: "The nation's defense programs lose far more to inefficiency than to dishonesty."[21] One could question whether this indeed was (and remains) the case as widespread inefficiency could arguably be equated with negligence, at best, if not with outright intentional misconduct or fraud, at worst.

2. *Ensure public support for defense initiatives.* The Packard Commission Final Report was concerned about public lack of support for defense programs that were critical to the nation. One mustn't forget that during the mid 1980s, the Cold War, with the development of exotic military technologies such as "Star Wars" antiballistic missile systems and other costly technological breakthroughs, had achieved new heights.

3. *Support for DOD management reforms.* The Packard Commission Final Report was also concerned that public skepticism and misperceptions, as they characterized them, would undermine the ability for DOD and the executive and legislative branches generally to undertake necessary management reforms within the DOD.
4. *Avoid harm to the U.S. industrial base.* The Packard Commission worried that misplaced and, in their opinion, overblown public concerns about widespread abuse and fraud would also harm the U.S. industrial base.
5. *Heighten defense industry accountability.* Finally, the Packard Commission also placed the majority of responsibility for the fraud and abuse that did exist on the shoulders of private industry. As the Packard Commission put it:

> [M]anagement and employees of companies that contract with the Defense Department assume unique and compelling obligations to the people of our Armed Forces, the American taxpayer, and out nation. They must apply (and be perceived as applying) the highest standards of business ethics and conduct.[22]

The Packard Commission also made it clear that it did not believe that the way to solve the fraud and waste problems was to create thick layers of auditors, monitors, and criminal sanctions. Indeed, it stated:

> Though government oversight is critically important to the acquisition process, no conceivable number of additional federal auditors, inspectors, investigators, and prosecutors can police fully, much less make it work more effectively. Nor have criminal sanctions historically proved to be a reliable tool for ensuring contractor compliance.[23]

In fact, the Packard Commission Final Report emphasized that criminal prosecutions were limited for a variety of reasons, including limited government resources yielding the reality that the Department of Justice "declines to prosecute approximately six in ten possible fraud cases referred to it by federal agencies."[24] The striking untold possibility laid bare by this statistic is that because of limited resources, the U.S. government at that time was only able to investigate 60 percent of the possible fraud that other agencies referred to it, not counting the other 40 percent of cases and any other possible instances of fraud and abuse that those agencies were unable to discover or pursue because of their limited resources.

While one of the themes clearly in evidence at the time of the Packard Commission Interim and Final Reports was that inefficiency (not only abuse) was a key concern, the other dominant theme was that there was a clear need to establish quality controls and better management on both sides of the procurement equation: the DOD and the private sector. Thus, the DII was borne as much from the need to impose quality and management improvement controls on the procurement process and a desire to create ethical business practices within the defense industry as it was from the perception that there were intolerable instances of fraud, waste, and abuse.

B. The Substance of the Packard Commission Work:
The Interim and Final Reports

The Packard Commission Interim Report made several recommendations—fleshed out more fully in the Packard Commission Final Report—designed to improve what it considered to be an increasingly deteriorating relationship between the DOD and the defense industry. Most of these recommendations focused on establishing procedures and practices around the procurement process both within the DOD bureaucracy as well as through the procurement process with the private defense industries.

However, regarding the role of the defense industry itself and the emergence of the DII, there were key final recommendations issued by the Packard Commission in its Final Report relating to business ethics and compliance. These recommendations were laid out in chapter four of the Packard Commission Final Report, entitled "Government-Industry Accountability."

Chapter four begins with the statement: "In our view, major improvements in contractor self-governance are essential."[25] The chapter then lists the following five key components of defense contractor self-governance or what could be called an effective ethics and compliance program:

1. *Creating well-defined codes of conduct.* In support of this objective, the Packard Commission commissioned the ERC, a leading think tank in the business conduct and ethics space, to analyze the issue of codes of conduct and the effective implementation of policies and procedures, and to recommend a course of action for the defense industry. In its report entitled "Final Report and Recommendations on Voluntary Corporate Policies, Practices, and Procedures Relating to Ethical Business Conduct," issued in February 1986,[26] the ERC recommended that companies develop codes of conduct that focus on the company's key and unique areas of need and risk. For example, within the defense industry the issue of conflicts of interest between private industry and the DOD in the procurement process is a very notable risk, where the appearance or reality of a conflict of interest can quickly emerge if DOD officials look for, or private sector companies offer, the promise of future employment to such officials.[27]

2. *Developing a system that tracks and vets conflicts of interest.* As the Packard Commission Final Report put it: "to ensure utmost propriety in their relations with government personnel, contractor standards of ethical business conduct should seek to foster compliance by employees of DOD with ethical requirements incident to federal service."[28]

3. *Developing an instructional and communications system.* A well-developed and targeted instructional system for employees must be in place that helps to implement and realize the policies contained in the code of conduct and make the code available to all employees.

4. *A system to monitor compliance and internal controls.* The Packard Commission Final Report zeroed in on another key element of a solid compliance and ethics program: monitoring and follow-up to ensure that the program is being implemented and is effective. A critical component of such an effective ethics and compliance program includes the establishment of a system of internal controls.

5. *Role of an independent audit committee.* A significant part of chapter four of the Packard Commission Final Report focused on the issue of contractor internal auditing. For this component of their recommendations, the Packard Commission hired the auditing and accounting firm Peat Marwick to examine the issue of the role of the audit committee of the board of private contractors and recommend best practices. It did so in its report to the Packard Commission entitled "Report on Survey of Defense Contractors' Internal Audit Processes," issued in February 1986.[29]

It is interesting to note that the Packard Commission Interim and Final Reports focused almost exclusively on the twin ideas that (a) public perception or misperception of fraud or alleged fraud would undermine the military readiness and capabilities of the United States, and (b) such negative public attitudes would also hurt the industrial growth and dominance of the private defense sector. Although much of the work emerging from the Packard Commission reports had other unintended—and salutary—consequences on the overall development of ethics and compliance programs within the private sector, it should not have been surprising to the observer that this would be the primary and almost sole focus of the Packard Commission given both the makeup of the commission (past, present, and future captains of industry and leaders of the defense establishment) and its mandate (cleaning up the military procurement process).

Despite the arguably somewhat limited perspective of the Packard Commission, that is, representing the viewpoint of the military-industrial complex, it is essential to underscore how truly revolutionary and groundbreaking the work of the Packard Commission was as it zeroed in on the fact that defense industry companies needed to do a better and more systematic job of developing internal governance, controls, and compliance. It is this aspect of the Packard Commission and its reports that became a clear and direct precedent for and influence on the emergence of the DII and the eventual rise, discussed later in this chapter, of a broader and more systemic approach to the creation and implementation of corporate compliance programs generally across industries.

C. The Interplay between the Packard Commission and the DII

At the same time that the Packard Commission was undertaking its work commissioning surveys and studies from the likes of the ERC, Peat Marwick, Arthur Andersen, and Market Opinion Research, behind the scenes leaders of several major defense contractors started to develop their own plans to deal with the growing tensions with the U.S. government, heightened attention from investigative reporters and organizations, and the apparent growing public distrust of the industry.

In parallel with the work of the Packard Commission and coinciding with the issuance of the Packard Commission Interim Report in February 1986, the seeds of the DII began to emerge. Jack Welch, then chief executive officer and chairman of the board of General Electric, one of the largest U.S. government defense contractors and no stranger to defense industry scandals in the 1970s and early 1980s, gathered an elite group of eighteen defense-industry chief executive officers to discuss the formation of an industry-wide voluntary compliance program in response to the increasing pressures from the government, most notably the work of the Packard Commission.

By July of that year, one month after the issuance of the Packard Commission Final Report, DII had thirty-one members that subscribed to its original principles (see table 4.1). Indeed, because of the interaction between the Packard Commission Interim Report and the emerging work of the original DII group of eighteen defense contractors, the original DII principles actually appeared as an appendix to the Packard Commission Final Report.[30]

D. The DII in 1986: The Original Principles and Governance

A. The Original Principles

The birth of the DII, the original principles of which were published almost simultaneously with the Packard Commission Final Report, represented a groundbreaking moment in the development of organized voluntary business conduct programs, not just internally by a company, but also across an industrial sector. Whether a defense contractor adopted the DII because of a deepseated sense of corporate responsibility or because it was feeling the heat from the U.S. government (especially on the heels of the Packard Commission's work), the defense industry was the first industry in the United States (and arguably anywhere else) that systematically and consciously created a system of internal governance intended to address and mitigate fraud and corruption, and to put systems and processes in place designed to enhance business conduct and legal compliance.

It should be emphasized that at the time of the creation of the DII—in mid-1986—there were no other visible or notable incentives in place for the creation

Table 4.1   DII Signatories as of July 3, 1986[1]

Aeronca Inc.	Hughes Aircraft Co.
Allied-Signal, Inc.	IBM Corporation
American Telephone & Telegraph Co.	Lockheed Corporation
The Boeing Company	Martin Marietta Corporation
Burroughs Corporation	McDonnell Douglas Corporation
E-Systems, Inc.	Parker Hannifin Corporation
Eaton Corp.	Pneumo Abex Corporation
FMC Corporation	Raytheon Company
Ford Aerospace & Communications Corp.	Rockwell International Corp.
General Dynamic Corporation	The Singer Company
General Electric Company	Sperry Corporation
Goodyear Aerospace Corporation	TRW, Inc.
Grumman Corporation	Textron, Inc.
Hercules Incorporated	United Technologies Corporation
Hewlett-Packard Company	Westinghouse Electric Corporation
Honeywell, Inc.	

[1] See http://www.dii.org/about-us/history.

of an internal system of business ethics or governance other than, of course, the existence of specific federal, state, and local laws forbidding all manner of wrongdoing. Constructive incentives to do the right thing from a preventative compliance standpoint did not exist until the U.S. Sentencing Guidelines indirectly created such a framework through chapter eight several years later.[31] Chapter eight of the U.S. Sentencing Guidelines, when adopted in 1991, provided the first cross-industry set of government incentives for corporate wrongdoers or potential wrongdoers to create an internal system of business conduct and compliance.

The DII served as a direct inspiration to and precedent to chapter eight. The Sarbanes-Oxley Act of 2002, which was designed to tackle, root out, and systematize internal controls and other compliance measures across the entire private sector in response to the Enron, WorldCom, and other significant corporate frauds of the 21st century, while indirectly related to these developments in corporate compliance programs, was still a distant and unfathomable development at the time of the DII's inception. However, it can be said to have also benefited directly from the work of the U.S. Sentencing Commission and the DII.

Thus, the original DII principles, which appeared in appendix M of the Packard Commission Final Report (and are listed verbatim in table 4.2), consisted of the following six fundamental principles:

Principle 1: Written Code of Business Ethics and Conduct. The need for a written code of conduct that provides a clear overview of business conduct expectations.

Principle 2: Employees' Ethical Responsibilities. The need for employees to undertake training and education about business conduct policies and procedures.

Table 4.2   The Defense Industry Principles 1986

Principle 1	Each company will have and adhere to a written code of business ethics and conduct.
Principle 2	The company's code establishes the high values expected of its employees and the standard by which they must judge their own conduct and that of their organization; each company will train its employees concerning their personal responsibilities under the code.
Principle 3	Each company will create a free and open atmosphere that allows and encourages employees to report violations of its code to the company without fear of retribution for such reporting.
Principle 4	Each company has the obligation to self-govern by monitoring compliance with federal procurement laws and adopting procedures for voluntary disclosure of violations of federal procurement laws and corrective actions taken.
Principle 5	Each company has the responsibility to each of the other companies in the industry to live by standards of conduct that preserve the integrity of the defense industry.
Principle 6	Each company must have public accountability for its commitment to these principles.

Principle 3: Corporate Responsibility to Employees. Companies need to encourage employees to report allegations and violations internally without fear of retribution.

Principle 4: Corporate Responsibility to the Government. The need for self-governance through monitoring of systems and procedures regarding federal procurement compliance and self-reporting of violations to the government.

Principle 5: Corporate Responsibility to the Defense Industry. Sharing of best practices and implementation principles with others in the defense industry through best-practice forums.

Principle 6: Public Accountability. Accountability to the public through periodic reporting of results.[32]

While the original DII principles were indeed groundbreaking and something that had not been done before by any industry, they were also fairly basic, limited, and generally superficial. They were basic in that they covered several obvious and fundamental issues, such as the need for a code of conduct and training. They were limited in that they focused almost exclusively on the idea of addressing and rooting out the principal problem identified by the Packard Commission Final Report, namely procurement fraud. Finally, the original DII principles were also in many ways superficial as they exhorted companies to follow their six principles, but these principles were largely vague and aspirational and did not create mechanisms for real accountability; for example, requiring independent third-party auditing of the implementation of the principles.

B. DII Governance and Membership

The creation of the DII also entailed the creation of infrastructure—an actual nonprofit organization based out of Washington, D.C.—to help run the initiative, assist members with developing best practices, and encourage new members to join. Early in the life of the DII, right after its creation, and as part of the development of this infrastructure, a high-level steering committee was formed, headed by none other than Jack Welch, chief executive officer of General Electric, the original corporate instigator of the development of the DII. The DII steering committee was made up of the chief executive officers of several leading defense contractors, and was put in place as the top governance body within the DII. The steering committee remains to this day the internal body that provides oversight to the overall organization and consists of chief executive officers of leading members with a rotating chair.[33]

In addition to a steering committee, the DII has a full-time DII coordinator who actually runs the organization and a working group of heads of ethics and compliance from some of the leading defense industry contractor members of the DII. The working committee focuses on tactical leadership of the organization as well as more specific guidance on what the overall DII organization should be devoted to, including keeping up with all manner of defense industry and other compliance developments in the United States and increasingly globally.[34]

What does it take to become a member of the DII? Any U.S. defense contractor (and that includes non-U.S. companies with a U.S. subsidiary that is a DOD contractor) can apply for membership in the DII. The defense contractor must fill out an application, be accepted, have its chief executive officer publicly commit to the DII principles, and remain a member in good standing. Indeed, the DII itself states that it is "selective, accepting only those defense companies whose CEOs personally commit the company to abide by the DII Principles."[35] Part of this commitment includes filling out an annual questionnaire, to be examined in greater detail below, the contents of which become part of a compiled annual report published by DII to the public. This published summary of the DII members' answers is meant to satisfy the DII principle of public accountability.

But what does it mean to be a DII member in good standing? A look at the period between 1986, when the DII was adopted, through today would indicate that to be a member in good standing of the DII, a company does not have to be in complete compliance with the DII principles.[36] Thus, a number of DII members over the years have had differing degrees of legal and regulatory difficulty (see table 4.4), but have not been asked to leave the DII. It would therefore seem that to be a member in good standing of the DII, it is sufficient for a company and its chief executive officer to make an internal commitment to establish and maintain a program of compliance and ethics and then provide responses to the annual public accountability questionnaire. This means living up to the six principles—having a code, educating employees, providing whistle-blowing solutions, conducting internal monitoring and auditing, sharing best practices across the industry, and providing public information on the compliance program—but as reported and determined by the member company itself. Thus it would seem that as long as the member provides these reports and appears to have an effective internal compliance and ethics program, it can continue to be a member of DII, with all the benefits appurtenant thereto.

II. From 1991 to 2010: The DII and the Emergence of an Ethics and Business Conduct Program Paradigm

A. The 1991 U.S. Sentencing Guidelines

It was only five years after the DII's first publication in 1986 that Congress legislated what has become the paradigm for compliance and ethics programs in the United States (and arguably even increasingly internationally over the past decade) through what is known as Chapter Eight of the U.S. Sentencing Guidelines, first passed in 1991 and subsequently amended in 2004 and 2010.[37] Primarily focused on the issue of how the judiciary is to calculate punishment for corporate criminal conduct under federal laws, the U.S. Sentencing Guidelines through Chapter Eight were directly and indirectly inspired by the DII principles adopted a half a decade earlier.

The guidance for creating and implementing a compliance and ethics program laid out in Chapter Eight of the Sentencing Guidelines has since become the recognized legal basis and standard in the United States for how a corporate compliance and ethics program should look.[38] The elements of an effective program first laid out in Chapter Eight have become the essential elements of

Table 4.3   Comparison of 1986 DII Principles to 1991 U.S. Sentencing Guidelines

DII Principle[1]	Chapter Eight of U.S. Sentencing Guidelines[2]
Principle 1: Written code of business ethics and conduct	Code of conduct and system of policies
Principle 2: Employees' ethical responsibilities	Training and communications programs
Principle 3: Corporate responsibility to employees	Anonymous and other reporting without fear of retaliation
Principle 4: Corporate responsibility to the government	Internal compliance risk assessments; monitoring; auditing
Principle 5: Corporate responsibility to the defense industry	
Principle 6: Public accountability	
	Effective, comprehensive, and fair system of internal discipline
	Delegation of approval authority (system of internal controls)
	Establishing and supporting proper internal resources in the form of an ethics and compliance officer and other personnel

[1] See the original DII Principles at http://www.dii.org/resources/dii-charter.pdf.
[2] See the U.S. Sentencing Guidelines at http://www.ussc.gov/2007guid/8b2_1.html. The U.S. Sentencing Guidelines were amended in 2004 and 2010. This summary adds all amendments through 2004.

an effective and recognized compliance program not only in the United States, but also increasingly globally, in one format or another.

In essence, Chapter Eight mimics many of the tenets of the DII principles. Table 4.3 summarizes the many areas of equivalency and similarity of the respective elements of a sound compliance program as set forth under each document:

Thus, the DII served as a precursor and in some ways an inspiration for much of what ended up as part of Chapter Eight of the U.S. Sentencing Guidelines and thus the law of the United States.[39]

B. The Emergence of a New Profession: The Ethics and Compliance Officer

Almost simultaneously with the issuance of the U.S. Sentencing Guidelines, a small group of little more than a dozen ethics officers of various industries, including from the defense industry, got together at Bentley College in Massachusetts to create the first nonindustry-specific association for the emerging ethics and compliance profession: the Ethics Officer Association, known today as the Ethics and Compliance Officer Association (ECOA).[40] By its own admission, the ECOA was created as a result of the concurrent activities elicited by the work of the DII as well as the U.S. Sentencing Guidelines. The ECOA has since become the largest professional association of its kind internationally and has been joined by a wide variety of professional, quasiprofessional, nonprofit, commercial, and consulting organizations all with the idea that companies need an internal ethics and compliance program to address both internal and external compliance and ethics needs and threats. Such expert entities, whether for profit or nonprofit, have developed a wide array of tools, techniques, training, auditing, and other products and services for the ethics and compliance professional to build an effective program. Central to this overall development in the field was and continues to be the work of the DII.[41]

C. Enron and Company: The Pendulum Swings in the Early 2000s

What eventually became one of the biggest frauds in corporate history—the Enron story—was brewing and began to bubble to the surface during the summer of 2001. Together with the occurrence of the terrorist attacks of September 11, 2001, and its concomitant impact on the conduct of international business, leading to a worldwide recession, the Enron scandal and several others that rose at its heels—Arthur Andersen, WorldCom, Global Crossing, Adelphia, Qwest, Parmalat, to name a few—had a major regulatory impact in the United States and Europe on issues of governance, internal controls, whistle-blowing programs, and compliance generally. Working at what could be considered warp speed for a legislative body anywhere, the United States Congress moved quickly after the collapse of Enron and enacted what came to be known as the Sarbanes-Oxley Act of 2002 (SOX). SOX emerged as the next big thing in compliance, focusing mainly on publicly traded companies and their internal controls, document retention programs, whistleblower protection programs, and other key risk-management processes.[42]

D. Amendments to the U.S. Sentencing Guidelines: The Role of DII as the Paradigm Evolves

There have been two major sets of amendments to the U.S. Sentencing Guidelines—one passed in 2004 and the other one in 2010. After its original adoption in 1991, the U.S. Sentencing Guidelines with its seven principal guidelines (many of which were inspired by the DII principles as discussed earlier) remained pretty much intact until 2004.[43] At that time, the U.S. Sentencing Commission completed its review of the 1991 Sentencing Guidelines by conducting hearings involving many experts in the field, some of whom had been direct contributors to and beneficiaries of the DII experience. These included the ERC and numerous ethics and compliance professionals who had been involved with the creation of the DII and the emergence of the ECOA.

The 2004 amendments to the U.S. Sentencing Guidelines revolved around several key components for an effective ethics and compliance program, the most important of which included a new requirement for conducting periodic compliance risk assessments, the need for the ethics and compliance functions to be allocated sufficient resources to build and maintain a program, and, very importantly, the need for governance and senior management oversight and ultimate responsibility for the program.[44]

The 2010 amendments to the U.S. Sentencing Guidelines, which became law on November 1, 2010, represent the latest thinking and action on the creation of an effective ethics and compliance program, and will require that a company's chief ethics and compliance executive have direct, personal access to the governing body or board when and if deemed necessary by such executive.[45] This requirement, once again, is something that several leading companies, including members of the DII, have already instituted as a best practice.[46]

E.   The Emergence of Mandatory Procurement Fraud Reporting: The 2008 Amendments to the Federal Acquisition Regulations

While the trends described above relating to the passage of the U.S. Sentencing Guidelines in 1991, emergence of an ethics and compliance profession within companies, and the adoption of SOX are applicable to all companies and all industries, it is possible to state that the defense industry, whether it is admired or not, and whether it adopted the DII principles for the right reasons or simply out of fear of government adverse action, was the precursor and instigator of many of these trends and, in turn, was a major contributor to the emergence over time of a set of compliance and ethics program best practices (see table 4.3).

Part of the rationale for the DII had always been to preempt further regulatory encroachment by the government by creating a strong voluntary program of ethics and compliance that would prevent the passage of more legal and compliance requirements. However, as much as it tried to convince the U.S. government not to require mandatory reporting of possible procurement fraud by implementing a best practices program of voluntary disclosure, the DII was not able ultimately to succeed on this particular issue. Part of the reason undoubtedly had to do with the fact that as much as the DII developed its compliance and ethics principles and practices, instances, and not just isolated ones, of defense industry procurement fraud cropped up regularly and sometimes dramatically both through investigative media reports and government investigations and prosecutions. Indeed, it was only within six years of the DII's and Jack Welch's championing of the adoption of the DII that GE was once again involved in a major defense industry scandal.[47]

But GE was certainly not alone. In a major investigative report published in *U.S. News and World Report* in 2002, it became clear that with or without a major initiative such as the DII, the old curse of procurement fraud and other compliance violations continued, it would seem, unabated. According to this report, "[I]n the past dozen years, 30 of the federal government's biggest contractors have accumulated more than 400 enforcement cases, resulting in at least $3.4 billion in penalties, settlements, and restitution."[48] Table 4.4 provides a summary of the number of cases and total fines paid (in millions) by the top ten corporate violators fined by the government over the ten-year period (1992–2002) examined in this investigative report.

Other cases of defense contractor misbehavior or wrongdoing have occurred throughout this period and doubtlessly will continue to occur. Some of the more notorious cases have involved defense contractors working for the U.S.

Table 4.4 Defense Industry Contractor Enforcement Cases Track Record 1992–2002[1]

Company	Number of Cases	Total Fines (in Millions)
General Electric	63	982
TRW	17	389
Boeing	36	358
Lockheed Martin	63	232
United Technologies	18	215
Archer Daniels Midland	8	208
Unisys	12	182
Raytheon	24	129
Litton (acquired by Northrup Grumman)	8	111
Cargill	8	102

[1] Christopher H. Schmitt, "U.S. Wages of Sin: Why Lawbreakers Still Win Government Contracts," *U.S. News and World Report*, May 13, 2002.

government in the two Iraqi wars, both in terms of pure procurement fraud, as in the case with Halliburton and KBR, and as part of the so-called UN Oil for Food scandal.[49] Moreover, Boeing was no stranger to scandal in the early 2000s when it became embroiled in one of the most-reported cases of pure conflict of interest between the DOD and defense contractor. Darleen Druyun, a high-ranking air force procurement officer, while negotiating with Boeing on behalf of the U.S. government to purchase military equipment, was also conducting parallel negotiations for a lucrative personal employment deal with none other than the chief financial officer of Boeing. Needless to say, once uncovered, this case blew up in the face of both people and both enti-ties—a defense contractor and the DOD, the two entities most targeted by the Packard Commission for avoidance of issues of exactly this kind. Both Doreen Druyun and Boeing's chief financial officer, Michael Sears, were prosecuted, found guilty, and served jail terms.[50]

Thus in the late fall of 2008, Congress once again addressed the issue of procurement fraud in the defense industry. This time the legislature focused on what had been one of the "best practices" tenets of the DII, the voluntary dis-closure of possible fraud. Given the continuing track record of defense industry fraud and abuse (so amply illustrated in table 4.4), Congress addressed the issue this time through amendments to the Federal Acquisition Regulations, which would now make it legally mandatory for defense contractors to have an inter-nal system to detect and address potential procurement fraud early and often, and would require companies to inform the government immediately of any sus-pected procurement fraud.[51] This new edict got the defense industry scrambling to find ways to convert their voluntary disclosure practices into a system for mandatory reporting of suspected fraud, which would require reporting of sus-pected or actual fraud at very low monetary thresholds and in connection with subcontractors as well.[52] See Table 4.5 for a summary of the impact of the 2008 amendments to the Federal Acquisition Regulations on defense contractors.

Table 4.5   The Impact of 2008 Amendments to the Federal Acquisition Regulations[1]

"The Contractor shall timely disclose, in writing, to the agency Office of the Inspector General (OIG), with a copy to the Contracting Officer, whenever, in connection with the award, performance, or closeout of this contract or any subcontract thereunder, the Contractor has credible evidence that a principal, employee, agent, or subcontractor of the Contractor has committed—

(A) A violation of Federal criminal law involving fraud, conflict of interest, bribery, or gratuity violations found in Title 18 of the United States Code; or
(B) A violation of the civil False Claims Act (31 U.S.C. §§3729–3733)"

1. Defense contractors may be debarred or suspended from a federal contract for failure to timely disclose to the U.S. government credible evidence of the following possible violations under a federal contract:
   a. Significant overpayments
   b. Civil false claims
   c. Bribery
   d. Gratuity
   e. Fraud (Title 18)
   f. Conflict of interest
2. Defense contractors must have a defined system of internal controls.
3. Contractor requirement to disclose if knowledge of subcontractor possible violation.
4. Applicable to contracts of $5 million-plus and 120 days or more performance.
5. Applicable to small businesses.
6. Subcontractor disclosure directly to the government, not through prime contractor.
7. Contractor must have an ongoing program of business ethics and conduct.

[1] United States Government Accountability Office, "Defense Contracting Integrity: Opportunities Exist to Improve DOD's Oversight of Contractor Ethics Programs," report to Congressional Committees, September 2009, p. 43.

F. The Financial Meltdown of the First Decade of the 21st Century

As if to bookend the beginning of the decade, with the eruption of Enron et al., the end of the first decade of the 21st century saw the overwhelming and pervasive global financial meltdown that began with the failures of Bear Stearns and Lehman Brothers in 2008 and still reverberates at the time of this writing. This closure to the first decade, as it were, is most dramatically underscored and exemplified by President Obama's signing into law on July 21, 2010, the Dodd-Frank Wall Street Reform and Consumer Protection Act of 2010, the most radical and comprehensive change in financial industry regulation since the 1930s and the establishment of the passage of the Securities and Exchange Act of 1934. This regulatory retort to the largest and most pervasive crisis in global finance the world has known was very similar to the adoption of the SOX 2002 on the heels of the pervasive fraud exemplified by the Enron and WorldCom cases, and perhaps even the U.S. Sentencing Guidelines of 1991 and the FCPA in 1977 as a result of some of the scandals in those days.[53]

The significance of these historical trends and changes to the DII has more to do with the emerging compliance environment that has been evolving over the past one to two decades, which is likely to continue to evolve over the next decade, affecting not only the defense industry, but also the national and international private sector.

III. The DII Today: Status, Challenges, and the Future

A. *The Principles Themselves: How Have They Changed?*

The DII website publishes information for its members, observers, and, by sharing its resources publicly, other industries. A recent look at the website revealed that the following components of an effective business conduct program were among the key elements endorsed by the DII:

- Company values
- Leadership commitment
- Risk assessment
- Ethics and business conduct policy
- Program assessment and evaluation
- Code of conduct
- Communications plan and awareness initiatives
- Inquiry and reporting mechanisms
- Awareness training

More interestingly, the original principles adopted by the DII back in 1986 have undergone a transformation as well, partly because of the need to adapt to changing circumstances, but also as part of the to and fro between the DII, the larger ethics and compliance community, and the government, as this chapter has tried illustrate.

Thus, the original DII principles have changed with the times. What follows is a principle-by-principle comparison and analysis of the current language of the DII principles as amended through March 2010 and the original principles created in 1986:

2010 Preamble:

We the members of the Defense Industry Initiative on Business Ethics & Conduct (DII), affirm our commitment to uphold the highest ethical standards in all our business dealings with the government, as expressed through the following principles:

The original 1986 DII principles did not include a preamble such as the one in the latest version. The latest version clearly attempts to emphasize key concepts of taking responsibility, assigning accountability, and setting expectations. Indeed, the preamble is prefaced with the following statement: "DII members, and the CEOs of every DII company, must abide by DII's core principles." It also contains what has become a much important component of business conduct programs in recent times, especially since the adoption of the 2004 U.S. Sentencing Guideline amendments—an emphasis on creating an ethical culture.

Principle 1:

1986: Each company will have and adhere to a written code of business ethics and conduct.

2010: We shall act honestly in all business dealings with the U.S. Government, protect taxpayer resources and provide high quality products and services for the men and women of the U.S. Armed Forces.

This latest version of the DII principles clearly emphasizes up-front and centrally the core objective of the principles themselves; that is, the true purpose of the DII principles is almost exclusively to ensure that no malfeasance takes place through member companies' dealings with three key stakeholders: the U.S. government, U.S. taxpayers (whose money, after all, goes to purchase defense industry products and services), and U.S. military personnel (whose health and safety is paramount). The original principle one, requiring a code of conduct, has been subsumed under the current principle two, below.

Principle 2:

1986: The company's code establishes the high values expected of its employees and the standard by which they must judge their own conduct and that of their organization; each company will train its employees concerning their personal responsibilities under the code.

2010: We shall promote the highest ethical values as expressed in our written codes of business conduct, nurture an ethical culture through communications, training, and other means, and comply with and honor all governing laws and regulations.

The second principle has become synchronized more closely to the state of ethics and compliance programs generally as influenced by Chapter Eight of the U.S. Sentencing Guidelines, Sarbanes-Oxley, and other recent developments. Its focus is more heavily directed at building an ethical culture, and its purpose is more aligned with compliance with all laws and regulations, not just procurement laws. An emphasis on training and communications also reflects the rise of these elements in an effective compliance and ethics program.

Principle 3:

1986: Each company will create a free and open atmosphere that allows and encourages employees to report violations of its code to the company without fear of retribution for such reporting.

2010: We shall establish and sustain effective business ethics and compliance programs that reflect our commitment to self-governance, and shall encourage employees to report suspected misconduct, forbid retaliation for such reporting, and ensure the existence of a process for mandatory and voluntary disclosures of violations of relevant laws and regulations.

There are clear and important changes to this principle. First and foremost, the whistle-blower protection language is stronger and the focus on having a proper system in place is keener. Moreover, changes have been made to clarify that voluntary disclosure of wrongdoing is no longer simply desirable but necessary; mandatory disclosure requirements are now in place and must be reflected internally within companies.

Principle 4:

1986: Each company has the obligation to self-govern by monitoring compliance with federal procurement laws and adopting procedures for voluntary disclosure of violations of federal procurement laws and corrective actions taken.
2010: We shall share best practices with respect to business ethics and compliance and participate in the annual DII Best Practices Forum.
This principle has been changed completely, with the content from the original principle four subsumed in other current principles, namely principle three. This new principle four focuses on the public accountability aspect of the principles originally under original principle six, which has now been eliminated.

Principle 5:

1986: Each company has the responsibility to each of the other companies in the industry to live by standards of conduct that preserve the integrity of the defense industry.
2010: We shall be accountable to the public, through regular reporting by DII to Congress and the public. These reports will describe members' efforts to build and sustain a strong culture of business ethics and compliance.
The current version of the DII principles expands the accountability concept from accountability strictly to one another as members of DII to a broader multi-stakeholder concept of actual accountability through regular reporting from each defense contractor member both to Congress and the public.

Principle 6:

1986: Each company must have public accountability for its commitment to these principles.
2010: The current version does not have a sixth principle.
The vague and aspirational public accountability language from the original principles is now contained in the current version of principle five as a more concrete requirement (see above).

Although the principles have changed somewhat with the passage of time, the focus of the principles and of the DII generally is on the questionnaire, which the DII requires all members in good standing to fill out and deliver to the DII coordinator every year. The questionnaire then becomes the basis for the public accountability aspect of the DII—the summary report prepared by the DII for public consumption. Let us turn to an examination of the questionnaire.

B. Converting Principles into Practices: The Original DII Questionnaire of 1986 Compared to Today's (2009) Questionnaire

The DII touts the fact that one of its principal contributions to the public is the fact that its members engage in public accountability. The principal manner in which members do this is by filling out each year a public accountability questionnaire. Below is an analysis of this questionnaire as it first existed in

1986 and as it exists today—substantial and constructive changes have been made. However, one important point remains and should be kept in mind throughout a reading of this analysis: while the questionnaire must be filled by a member in good standing of the DII, the information each company submits to the DII coordinator is not in itself made public. In fact, what is claimed to be public accountability really remains fairly behind the scenes as the DII coordinator collects and reviews the information, and in turn provides a public report that discusses trends and activities, revealing no individual company information.

Both the original and current DII principles include a questionnaire to help each member conduct an internal survey of the state of business ethics and conduct within their organization and to assist in the preparation of the accountability report. Table 4.6 shows the original questionnaire as it was first created in 1986, and the questionnaire as it exists at the time of this writing. It is clear that some major changes—most for the better—have taken place over the questionnaire's two and a half decades of existence. However, a fundamental concern must be kept in mind throughout a consideration of these questions: they are voluntarily collected and reported by companies to the DII coordinator, and the DII coordinator in turn prepares a collective, anonymous, and voluntary public report.

An analysis of the original 1986 questionnaire shows that while the questions were important and critical to understanding the relative robustness of an ethics and business conduct program (and frankly, these questions had never been asked before), in and of themselves, the 1986 questions weren't that useful, as they often required a simple yes or no answer, did not require proof or follow-up, and provided a generally superficial treatment of the issues raised. For example, the first four questions of the 1986 questionnaire could be answered with a simple yes or no:

- Yes, we have a code of conduct.
- Yes, we circulate the code to all employees.
- Yes, employees receive orientation and training on the code.
- Yes, we assign accountability for implementation of the code to operating personnel.

However, some of the other questions in the 1986 questionnaire began to address the more difficult to measure but nevertheless core aspects of a program, which, if demonstrable, could help to create a culture of business ethics over the longer term. Among these kinds of questions from the 1986 questionnaire were:

- Question 7, which addressed the issue of the creation of concrete internal resources to help employees with their concerns and questions.
- Question 9, which addressed the need for follow-up and resolution of suspected violations that may have been reported by employees or others.
- Question 10, which raised an issue of great importance: creating a sense among employees that the company would listen to their concerns and follow up to create solutions and closure.

Table 4.6 Original (1986) DII Questionnaire Compared with the Current (2009) DII "Public Accountability" Questionnaire[1]

1986 Questionnaire	2009 Questionnaire
1. Does the company have a written code of business ethics and conduct?	Does the company have a written Code of Business Ethics and Conduct? *(Please provide link to the current version).*
	See 1986 question 1.
	NEW: *Describe any code provisions or policies or supplemental materials that require prompt internal reporting of violations of the code to an appropriate person or persons identified in the code. If reporting is not required, describe any code provisions that encourage such reporting and identify to whom the reports are to be made.*
2. Is the code distributed to all employees principally involved in defense work?	NEW: *Describe any code provisions, policies or other supplemental materials that address Government contracting compliance risk areas.*
3. Are new employees provided any orientation to the code?	Describe any code provisions, policies or other supplemental materials that call for fair dealing and identify standards for governing conduct with customers, suppliers and competitors.
	See 1986 question 6.
4. Does the code assign responsibility to operating management and other for compliance with the code?	NEW: *Describe any code provision or associated policy that requires that outside marketing and sales consultants are governed by, and informed of the company's code of conduct and relevant associated policies.*
5. Does the company conduct employee training programs regarding the code?	NEW: *What is the title of the senior person or persons assigned responsibility for the company's ethics and business conduct program?*
6. Does the code address standards that govern the conduct of employees in their dealings with suppliers, consultants and customers?	Does the company distribute the code to all employees *(including agents and contract employees)* principally involved in defense contract work? *(Describe.)*
	See 1986 questions 2 and 3.
7. Is there a corporate review board, ombudsman, corporate compliance or ethics office or similar mechanism for employees to report suspected violations to someone other than their direct supervisor, if necessary?	NEW: *Describe the company's efforts, if any, to make the code known to subcontractors.*
8. Does the reporting mechanism protect the confidentiality of employee reports?	Are new employees provided an orientation to the code? *If so, describe when and how.* See 1986 question #3.

Continued

Table 4.6 Continued

1986 Questionnaire	2009 Questionnaire
9. Is there an appropriate mechanism to follow-up on reports of suspected violations to determine what occurred, who was responsible, and recommended corrective and other actions?	Does the company conduct employee information and training programs regarding employee obligations under the code? *(Describe best examples).* See 1986 question 5.
10. Is there an appropriate mechanism for letting employees know the result of any follow-up into their reported charges?	NEW: *a. Describe the company's internal mechanism(s) for employees and others to seek ethics guidance and report suspected instances of misconduct.* *b. Describe the ways in which the reporting mechanism(s) is publicized.* See 1986 questions 9 and 10.
11. Is there an ongoing program of communication to employees, spelling out and re-emphasizing their obligations under the code of conduct?	Describe any code provisions or company policies or practices which seek to protect the confidentiality if a reporting employee's identity *and prohibit retaliation for good-faith use of the reporting mechanism?* See 1986 question 8.
12. What are the specifics of such a program? • Written communication? • One-on-one communication? • Group meetings? • Visual aids? • Others?	NEW: *Describe any code provisions or company policies or procedures that govern the review or investigation of possible violations of the code (including matters reported by employees or third-parties).*
13. Does the company have a procedure for voluntarily reporting violations of federal procurement laws to appropriate governmental agencies?	NEW: *Describe any code provision or company policies or procedures for letting those who report possible violations know the result of the company's follow-up.*
14. Is implementation of the code's provisions one of the standards by which all levels of supervision are expected to be measured in their performance?	Describe any code provision or company policies or procedures for voluntarily reporting violations of federal procurement law to appropriate governmental authorities. See 1986 question 13.
15. Is there a program to monitor on a continuing basis adherence to the code of conduct and compliance with federal procurement laws?	Is implementation of the code's provisions one of the standards by which all levels of supervision are expected to be measured in their job performance? *(Describe).* See 1986 question 14.
16. Does the company participate in the industry's "Best Practices Forum"?	Is there a program to monitor, on a continuing basis, adherence of the code and compliance with federal procurement laws? *(Describe how monitored.)* See 1986 question 15.

Continued

Table 4.6 Continued

1986 Questionnaire	2009 Questionnaire
17. Are periodic reports on adherence to the principles made to the company's Board of Directors or to its audit or other appropriate committee?	NEW: *Describe any process the company uses to periodically review the effectiveness of its ethics and business conduct policies, procedures and program.*
18. Are the company independent public accountants or a similar independent organization required to comment to the Board of Directors or a committee thereof on the efficacy of the company's internal procedures for implementing the company's code of conduct?	NEW: *Does the company periodically modify its program to ensure that existing or emerging risks are addressed appropriately? If so, describe the process used.*
19.	NEW: *Describe any code provision or company policy or procedure governing discipline and corrective actions which are responsive to violations of the code.*
20.	*Did the company fulfill its obligation to share best practices with respect to adherence to standards of ethical business conduct? Did the company attend the most recent Best Practices Forum? Who from the company attended?* See 1986 question 16.
21.	NEW: *Describe any periodic reports on the company's ethics and conduct program that are made to the company senior management and/or the Board of Directors or governing body.* See 1986 question 18.
22.	NEW: *What does the company do to promote an organizational culture that encourages ethical conduct and a commitment to compliance with the law?*
23.	NEW: *What does the company do to promote or require implementation of ethics and business conduct programs consistent with the DII principles within your Supply Chain?*
24.	NEW: *Provide the name and contact information of the company individual best informed to respond to questions about these responses.*

[1] Information in this table was gathered from DII's original questionnaire, issued in 1986, and the current (2009) questionnaire, which can be found as attachment B to "Public Accountability Report of the Defense Industry Initiative on Business Ethics and Conduct," January 1, 2008–June 30, 2009, http://www.dii.org. All new questions not originally part of the original 1986 questionnaire have been italicized in this table for ease of reference.

Next were several questions in the 1986 questionnaire that dealt directly with the issues of procurement and government relations. (See questions 6, 13, and 15.) These questions, however, largely reflect the fact that the genesis of the DII program can be attributed to the need for the defense industry to react quickly to an increasingly negative public and legislative perception of the industry on the heels of the defense procurement scandals of the early 1980s.

The 1986 questionnaire also has a few questions that focus on one of the most difficult issues of all in the creation and implementation of an effective ethics and compliance program: how to measure its effectiveness; its reality; the fact that it is not only a set of words, policies, and aspirations, but also something that is taken seriously and actually implemented and for which results can be measured. Questions 14, 15, 17, and 18 address the measurability issue to a certain extent, but not fully. While these questions encourage review by or reporting to important third parties such as a company's board of directors, outside auditors, and the government itself, such reporting is wholly voluntary, still woefully lacking in rigor, and the requirement of demonstrable results and guidance on what constitutes success.[54]

Finally, the 1986 questionnaire pointed to another innovation (certainly at the time and with regard to compliance programs) in question 16, which asked whether the defense contractor belongs to the industry's "Best Practices Forum." Under the DII, the creation of an ongoing forum became one of its enduring marquee creations; DII members could participate in an annual forum in which the latest industry programs, policies, practices, and trends are discussed.[55]

As to the recent 2009 questionnaire, it is possible to distinguish some major improvements that have taken place, many of them reflective of both the U.S. Sentencing Guidelines as adopted in 1991 and revised through 2004,[56] as well as other best practices that have been generally developed in the ethics and compliance community. The most important improvements include:

- A much heavier emphasis on the need for employee reporting and guidance seeking on issues of ethics and business conduct.
- Asking more probing questions that require details and specifics about policies, practices, and mechanisms (and not merely requiring a yes or no answer).
- Requiring proof of certain matters—names, dates, details, meetings, et cetera. For example, one question requires the specific name and title of the person in charge of the company's business conduct program.
- Featuring compliance with heightened federal procurement laws requiring mandatory disclosure of possible violations through beefed-up employee and third-party reporting mechanisms, including a specific requirement to show how the company guarantees nonretaliation against employees who report in good faith.
- Focus on understanding and revealing periodically risk areas as required under the 2004 amendments to the U.S. Sentencing Guidelines.
- Driving the compliance and ethics program accountability issue upward to senior management and the board as required under the 2004 amendments to the U.S. Sentencing Guidelines.
- Driving compliance and ethics program accountability sideways and down to the supply chain, outside marketing and sales consultants, subcontractors, and contract employees.

- Requiring explanations of how the company metes out discipline for ethics and business conduct violations.
- Asking probing questions on how the company measures the effectiveness of its program as required under the 2004 amendments to the U.S. Sentencing Guidelines.
- Asking how the company implements corrective action after it has found that violations have occurred.

Finally, it also bears mentioning that partially in response to new requirements under the U.S. Sentencing Guidelines and no doubt partially a result of its own development of best practices, the DII has developed other useful tools, techniques, and practices for members. Among them, for example, is assistance in understanding the key risks of a defense industry contractor; see table 4.7 for a summary of some of the primary defense contractor compliance and ethics risks that the DII has put together for its members. Very notably, and in contrast with the early days of the DII, this best practices guidance goes well beyond the issue of procurement fraud avoidance and demonstrates a much more holistic view of ethics and compliance risk management.

By assembling this type of risk management information from across its now ninety-member base (see table 4.8 for a full list of DII members as of March 2010), the DII is providing a very valuable benchmarking and best practices service not only to its own members, but also to the larger corporate, organizational and ethics and compliance community.

C. DII: Final Assessment and Recommendations

As we conclude this chapter, it may be worth asking once again: Is there a difference between the defense industry companies that subscribe to the DII and those that do not? Does it make a difference to the company itself to be a member of DII? In other words, does the need to adhere to the requirements of DII membership actually improve a company's compliance and ethics track record? Does the DII make a difference to the overall track record of the industry regarding the breadth and depth of procurement fraud and its prevention, which after all is the stated raison d'être of the DII? Does the fact that the DII does not actually require individual public accounting by its members work against internal improvements, or, to the contrary, does this commitment by a company to be part of a best practices forum have direct and indirect intended and unintended positive consequences?

While it is not possible to answer these questions scientifically based on the evidence available, it is possible to look back at the twenty-five years of the DII and make a number of remarks.

The DII took it upon itself to issue annual reports summarizing the progress, or lack thereof, of the DII program elements of its member companies. As with any self-reporting process that is not open to outside, independent, expert third-party review, these annual reports, while descriptive and somewhat substantive, are also fairly bland aggregations of data that members, at the end of the day, are willing to share. The Public Accountability Reports do not reveal details of any members' particular answers and do not delve deeply or critically into the details of each company's performance. While this is not necessarily true of all members of the DII, as some of them do produce their own ethics and compliance public reports, the DII Public Accountability Reports are useful overviews but do not amount to auditable public accountability.[57]

The DII effort started as and, for all intents and purposes, continues to be a fairly narrowly focused effort in a number of respects: it is open exclusively to the defense industry, it is U.S.-centric because it caters to relations with the U.S. government, and it is narrowly focused on relations with only one U.S. government entity—the DOD. Most critically, however, the DII's roots and even its development over the past quarter-century remain limited intellectually as the almost exclusive focus of the effort has been on addressing the issue of procurement fraud, although to its credit the DII has recently expanded its repertoire to include related themes, policies, tools, and techniques.[58]

However, the DII lacks teeth, for lack of a better word. It remains a voluntary mechanism used to develop best practices but lacking in rigorous testing, independent auditing, or enforcement. While this may very well be what was originally intended and continues to be currently intended by the organization, as its own annual reports and that of the Government Accountability Office (GAO) demonstrate, this approach does not ensure fundamental compliance or the rooting out of procurement fraud, its original objective.[59]

As table 4.9 demonstrates, while some of the biggest DOD contractors are members of the DII, many defense contractors are not members thus leaving open several critical questions:

- Do the non-DII contractors have an ethics and compliance program in place, let alone an "effective" one?
- Why don't the non-DII top-sixty DOD contractors belong to the DII?
- Is the DII itself an effective "industry" initiative if it has only ninety members (out of tens of thousands of contractors and subcontractors), with more than 50 percent of the sixty biggest DOD contractors (with $500 million or more in DOD-related revenues) not feeling compelled to become members of DII?

So, was the DII a business conduct program trendsetter, and has the DII become the business conduct program standard? From the analysis provided in this chapter, it is possible to make a couple of observations with some certainty. First, the DII was indeed a trendsetter, or perhaps more accurately, an innovator in the creation of internal business conduct programs within companies; at the time of its creation in 1986 there was no other industry-wide (let alone internal) corporate code of conduct program standard that had been developed at any scale by any one company or industry.

It is a little more difficult to categorically state that the DII has become the industry standard for a couple of reasons. While the DII has been a very active and sharing organization in that it has developed and made publicly available many of its best practices, it has remained a somewhat limited organization for some of the reasons described above.

The DII is designed as a set of guidelines to help defense contractors sign on to aspirational principles, devote proper resources to accomplishing the principles, and account publicly with the remainder of the DII membership annually on how it has done in regard to the principles. It is not an organization that polices its members' compliance or otherwise tries to gauge the level of compliance and ethics within a member company. So long as a defense company

Table 4.7   Typical Compliance Risk Areas Identified and Provided for by DII Companies[1]

- Offering business courtesies to government personnel, which may be perceived as gratuities or kickbacks
- Personal and organizational conflicts of interest
- Time charging and expense reporting
- Use of company property, equipment, and facilities
- Use of copyrighted or licensed materials
- Accurate representation in proposals of data or credentials and employee qualifications
- Proper recording and disbursement of funds and other assets
- Prohibitions on customer and competitor proprietary data/source selection information
- Quality assurance
- Prohibiting kickbacks from suppliers and subcontractors
- Relationships with customers and suppliers
- Engagement and control of agents, including consultants and sales representatives
- Lobbying and political contributions
- Drug and substance abuse
- Equal opportunity employment
- Sexual harassment
- Inventions/patent policy
- Government audits and investigations
- Control of technology transfer to foreign persons
- Hiring former government employees and other "revolving door" issues
- Restrictions on duty assignments to former government employees
- Misconduct in science
- Computer system usage and Internet use
- Money laundering
- Protecting government property
- Insider trading
- Security and crisis management

[1] DII 2009 Public Accountability Report, pp. 32–33.

member complies—or appears to comply through its voluntary disclosure—with the principles, no other requirement seems to be in place.

Thus, ostensibly, a member could engage in procurement fraud, but as long as it seemed to be following the DII principles, paid its dues, and provided public accountability reporting, it would not have to fear being delisted from the DII itself. Whether this is a form of membership that actually breeds better practices and overall compliance, or simply provides the membership with a veneer of compliance is a question that remains unanswered and is probably unanswerable. A defense contractor with deep pockets can hire a team of compliance professionals to put together a gold-plated ethics and compliance program, and might get away with looking good but not necessarily doing good; that is, the ethics and compliance program becomes a matter of effective public relations but not effective internal controls and culture.

The DII has, however, made a number of very positive contributions to the overall dialogue about and development of an effective ethics and business conduct program over its quarter-century of existence. The DII represented a groundbreaking initiative at the time of its inception, and it continued to interact proactively and constructively with the ethics and compliance community over

Table 4.8 2010 DII Members[1]

3M	ITT Industries
Aerojet	Kellogg Brown & Root
AgustaWestland North America, Inc.	L-3 Communications Corporation
Alcoa, Inc.	Leader Communications, Inc. (LCI)
Allfast Fastening Systems, Inc.	LMI Aerospace, Inc.
Alliant Techsystems, Inc.	Lockheed Martin Corporation
American Ordnance	MER Corporation
AT&T	MIT Lincoln Laboratory
Babcock & Wilcox	Natel Engineering Company
BAE Systems	National Air Cargo
Boeing Company	National Technical Systems
Booz Allen Hamilton	Northrop Grumman Corporation
CA, Inc.	Omega Technologies Company
CFM International	Orbital Sciences Corporation
Ciber, Inc.	Parker Hannifin Corporation
CNA Corporation	PGBA, LLC
Concurrent Technologies Corporation	Protective Products International
Crane Co.	Proteus Technologies
CSC	QinetiQ
Cubic Corporation	Raytheon Company
Curtiss-Wright Corporation	Rockwell Collins, Inc.
DataPath, Inc.	SAIC
Day & Zimmermann, Inc.	SELEX
DRS Technologies, Inc.	SENTEL Corporation
DS2 (Defense Support Services LLC)	Sequa Corporation
DynCorp International LLC	Serco
EADS North America	Siemens Government Services, Inc.
Earl Industries, LLC	SkyLink USA
EarthTech (Tyco International)	Sodexo Federal Services, Inc.
EG&G Technical	Solers, Inc.
Esterline Corporation	Standard Aero
Frequency Electronics, Inc.	Teledyne Technologies Incorporated
General Atomics	Textron, Inc.
General Dynamics	Thales USA, Inc.
General Electric	Timken Company
Georgia Tech Research Institute	TriWest Healthcare Alliance
Goodrich Corporation	Tybrin Corporation
Harris Corporation	United Launch Alliance
HealthNet Federal Services, LLC	United Space Alliance (Boeing Company)
Herley Industries, Inc.	United Technologies Corporation
Honeywell International, Inc.	University of Dayton Research Institute
Humana Military Health Services	URS Corporation
IAP Worldwide Services	Verizon
IBM Corporation	Vought Aircraft Industries, Inc.
Immix Group	Williams International
Institute for Defense Analyses (IDA)	Woodward Governor Company

[1] Defense Industry Initiative, March 13, 2010, http://www.dii.org/our-companies.

Table 4.9 Companies with $500M+ in DOD Revenue, Fiscal Year 2006[1]

CONTRACTOR NAME	REVENUE (IN MILLIONS) FOR FISCAL YEAR 2006	DII MEMBER?
Lockheed Martin Corporation	26,620	Y
Boeing Company	21,721	Y
Northrup Grumman Corporation	16,627	Y
General Dynamics Corporation	11,942	Y
Raytheon Company	10,069	Y
BAE Systems PLC	6,192	Y
KBR, Inc.	6,060	Y
L-3Communications Holding, Inc.	5,197	Y
United Technologies Corporation	4,453	Y
Science Application International Corporation	3,211	Y
Computer Sciences Corporation	2,884	N
Humana, Inc.	2,642	Y
ITT Corporation	2,522	Y
General Electric Company	2,328	Y
Heath Net, Inc.	2,119	Y
Triwest Healthcare Alliance Company	2,022	Y
Electronic Data Systems Corporation	2,008	N
AM General, LLC	1,944	N
Agility Logistics	1,838	N
Honeywell International, Inc.	1,679	Y
Textron, Inc.	1,369	Y
URS Corporation	1,369	Y
Amerisourcebergen Corporation	1,346	N
Harris Corporation	1,339	Y
FedEx Corporation	1,303	N
Bechtel Group, Inc.	1,264	N
Booz Allen Hamilton, Inc.	1,245	Y
BP America, Inc.	1,199	N
Exxon Mobil Corporation	1,176	N
Shell Oil Company	1,151	N
Alliant Techsystems, Inc.	1,128	Y
Oshkosh Truck Company	941	N
Rockwell Collins, Inc.	824	Y
Korea Agricultural Cooperative	761	N
DRS Technologies	730	Y
Philips & Jordon, Inc.	705	N
CACI International, Inc.	681	N
General Atomic Technologies Company	670	Y
McKesson Corporation	670	N
Valero Energy Corporation	661	N
Thales	657	Y
Aerospace Corporation	654	N
Mitre Corporation	652	N
Massachusetts Institute of Technology	640	Y
Dell, Inc.	636	N
Cardinal Health, Inc.	635	N
Syracuse Research Corporation	613	N
Chugach Alaska Corporation	593	N
Refinery Associates of Texas	577	N

Continued

Table 4.9   Continued

CONTRACTOR NAME	REVENUE (IN MILLIONS) FOR FISCAL YEAR 2006	DII MEMBER?
Environmental Chemical Corporation	570	N
Parsons Corporation	526	N
Johns Hopkins University	525	N
Battelle Memorial Institute	519	N
Shaw Group, Inc.	519	N
Maersk Line Ltd.	516	N
Jacobs Engineering Group, Inc.	505	N
Kraft Foods, Inc.	501	N

TOTAL DOD CONTRACT AWARDS FOR TOP 57 COMPANIES IN 2006: $164,448

TOTAL DOD CONTRACT AWARDS TO ALL CONTRACTORS IN 2006: $294,976

[1] "Defense Contracting Integrity: Opportunities Exist to Improve DOD's Oversight of Contractor Ethics Programs," pp. 35–36.

time, making a number of distinct contributions to the development of tools and techniques, policies, and procedures that are usable by other companies and industries. Its success can also be measured in the number of companies that have joined the DII, now amounting to approximately ninety members (see table 4.8). The DII's example was also an inspiration for other cross-sectoral efforts, such the Extractive Industry Initiative, which has brought together many of the world's leading mining and oil and gas companies around the issue of bribery and corruption.[60]

With the recent addition of mandatory disclosure of potential procurement fraud under the Federal Acquisition Regulation amendments of 2008, the DII is in a good position to serve its members in providing real-time compliance information and helping to develop best practices techniques and tools to meet such challenges. With some additional rigor and discipline added to the mix over the next few years, the DII, and other similar programs whether company-centric or industry-wide, can provide greater assurance to stakeholders everywhere—including employees, customers, the government, the media, nonprofits, or NGOs—that informed and substantive attempts at rooting out at least the worst kinds of violations and building a more effective and practical culture of integrity within organizations is something that is taken seriously within the organization.

The DII is a complex and sometimes perplexing organism. It is simultaneously constructive, productive, and highly useful, and not quite as rigorous or accountable as it would claim. Without the DII, the world of corporate ethics and compliance programs would not have developed as robustly as it has. The inner contradictions of the DII are also visible within its particular members. Take the case of GE, for example, which has probably the best and most developed internal ethics and compliance program of any company in the world, while simultaneously finding itself in the thicket of a compliance problem on a fairly periodic basis.[61]

Thus, while the overall legacy of DII is positive, its members would be wise over the next few years to consider invigorating some of the more rigorous aspects of maintaining a strong ethics and compliance program by focusing especially on two major initiatives: 1) developing independent third-party monitoring, testing, and auditing of the effectiveness of the internal ethics and compliance program (and considering publishing the results thereof); and 2) providing their chief ethics and compliance officers and teams with real tools and resources to do their work effectively internally, with real access to the company's highest governing body—the board of directors—before the government begins to mandate such actions in reaction to the next great wave of corporate scandals.

Notes

1. Andrea Bonime-Blanc has served as general counsel, chief ethics and compliance officer, corporate secretary, and risk officer for several global organizations for the past fifteen years. She is chairwoman of the board of directors of the Ethics & Compliance Officer Association and the author of numerous books and articles on business ethics, compliance, risk management, governance, constitutional change, and democratization, and she speaks and teaches frequently. She holds a joint JD and PhD from Columbia University and grew up in Europe.
2. "Defense Industry Initiatives on Business Ethics and Conduct," June 9, 1986.
3. The DII was created by a group of U.S.-based defense industry contractors. However, as it grew over the years, DII membership, as is evident from the current membership listed in table 4.8, also includes U.S. subsidiaries of non-U.S.-based defense contractors, such as U.K.-based BAE Systems, with defense contracts in place with the DOD.
4. See the next sections examining the composition and work of the Packard Commission.
5. This chapter uses the following terms to describe internal business conduct programs at corporations fairly interchangeably: "ethics and compliance (or compliance and ethics) program," "code of conduct program," and "business conduct program."
6. Today, several major organizations exist in the United States and Europe that are devoted to the issue of building internal organizational business conduct programs. Among them are the original associations of this kind, the Ethics Resource Center (ERC) and the Ethics Officer Association, today known as the Ethics and Compliance Officer Association (ECOA); and a number of other U.S.- and non-U.S.-based organizations such as the Society for Corporate Compliance and Ethics, the Open Compliance and Ethics Group, the Institute for Global Ethics, the U.K.-based Institute of Business Ethics, the France- and Belgium-based Cercle D'Ethique des Affaires/Cercle Europeen des Deontologues; and a number of national associations such as the Association of Compliance Officers of Ireland or regional associations such as the Australasian Compliance Institute and the European Business Ethics Network. Few of these organizations, except for the ERC, which played a major role in the creation of the DII, existed before 1992, when the ECOA was founded. Few of this addresses, however, another key parallel development over the past two to three decades, which has also had an indirect effect on the field of ethics and compliance but which is beyond the scope of this chapter, namely the development of the field of corporate social responsibility.
7. See http://en.wikipedia.org/wiki/Lockheed_bribery_scandals. Also see S. Hamilton, E. Eckardt, *The Lockheed Bribery Scandal*, www.CasePlace.org.
8. The Foreign Corrupt Practices Act of 1977, as amended, 15 U.S.C. §§78dd-1, et seq. (FCPA). For the legislative history of the FCPA, see www.justice.gov/criminal/fraud/fcpa/history/.

9. See Organization of Economic Cooperation and Development, "Update of Country Descriptions of Tax Legislation on the Tax Treatment of Bribes to Foreign Public Officials," June 2009, www.oecd.org/dataoecd/58/10/41353070.pdf.

10. Andrea Bonime-Blanc and Mark Brzezinski, "A New Era in Anti-Corruption: Governments Get Serious About Enforcement." Conference Board Executive Action Report, April 2010; Francois Vincke and Fritz Heimann, *Fighting Corruption: A Corporate Practices Manual*, ICC Publishing, 2003.

11. For the companies' own descriptions of their global ethics and compliance programs, see the following websites: EADS, www.eads.com/eads/int/en/our-company/our-governance /ethics-and-compliance.html; BAE, www.baesystems.com/CorporateResponsibility/ ResponsibleBusinessConduct/index.htm.

12. The Project on Government Oversight continues to this day to provide investigative reports and other resources aimed at exposing and eliminating government corruption. See www.pogo.org.

13. James Fairhall, "The Case for the $435 Hammer: Investigation of Pentagon's Procurement," *Washington Monthly*, January 1987; and Evan Thomas, Barrett Seaman, and Bruce Van Voorst, "Defensive About Defense," *Time*, March 10, 1986.

14. Defense Industry Initiative, "Origins and Development of the Defense Industry Initiative," www.dii.org.

15. The President's Blue Ribbon Commission on Defense Management, *A Quest for Excellence: Final Report to the President*, June 1986, p. 1 (herein referred to as the "Packard Commission Final Report"). Also see "The Government's Role in Preventing Contractor Abuse: Hearings Before the Subcommittee on Oversight and Investigations of the House Committee on Energy and Commerce," 99th Congress, First Session 402 (1985) (Statement of Joseph H. Sherick, Inspector General, DOD).

16. The Packard Commission Final Report, p. 75.

17. See www.en.wikipedia.org/wiki/The_Packard_Commission.

18. The Packard Commission Final Report, p. 75.

19. The Packard Commission Final Report, p. 76.

20. The Packard Commission Final Report, p. 76. Also see Market Opinion Research, U.S. National Survey: Public Attitudes on Defense Management, Appendix L in the Packard Commission Final Report, June 1986.

21. The Packard Commission Final Report, p. 77.

22. The Packard Commission Final Report, p. 77.

23. The Packard Commission Final Report, pp.77–78.

24. The Packard Commission Final Report, p. 78. Also see U.S. General Accounting Office, *Fraud in Government Programs: How Extensive Is It? How Can It Be Controlled?*, GAO/AFMD-81-57, at 28–30 (May 7, 1981).

25. The Packard Commission Final Report, pp. 81–83.

26. Ethics Resource Center, "Final Report and Recommendations on Voluntary Corporate Policies, Practices and Procedures Relating to Ethical Business Conduct," Appendix N in the Packard Commission Final Report.

27. As will be discussed later in this chapter, a famous procurement conflict-of-interest case yielding the conviction and incarceration of both a U.S. government DOD official and the chief financial officer of defense contractor Boeing took place in the early 2000s and involved exactly this type of risk.

28. The Packard Commission Final Report, p. 83.

29. The Packard Commission Final Report, p. 84.

30. Packard Commission Final Report, Appendix M, pp. 251–254.

31. Chapter Eight specifically provides that organizations that are found to have committed a crime and do not have compliance and ethics program elements in place to prevent or detect such a crime may not get the benefit of reductions in fines, jail terms, and other penalties. U.S. Sentencing Guidelines Manual Section 8B2, at www.ussc. gov/2007guid/8b2_1.html.

32. Defense Industry Initiative on Business Ethics and Conduct, "Origins and Development of the Defense Industry Initiative," in 2008 Public Accountability Report, available at www.dii.org/resources/annual-report-2008.pdf.

33. "Origins and Development of the Defense Industry Initiative," p. 25. For a roster of the members of the DII Steering Committee at the time of this writing, including such notables as the chief executive officers of UTC, Honeywell, Northrop Grumman, and Raytheon, see www.dii.org/our-companies/dii-steering-committee.

34. See the composition of the current working group, which includes the chief ethics and compliance officers of General Dynamics, Lockheed Martin, and Boeing, to name a few, at www.dii.org/our-companies/dii-working-group. There are publicly available resources on the DII website, including all of the presentations made at the annual DII conference, which usually takes place in June of each year.

35. DII 2009 Public Accountability Report, p. 29.

36. Only six years after the adoption of the DII principles, General Electric found itself in a major defense industry bribery scandal. See Richard W. Stevenson, "Pentagon Disciplines GE for Bribe Scandal," *New York Times*, June 3, 1992. Also, see table 4.4 for a summary of defense industry enforcement cases from 1992 through 2002, which include many of the leading members of the DII.

37. The U.S. Sentencing Guidelines were first adopted in 1991 and amended in 2004; in 2010 new amendments providing for further strengthening of the role of chief compliance officers within organizations became law on November 1, 2010.

38. For a comprehensive overview and analysis of the elements of an effective ethics and compliance program as inspired by Chapter Eight of the U.S. Sentencing Guidelines, see *The Ethics & Compliance Handbook: A Practical Guide from Leading Organizations*, Ethics & Compliance Officer Association Foundation, Waltham, MA, 2008.

39. The oddity about Chapter Eight of the U.S. Sentencing Guidelines is that it does not represent a law that is proactively enforced. It is a law that is applied in retrospect when a potential or actual corporate wrongdoer is under investigation or prosecution by the U.S. government. U.S. prosecutors will ask the corporation whether it has a compliance program in place, and will measure, through tools and practices developed by the DOJ, whether such a program is indeed in place. If the company does not seem to have a compliance program or has what appears to be only a veneer of a program, the DOJ will potentially charge the company with greater wrongdoing and or seek higher fines and penalties.

40. See www.theecoa.org/imis15/ECOAPublic/ABOUT_THE_ECOA/History _of_the_ECOA/ECOAPublic/AboutContent/History.aspx?hkey=43ce057e- 1870–408c-a6b3-b2f27c5b2950.

41. Ethics and Compliance Officer Association, www.theecoa.org.

42. The literature on the Enron and post-Enron scandals is vast, as is the literature on SOX. See bibliography appended to this chapter for a variety of useful resources relating to this period.

43. See table 4.3 in this chapter.

44. For a reader-friendly version of these amendments, see www.ussc.gov/2004guid /RFMay04.pdf.

45. A full statement of the 2010 amendments to Chapter Eight of the U.S Sentencing Guidelines can be found at www.ussc.gov/2010guid/finalamend10.pdf.

46. Ethics Resource Center, Ethics and Compliance Officer Association, et al., "Leading Corporate Integrity: Defining the Role of the Chief Ethics and Compliance Officer," January 2008. This paper is available at www.ethics.org/files/u5/CECO_Paper _UPDATED.pdf.

47. See Richard W. Stevenson, "Pentagon Disciplines GE for Bribe Scandal," *New York Times*, June 3, 1992.

48. Christopher H. Schmitt, "U.S. Wages of Sin: Why Lawbreakers Still Win Government Contracts," *U.S. News and World Report*, May 13, 2002.

49. See Sharon Otterman, "Iraq: Oil for Food Scandal," *Council on Foreign Relations*, October 28, 2005, available at www.cfr.org/publication/7631/iraq.html.

50. Jerry Markon and Renae Merle, "Former Boeing Executive Pleads Guilty," *Washington Post*, http://www.washingtonpost.com/ac2/wp-dyn?pagename=article&contentId=A27573–2004Apr20&notFound=true. Also see *60 Minutes*, "Cashing in for Profit? Who Cost Taxpayers Billions in Biggest Pentagon Scandal in Decades?", available at www.cbsnews.com/stories/2005/01/04/60II/main664652.shtml; and Leslie Wayne, "A Growing Military Contract Scandal," *New York Times*, November 8, 2004, available at www.query.nytimes.com/gst/fullpage.html?res=9C02E4DB153BF93BA35753C1A9629C8B63&sec=&spon=&pagewanted=all.

51. November 12, 2008, at 73 Fed. Reg. 67,064–67,093.

52. For a copy of the regulations, see www.edocket.access.gpo.gov/2008/E8–26906.htm. For a good summary of the implications of the new regulations to the defense industry, see Scott W. MacKay, Angela B. Styles, Carl Buzawa, and Douglas E. Perry, "Mandatory Disclosure: A New Reality," December 3, 2008, available at www.dii.org.

53. See the following contemporaneous accounts of several recent scandals: Barbara Ley Toeffler and Jennifer Reingold, *Final Accounting: Ambition, Greed, and the Fall of Arthur Andersen* (New York: Currency Doubleday, 2003); Cynthia Cooper, *Extraordinary Circumstances: The Journey of a Corporate Whistleblower* (New York: Wiley, 2008); and Bethany McLean and Peter Elkind, *The Smartest Guys in the Room: The Amazing Rise and Scandalous Fall of Enron* (Portfolio Hardcover, 2003).

54. In defense of the defense industry on this issue, especially at the time that the DII was launched and the DII questionnaire was created, this was all virgin compliance territory for any business or industry, and thus their ability to actually ask the right questions without necessarily having all the answers was admirable and prescient. To this day, the single most difficult and challenging part of implementing an organizational ethics and compliance program is measuring its effectiveness.

55. In 2010, the industry held its forum from June 14 to 16 in Washington, D.C., as it has every year since the founding of the DII. The agenda included a wide variety of ethics and compliance topics, including some recent developments the DII intended to avoid: the emergence in the past two years of mandatory disclosure of possible ethical and compliance violations to the government under the new procurement rues enacted in the 2008 Federal Acquisition Regulations, discussed earlier in this chapter. See www.crowell.com/pdf/2010-DII-BPF-Tentative-Agenda.pdf.

56. The 2009 questionnaire does not reflect the changes to be brought about by the 2010 amendments to the U.S. Sentencing Guidelines, which were enacted on November 1, 2010. The focus of these amendments has to do with providing compliance and ethics professionals with the ability to access and report directly to the highest governing body of a company when and if deemed necessary. A full statement of the 2010 amendments to Chapter Eight of the U.S Sentencing Guidelines can be found at www.ussc.gov/2010guid/finalamend10.pdf.

57. For example, GE provides a fairly detailed and open report on the elements of its business conduct program, including references to exactly how many and the nature of complaints received via its corporate whistle-blower hotline.

58. See the DII website for a variety of presentations and explanations of current initiatives: www.dii.org.

59. "Defense Contracting Integrity: Opportunities Exist to Improve DOD's Oversight of Contractor Ethics Programs," United States Government Accountability Office, Report to Congressional Committees. September 2009; pp. 35–36.

60. See the Extractive Industries Transparency Initiative website: www.eiti.or.

61. GE represents both the paradigm and the paradox of both the good corporate citizen—as the founder of the DII and a major contributor to the creation of effective ethics and compliance programs over the years—and as the recidivist, having been repeatedly in

the crosshairs of U.S. government enforcement agencies over the years for a variety of corruption, procurement fraud, and other cases. This was exemplified once again at the time of this writing by the imposition by the Securities and Exchange Commission of a $23.4 million FCPA-violation fine relating to the UN Oil for Food scandals. See www. sec.gov/news/press/2010/2010–133.htm.

5

International Council on Mining and Metals Sustainable Development Framework (ICMM)*

S. Prakash Sethi and Olga Emelianova

Mining Industry's Code of Conduct: Sustainable Development (SD) Framework

There has been growing recognition on the part of the mining companies that the *status quo* has become untenable. Mining companies around the world are being confronted with protests and demonstrations that often turn violent and lead to loss of human life, damage to property, and disruption in production operations. At the same time, they are being subjected to lawsuits in their home countries with potential damage awards in the billions of dollars.

In response, a group of mining companies organized under the aegis of the International Council on Mining and Metals (ICMM), created a set of guiding principles called the Sustainable Development (SD) Framework.[1] The ICMM SD Framework included ten main principles covering issues of concern in the mining industry (Exhibit 5.1).

The initiative, however, instantly became a subject of intense criticism by some of the largest and influential nongovernmental organizations in the area of environmental protection and sustainable development. These groups accused the industry of creating an organization that is completely controlled by the industry. The SD Framework defined the issues from the perspective of the industry and offered solutions advocated by the industry. They also described the code as devoid of specificity, requirements for compliance, and independent assurance of compliance verification.

ANTECEDENTS TO THE ICMM

The MMSD Project

In the late 1990s, rising public concern over environmental and social harm attributed to the extractive industry induced some of the leading companies

---

Exhibit 5.1   ICMM Sustainable Development Framework

Principle 1: **Corporate Governance**—Implement and maintain ethical business practices and sound systems of corporate governance.

Principle 2: **Corporate Decision Making**—Integrate sustainable development considerations within the corporate decision-making process.

Principle 3: **Human Rights**—Uphold fundamental human rights and respect cultures, customs, and values in dealings with employees and others who are affected by our activities.

Principle 4: **Risk Management**—Implement risk management strategies based on valid data and sound science.

Principle 5: **Health and Safety**—Seek continual improvement of our health and safety performance.

Principle 6: **Environment**—Seek continual improvement of our environmental performance.

Principle 7: **Biodiversity**—Contribute to conservation of biodiversity and integrated approaches to land-use planning.

Principle 8: **Material Stewardship**—Facilitate and encourage responsible product design, use, reuse, recycling, and disposal of our products.

Principle 9: **Community Development**—Contribute to the social, economic, and institutional development of the communities in which we operate.

Principle 10: **Independent Verification**—Implement effective and transparent engagement, communication, and independently verified reporting arrangements with our stakeholders.

---

in the industry to take steps to assure the public that their operations were conducted in a socially responsible manner and were compatible with sustainable development. One outcome of this movement was a new Global Mining Initiative (GMI), and through it the creation of the Mining, Minerals, and Sustainable Development (MMSD) project.

From its very inception, the GMI effort was spearheaded by three of the world's largest mining companies: Rio Tinto, Western Mining Corporation, and Phelps Dodge Corporation[2]. The companies' CEOs, Robert Wilson, Hugh Morgan, and Douglas Yearley, played leadership roles in creating the project. The start-up funds for the MMSD project were provided by twenty-seven companies, with each contributing at least $150,000, for a total of approximately $4 million. However, by the time its initial report was completed, the project had exceeded $7 million.

Launched in April 2000, MMSD was conceived as a wide-ranging research and consultation project. Therefore, it was felt that the study should be conducted in an objective and independent manner to ensure its credibility to the industry's external stakeholders. Consequently, conducting the study was contracted to the International Institute for Environment and Development (IIED). The governance structure of the MMSD project was composed of three groups: the Sponsors Group, the Assurance Group, and the Work Group, which were governed by a set of charters. The World Business Council for Sustainable Development (WBCSD) was responsible for coordinating the activities of the three groups.

The Sponsors Group was composed of twenty-seven commercial and thirteen noncommercial sponsors, who were engaged in planning and budgeting the research project. They also contributed to reviewing research materials. Assurance Group was represented by twenty-five experts from academic, industry, government, and civil society groups. However, these specialists served in the Assurance Groups on an individual basis and not as representatives of their respective organizations. The Assurance Group was responsible for reviewing the project and making decisions for future direction. The Work Group managed regional and national partnerships and commissioned research projects.[3]

The MMSD project took two years to set up multi-stakeholder dialogue and conduct thorough research. It included four regional partnerships, each with its own governance structure; about twenty national projects; twenty-three global workshops; and 175 working papers. According to the project documents, it involved more than 5,000 participants from various stakeholder groups from all over the world. During this period, twenty-one project bulletins were issued and sent to 5,000 stakeholders to report on the progress and to seek feedback on the draft report.

In one sense, the MMSD project was a model of deliberate planning, inclusive participation by all major stakeholders, open dialogue, transparency in external communications, and public disclosure (Hamann, 2003).[4] The final report called for the creation of the International Council on Mining and Metals (ICMM), which would develop and implement a Declaration on Mining, Minerals, and Sustainable Development. The report recommended that the declaration should include a commitment to periodic independent auditing of compliance. It stated that the declaration would be effective "if it includes a commitment to develop specific, measurable criteria as a set of protocols, along with a system of verification of performance."[5]

Critics of the industry, however, remained skeptical and unconvinced. They argued that the process was stage managed to stretch it over a long period of time to avoid the necessity of substantive action by way of changing mining practices. The industry was also accused of selecting NGOs that were friendly to its perspective and who may otherwise be relatively uninformed about the environmental and sustainability issues pertaining to the industry. Alternately, well-informed NGOs that participated in the process complained that their views were not given serious consideration. This led to a boycott of the MMSD project by many NGOs who were considered knowledgeable and experienced about issues pertaining to the extractive industry and sustainable development. The MMSD project was also criticized for a similar inadequacy in participation on the part of indigenous peoples and other affected groups.

Creation of a Certification System

One of the key efforts of the MMSD report was to articulate the role and creation of a certification system that would lend credence to and enhance public trust in the industry's efforts toward improved mining operations and that would contribute to an environmentally friendly, sustainable development. Having analyzed existing certification methods, the MMSD report suggested that extractive-industry certification, among other things, should:

- be based on the existing codes of conduct, policies, and procedures;
- provide a global framework, which would be implemented locally;
- provide a structure for stakeholder consideration;
- focus on addressing business needs;
- be initiated as an internal process; and,
- be gradually rolled out to include a wide group of stakeholders.

ICMM'S STRUCTURE AND MODUS OPERANDI

ICMM's Governance and Structure

ICMM is governed by its members, which currently include nineteen major companies and thirty commodity and regional trade and industry associations.[6] These include Africa Rainbow Metals (South Africa), Anglo American (South Africa), AngloGold Ashanti (South Africa), Barrick (Canada), BHP Billiton (Australia), Freeport-McMoRan Copper & Gold (United States), GoldCorp (Canada), Gold Fields (South Africa), Lihir Gold (Australia), Lonmin (South Africa), Minerals and Metals Group (Australia), Mitsubishi Materials (Japan), Newmont (United States), Nippon Mining & Metals (Japan), Rio Tinto (Australia), Sumitomo Metal Mining (Japan), Teck (Canada), Vale (Brazil), and Xstrata (Switzerland). The trade associations are a veritable group of intra-country industry groups and national and multinational organizations.

It should be noted at the outset that ICMM's governance structure is completely insular and has no formal representation from outside the industry. Its first chairman was Douglas Yearley, the retired chairman and CEO of Phelps Dodge Corporation. He was succeeded by Rio Tinto's CEO, Robert Wilson, who in turn was replaced by former executive chairman of Noranda, Inc, David Kerr, who is the current chairman of the ICMM's council.[7] Association members are represented by the Associations Coordination Group.

Creation of Sustainable Development Framework: The Core Principles

ICMM was established in October 2001 by the extractive industry leadership through the expansion of duties of another mining industry association—International Council on Metals and the Environment (ICME). Subsequently, at a 2002 conference in Toronto, the responsibilities to implement the recommendations of the MMSD report were given to the newly formed council. Between October 2001 and May 2003, ICMM initiated a wide variety of programs and activities that focused on setting standards for the industry's performance, creating international policy and collaborative networks, and catalyzing change for sector-wide action.

Finally, in May 2003, more than three years after the creation of the MMSD project, ICMM announced—with considerable fanfare by the industry—the result of this enormous effort in the form of the Sustainable Development (SD) Framework, which would henceforth guide the actions of the extractive industry. The intent of the SD Framework was to create a uniform set of principles that individual companies would adapt to their own situation either by following the Framework as currently redacted, or by creating their own codes of conduct to respond to their specific concerns within the Framework. The SD Framework outlined ten core principles against which the ICMM's members would measure their sustainable development performance.

The ten core principles were essentially inspirational by nature. They lacked specificity as to how they would be implemented and how they would allow member companies to measure their performance. Therefore, ICMM created a set of forty-six explanatory statements that would explicate and amplify the core principles (exhibit 5.2).

Exhibit 5.2   ICMM SD Framework: Explanatory Statements

Corporate Governance
Principle 1: Implement and maintain ethical business practices and sound systems of corporate governance.

Develop and implement company statements of ethical business principles and practices that management is committed to enforcing.

Implement policies and practices that seek to prevent bribery and corruption.

Comply with or exceed the requirements of host-country laws and regulations.

Work with governments, industry, and other stakeholders to achieve appropriate and effective public policy, laws, regulations, and procedures that facilitate the mining, minerals, and metals sector's contribution to sustainable development within national sustainable development strategies.

Corporate Decision-Making
Principle 2: Integrate sustainable development considerations within the corporate decision-making process.

Integrate sustainable development principles into company policies and practices.

Plan, design, operate, and close operations in a manner that enhances sustainable development.

Implement good practice and innovate to improve social, environmental, and economic performance while enhancing shareholder value.

Encourage customers, business partners, and suppliers of goods and services to adopt principles and practices that are comparable to our own.

Provide sustainable development training to ensure adequate competency at all levels among our own employees and those of contractors.

Support public policies and practices that foster open and competitive markets.

Human Rights
Principle 3: Uphold fundamental human rights and respect cultures, customs, and values in dealings with employees and others who are affected by our activities.

Ensure fair remuneration and work conditions for all employees, and do not use forced, compulsory, or child labor.

Provide for the constructive engagement of employees on matters of mutual concern.

Implement policies and practices designed to eliminate harassment and unfair discrimination in all aspects of our activities.

Ensure that all relevant staff, including security personnel, are provided with appropriate cultural and human rights training and guidance.

Minimize involuntary resettlement and compensate fairly for adverse effects on the community where they cannot be avoided.

Respect the culture and heritage of local communities, including indigenous peoples.

Risk Management
Principle 4: Implement risk management strategies based on valid data and sound science.

Consult with interested and affected parties in the identification, assessment, and management of all significant social, health, safety, environmental, and economic impacts associated with our activities.

Ensure regular review and updating of risk management systems.

Inform potentially affected parties of significant risks from mining, minerals, and metals operations and of the measures that will be taken to manage the potential risks effectively.

Develop, maintain, and test effective emergency response procedures in collaboration with potentially affected parties.

Health and Safety
Principle 5: Seek continual improvement of our health and safety performance.

Implement a management system focused on continual improvement of all aspects of operations that could have a significant impact on the health and safety of our own employees, those of contractors, and the communities where we operate.
Take all practical and reasonable measures to eliminate workplace fatalities, injuries, and diseases among our own employees and those of contractors.
Provide all employees with health and safety training, and require employees of contractors to have undergone such training.
Implement regular health surveillance and risk-based monitoring of employees.

Rehabilitate and reintegrate employees into operations following illness or injury, where feasible.

Environment
Principle 6: Seek continual improvement of our environmental performance.

Assess the positive and negative, the direct and indirect, and the cumulative environmental impacts of new projects, from exploration through closure.

Implement an environmental management system focused on continual improvement to review, prevent, mitigate, or ameliorate adverse environmental impacts.

Rehabilitate land disturbed or occupied by operations in accordance with appropriate post-mining land uses.

Provide for safe storage and disposal of residual wastes and process residues.

Design and plan all operations so that adequate resources are available to meet the closure requirements of all operations.

Biodiversity
Principle 7: Contribute to conservation of biodiversity and integrated approaches to land use planning.

Respect legally designated protected areas.

Disseminate scientific data on and promote practices and experiences in biodiversity assessment and management.

Support the development and implementation of scientifically sound, inclusive, and transparent procedures for integrated approaches to land use planning, biodiversity, conservation, and mining.

Material Stewardship Principle 8: Facilitate and encourage responsible product design, use, reuse, recycling, and disposal of our products.

Advance understanding of the properties of metals and minerals and their life-cycle effects on human health and the environment.

Conduct or support research and innovation that promote the use of products and technologies that are safe and efficient in their use of energy, natural resources, and other materials.

Develop and promote the concept of integrated materials management throughout the metals and minerals value chain.

Provide regulators and other stakeholders with scientifically sound data and analysis regarding our products and operations as a basis for regulatory decisions.

Support the development of scientifically sound policies, regulations, product standards, and material choice decisions that encourage the safe use of mineral and metal products.

Community DevelopmentPrinciple 9: Contribute to the social, economic, and institutional development of the communities in which we operate.

Engage at the earliest practical stage with likely affected parties to discuss and respond to issues and conflicts concerning the management of social impacts.

	Ensure that appropriate systems are in place for ongoing interaction with affected parties, making sure that minorities and other marginalized groups have equitable and culturally appropriate means of engagement.
	Contribute to community development from project development through closure in collaboration with host communities and their representatives.
	Encourage partnerships with governments and non-governmental organizations to ensure that programs (such as community health, education, and local business development) are well designed and effectively delivered.
	Enhance social and economic development by seeking opportunities to address poverty.
Independent Verification Principle 10: Implement effective and transparent engagement, communication, and independently verified reporting arrangements with our stakeholders.	Report on our economic, social, and environmental performance and contribution to sustainable development.
	Provide information that is timely, accurate, and relevant.
	Engage with and respond to stakeholders through open consultation processes.

Unfortunately, these explanatory statements also suffered from the same flaws as the core principles that they were intended to clarify. Even a cursory analysis reveals these amplificatory statements to be broad and vague enough to accommodate elephantine variations from the core values of the ICMM SD Framework and still qualify a company as meeting code standards. Rather than alleviating the problem of overly generalized principles, the amplifications have further exacerbated the problem by overly simplistic explanations.

ICMM's Programs and Activities, 2003–2009

Even a brief review of ICMM's activities would suggest that the organization has been expanding its reach by increasing its membership, which now consists of the seventeen largest mining companies. In addition, ICMM has thirty association members, including nineteen national and regional mining associations, and eleven regional and global commodity associations.

Over the period of 2003–2009, ICMM has primarily focused its efforts and resources in two areas:

(1) Developing a series of position papers that would clarify its principles.
(2) Preparing toolkits and participating in evaluation studies to assist industry members in implementing ICMM principles and to enhance sustainable business practices in their operations.

From all accounts, it has been a prodigious effort, if progress can be defined in terms of sheer volume of paperwork. More than 700 documents were produced and included in ICMM's online library over that period. ICMM has also engaged in a broad range of activities that would suggest progress in implementing the substance of its ten core principles. For example, ICMM currently has task forces in the six areas: environmental stewardship; health and safety; materials stewardship; socioeconomic development; reserves and resources; and communications.

Time and space do not allow a detailed description of the areas undertaken by the organization. However, a brief description of some of the more notable developments illustrate the point:

1. In August 2003, ICMM launched its first position statement, "Mining and Protected Areas." ICMM members agreed to a set of ten recognition statements with respect to mining and protected areas, and made a commitment to respect legally designated protected areas and not conduct exploration or mining operations in World Heritage areas. ICMM members also committed to working with the International Union for Conservation of Nature (IUCN), governments, intergovernmental organizations, and NGOs to develop tools for biodiversity conservation and best practice guidance for the industry.

2. In October 2004, ICMM came out with the position statement "Mineral Resources and Economic Development." This position statement was supposed to draw its guidelines from the Resource Endowment Project after its scheduled completion in 2005. A set of nine statements was substituted for ICMM's policy position in the interim to enhance the economic outcomes of investments in mineral resource development.

3. In May 2006, the Supplement on Climate Change was introduced. It consisted of six points that summarized ICMM members' positions in regard to the issue of climate change and outlined specific commitments. Member companies were expected to:
   a. continue to meet or exceed government requirements, contributing positively wherever they operate;
   b. monitor and report GHG emissions consistent with international standards, in line with their commitment to report in accordance with the Global Reporting Initiative framework;
   c. reduce GHG emissions as measured in absolute terms or per unit of production or through improved; and,
   d. strive toward energy efficiency.

4. In May 2008, ICMM developed the position statement "Mining and Indigenous Peoples," which elaborated on the issues of human rights, cultural heritage of traditional settlements, and sociopolitical development. The statement also amplified on the mining industry's commitments and future goals.

5. In February 2009, ICMM added another position statement, "Mercury Risk Management." The statement is composed of an introductory section outlining the relevance of the issue to the ICMM's ten principles, a list of eight recognition statements, and seven commitment statements. The supplement states that although organized mining no longer uses mercury in the production cycle, the issue is relevant with regard to artisanal small-

scale mining as well as in side operations and mercury-bearing products (e.g., lamps and switches). The supplement elaborated on the commitments of industry participants to provide better oversight of mercury-bearing materials and prevent potential contamination. The statement also indicated that mining companies commit to not opening any mines specifically for mercury production. It also notes ICMM members' commitment "to work on an integrated multi-stakeholder strategy through ICMM to reduce and eventually cease supplying mercury into the global market once policy and economically viable long-term technological solutions for the retirement of mercury are developed."

6. In May 2009, ICMM produced the position statement "Transparency of Mineral Revenues." This latest release integrated three other statements produced between 2003 and 2007 to support the Extractive Industries Transparency Initiative (EITI). This integrated document talks about the potential social, economic, and institutional benefits of mining that gives rise to the need of transparency in revenues in the mining industry. The previous position statements were named "ICMM Statement on the Extractive Industries Transparency Initiative" (2003), "Position Statement on Extractive Industries Transparency Initiative" (2005), and "ICMM Statement on the Extractive Industries Transparency Initiative" (2007).

Environmental Stewardship

Among its principles, the ICMM SD Framework calls for sustainable development and environmental stewardship of global mining operations. Under the umbrella of the Environmental Stewardship program, ICMM is currently working on two projects: integrated mine closure, and biodiversity, good practice, and offsets.

Integrated Mine Closure

In 2006, ICMM conducted an internal survey to review and assess existing practices on integrated environmental and social closure planning pertaining to mining operations and mine closing. The survey revealed mixed findings. Consequently, in 2008 the council prepared and released a toolkit called "Planning for Integrated Mine Closure."[8] This document provides details on managing all stages of mine planning and operation, models of risk and cost assessment, and checklists for various stages of planning. It also incorporates community development toolkit, stakeholder engagement, and biodiversity management. In 2009, a Spanish version of the toolkit was released for transparency in wider communities.

Biodiversity, Good Practice, and Offsets

In collaboration with International Union for Conservation of Nature, in 2006 ICMM released the document "Good Practice Guidance for Mining and Biodiversity."[9] The document provided details on specific tools and techniques of integrating biodiversity into project development, operations, planning, and implementation of mine closure. In addition, it offered tools for assessment, system management, stakeholder engagement, rehabilitation, and mitigation.

Resource Endowment Initiative

Another one of ICMM's projects is called the Resource Endorsement Initiative (REI), which was developed in collaborative effort with multi-stakeholder groups, and included the World Bank, UNCTAD, and the ICMM-led industry working group. It aims to assist governments, industry groups, and society at large to identify and manage factors that allow countries to benefit from their substantial resource endowments through economic growth and poverty reduction. As a part of the Resource Endorsement Initiative program, several projects are currently underway. ICMM is working on the final phase of REI by establishing partnerships in Tanzania, Ghana, and Peru. The council has also initiated a project on mining taxation review.

Community Development Toolkit

The Community Development Toolkit was published in November 2005 in collaboration with the World Bank and Energy Sector Management Assistance Program (ESMAP).[10] The 165-page document provides background information on mining policies and laws, and offers seventeen specific tools designed to be used throughout a project cycle, and cover assessment, planning, management, and evaluation phases of community development, as well as stakeholder relationships. The document is divided into five categories: assessment, planning, relationships, program management, and monitoring and evaluation.

Minerals Taxation

The rationale behind the minerals taxation initiative, developed in 2006, was the recognition that a country's tax policy exerts significant influence on the resources available for social and economic development. An independent consulting firm, Oxford Policy Management, was selected to review the issues and challenges in the design and application of minerals taxation regimes. To ensure the integrity of the review, an independent advisory board was created to oversee the project. It was composed of four specialists in mining taxation: Philip Daniel (IMF), Tom King (KPMG), Ted Moran (Georgetown University), and Jim Otto (University of Denver). The first draft of the report was completed in March 2008. After a thorough review by the advisory board and ICMM member companies, the final version of the review was released in March 2009.[11] The review examined different types of regimes and taxation systems, and concluded that there was an obvious need and interest both on the part of local governments and mining companies to establish clear and legitimate taxation regimes.

Socioeconomic Development

ICMM's work with socioeconomic development of the regions with mining operations pertained to the designing of a Community Development Toolkit covering two programs: business and human rights, and treatment of the indigenous people. In the area of business and human rights, ICMM has been granted observer status for the Voluntary Principles on Security and Human Rights (VPs). In September 2008, during the Senate Judiciary Committee Subcommittee on Human Rights and Law hearing on voluntary principles, ICMM endorsed and expressed strong support to the VPs. The council also worked with John Ruggie, special representative for business and human rights to the United Nations, to provide updates on the mining industry's initiatives and collaborative action in preventing human rights abuses. All together, ICMM has made three submissions to the UN Special Representative since 2005. In July 2009, ICMM came out with its first human rights publication, "Human Rights in the Metals and Mining Industry: Overview, Management Approach, and Issues."[12] The publication reviews how ICMM member companies deal with human rights challenges, and is aimed at reducing the dilemmas of ICMM members and other companies in the mining industry. The theoretical basis of this publication is based on the "protect, respect, remedy" framework produced by John Ruggie in 2008.

ICMM's work on the issues of indigenous peoples was initiated in 2002. In May 2005, a detailed review called "Mining and Indigenous Peoples Issues" was prepared. Later in the same year, ICMM started a dialogue with IUCN (the World Conservation Union) on the issue of indigenous peoples rights. A result of these two processes was the formulation of a position statement that was accepted and approved by the ICMM Member Council in 2008. Ethical Investment Research Services (EIRIS) recognized ICMM's commitment to the practices involving indigenous people as a good industry practice. According to a report titled "Indigenous Rights: Risks and Opportunities for Investors," released by EIRIS, the mining sector was recognized as a best-performing sector in dealing with indigenous peoples' issues.[13]

Material Stewardship

ICMM has produced a number of position papers and toolkits that promote, among others, responsible design, use, reuse, recycling, and disposal of the materials produced. These toolkits cover a variety of topics, such as life-cycle management, chemical management, and sustainable consumption and production.

In May 2009, ICMM launched the Minerals and Metal Management 2020 Strategy[14]—an action plan consisting of twenty-three priority actions for safe and responsible production in the mining and metals sector. The plan's main goal, that minerals and metals should be "used and produced in ways that minimize significant adverse effects on human health and the environment by 2020," supports the objective of the UN's Strategic Approach to International Chemicals Management (SAICM). Reviewed by a key group of stakeholders, these actions promoting integrative chemical management extend to 2020 and beyond.

According to Angel Gurria, secretary-general of the OECD, "The action plan clearly demonstrates the commitment of the ICMM members to take responsibility of the safety of their products at all stages of the life cycle." In a letter to ICMM, Achim Steiner, executive director of the United Nations Environment Programme (UNEP), states, "The ICMM Global Action Plan initiative [demonstrates] commitment to the implementation of the Strategic Approach as well as providing an example for others to follow."[15]

Health and Safety

In November 2006, ICMM held an international health and safety conference in Johannesburg, South Africa. The event brought together more than 300 participants from the mining sector, and offered seminars and workshops on issues of employee work safety, community relations, and health-related programs. In 2007, ICMM put together a database of materials and agents of concern within the minerals sector with corresponding data on occupational exposure limits (OELs). Another important document with respect to health and safety was "Good Practice Guidance on HIV/AIDS, TB, and Malaria," produced in August 2008. The document provided step-by-step descriptions of HIV/AIDS, tuberculosis, and malaria medical programs management, offered information on preventive health-care programs, and resources management. A year later, in August 2009, ICMM published another important document called "Good Practice Guidance on Occupational Health Risk Assessment (HRA)."[16] This document is a step-by-step information resource that helps HRA commissioners identify health hazards and their effects, assess exposure levels, analyze the effectiveness of existing control measures and other steps in carrying out an HRA.

ANALYSIS AND EVALUATION

Notwithstanding the massive scale of activities described in the previous section, it is not clear what, if anything, these activities has achieved in the more effective implementation of ICMM principles. All of these so-called toolkits and evaluative efforts imply that the mining industry is in a nascent stage of development and thus needs a coordinated effort to develop implementation tools that are both cost efficient and operationally effective. In reality, the mining industry includes some of the largest and most capital-intensive companies with decades of operations experience in the most difficult natural and human environments. The problems confronting the industry are also well known. What is necessary, therefore, are not new tools, but determination to take effective action.

In an earlier section of this book, we outlined eight necessary preconditions for a voluntary code of conduct to be efficient, effective, and credible. These preconditions require that an industry-wide code of conduct addresses substantive issues that underlie society's concerns about the industry's operating practices. The principles outlined must be specific, and the performance measured must be realistic in magnitude and time frame. There must be an effective internal implementation system, management performance evaluation, independent governance structure, and an independent external monitoring and compliance verification system. Finally, there must be maximum transparency and disclosure to the public.

In this section we undertake a systematic analysis of the ICMM's principles, policies, programs, and implementation procedures in the context of their intended goals, and the extent to which they have been achieved and are likely to be achieved in the foreseeable future. In particular, we examine (a) the specific elements of the program content; (b) the operational framework; (c) the governance structure; and (d) accountability assurances that are intended to enhance or deter the industry in meeting its promises to society.

ICMM's Principles: Gap between Promises and Performance

It has been almost nine years since the extractive industry launched its initiative to respond to public concerns about its operational practices and their potential negative side effects on the environment and the people who are affected by the industry's activities. The industry has spent millions of dollars in developing new programs intended to demonstrate the sincerity of its commitment toward meeting its self-professed goals.

ICMM Core Principles and Amplifications

A careful reading of the ten principles in the SD Framework suggests that they are primarily inspirational in character, with heavy emphasis on "intent" and calls for "commitment" on the part of member companies to improve their performance along indicated dimensions. As such, any knowledgeable expert, or a good PR person, could have written them in a relatively short time.

A major flaw of these principles lies in their lack of specificity. For example, the first principle states its goal to "implement and maintain ethical business practices and sound system of corporate governance." However, there is no discussion of what constitutes "ethical business practices," or a "sound system of corporate governance." While we may all agree with the spirit of these principles, we may be far apart as to their transformation in actual business practices. As discussed earlier, the system of corporate governance as outlined in the MMSD report and incorporated in ICMM structure fails to meet the spirit of these principles.

To take another example, consider principle six, which calls for "continual improvement of our environmental performance." Unfortunately, such a statement asks a question rather than answers one—that is, what is a company's current level of environmental performance and what would constitute acceptable level of improvement? Even at a conceptual level, the principle could have been more specific. For example, there could be a minimum level of performance-specific environmental practices to which all industry members would be expected to adhere. From this standard, one could measure "improvement" in two ways: (a) the capacity of a company to improve versus its actual performance, and (b) the narrowing of the gap between a company's performance and societal expectations. Unfortunately, the principle is silent on these issues. The current approach provides a "safe harbor" for companies that are lagging in meeting the minimal standards of performance simply because the "minimum level" has not been specified. Under these conditions, "continual improvement" is a meaningless standard and may end up misleading the public as to a company's performance on this issue.

Principle ten calls for effective and transparent engagement with stakeholders, including "independently verified reporting arrangements." However, ICMM does not provide any information regarding how company performance would be independently verified and how results would be reported to the public. Equally important, ICMM does not suggest any approaches to what the industry would do in the event that a member company's verification procedures are lacking in independence. Nor does it indicate what the industry might do in the event that a member company declines to make its findings public with regard to its compliance with the ICMM framework. When viewed in the context of analytical framework presented earlier, it becomes apparent that ICMM's process of code formulation, rules of governance, and code provisions fall within the purview of what we consider to be drawbacks of group-based code formulation. The overwhelming dominance of industry interests has been pervasive in every aspect of ICMM's deliberations. Code formulation, when there is no prior established standards, must be largely independent (but not hostile) to industry's interests in order to have realistic inputs from other segments of society that are adversely affected by the industry's current practices.

ICMM's Governance Structure

The SD Framework was created through an extensive consultative process and supported by a budget of more than $7 million. There is, however, little evidence to show that it benefited in any meaningful manner from the intensive, multi-stakeholder participation and production of voluminous reports. The MMSD report had called for a new governance structure that would have industry involvement but would not be dominated by it. This has turned out not to be the case.

ICMM's governance structure is completely insular and controlled entirely by the member companies. From its very inception, its governance council has been made up of the CEOs of all ICMM member companies, two elected representatives from the member associations, and ICMM's president. It meets twice a year to set the strategic direction for ICMM and decide on policy. The current chairman of ICMM Council is Richard Adkerson, president and chief executive officer of Freeport-McMoRan Copper & Gold. The council is composed of seventeen members, who are senior executives of ICMM's member companies.

The report had also recommended that the industry itself should be the primary provider of funds for the initiative. The combination of the two factors, control of decision making and funding, would raise serious questions about the effectiveness of the organization in implementing its principles and its credibility as to the industry's assertions of progress in implementing ICMM's principles. It would also require a higher burden of proof to demonstrate its responsiveness to society's needs where they are found to be inconsistent with and unacceptable to the industry members' economic interests.

The council is supported by the Executive Working Group, which meets four times a year and is the primary vehicle through which members engage with each other and the ICMM secretariat. It is composed of nominated representatives (known as principal liaisons) from each of the company and association members.

The Executive Working Group is responsible for the effective implementation of the ICMM work program and budget. It is supported by a number of specialist task forces, through which members actively participate in ICMM projects. In addition, ICMM has an Associations Coordination Group. This group meets twice a year, and is the vehicle for associations to discuss common strategic issues and provide input to the council and Executive Working Group. It also elects two representatives (the group chairman plus one other) to sit on the ICMM council for a two-year term.

In this sense, ICMM's current governance structure is closer to that of industry-based trade associations, which are formed to protect industry members' interests in their traditional business activities. It fails to meet the criteria of independence. It even falls below the standards adopted by other industry groups in natural resources, manufacturing, and internationally oriented industry-trade associations, which seek to involve nonindustry stakeholders at the governance and consultative levels.[17]

It can be stated without exception that ICMM's governance structure and financial support are in clear violation of MMSD recommendations, which were quite weak to begin with. This structure does not allow for any meaningful participation from knowledgeable experts or public representatives that would allow for independent external input and a measure of transparency to the board's deliberations.

It should also be noted that ICMM's has not taken any action to another of the MMSD recommendation—to create a certification system to verify individual company compliance with ICMM principles and performance standards. An effective and transparent system of verification would go a long way in enhancing the industry's credibility and public trust.

As a matter of common sense, it would seem illogical for an industry to opt for such a governance structure where (a) it is under severe public criticism; (b) lacks public trust and confidence and industry's assertions of responsible behavior; and (c) the industry needs to demonstrate a good-faith effort and transparency in its conduct. The governance structure in this instance is akin to that of trade groups where inclusiveness and insularity are designed to keep all members in line to protect an industry-wide position, and to ensure that the group's findings and recommendations do not deviate from the intentions of the industry leaders. The control over budget ensures that ICMM will undertake only those activities that are approved by industry leaders and that all actions and pronouncements by ICMM would be nothing more than the industry leaders' preferred position. In other words, ICMM provides a "respectable cover" for packaging the industry's viewpoint. Therefore, it becomes inevitable that no outsider should be allowed access to real deliberations and decision making at the top level of governance.

It should, therefore, come as no surprise that industry's performance has the hallmark of extensive and intensive activity, but with results that are hard to measure and members' compliance seldom confirmed through independent external verification. A review of ICMM's plans indicate that even if all of the proposals currently under review are implemented, they are unlikely to improve the quality of code implementation in terms of delivering results that are meaningful; have direct relation to societal expectations; and accurately and objectively measure individual company performance, which is independently monitored and verified and also provide maximum transparency in public disclosure.

ICMM's Activities, Compliance, and Reporting Guidelines

Program Development and Implementation Procedures

From its inception in 2001 and continuing through 2009, ICMM has embarked upon a host of studies covering almost every conceivable area of activity where issues have been raised concerning the industry's activities and performance. Even a brief summary of these activities—outlined in an earlier section—would suggest that ICMM has been hyperactive in organizing multistakeholder groups, preparing comprehensive reports on specific issues, and even preparing toolkits for member companies to assist them in implementing various programs.

From the industry's perspective, these programs provide strong evidence of its efforts toward progressive reform. Nevertheless, an overall review of their actual implementation leaves considerable room for skepticism.

The plethora of detailed studies, reports, and toolkits, which to date have consumed an overwhelming majority of ICMM's resources, would suggest that the extractive industry must have been living in the Stone Age prior to the incarnation of ICMM. One wonders why the leading companies in the mining industry did not take many of the actions that were known to them long before ICMM was created. A cynic might also argue that this hyperactivity is designed to distract public attention from the actual compliance and toward implementing reform. Moreover, almost every recommended measure for compliance leaves much wiggle room for member companies to postpone and to modify their compliance with ICMM standards.

It is no wonder, therefore, that industry critics have remained dissatisfied with the gap between the promises and performance of ICMM and its member companies.[18] For example, Brandon Prosansky, in his article "Mining Gold in Conflict Zone: The Context, Ramifications, and Lessons of AngloGold Ashanti's Activities in the Democratic Republic of the Congo," described AngloGold Ashanti's operational environment in DRC and its indirect involvement in human rights abuses in the area. The article provided explicit evidence of AngloGold Ashanti's interactions with the Nationalist and Integrationist Front (FNI), a powerful, armed group responsible for violent actions against the local Congolese population. While the company claimed that contact and interaction with FNI was unavoidable since FNI was in de facto control of the mines in the Ituri area, AngloGold Ashanti did not make any effort to regulate the situation and prevent possible human right conflicts. In regard to AngloGold Ashanti's commitment to the ICMM principles to uphold fundamental human rights, Prosansky states that the company "arguably violated that commitment by failing to take action to prevent FNI abuses."[19]

In 2007, Newmont's shareholders passed a resolution asking the company to begin a Community Relations Review (CRR) of the company's operations. The review, commissioned and funded by Newmont, took two years. The report noted that despite its efforts, the company failed to build strong community relations at five of its principle mine sites in Nevada, Peru, Indonesia, Ghana, and New Zealand.[20]

Other researchers have claimed that mining operations do not guarantee future economic development of the region. A study produced by Oxfam America in 2008 on the economic development of Central America argues that there is no long-term increase in the economic growth among Latin American countries that have experienced a natural resource boom.[21] The study refers to the issue of expatriation of profits, reduction in local employment due to the availability of technology and opportunities to bring experienced and qualified people from other regions, and overall cost of the operations. In addition, local communities are left to deal with the social and environmental effects of the mining operations for years ahead.[22] ICMM's Resource Endorsement Initiative study offers contrary findings: "Undertaken in the right way, investment in the extractive industries can provide a critical kick-start to broader economic and social development."[23]

In November 2007, the British group War on Wants produced a report that provided a list of human rights violations in which mining companies were complicit. It distinguished three types of such involvement.

1. "Silent complicity" is held to exist where companies fail to speak out against clear patterns of human rights violation in the areas where they are operating.
2. "Beneficial complicity" pertains to when companies are the beneficiaries of human rights abuses committed by state forces—as in many of the cases described in this report.
3. "Direct complicity" occurs when a company provides assistance to a body, which then commits a human rights violation.[24]

The report claimed that industry self-regulation in the form of voluntary codes had been shown to be ineffective, and urged the UK government to take action in acknowledging the harm caused by British mining companies to the communities, and designing new standards and regulations to ensure corporate accountability in the international arena.[25]

Paul Mitchell, ICMM's president at that time, expressed strong disagreement with the claims and accusations in the report, and called it "a selective and inaccurate account of a complex subject." He argued that mining companies were among the very few sources of investment in the world's poorest countries, and that investment is essential for economic growth and peace.[26]

Another report, prepared jointly by Earthworks and Oxfam America as a part of the No Dirty Gold campaign, once again called for public attention to numerous violations of human rights caused or neglected by mining companies' operations. The report proposed an alternative set of rules of operations for mining companies, called "The Golden Rules."[27] The response letter from Paul Mitchell noted that criticism of the report was based on "stale, dated, and incorrect information," and that the report did not recognize progress made by ICMM and ICMM member companies in regard to implementing the SD Framework.[28]

Corporate Accountability and Performance Verification

ICMM's current guidelines indicate that independent monitoring and public reporting are to be voluntary and at the discretion of individual companies. Principle ten calls for implementation of effective and transparent engagement, communication, and independently verified reporting arrangements with all relevant stakeholders.

ICMM members' commitment to provide periodic reporting along GRI requirements specified that for the first reporting cycle, the 2006 annual reports, the member companies were to report "informally" against the guidelines. This meant that the companies were not required to cover all of the content of the GRI Framework, but should gradually introduce the GRI Framework in preparation of reports in the future.

ICMM's motion further stated that within two reporting cycles, companies-signatories would proceed to reporting "in accordance" with the GRI Framework. This commitment to report "in accordance" with GRI Framework, however, was subject to possible extension: "[I]t is recognized that some members may require an additional reporting cycle," and the transition to the new reporting level should be done "as soon as practical."

It should be noted here that GRI reporting procedures have their primary focus on self-reporting, where organizations are provided with a large measure of flexibility in choosing and interpreting various standards of performance. The system is almost entirely process-oriented, with inadequate emphasis on outcome-oriented measures. Therefore, it seems that ICMM's concerns for external reporting envisaged an unusually slow and deliberate process to postpone any meaningful disclosure as far into the future as possible.

ICMM's Framework, however, has no provision as to how the industry will monitor member companies' compliance with principles and how it would persuade the recalcitrant members to improve their compliance. In early 2010, ICMM announced acceptance of the Global Reporting Initiative Framework for corporate performance reporting. While the reporting framework set up by GRI provides a mechanism to report performance—however defined—it does not provide any standards against which individual company performance could be measured or evaluated for adequacy. Nor does it set minimum standards in any area of the mining industry's operations. A review of ICMM's plans for the future suggests that even if all of the proposals currently under review are implemented, they are unlikely to improve the quality of code implementation. Therefore, in the absence of standardized measures of performance, uniformity in reporting, and transparency in full disclosure, the notion of voluntary codes of conduct is rendered almost worthless since it lacks any assurance of credibility and accuracy.

Reporting Guidelines

Initial formulation of ICMM's principles and procedures called for the desirability of adequate public reporting of individual company compliance with ICMM's principles. In the beginning of 2005 and two years after the launch of the principles, ICMM added a commitment to report companies' performance along the Global Reporting Initiative (GRI) Guidelines. A draft GRI Supplement for the Mining and Metals Sector was released and reviewed by a working group composed of twenty members (ten industry representatives and ten stakeholders).

In October 2006, GRI launched its G3 Sustainability Reporting Guidelines, which provided a reporting framework for mining companies. In response, ICMM prepared a detailed resource guide to assist member companies in preparing annual CSR sustainability reports "in accordance" with GRI guidelines. The guide links ICMM principles with relevant GRI requirements, and refers to various resources, tools, protocols, codes, policies, and assurance standards used in submitting required information, such as the GHG protocol, water protocol, ICTI, London Benchmarking Group, IFRS and IASB standards, ISO1400, SA8000, OECD Guidelines, et cetera.

ICMM's Integrity Assurance

ICMM's SD Framework requires the signatory companies to provide independent assurance that ICMM commitments are met. In May 2006, the ICMM council approved a pilot assurance procedure to establish the requirements for member companies to meet the ICMM assurance commitment. These requirements include:

1. Providing a statement in the annual public report on how the company complies with the ICMM SD Principles and Reporting commitments.
2. Seeking confirmation that its SD report meets Level A+ of the G3 Guidelines.
3. Having its SD report assured by a third party consistent with this procedure.

The assurance procedure guidelines are linked to assurance requirements of GRI and ICMM Frameworks. They suggest practical steps that must be taken in preparing assurance statements. The guide also provides a list of necessary requirements to ensure the independence of the assurance body and sets boundaries of assurance scope. ICMM requires companies to provide independent assurance and conclusions/opinions relating to the content and integrity of reported information for the following subject matters:

Subject Matter 1: The alignment of a member company's sustainability policies to ICMM's ten principles and any mandatory requirements in ICMM position statements.

Subject Matter 2: The company's material SD risks and opportunities based on its own review of the business and the views and expectations of its stakeholders.

Subject Matter 3: The existence and status of implementation of systems and approaches that a company is using to manage each (or a selection) of the identified material SD risks and opportunities.

Subject Matter 4: The company's reported performance during the given reporting period for each (or a selection) of the identified material SD risks and opportunities.

Subject Matter 5: The company's self-declared application level of the G3 Guidelines.

The timeline included in the assurance procedure guide indicates that companies/signatories are required to include independent assurance in the annual public report starting in 2009 (for the fiscal year 2008) on subject matters one and five, and beginning in 2010 on all five subject matters.

There is some ambiguity in ICMM's requirements for compliance. Contrary to ICMM's previously stated commitment, its website states (as of May 19, 2009) that the assurance procedure "also takes into account recent developments in the external reporting and assurance environment, and in particular the May 2008 commitment of ICMM members to report in accordance with the G3 Guidelines." As noted previously, ICMM made a commitment in regard to the annual reporting along GRI requirements in 2005 and in 2006 created a resource guide to respond to the Mining and Metal Supplement.

Concluding Observations

On the surface, ICMM's Sustainable Development Framework offers one of the most significant opportunities to demonstrate the effectiveness of an industry-based framework for sustainable development. If implemented properly, it could have far-reaching consequences for the industry's economic and financial health.

In so doing, it would also go a long way in engendering greater public trust in the industry's promises and assertions of progress. Unfortunately, the industry's chosen course in the form of governance structure and program implementation makes it all but impossible for ICMM to succeed in its claimed objectives. It has become an elaborate edifice for project activities with little possibility of achieving intended outcomes.

In this sense, ICMM's response to its critics is quite revealing and tends to confirm the pessimism expressed by the industry's critics when it defends its performance to date more in the nature of "work in progress" rather than goals accomplished. For example, in a recent communication with the authors, ICMM provided the following information concerning its progress toward implementation of its sustainable framework.

- Reporting procedures for SD principles: The procedures have been developed in partnership with the GRI through a multi-stakeholder process. It will soon be published by GRI as the Mining and Metals Reporting Supplement and details of the current document are available on both of our websites. After a phase in period all ICMM member companies will be required to report against these indicators, making ICMM the largest industry group reporting "in accordance" with GRI procedures.

- We agree that the mining industry should adopt good practices whenever it is practical and possible to do so. I cannot speak on behalf of the whole mining sector, only ICMM's members, but believe that our members have gone to considerable lengths to better understand good practices and to develop techniques to enable these to be implemented. Examples of this are the MMSD process and joint projects with organizations like the World Bank, UNEP, the GRI and IUCN on a range of key issues including biodiversity, community and national economic development, transparency and public reporting, materials stewardship and responding to emergencies.

The reality is that it takes some time to develop and apply good practices in any economic sector. One example is reporting sustainable development performance; we have adopted a set of SD principles, are just about to adopt a formal reporting arrangement, and in the coming year will develop procedures for verification. Thus this process, undertaken collaboratively with the GRI and a multi-stakeholder group, will take about three years to complete although where possible results have been progressively adopted. I do not believe that any shorter period would have been realistic. In the interim it would be possible to be critical about not following "best practice." However, any fair or pragmatic analysis would have to acknowledge the range of initiatives we are pursuing and compare them to other sectors nearly all of which are doing much less. The latter is a valid benchmark just as much as a theoretical notion of what might be best practice.

- At present we have no means of pursuing complaints against members other than referring them to our Council for consideration and, possibly, disciplinary action. It is important to note that we have not received any such complaints to date but the Council does have powers to suspend or terminate membership if it felt this was appropriate.[29]

In the opinion of the authors, and given the long history of the mining industry, these efforts are too tame and their progress is too slow. The mining industry has had decades of experience in dealing with environmental issues and coping with the problems of corruption, unstable governments, human rights abuses, and protecting the legitimate rights of the indigenous peoples.

Based on the developments of ICMM's programs and its progress to date, the mining industry cannot assert that it intends to make substantive improvements in alleviating environmental and social problems through its commitment to ICMM. For this to happen, both the issues and the measures of compliance must be clearly specified a priori before an industry-based framework can provide guidance to member companies that would be viable and credible to the industry's external constituencies. Any such framework must explicitly recognize the need for outcome-oriented standards that can be objectively measured and independently verified.

As currently stated, neither the principles nor their amplifications provide any standards that are:

a. clearly stated as "absolute minimum" in a manner that is quantitatively defined and objectively measured. Is there anything that the industry asks its member companies to do or refrain from doing which leaves no wiggle room? Are there any issues and standards that are considered to be of "zero tolerance" and where less than full compliance is not an option?

b. Why is it that no amplification indicators call for "outcome-oriented" standards of performance? Why can't there be minimum quantitative standards with regard to toxic waste, wastewater treatment, or disposal of mine waste, to name a few?

c. How does the industry define fair remuneration and working conditions? What if the local government's minimum wages and working conditions are considered grossly inadequate and are widely violated? What if the companies themselves have played an important role in encouraging local governments to keep these wages deliberately low and impose working conditions that border on involuntary servitude? And where does the notion of "living wage" fit in this equation?

d. How does the industry plan to protect the property rights and cultural heritage of indigenous peoples where the host country's governments, with or without the complicit acquiescence of the mining companies, are involved?

Individual Member Companies' Compliance Efforts

The success of an industry- or group-based voluntary code depends on the extent to which member companies comply with the code in their own operations. The voluntary nature of the Framework means that members of ICMM must press forward to make the general and aspirational Framework set out by ICMM into (1) concrete codes of conduct that address specific countries and sites in which mines are operated, and (2) actual deliverable results that can be audited and reported to company management, local communities, and the general public. Without such an amplification of the Sustainable Development Framework, the efforts of the ICMM and its members will not only be unproductive, but also will further hurt the reputation of the industry.

It follows, therefore, that the performance-compliance level of the group's weakest member will adversely affect that of the entire group.

Mining companies, even when acting individually, possess tremendous economic leverage to induce host countries into adopting policies advocated by these companies. When acting collectively, they can be a force for positive change that would generate tremendous aggregate wealth. They can also influence host countries to adopt policies to ensure that this wealth is used prudently so as to benefit both current and future generations.

To date, the record of companies in the mining as well as oil and gas industries has not been encouraging in this respect. However, this need not be the case for the future. Through ICMM, the extractive industry has recognized the problems that it must confront. It has also established general guidelines to address those issues. Now the companies that helped to establish those guidelines must be willing to take the next and more difficult step—to put the ICMM Sustainable Development Framework into real operational form, company by company and site by site. They must prove to the world through actions and accurate auditing and reporting that the mining industry can walk the walk as well as talk the talk.

Principle ten of ICMM's SD Framework and its amplifications calls for timely, accurate, and relevant reporting of economic, social, and environmental performance of ICMM member companies and their contribution to sustainable development. In our discussion of the preconditions to effective implementations of group-based voluntary codes of conduct, we argued that code compliance must be integrated into the firm's normal decision-making structure and systems. Furthermore, the organization must have internal monitoring and compliance assurance systems to ensure the accuracy and integrity of the company's sustainability reports.

In evaluating the performance of individual companies, we took a somewhat different approach, which would tilt the performance-evaluation measures in favor of the industry. Rather than looking at the weakest members of the group, we chose for our analysis the sustainability reports of four of the leading companies in the industry whose CEOs hold leadership positions in ICMM. The companies included in our analysis are Anglo-American, Newmont Mining, BHP Billiton, and Rio Tinto.

The overall picture revealed in these reports was quite disappointing. Very large parts of the reports were pictorial and descriptive. They emphasized process rather than output, and provided information that the companies would like the public to know rather than the information that the public would want the companies to provide. Where data were provided, they were essentially descriptive facts and lacked relevant context. The reports did not have any comparative analysis or points of reference where individual company performance is measured against best practices, targets to be achieved, and shortfalls, if any. There was little information as to the company's actions where its operations had been previously criticized by external stakeholders.

Another glaring absence in the reports was a complete absence of systematic analysis of the companies' operations and their compliance with the ICMM's ten principles and their amplifications. It would be impossible for a person analyzing these reports to state that Company A has reached a certain percentage of compliance with individual principles and that its overall compliance with the ICMM principles has reached, say, 80 percent compared with 60 percent in the year before.

For ICMM to be the voice of the mining industry, and in particular its member companies, which are among the largest and most successful mining companies, it must take steps toward a more meaningful implementation of the Sustainable Development Framework.

1. Establish clear-cut standards of conduct that would be the most attainable and best possible standards given in the current state of technology and

societal expectations. Furthermore, these standards should not be limited to environmental issues, but must encompass any others, including the issues of bribery and corruption, human rights abuses, rights of the indigenous people, and transparency in its dealing with local governments and especially the army and police in the host country. A starting point in this direction would be the Voluntary Principles on Security and Human Rights, jointly promulgated by the governments of the United States and the United Kingdom on December 19, 2000.

2. Establish minimum standards of conduct in the above-mentioned areas that would be considered inviolate under any set of conditions and that the member countries would pledge never to violate.

3. Review the current policies and practices of member companies to ensure their total compliance with the inviolate minimum standards of conduct.

4. Require member companies to develop their own codes of conduct. They would comply with the broad principles enumerated in the SD Framework, but would also be cognizant of unique conditions prevalent in different countries with mining operations.

5. Establish criteria for creating standards for performance evaluation and independent external monitoring systems for compliance verification. Any monitoring system must be an integral part of code compliance on a regular basis.

6. Ensure maximum transparency in public disclosure of member companies' performance with its code compliance.

Appendix 5.1

MEMBER ASSOCIATIONS

Cámara Argentina de Empresarios Mineros (CAEM)
Cámara Asomineros Andi—Colombia
Cámara Minera de México
Cámara Minera de Venezuela (CAMIVEN)
Chamber of Mines of South Africa
China International Mining Group
Cobalt Development Institute
Consejo Minero de Chile A.G.
Eurometaux
Euromines
Federation of Indian Mineral Industries
Indonesian Mining Association
Instituto Brasileiro de Mineraçao
International Aluminium Institute
International Copper Association (ICA)
International Lead Association
International Molybdenum Association (IMOA)
International Wrought Copper Council
International Zinc Association
Japan Mining Industry Association
Minerals Council of Australia
Mining Association of Canada
Mining Industry Associations of Southern Africa (MIASA)
National Mining Association (NMA)—United States
Nickel Institute
Prospectors and Developers Association of Canada
Sociedad Nacional de Minería (SONAMI)—Chile
Sociedad Nacional de Minería, Petróleo y Energía (SNMPE)—Peru
World Coal Institute
World Gold Council

Notes

International Council on Mining and Metals Sustainable Development Framework

* This chapter is a revised, updated, and expanded version of two earlier papers by the authors: S.P. Sethi, "The Effectiveness of Industry-Based Codes in Serving Public Interest: The Case of International Council on Mining and Metals," *Transnational Corporations* (United Nations Conference on Trade and Development, Geneva, Switzerland), vol. 14, no. 3 (2005), pp. 55–99; and S.P. Sethi and O. Emelianova, "A Failed Strategy of Using Voluntary Codes of Conduct by the Global Mining Industry," *Corporate Governance: The International Journal of Business and Society*, vol. 6 no. 3 (2006), pp. 226–238. Additional research support for the current chapter was provided by Suparna Ray and is gratefully acknowledged.

1. See details at www.icmm.com.
2. Phelps Dodge was a U.S. mining company that was acquired by Freeport-McMoRan Copper & Gold, Inc., in March 2007.
3. For details on MMSD's governance and organizational structure, see http://www.iied. org/mmsd/governance.html.
4. For details on MMSD's working papers, see http://www.iied.org/mmsd/wp/index. html.
5. For details, see MMSD's final report "Breaking New Ground."
6. See appendix 5.1 for details.
7. For details on ICMM's governance and organizational structure, see ICMM's website, www.icmm.com.
8. An 86-page document is available for download at ICMM's website, http://www.icmm. com/document/310.
9. A 148-page document is available for download at ICMM's website, http://www.icmm. com/document/13.
10. This document is available for download at ICMM's website, http://www.icmm.com/ document/2.
11. An 84-page document is available for download at ICMM's website, http://www.icmm. com/document/520.
12. Report available at http://www.icmm.com/document/642.
13. For more details, see "Experts in Responsible Investment Solutions" at http://www. eiris.org/files/research%20publications/indigenousrightsjun09.pdf.
14. "Minerals and Metal Management 2020," available at http://www.icmm.com/ document/583.
15. "ICMM Launches Minerals and Metals Management 2020 Strategy," October 30, 2009, ICMM press release, http://www.justmeans.com/press-releases/ICMM-launches-Minerals-and-Metals-Management-2020-Strategy/4198.html.
16. Report available at http://www.icmm.com/document/629.
17. For examples of industry-based CSR-related codes of conduct involving NGOs and other external stakeholders, see Fair Labor Organizations (www.fairlabour.org), the Forest Stewardship Council *(www.fscus.org), and Rainforest Alliance (www.rainforest-allianve.org).*
18. Jane Perlez, Kirk Johnson, and Somi Sengupta, "Behind Gold's Glitter: Torn Lands and Pointed Questions," *New York Times*, October 24, 2005.
19. Brandon Prosansky, "Mining Gold in Conflict Zones: The Context, Ramifications, and Lessons of AngloGold Ashanti's Activities in the Democratic Republic of the Congo," *Northwestern University Journal of International Human Rights* 5, no. 2, (2007): 236–274.
20. Earthworks, "Earthworks Calls on Newmont to Respect Community Rights," (March 2009), available at http://eathworksaction.org/PR_Newmont2.cfm. Synergy Global Consulting, "Global Community Relations Review: Site-Based Assessment of Ahafo

Mine, Ghana," (2008), available at http://newmontghana.com/images/stories/ahafo_pdf/ahafo_community_relations_review_2009.pdf.

21. Thomas M. Power, "Metals Mining and Sustainable Development in Central America," *Oxfam America* (2009), http://www.oxfamamerica.org/newsandpublications/publications/research_reports/metals-mining-and-sustainable-development-in-central-america/metals-mining-and-sustainable-development-in-central-america.pdf.

22. Keith Slack, "Mining Conflicts in Peru: Condition Critical," Oxfam America (2009), http://www.oxfamamerica.org/publications/mining-conflicts-in-peru-condition-critical/?searchterm=Mining%20Conflicts%20in%20Peru:%20Condition%20Critical.

23. Oliver Balch, "Extractive Industries: Communities Halt El Salvador Gold Grab," *Ethical Corporation* (2008), http://www.ethicalcorp.com/content.asp?ContentID=6119&newsletter=24.

24. Mark Curtis, "Fanning the Flames: The Role of British Mining Companies in Conflict and the Violation of Human Rights," (2007), http://www.waronwant.org/attachments/Fanning%20the%20Flames.pdf.

25. Mark Curtis, "Fanning the Flames: The Role of British Mining Companies in Conflict and the Violation of Human Rights," (2007), http://markcurtis.wordpress.com/2007/11/20/fanning-the-flames-the-role-of-british-mining-companies-in-conflict-and-the-violation-of-human-rights.

26. Paul Mitchell, "ICMM Responds to War on Want Report," International Council on Mining and Metals (2007), http://www.icmm.com/document/221.

27. Earthworks and Oxfam America, "Golden Rules: Making the Case for Responsible Mining," (2008), http://www.asiaing.com/golden-rules-making-the-case-for-responsible-mining.html.

28. Paul Mitchell, "2008 No Dirty Gold Campaign: ICMM Response," International Council on Mining and Metals (2008), http://www.icmm.com/document/33.

29. Excerpts from various communications between the author and Paul Mitchell, secretary general, ICMM.

IV

Industry-Wide Voluntary Codes
of Conduct in Collaboration with
Civil Society Organizations

6

The Role of Certification in Protecting the World's Forests

Tensie Whelan and Emily Dwinnells

Since the Industrial Revolution, the global population has grown from 1.6 billion to 6.1 billion, with 80 percent of the growth occurring between 1950 and 2000. The United Nations has projected that the world's population will surpass 9 billion people by 2050.[1] One significant side effect of this growth has been the destruction of the world's forests—the repository of biodiversity, medicines, livelihoods, water, and carbon. In the past 300 years, forest cover has decreased by nearly 40 percent, with approximately three-quarters disappearing within the past two centuries.[2]

The causes of deforestation are many, though agricultural conversion is the primary culprit, responsible for 70 percent of deforestation.[3] Different approaches have been developed to address this problem, ranging from full protection as parks and wilderness areas, to required set-asides on private lands, to certification of sustainable forest management practices and green procurement policies.

This chapter will focus on the role of certification, a standard-setting process for responsible forest management that uses market forces to encourage voluntary compliance. Since its development in the late 1980s, certification has emerged as a powerful code of conduct for society in meeting the challenges of natural resource conservation, including large-scale deforestation and ecosystem degradation, while also addressing the rights of forest-dwelling indigenous peoples throughout the world.

State of World Forests

Currently, forests cover approximately 30 percent of the world's land area, or just fewer than 4 billion hectares.[4] Although this represented an average of .62 hectares per capita in 2005, the distribution of forest land among nations varies widely.[5] The top ten most-forested countries account for 66 percent of the world's total forest area, and the remaining 34 percent is split among the other 212 countries. The top five most heavily forested countries—the Russian Federation, China, Brazil, Canada, and the United States—claim more than half of all forests worldwide, with the Russian Federation alone accounting for 20 percent.[6]

Between 1990 and 2005, the rate of deforestation averaged 13 million hectares per year.[7] Although total deforestation continues at an alarming pace, forest plantations, landscape restoration, and the natural expansion of forests have significantly reduced the net loss of forest area in some countries over the past fifteen years.[8] Plantation forests, consisting primarily of introduced species, make up an estimated 3.8 percent of the total forest area globally.[9]

Although plantations are slowing the net rate of deforestation, the loss of high biodiversity primary forest—forests of native species that do not show signs of human intervention and where ecological processes are not significantly disturbed—has continued at a constant rate of 6 million hectares per year since the 1990s.[10] While tropical forests account for less than 10 percent of forests worldwide, scientists believe that 50 to 90 percent of terrestrial plant and animal species reside in these habitats. For instance, the ancient tropical forests of Malaysia are home to 2,650 species of trees, 700 species of birds, 350 species of reptiles, 300 species of freshwater fish, 165 species of amphibians, and millions of invertebrate species.[11]

Not only do tropical forests contain some of the highest levels of biodiversity, they are also home to some of the world's poorest people. It is estimated that in developing countries, forests sustain up to 1.4 billion of the world's rural poor.[12] Increasing demographic pressures in the absence of viable economic alternatives in rural areas accelerate the cycle of environmental degradation and poverty resulting in deforestation from slash-and-burn agriculture, unregulated logging, non-timber forest product extraction and unsustainable cattle ranching. The World Bank estimates that approximately two-thirds of tropical forests are under moderate to high pressure from agricultural expansion and timber extraction.[13]

In two of the most severely affected regions, Africa and Latin America, considerable efforts are being made to reverse this trend. The African Conference of Ministers in Charge of Forests Central Africa (COMIFAC) has successfully led a regional initiative to designate 70 million hectares of forest for conservation of biological diversity.[14] Similarly, forest designated for biodiversity conservation in South America has increased by 2 percent between 2000 and 2005. In 2005, 11 percent of forests worldwide were designated for biological diversity conservation, representing an increase of 96 million hectares since 1990.[15]

Although encouraging, many of these protected areas are "paper tigers," with illegal logging and forest fires reducing their forest cover. Most forest-related production activity occurs in the absence of any responsible management planning and therefore does not allow for conservation and regeneration. Developing countries report that only 3 percent of their forest areas are managed.[16] When adequately enforced, protection of forests can contribute to the solution; however, it will never become the sole answer. Additional approaches that preserve forest cover and provide sustainable livelihoods for the people living in and around these forests are critical to maintaining and increasing forest cover globally. In the past fifteen years, certification of sustainable forest management practices has emerged as an important solution to this challenge.

Forests and Climate Change

To avoid profound and irreversible changes to the earth's climate, the International Panel on Climate Change (IPCC) recommends that the global community must reduce greenhouse gas (GHG) emissions by 60 to 80 percent from current levels by 2050.[17] Global forest loss contributes more to global GHG emissions than all the trains, planes, and automobiles combined—20 percent of the total. In some tropical countries, such as Brazil and Indonesia, deforestation is the leading cause of GHG emissions and can be as high as 50 to 70 percent of the total.

The international response to climate change was launched at the Earth Summit in Rio de Janeiro in 1992 with the signing of the UN Framework Convention on Climate Change. Several years later, in 1997, the Kyoto Protocol was developed to set binding targets to significantly reduce GHG emissions. However, the Kyoto Protocol failed to address deforestation, focusing almost exclusively on reducing industry-related emissions.

During negotiations in Copenhagen scheduled for 2009, the global community convened for the last time before the Kyoto Protocol expires in 2012 and to lay the groundwork for a new climate regime. Reduced Emissions from Deforestation and Degradation in Developing Countries (REDD), a program launched by the United Nations to equip several developing countries with systems to monitor, assess, and report forest cover, will provide support for developing countries to improve governance, monitor deforestation and land use, and implement effective economic and social programs to address deforestation and land-use change. Mechanisms that reduce deforestation are expected to be a key component of the resulting solution, and certification or verification of compliance—both of forest set-asides and of sustainable forest management—will be part of the implementation plan.

History of Forest Certification

Forest-based activities have provided mankind with material and economic resources for hundreds of years. Government controls—such as the establishment of national forest reserves, forestry services, training facilities, and a variety of laws and regulations—have historically provided adequate industry oversight and lent institutional, technical, and legal strength to modern concepts of forest ownership, management planning, and yield control. However, the post–World War II era witnessed an unprecedented increase in demand for timber for reconstruction and accelerated consumption due to growing economies and an increase in trade. The rise of the logging industry eroded government controls in the name of progress and led to a gradual decline in forestry management and protection (Synott, p. 5). According to the United Nation's Food and Agriculture Organization (FAO), approximately 17 million hectares of tropical forests were cleared in 1990, a rate of one acre per second.

During the 1980s, budding global concern around the rapid deforestation and biodiversity loss in the Amazonian rainforest brought the issue of forestry management into the international policy spotlight. In 1988, the International Tropical Timber Organization (ITTO), an organization created under the auspices of the United Nations to analyze and provide solutions to tropical deforestation, commissioned a study and found virtually no sustainable forestry management controls in place in tropical member countries (Synott, p. 6). The failure of governmental controls coincided with the birth of corporate campaigns, a tactic employed by environmental organizations to raise public awareness around the environmentally destructive business practices of various corporations. Friends of the Earth and other environmental nongovernmental organizations (NGOs) began to publicly call for boycotts of all tropical timber after linking UK timber companies with tropical deforestation (Synott, p. 7). Such campaigns played an important role in developing broad-based consumer awareness, and mobilized public opinion to create market incentives that eventually led some retailers to react to these accusations and change their negative behaviors.

Multilateral governmental attempts to confront deforestation provided early, but unsuccessful, responses to address the destruction of Amazonian rainforests. The Rainforest Alliance launched the first sustainable forestry certification program of its kind, called SmartWood, in 1990 as a result of several meetings organized to debate alternatives to boycotting timber products. Attendees included Dr. Thomas Lovejoy, a tropical biologist with the Smithsonian at the time, and Dr. Ghillean Prance of Kew Botanical Gardens in the UK, as well as foresters, timber company executives, loggers, environmentalists, and others. SmartWood developed a system for identifying "well-managed tropical woods" and performed the first third-party field evaluation of logging concessions in Indonesia in 1990. The SmartWood standard was based on watershed stabilization, sustained yield production, and a positive impact on the well-being of local people.

Driven in part by the failure of previous intergovernmental processes, a variety of social groups, environmental nonprofits, academics, forestry professionals, and businesses began attending parallel meetings to develop the concept of an international sustainable forest certification system. In 1993, the Rainforest Alliance, World Wildlife Fund, Greenpeace, timber traders, indigenous peoples groups, government representatives, forest worker organizations, and industry leaders were among the 134 invitees that met in Toronto, Canada, to establish the Forest Stewardship Council (FSC). By August 1994, a definitive set of principles and criteria and statutes for the council were voted on and approved by the founding members. The FSC secretariat was established in Oaxaca, Mexico, and Timothy Synott was hired as the first executive director. Since its establishment, a number of industry-based certification initiatives have been developed.

The FSC System

The FSC standard is widely considered to be the highest social and environmental standard in the forestry sector and across continents, forests types, sizes, and various kinds of ownerships due to its equitable approach to improving environmental, social, and economic performance. The attributes that distinguish it from other industry-based certification schemes are its strict adherence to third-party auditing and its democratic, public, and transparent method for developing standards. The ability to involve environmentalists, social scientists, business representatives, indigenous group leaders, local governments, and a variety of other interests in the development of principles and criteria has provided the FSC standard with a great deal of legitimacy within the marketplace and among stakeholders. Although relatively new to the world of certification and standards, forest certification has had a major impact on the forestry industry and the management of forests worldwide.

The creation of the FSC illustrates the opportunities and the challenges of building a stakeholder-based global standard. The ability to meet the diverse needs of social groups, environmentalists, and business is largely dependent upon the highly democratic governance structure. Although it has become a legitimate model of consensus building, during its development, business interests opposed the FSC, feeling that environmental NGOs, which comprised part of the founding assembly, would gain too much influence over the forestry industry and create a monopolistic standard. Small landowners worried certification would reduce control over their lands and increase the costs and bureaucracy of management. Similarly, national governments were concerned that the multi-stakeholder approach and international scope of the FSC standard would undermine national sovereignty of forests. Initially, these opposing interests resisted the standards altogether. However, as independent verification gained popularity, it became evident that industry and governmental interests had to react. This led to the development of national certification schemes intended to compete with the FSC.

The decision to make the FSC a membership organization allowed for a wide variety of interests across the forestry industry to participate in the standard development process. Understanding that the division of the decision-making power would determine the balance and legitimacy of the standard, the founding members created the FSC as a membership organization open to all stakeholders within the forestry sector. Both institutional and individual membership was permitted. Membership, also called the General Assembly of the FSC, was established as the highest decision-making body in the organization and was broken down into an environmental, social, and economic chambers with equal weight in the voting process. All chambers must approve major decisions to be enforced. Each of these chambers is further divided into sub-chambers according to the World Bank definition of northern (developed) and southern (developing) countries. The social chamber includes a variety of non-profit, NGO, indigenous peoples associations, unions, research, academic, technical institutions, and individuals that have demonstrated a commitment to socially responsible forestry. The environment chamber includes a similar composition of members focused on environmentally viable forest stewardship. Lastly, the economic chamber includes individuals and organizations with commercial interests. Members include industry and trade associations, wholesalers, retailers, traders, consumer associations, and consulting companies. Membership in the economic chamber is contingent upon a demonstrated commitment to the implementation of FSC Principles and Criteria.[18]

The creation of three separate chambers allows for equal representation and the maintenance of balance of voting power between critical interests and geographies without having to limitlimiting the number of members. The decision-making body below the General Assembly is a group of nine individuals comprising the Board of Directors. Three members are elected from each of the chambers for a three-year term, during which they are accountable to FSC members.[19] Directors must be individual members of the FSC or the designated delegates of a member organization. At the end of each calendar year, three directors retire and are replaced through a postal ballot or general assembly vote. The Executive Director of the FSC reports to the Board of Directors.

Accreditation

The FSC accredits certification organizations to perform audits of forestry operations and confer FSC certification. Accreditation Services International (ASI) manages the FSC accreditation program. ASI conducts an office audit of the potential certification body and witnesses trial audits in the field. Once accreditation is achieved, ASI performs one office and field audit for each FSC-accredited certification body annually. In addition, the FSC requires that all accredited bodies comply with relevant International Standard Organization (ISO) standards to achieve accreditation.[20]

If an accredited certification body is found not to be fully in compliance with all FSC stipulations, a Corrective Action Request (CAR) is filed. If the CAR is fulfilled within a certain time frame, accreditation powers remain. The length of time granted depends on the seriousness of the infringement and can vary from three months or less to one year. However, after this time frame lapses and the certification body fails to improve, the accredited body will be suspended and eventually lose its FSC accreditation.[21]

Since its inception, the FSC has certified more than 100 million hectares of forests and issued more than 13,000 certificates in eighty-one countries. According to the FSC, the certified area is equivalent to around 8 percent of the world's total forest area. The following ten principles describe environmentally responsible, economically feasible, and socially equitable forest management practices that form the basis for all FSC forest management certification.

Principle 1: Compliance with all applicable laws and international treaties.
Forest management shall respect all applicable laws of the country in which they operate as well as international treaties and agreements to which the country is a signatory, and shall comply with all FSC Principles and Criteria.
Principle 2: Demonstrated and uncontested, clearly defined, long-term land tenure and use rights. Long-term tenure claims and use rights for land and forests resources shall be clearly defined, documented. and legally established.
Principle 3: Recognition and respect of indigenous peoples' rights.
The legal and customary rights of indigenous peoples to own, use, and manage their lands, territories, and resources shall be recognized and respected.
Principle 4: Maintenance or enhancement of long-term social and economic well-being of forest workers and local communities and respect of worker's rights in compliance with International Labor Organization (ILO) conventions.
Forest management operations shall maintain or enhance the long-term social and economic well-being of forest workers and local communities.

Principle 5: Equitable use and sharing of benefits derived from the forest.
Forest management operations shall encourage the efficient use of the forests multiple products and services to ensure economic viability and a wide range of environmental and social benefits.

Principle 6: Reduction of environmental impact of logging activities and maintenance of the ecological functions and integrity of the forest.
Forest management shall conserve biological diversity and its associated values, water resources, soils, and unique and fragile ecosystems and landscapes, and, by so doing, maintain the ecological functions and integrity of the forest.

Principle 7: Appropriate and continuously updated management plan.
A management plan appropriate to the scale and intensity of the operations shall be written, implemented, and kept up to date. The long-term objectives of management and the means of achieving them shall be clearly stated.

Principle 8: Appropriate monitoring and assessment activities to assess the condition of the forest, management activities, and their social and environmental impacts. Monitoring shall be conducted, appropriate to the scale and intensity of the forest management, to assess the condition of the forest yields of forest products, chain of custody, management activities, and their social and environmental impacts.

Principle 9: Maintenance of High Conservation Value Forests (HCVFs), defined as environmental and social values that are considered to be of outstanding significance or critical importance. Management activities in high conservation value forests shall maintain or enhance the attributes that define such forests. Decision regarding high-value forests shall always be considered in the context of a precautionary approach.

Principle 10: In addition to compliance with all of the above, plantations must contribute to reduce the pressures on and promote the restoration and conservation of natural forests. Plantations shall be managed in accordance with Principles 1–9 above. While plantations can provide an array of social and economic benefits and can contribute to satisfying the world's needs for forest products, they should complement the management of, reduce pressures on, and promote the restoration and conservation of natural forests.

These overarching principles are further defined by a set of fifty-six verifiable criteria that outline the conditions that must be met to achieve each of the principles. These criteria minimize the negative impacts of forestry operations on the environment, maximize social benefits, and maintain the important conservation values of the forest. Together they provide a basis for operational forest management and are designed for application to all forest types from boreal to tropical, which can be further interpreted to account for specific national or regional contexts in both the developing and developed world.

The FSC has stipulated a process to determine national or regional interpretations. Actors that wish to develop national initiatives first create interpretations of the principles listed above and adapt its management and operations to conform to all applicable FSC requirements. Once this is accomplished, they submit their interpretations to the FSC for formal accreditation. A national working group needs to be accredited by the FSC board before a national or regional standard can be submitted to the FSC for accreditation.[22]

In addition to certification of forestry management, FSC offers a chain-of-custody (CoC) certification that certifies industries that process and sell forest products. In this instance, products are tracked from the forest, through processing, shipping, and manufacturing, to the wholesale and distribution stages. Certified operations are allowed to use the FSC trademark to give consumers a seal of approval. CoC certification can be used to demonstrate compliance with public or private procurement, such as the U.S. Green Building Leadership in Energy and Environmental Design (LEED) rating system.[23]

Acknowledging that some shortages occur in the supply of certified material, the FSC allows manufacturers to use three different types of seals that allow companies to avoid unsustainably produced wood. The "FSC Pure" seal certifies that the material was produced with materials extracted from 100 percent certified forests. The "FSC Mixed Sources" seal signifies that the product was made with a mix of FSC-certified and controlled wood sources. The "Controlled Wood" standard requires that wood is not harvested illegally, in violation of traditional and civil rights, harvested in forests where management threatens High Conservation Value (HCV) areas, or harvested from conversion of natural forests or from areas where genetically modified trees are planted. Controlled wood must be independently verified before it is mixed with FSC-certified materials to be sold using the mixed-sources symbol.[24]

In addition to individual certification of a company or an individual, the FSC certification can also be granted to a cooperative of forest producers or communities that manage timber and non-timber forest products like resins, rattan, and fruits. This is called Group Certification. Community forest management differs from conventional forest management in that it occurs within a specific social context that involves a group that has developed a traditional way of life and takes into consideration the community's livelihood and its relationship with the forest. This type of certification aims to add value to managed forest resources and encourage social organization, worker safety, and efficient production.[25]

Forestry Certification Schemes

The industry-led Programme for the Endorsement of Forest Certification schemes (PEFC) was created in Finland in 1999. It acts as an umbrella organization that endorses various national forest certification schemes. The PEFC Council, composed of national governing bodies representing forest owner associations and other industry interests, approves national schemes that are developed in compliance with the umbrella scheme. It started as a European-driven scheme and has since spread to parts of Central and South America, Asia, and Africa. Currently, the PEFC has thirty-five independent national forest certification schemes in its membership, accounting for nearly 200 million hectares of certified forests, making it the world's largest certification system. PEFC endorses a variety of systems, including SFI and CSA, all with differing levels of rigor and credibility.

The American Forest and Paper Association (AFPA), a national industry association, founded the Sustainable Forestry Initiative (SFI) in 1994. Initially an industry code of conduct with mandatory member self-reporting, the SFI added third-party verification in 1998. The SFI standard focuses mainly on large forests throughout the U.S. and Canada. It has 219 program participants and has certified 61,556,494 hectares throughout this region.[26]

The Canadian Standards Association (CSA) is a national standard-setting organization that sets a broad array of standards in Canada. Industry members of the Canadian Pulp and Paper Association approached the CSA about developing a standard in the early 1990s. It completed its first voluntary forest certification in 1999 and has certified more than 82 million hectares.

Established in 1941, the American Tree Farm System (ATFS) is one of the oldest forest management programs. This organization focuses on private, nonindustrial forests in the United States and has certified 88,000 tree farmers in forty-six states.[27] It certifies to the American Forest Foundation's Standards of Sustainability for Forest Management using a network of volunteer inspecting foresters.

In addition to the systems previously mentioned, a variety of national and regional programs have been developed specifically for the tropics. The International Tropical Timber Organization (ITTO), an intergovernmental organization promoting conservation and sustainable management practices, was established in Japan under the auspices of the UN in 1986.[28] It first put forth criteria and indicators for sustainable forestry management in 1990. These were later revised and used by tropical governments such as Brazil, Malaysia, and various African countries to form national criteria.

Since its introduction in the early 1990s, forest certification has become a worldwide movement and has had a greater impact on forest management practices than any other effort in hundreds of years. This market-based mechanism is a huge boon to the development of natural resources management and has given consumers the ability to identify legal forest products.

Certifiers and Portfolios

Currently there are twenty-two FSC-accredited certifying bodies working in eighty-four countries around the world to audit forestry operations, manufacturers, traders, pulp producers, printers, and many other kinds of operations. The FSC accredits certifiers of both Forest Management (FM) and Chain-of-Custody (CoC) Certification. Large accredited certifiers include the Rainforest Alliance's SmartWood program, Bureau Veritas Certification, QMI-SAI Global, SGS Systems and Services Certification USA, and Scientific Certification System, Inc. In terms of total area certified by Forest Management or Forest Management/Chain-of-Custody, tropical/subtropical forests account for 14 percent of the total area, temperate forests 39 percent, and boreal forests 47 percent. Some 954 forest management certificates and 12,930 in chain-of-custody certificates have been issued to date. Another measure by forest type shows that the majority of certification occurs within natural forests at 58 percent, followed by seminatural and mixed plantation and seminatural forests at 34 percent, and plantations at 8 percent.[29] Public lands accounted for 55 percent of the total certified area, whereas private lands accounted for 40 percent, with community and concessions making up the remaining 4 percent.

Meeting the FSC Standard

Companies and organizations applying for FSC certification are usually required to make significant management changes before they are able to meet the FSC standard. Preconditions and conditions are corrective actions that must take place according to an agreed schedule subsequent to obtaining certification.

A recent impact study created by the Rainforest Alliance's SmartWood division found that certified operations in twenty-one counties were required to make changes during their certification assessments. The study showed that the conditions for certification were not skewed in any one direction. There was a roughly equal emphasis on improving environmental, economic, and legal forest management and systems issues. In each of these categories, at least 60 percent of certified operations surveyed were required to make changes.

The issues that certified operations were required to address most often included three social issues (worker safety, training, and communication and conflict resolution with stakeholders), three environmental issues (aquatic and riparian area, sensitive sites, and high conservation value forests (HCVF)), and four systems issues (management plans, monitoring, chain of custody, and inventory).

The most prevalent environmental impact of FSC certification was an improvement of riparian and aquatic management in 63 percent of the operations. The habitat along the banks of natural watercourses is very important to both wildlife species and water quality, so it is not surprising this would be a common issue during assessments for certification. Another frequently cited issue was the treatment of sensitive sites and HCVFs in 62 percent of the operations. The identification, conservation, and protection of these areas were the central focus of the changes required. Stakeholder consultation with regard to sensitive sites and HCVFs, as well as the expansion of inventory, monitoring, and mapping activities to include these features, was often required before passing the assessment. The improved treatment of threatened and endangered species in 62 percent of the operations was another frequently occurring issue. Operations dealing with threatened and endangered species were required to ensure species protection, but details such as particular protection strategies were chosen by the operation and assessed by Rainforest Alliance/SmartWood in the annual audit.

Among the most prevalent social changes required were improved communication and conflict resolution with stakeholders, neighbors, and communities (75 percent of operations); improved worker training (64 percent); and improved treatment of illegal activities and trespassing (25 percent). Tropical forestry operations, which are often located in regions with weaker workers' rights laws and operate on slimmer economic margins than their temperate counterparts, experience significantly higher social changes than temperate region operators.

Systems impacts of SmartWood certification led to improved management planning in 93 percent of the operations, improved monitoring (86 percent), and improved chain-of-custody management. In the area of forestry management, 60 percent of operations were required to improve their roads and skid trails for extracting timber. Another 55 percent were asked to improve regeneration and reforestation activities, and 48 percent improved management of chemicals in their operations.

Environmental Impacts of FSC Certification

The Rainforest Alliance is also tracking the social, environmental, and economic impacts of certification through its annual audits. The Rainforest Alliance began collecting data on twenty key indicators in 2007 and issued a report on data gathered to date in 2008. Among the 150 operations assessed, 16 percent of their total forest area was designated as a strict reserve. The combined reserve area on this sample amounted to an area more than twice the size of Yellowstone National Park—nearly 2 million acres. The average reserve size was 13,450 hectares. Forestry operations with a greater percentage of plantation area tended to have significantly larger reserve areas.

This study conducted by the Rainforest Alliance also found that certified operations designated an average of 22,000 hectares or 22 percent of their total area as high conservation value forest (HCVF). The combined sum of HCVF land for the 118 operations that reported data during the study was 2.5 million hectares. HCVFs are subcategorized into a series of six types. Publicly owned forests tended to have a greater amount of area designated as HCVF than privately or community owned operations, and this area was most frequently defined as HCVF Types 1–4, which cover biodiversity, landscape-level issues, threatened and endangered species, and ecosystem services. The types most commonly represented in this study were Type 1 and Type 2.

Nearly all FSC regional standards include management requirements for streamside management zones. FSC criterion 6.5 stipulates the control of erosion and protection of water resources. The impact of certification on water quality and aquatic vertebrae is assessed using an indicator that tallies the length of streams flowing through certified lands. This indicator was adapted to become a general measure of impacts by measuring the amount of water resources managed in accordance with FSC criteria. The indicator revealed that the sixty-one operations that reported data have a combined total of 51.500 linear kilometers of perennial streams flowing through them. If these streams were placed end to end, they would span the circumference of the earth.

The Guatemala Case Study

An excellent example of the improved environmental services of FSC certified forests can be found in the Maya Biosphere Reserve of Guatemala. This 2 million–hectare reserve includes 820,000 hectares of protected area, 780,000 hectares of community logging concessions, and 315,000 hectares of buffer zone. The reserve holds more than a dozen important archaeological sites and rare wildlife such as jaguars, brocket deer, and scarlet macaws. The Rainforest Alliance has certified twelve community and two private forestry operations in the reserve to FSC standards, and assesses them annually to ensure that they follow strict standards for protection of the environment and people. Researchers also found that the deforestation rate within the FSC-certified concessions was twenty times lower than in the protected areas. The areas devastated by fires in the FSC-certified logging concessions decreased steadily from 6.5 percent in 1998 to 1 percent in 2007, while fires affected 7 to 20 percent of the surrounding protected area.

According to José Román Carrera, Rainforest Alliance forestry manager for Central America, the export of new products—and the access to buyers willing to pay higher prices for value-added certified wood—has provided much-needed additional income for more than 6,000 people in the region. More than 2.6 million board feet of certified wood and wood in the process of certification has sold, totaling more than $4.7 million. More than $5.2 million has been invested by partners in building new factories and mills, and in repairing and upgrading old ones. As a result, more than 2,000 temporary jobs and 500 permanent jobs have been created. This has led not only to improved household incomes, but also to profits being invested in community works such as a potable water system, new schools, clinics, and an emergency medical fund for poor families. "The increased earnings not only raise living standards, they also raise people's awareness of the need to manage the forest in a sustainable manner," says Carrera.

The community of Uaxactún, set in the rainforest north of Tikal National Park, has sold nontraditional wood species to several companies, produced special cuts of mahogany for Gibson Guitar, and exports weekly shipments of jade palm leaves to the U.S. floral supplier Continental Floral Greens. According to Floridalma Ax, a member of the organization that administers Uaxactún's forest concession, community members have invested part of the money from those sales to hire teachers for the town's understaffed school and to provide scholarships for older students to take computer courses in the nearest city.

The impacts of FSC certification are apparent, especially when contrasted with the conditions found in nearby national parks. Laguna del Tigre National Park, the reserve's largest protected area, has already lost more than 40 percent of its forests to illegal loggers and slash-and-burn farmers, whereas the concessions have lost less than 4 percent of their forest cover. According to Benedín García, a former forest ranger and one of the founders of the organization that administers Uaxactún's forest concession, the reason the FSC-certified concessions are better conserved than the parks is that they are protected by the people who rely on them for their livelihoods. He explains that part of the money earned from the sale of certified wood is used to pay local forest guards who patrol the concession every day, but all of the town's residents also contribute to that duty. "Our secret is that we have more than 150 people working in this forest, collecting palm leaves, chicle, and allspice, and if one of them sees something happening that shouldn't be, they report it to us, and we send a delegation to that area immediately."

For Carrera, this community approach to conservation is not only the best means of protecting the Maya Biosphere Reserve, but also could be the key to saving the region's other large wilderness tracts, all of which are threatened. A career conservationist, Carrera was the regional director of Guatemala's National Council of Protected Areas, having joined the organization when the biosphere reserve was created, and spent years battling illegal loggers and squatters before going to work for the Rainforest Alliance.

"I used to think that the way to protect the forest was to say, 'Stop, don't touch.' We put people in jail and confiscated the illegal wood, but the forest just kept getting smaller and smaller," explains Carrera. "I realize now that a more effective way to conserve the rainforest is to show the people who live there that they can make a better living by managing the forest sustainably than they would it if they cut it down. This is something we are accomplishing in Guatemala and that we would like to repeat in and around Central America's other biosphere reserves in order to ensure the survival of this region's endangered wilderness."

Social Impacts of FSC Certification

The Rainforest Alliance has developed social indicators to track the number of people employed in certified companies, the number of sites conserved of importance to indigenous peoples and communities, the number of serious accidents per one hundred workers, and the number of fatalities per one hundred workers.

The indicator study found that sample operations certified by the Rainforest Alliance employed 37,361 people directly, including both full- and part-time workers. Another indicator, developed to determine employee well-being relative to the fourth FSC principle, focused on workers' rights and community relations, is the number of accidents leading to serious injury or death within the previous twelve months. A serious accident is defined as an incident that cannot be treated with basic first aid and requires professional medical treatment. Examples include significant strains, severe lacerations requiring stitches, hyper/hypothermia, heart attacks, strokes et cetera. On average, .4 percent of workers at certified operations have experienced a serious accident in the past twelve months.

The International Labour Organization (ILO) publishes accident and fatality rates from the broader forest sector by country. For the three countries in the Rainforest Alliance study that were also tracked by the ILO—Canada, Argentina, Estonia—the serious accident rate on FSC-certified operations was .61 percent versus the industry standard of .75 percent.

Another important value incorporated into the FSC's third principle is the recognition and respect of indigenous rights. Operations were asked to report on the number of special cultural sites for which explicit language specified the protection of or access measures in the management plan. They reported a total of 1,558 special sites, which is an average of 21.6 per operation. It was also discovered that community- or indigenous-owned operations designated a relatively large percentage of their area as HCV Type 5, which describes a subcategory of HCVF related to areas fundamental to meeting basic needs of local communities.

The University of São Paulo College of Agriculture (ESALQ/USP) recently conducted a study of FSC certification on behalf of IMAFLORA, a Brazilian environmental nonprofit organization that certifies farms and forestry operations in partnership with the Rainforest Alliance. The researchers compared

FSC-certified plantations and a control group of noncertified operations in the states of Santa Catalina and Rio Grande do Sul. The two groups were similar in terms of size of the planted area, employees, and outsourced workers. Safety in the workplace, professional training, working conditions, hiring, access to education and health services, social organization, and relationship with the community were the main indicators researched in the study.

The study found that although the majority of workers on both certified and noncertified operations had not completed primary school, there was a significant difference in the number of children of resident workers enrolled in school on certified operations (85 percent) compared to noncertified operations (15 percent).

Preventative health measures practiced in both groups were of high quality. FSC preventative health requirements include a health examination for admission and regular examinations thereafter, and can be measured by the absence of work-related health injuries. In these categories, certified operations performed slightly better than the control group. Although not a formal certification requirement, 72 percent of the certified operations provided professional medical care compared to only 45 percent in the control group.

Certification had a positive impact on the training of forest workers. Almost all of the workers received initial instruction on certified plantations (87 percent), whereas only 47 percent of workers participated in training in the control group. In addition, 100 percent of workers on certified plantations were given written reference materials addressing health and safety at work, education and environment, forest machines and mechanics, pesticide application, information on the firm and its rules, chainsaw operation, crop handling, and certification, among other topics. All workers believed these materials were of high importance. Only 14 percent of the control group received written materials.

Linked to training, the study found that few workers on certified operations used burnt oil in their chainsaws, a practice discouraged by the FSC, whereas the majority (65 percent) of control group workers engaged in this risky behavior. In addition, 100 percent of employees at certified operations wash and store pesticides correctly, although neither group sufficiently offered water, soap, and paper during the application of these chemicals.

In the field, the study showed that certification contributed to the well-being, health, and safety of workers engaged in forest activities in the field. Although not all certified operations met FSC standards in the field, they surpassed the control group in each of the following categories related to work in the field: availability of water (99 versus 89 percent), a person trained for emergencies (63 versus 16 percent), a vehicle on call (86 versus 75 percent), means of communication (83 versus 59 percent), first-aid materials (43 versus 0 percent), and sanitary facilities (57 versus 0 percent). In addition, the provision and quality of meals in the field and a place to eat them was higher in certified versus noncertified operations.

Forest machinery, including farming tractors, track loaders, bulldozers, skidders, and chainsaws, used by workers were observed for a variety of safety components, including safety belts, rollover protective structures, and protection against power transmissions. In addition, the headlights, lights, reverse-gear warning signal, horn, and rear-view mirror were checked. There was little difference between the two groups with regard to chainsaw safety devices; however, 100 percent of certified operations' machines had all safety structures and 80 percent had all safety elements intact, whereas 0 percent of the control groups' machinery met either standard.

The positive influence of certification was also visible with regard to transportation. The majority (65 percent) of certified operations in the sample provided company transportation, whereas less than half (39 percent) of the noncertified operations fulfilled this FSC requirement. Of the company transportation provided, 98 percent of certified outfits provided appropriate transportation, which was slightly higher than noncertified operations (87 percent). Inappropriate transportation includes riding on a tractor or in the dumpcart of large trucks and pickup trucks, in a derelict cab, or in a cab where fuel was transported along with the workers. Tools were transported in a separate compartment in 96 percent of certified operations compared to 61 percent in the control group.

Overall, a greater percentage of forest workers at certified operations received higher wages. The same was true of outsourced workers. Housing and lodging indicators were considered but showed little difference. One positive impact of certification on housing was the availability of water treatment for human consumption. Sanitation, as measured by appropriate sewage destination and disposal of garbage for housing and lodging, was positively affected by certification. Appropriate sewage destination rates were similarly high for both groups.

The Impact of FSC Certification on Indigenous Communities

The subtropical to temperate forests in the mountain districts of Bajhang and Dolakha of Nepal are government-owned but managed by local people organized into legally recognized Community Forest User Groups (CFUGs). Currently, some 14,387 CFUGs manage approximately 1.2 million hectares of forest in Nepal. Non-timber forest products (natural medicines and supplements, essential oils, and variety of other herbal medicinal and beauty products) are an important source of income for these groups.

Working with local partners, the initial assessment covered eleven CFUGs selected by the Alliance for pilot certification. Today the certificate covers twenty-one CFUGs, managing 14,086 hectares. The user groups range from sixty-five to 544 households in size and cover anywhere from twenty-eight to 1981 hectares per group. Additionally, eight forest enterprises received FSC Chain-of-Custody certification, which includes the first handmade FSC-certified paper in the world, which was used by cosmetics company Aveda for gift boxes in 2007.

In a process led by the Asia Network for Sustainable Agriculture and Bioresources (ANSAB), some twenty-one CFUGs have been certified for NTFP extraction under FSC. As part of the certificate, CFUGs were trained to map areas set aside for the protection of sensitive wildlife habitat, cultural sites, and streams, and identified two threatened bird species, which they are now protecting. CFUG members now monitor changes in forest conditions and have been trained in accounting practices to ensure transparency. Additionally, certification has helped strengthen the democratic institutions of these communities. CFUGs in Boakha have negotiated settlements with yak grazers over tenure and territorial issues, and have created a microloan program for its poorest members.

In the Brazilian municipality of Xapuri, Acre, community forest management to Forest Stewardship Council standards enabled indigenous communities to preserve their traditional forest-dependent livelihoods. The Chico Mendes Association, for example, relied on NTFPs such as latex and Brazil nuts as its main source of income for decades. However, as the population increased, this production could no longer adequately support the community. The association decided to integrate its traditional activities with the sustainable harvest of wood and obtained FSC certification in March 2002. The wood is sold to a furniture factory in the heart of the forest, providing revenue and jobs to the community.[30]

FSC and Community Issues

FSC certification requires that producers work closely with surrounding communities—criteria especially important for large companies. When Mil Madeireira, a forest products company in Brazil, first sought certification for its 82,000 hectares, it did not know or communicate with families living near its forest. During the certification process it became clear that although there was no conflict at hand, the potential for future conflict existed. The families did not recognize Mil Madeireira as the legitimate owner of the area; in addition, they used fire to clear their agricultural plots, thereby threatening the resources under management. Certification served as the impetus for issuing all 142 families land titles in September 2008. A condition for certification stipulated that no forest management activities would take place in the forest area bordering the occupied land. The Amazonas government and certified company Mil Madeireira signed an agreement to compensate agrarian communities for the loss of forest use.

Economic and Market Impacts

FSC is currently one of the fastest-growing certification programs in the world. In 2006, it increased by 20 million hectares, by 10 million hectares in 2007, and by more than 10 million in 2008. The number of active certifications including both CoC and forest management totals 13,884. Based on an FSC survey, the overall value of FSC-labeled sales estimates in 2007 was $20 billion, four times its $5 billion market value in 2005. Companies with a combined turnover value of $250 billion in wood products are committed to FSC certification.

The FSC supply chain also continues to grow rapidly. The estimated supply of FSC-certified pulp in the market is 4.7 million tons, about 9 percent of the total global supply. Despite a slight dip in the global industrial roundwood volumes in 2006, FSC roundwood increased from 21 to 24 percent of the market share. The FSC impact study conducted on behalf of

IMAFLORA discovered that the majority of the certified organizations in the sample acquired certification to improve access to markets.

Surveys conducted by the FSC also show that consumer recognition is rising. In the Netherlands, the FSC places fourth in a ranking of the country's best-known quality assurance trademarks. Upon prompted recognition, FSC reaches 67 percent of the population in the Netherlands, 56 percent in Switzerland, and 23 percent in the UK, with the highest recognition coming from residents under the age of twenty-five.

FSC Certification Brings Increased Revenue to Pennsylvania

Between the years 1997 and 1998, the state of Pennsylvania certified 2.1 million acres to FSC standards. The Pennsylvania Bureau of Forestry was motivated to pursue FSC certification for a number of reasons. The bureau felt that its forest management practices would strengthen key aspects of its management system, such as the implementation of a timber harvest allocation model. Through the certification process, the bureau was able to highlight major areas of concern, like the impact of deer populations on regeneration. It also wanted to establish a model for other large public and private forests.

To learn more about the economic impacts of FSC certification, the Rainforest Alliance examined six years of timber sales data provided by the bureau to determine whether higher prices are being paid for state forest timber as a result of certification.

Between 2001 and 2006, buyers of Pennsylvania state forest timber paid approximately $7.7 million more for FSC-certified timber. The higher bid prices equated roughly to a 10 percent increase in revenue for the Pennsylvania state forest timber over what would have been earned in the absence of certification. A dramatic increase in timber sold to FSC-certified buyers and the dollar value of those sales occurred after the forests were certified. The percentage of timber bought by FSC-certified buyers went from less than 10 percent in 1998 to over 40 percent in 2006, while the total acreage producing wood sold to FSC-certified buyers increased from 7 percent to nearly 30 percent over that time period. By 2006, FSC-certified timber sales accounted for almost two-thirds of the dollar value of all state forest timber sales, up from less than 15 percent.

Challenges

As demonstrated by these examples, certification can have a significant impact on improving responsible forest management, and can help provide sustainable livelihoods as well. At the same time, certification has many limitations. First, different standards have varying degrees of rigor and credibility, and the proliferation of certification schemes has made it difficult to easily distinguish the best practices and has the potential to lead to consumer confusion in the marketplace.

Second, more forests have been certified where forests are better protected in the first place—only 14 percent of tropical forests have been certified by FSC, for example, versus 39 percent of temperate forests and 47 percent of boreal forests. The underperformance in the tropics is due to a variety of factors, ranging from the large volume of illegal logs sold so cheaply that responsibly managed forest products cannot compete, to corruption and weak governance by host governments, to the high cost of reaching compliance when practices have been severely subpar. Large natural forest operations in the tropics often must completely overhaul their equipment, forestry practices, and labor practices. To gain FSC certification, plantations must prove they have not deforested virgin forest after November 1994.

Fortunately, the European and U.S. governments are addressing the illegal logging problem with recent legislation that aims to stop the import of illegal timber into those countries. Different systems for verifying legality are being tested and developed. It will likely be several years before a functioning system is up and running, but the threat of it may begin to help the uptake of forest certification.

The length of time and expense of coming into compliance can be addressed by a step-wise approach of verifying progress against the standard on an annual basis, giving an operation five years to reach certification but providing them with recognition in the marketplace in the meantime.

Another weakness of forest certification to date is the difficulty for small operations to meet the standard. FSC has made some efforts to develop a streamlined standard for small operations, but it still remains too difficult for many. In some countries, this problem is being addressed through a program to certify loggers, because many small landholders turn over their forests to loggers for management.

Forest certification is also criticized by a few environmental and social groups who either oppose logging on principle or oppose specific companies and operations. One dilemma certification presents is how to treat a company that has some holdings certified to best practice but is pursuing unsustainable forest practices in other areas. FSC has put forward a policy to address this, but other certification systems have not done so. In some cases, critics have identified weaknesses in specific certifications where the certification has not met the standard it is supposed to meet. The FSC has a process for protesting such issues, forcing certifiers to respond to and address concerns. Certifiers that have demonstrated consistent problems with the quality of their audits have been delisted by the FSC. This has generally not been the case with other certification systems.

Conclusion

Certification of responsible forest management has had a greater positive impact on forests than any other approach in the past one hundred years. Only about 11 percent, or 470 million hectares of the world's 4.5 billion hectares of forests are under full park or wilderness protection status, and those are often protected only on paper.[31] The lack of active management opens these nominally protected areas to illegal logging, wildlife poaching, agricultural encroachment, and settlement. In addition, international treaties on forest management have stalled or have been inadequately enforced. By contrast, forest certification—by all of the systems together—has improved practices on more than 320 million hectares of forest globally, or 8.3 percent of all forests and 13.4 percent of all working forests in the world. FSC, the most rigorous system, has certified 32.3 percent.[32]

If we are to protect the forests of the world, we must provide the people living in and around them the means to support themselves. Sustainable forest management can provide those means, and certification can ensure that forests are truly being managed responsibly. Government policy can support responsible forest management by stopping illegal logging and by creating procurement policies that require FSC-certified forest products. The private sector can also help by specifying FSC, and indeed, some sectors, such as the paper industry, are making great strides.

Governments, consumers, and the private sector need to pressure all certification systems to become equivalent in rigor and credibility to FSC. The multistakeholder governance structure of FSC encourages it to engage in continual improvement, as it too needs to adapt and improve both its standard and its rules.

Forest certification is here to stay. It also seems close to the tipping point where it will become a standard part of doing business. The next five years will be critical in determining how well it can make inroads in the tropics, where it is most needed. The current negotiations around avoiding deforestation and encouraging reforestation as part of a global climate regime should help encourage more governments to support responsible forest management through certification as a way to ensure reduced deforestation while still addressing poverty-alleviation goals.

Notes

1. United Nations Department of Public Information, News And Media Division, "World Population Will Increase by 2.5 Billion by 2050; People Over 60 to Increase by More Than 1 Billion," *Press Release POP/952*, (2007), retrieved from http://www.un.org/News/Press/docs/2007/pop952.doc.htm.
2. *Global Forest Resources Assessment 2005*, (Rome: Food & Agriculture Org., 2006), Chapter 2, pp 11–36, retrieved from ftp://ftp.fao.org/docrep/fao/008/A0400E/A0400E03.pdf.
3. Markku Kanninen et al., *Do Trees Grow on Money? The Implications of Deforestation Research for Policies to Promote REDD*, (2007), retrieved from http://www.cifor.cgiar.org/publications/pdf_files/cop/REDD_paper0712 07.pdf.
4. *State Of The World's Forests 2007*, (Rome: Food & Agriculture Org., 2007), retrieved from ftp://ftp.fao.org/docrep/fao/009/a0773e/a0773e08.pdf.
5. *Global Forest Resources Assessment 2005*, (Rome: Food & Agriculture Org, 2006), chapter 2, pp. 11–36, retrieved from ftp://ftp.fao.org/docrep/fao/008/A0400E/A0400E03.pdf.
6. Ibid.
7. Ibid.
8. Ibid.
9. Ibid.
10. Ibid, chapter 3, pp. 37–56.
11. Patrick Gonzalez et al., "Forest and Woodland Systems," in *Ecosystems and Human Well-Being: Current State and Trends*, (Washington, D.C.: Island Press, 2005), pp. 585–614, retrieved from http://www.millenniumassessment.org/documents/document.290.aspx.pdf.

12. Gareth Thomas, *Fourth Global Environment Outlook Report*, (October 25, 2007), retrieved from https://www.dfid.gov.uk/Media-Room/Speeches-and-articles/2007-to-do/Speech-by-Gareth-Thomas-Minister-for-Trade-and-Development-at-the-launch-of-the-fourth-Global-Environment-Outlook-report-25-October-2007/.

13. See http://siteresources.worldbank.org/EXTCC/Resources/407863–12131225462243/5090543–1213136742584/May27 Agenda.pdf.

14. Markku Kanninen et al., *Do Trees Grow on Money? The Implications of Deforestation Research for Policies to Promote REDD*, (October 25, 2007), retrieved from http://www.cifor.cgiar.org/publications/pdf_files/cop/REDD_paper071207.pdf.

15. See http://www.fao.org/forestry/foris/data/fra2005/kf/common/GlobalForestA4-ENsmall.pdf.

16. Patrick Gonzalez "Forest and Woodland Systems," in *Ecosystems and Human Well-Being: Current State and Trends*, (Washington: Island Press, 2005), chapter 21, pp 585–621, retrieved from http://www.millenniumassessment.org/documents/document.290.aspx.pdf.

17. Markku Kanninen et al., *Do Trees Grow on Money? The Implications of Deforestation Research for Policies to Promote REDD*, (2007), retrieved from http://www.cifor.cgiar.org/publications/pdf_files/cop/REDD_paper071207.pdf

18. Michael E. Conroy (2007). Branded! How the 'Certification Revolution' is Transforming Global Corporations. Philadelphia: New Society Publishers, p.62

19. FSC Chain of Custody Certification, *FSC Rules & Program, Types of FSC certificates, Chain of Custody*. Retrieved from http://www.fsc.org/134.html?&L=0

20. Ibid.

21. Ibid.

22. Sophie Higman et al., eds., *The Sustainable Forestry Handbook*, (London: Earthscan, (2005), p. 24.

23. FSC Chain of Custody Certification, *FSC Rules & Program, Types of FSC Certificates, Chain of Custody*, retrieved from http://www.fsc.org/134.html?&L=0.

24. Ibid.

25. *Does Certification Make a Difference?*, (Piracicaba, Brazil: National Union of Book Publishers, 2009), retrieved from http://www.imaflora.org/arquivos/Does_certification_make_a_difference.pdf.

26. For details, see www.sfiprogram.org.

27. For details, see www.treefarmsystem.org.

28. For details, see www.itto.int.

29. "Global FSC Certificates: Type and Distribution," *Forest Stewardship Council* (2008), retrieved from http://www.fsc.org/fileadmin/web-data/public/document_center/powerpoints_graphs/facts_figures/08–12–31_Global_FSC_certificates_-_type_and_distribution_-_FINAL.pdf.

30. "FSC Brings New Prosperity to Legendary Community," *Forest Stewardship Council* (1996), retrieved from http://www.fsc.org/fileadmin/web-data/public/document_center/publications/case_studies/FSCBrings Prosperity_Chico_Mendes_1p.pdf.

31. *Global Forest Resources Assessment 2005. 15 Key Findings*, (Rome: Food & Agriculture Org., 2006), retrieved from http://www.fao.org/forestry/foris/data/fra2005/kf/common/GlobalForestA4-ENsmall.pdf.

32. Kraxner, Florian, Catherine Mater, Toshiaki Owari "Green Building Drives Construction Market and Forest Certification: Certified Forest Products Markets, 2007–2008," *UNECE/FAO Forest Products Annual Market Review, 2007–2008* (2008), pp. 1–16, retrieved from http://www.unece.org/timber/docs/certification/2008-cert.pdf.

V

Universal Multi-Industry and Multipurpose Voluntary Codes of Conduct

7

Kimberley Process Certification Scheme (KPCS): A Voluntary Multigroup Initiative to Control Trade in Conflict Diamonds

S. Prakash Sethi and Olga Emelianova

The Kimberley Process Certification Scheme (KPCS) was created in 2003 to control the illegal mining and trade of diamonds, variously called "conflict diamonds" or "blood diamonds," from war-torn countries in Africa. Money earned from the sale of these diamonds has been used to finance ethnic and territorial fights by local warlords and tribal chiefs, culminating in systematic mass killings, gross human rights violations, atrocities against women and children, genocide and ethnic cleansing, forced migration, and sectarian violence against civilians. More often than not, these atrocities have been concentrated among the poorest countries in Africa.

Even a brief history of bloody conflicts in these countries makes it imperative that every effort should be made to contain them to minimize loss of human life and economic devastation. Local wars and crimes against unprotected communities and civilians have been a recurring phenomenon through our history. While financing is a prerequisite for such activities, ethnic and sectarian hatred are the primal driving forces. Therefore, while every effort needs to be made to deny the funding that fuels these conflicts, this alone would not be sufficient. We must also find means to extinguish the more fundamental reasons that underlie these conflicts. Otherwise, lack of funding may exacerbate the problem by increasing the scope and intensity of atrocities that would be necessary to wage wars of hatred.[1]

The KPCS is a collective effort combining the resources and cooperation of global governing bodies, national governments, the business community, and civil society organizations. In this sense, the initiative belongs to a genre of "global governance systems" that attempts to bring together private-sector players and national governments, and cooperates with nongovernmental organizations (representing the public interest or speaking for disenfranchised groups). The philosophical approach is that of consensus building wherein all participants would voluntarily agree to regulate their conduct to achieve a commonly agreed end goal. There is greater emphasis on creating incentives—both financial and nonfinancial—that would motivate all parties to create common good while protecting and enhancing their self-interest. Sanctions, where necessary and justified, are imposed with extreme reluctance, if ever. Instead, transparency and peer pressure are applied to encourage the recalcitrant members to become participants in good standing.[2]

Unfortunately, the scorecard with regard to global governance systems has not been encouraging even where the primary parties are national governments operating under the aegis of well-established global organizations, such as the United Nations and its Security Council or the European Union. Nation-states have often brazenly exercised their power to pursue their respective political agendas and protect vested interests even in the face of a potential global crisis, such as nuclear proliferation or territorial wars. The challenges of multiparty coordination are far more complex, because national governments, business groups, and NGOs often have conflicting agendas and utilize differing means to achieve desired outcomes. These sharp disagreements are inevitable where gains from becoming a free rider can be substantial and where any sanctions for noncompliance are likely to be perfunctory.

In evaluating the effectiveness of the KPCS, we should examine the following issues:

1. The nature and scope of the initiative and the extent to which it defines the underlying problem.
2. The quality and independence of the governance structure in ensuring performance accountability.
3. The characteristics of the decision-making infrastructure and its ability to effectively implement the organization's mandate and connect it to the organization's principles.
4. A critical analysis of incentives and reward structures to ensure that their benefits are positively related to the various actors' self-interest while discouraging free riders, adverse selection, and creation of negative externalities.
5. A realistic assessment of the impact of the KPCS on the parties who would be adversely affected by its activities, that is, warlords and mercenaries, who stand to lose with every increase in the effectiveness of the KPCS.
6. The scope and extent of independent, third-party monitoring, and public disclosure of its findings, including follow-up of corrective efforts.

Antecedents to the Creation of the KPCS

The diamond industry has never been without severe conflicts and human rights abuses or environmental degradation regardless of whether they were committed by Western colonizers, leaders of diamond mining industry, and, more recently, corrupt governments and self-styled freedom fighters. Most conflict diamonds are produced in the economically underdeveloped African countries that also suffer from ineffective and corrupt government bodies and a general lack of judicial systems and oversight. These countries are often subject of political instability and long histories of human rights abuses.[3] The second half of the twentieth century was marked by a series of violent political conflicts, civil wars, and rebel movements in Central and Western Africa, including Sierra Leone, Angola, Liberia, and other African countries. Reports produced by the United Nations and many reputable nongovernmental organizations indicate that diamond exploration in Western and Central Africa was largely conducted under the direct or indirect oversight of national governments or rebel groups. The proceedings of this rough-diamond trading were used to fuel violent conflicts that resulted in the destruction of villages and towns, and death and injury to millions of civilians.[4]

Impetus for the Establishment of the KPCS

In July 1998, Global Witness, with support from Partnership Africa Canada and other NGOs, spearheaded a campaign to expose the nexus between diamond smuggling and the civil war. Whether they liked it or not, transnational corporations engaged in these operations found themselves accused of cooperating, or at the very least, benefiting from the environmental degradation and human rights abuses emanating from these operations.[5] The NGOs' campaign and the widely reported war horrors drew the attention of the international community to investigate the diamonds-for-arms trade that has been ravaging the African states.

The campaign and intense public scrutiny prompted the United Nations Security Council to impose sanctions on the Angola government, prohibiting the direct or indirect export of rough Angolan diamonds.[6] In May 2000, driven by the common goal to regulate illicit diamond trade, the South African diamond-producing states, representatives of the diamond industry, and the NGOs came together in Kimberley, South Africa, to formulate an action plan to end the conflict-diamond trade and debilitate the diamond-funded violence in the war-torn regions of southern Africa.[7] This meeting marked the beginning of a collaborative effort known as the Kimberley Process.

In December 2000, the United Nations General Assembly endorsed the creation of a global certification scheme to legitimize the trade of rough diamonds.[8] It became apparent to industry leaders that the diamond industry faced a major challenge to its business if diamonds were perceived not as symbols of long-lasting love, luxury, and wealth, but as symbols of corporate greed and exploitation, and drenched in the blood of innocent victims. The campaign against blood diamonds, complete with portrayals of the limbs of children cut off by rebels in Sierra Leone, effectively countered the soft focus of the diamond ring as an object representing love and commitment.[9] The drive for the industry's change from resistance to cooperation was spurred by De Beers, the industry leader that stood to lose the most from declining diamond sales.[10] In the same year, the World Federation of Diamond Bourses and the International Diamond Manufacturers Association jointly created the World Diamond Council (WDC) with the mandate to develop a tracking system for trade in rough diamonds and to prevent their illicit use.[11]

After two years of discussions, in November 2002, the UN, state governments, the diamond industry, and nongovernmental organizations launched the Kimberley Process Certification Scheme, an international certification scheme for rough diamonds based primarily on national certification schemes with internationally agreed minimum standards.[12]

The deadline for implementing the scheme was January 2003, with the participating members being granted until February 1 to begin checking procedures at national borders. Additionally, the period from January until February 2003 was declared the tolerance month, providing participants some leeway and avoiding imposition of any penalties where certificates could not be issued due to technical glitches.[13] However, several participating countries were underprepared, prompting a deadline extension to May 1, 2003.[14] From initiation of the Kimberley Process in 2000 until its implementation in May 2003, the UN, diamond industry trade bodies, civil society groups, and participating governments assembled approximately twenty-four times to draft, polish, and finalize the Kimberley Process Certification Scheme.

Implementing the KPCS

The Kimberley Process Certification Scheme implementing document describes the goals of the project, its governance-system deliberative bodies, organization and decision-making structures, responsibilities for monitoring performance, and public disclosure (see appendix 7.1). The KPCS exhibits all the hallmarks of a highly bureaucratic and structured system that is intended to coordinate and manage the activities of various stakeholders—nations, business groups, and nongovernmental organizations. It sets out not only procedures, but also detailed instructions for implementing them. Consensus building and deliberate negotiations are of paramount importance, and the leadership is rotated to indicate a sense of equality and egalitarianism.

The KPCS presents a paradox in terms of goal and means, performance, and accountability. In one sense, the organization's entire focus is devoted to managing conflicts among the participating groups to prevent the trade in illicit diamonds. All activities are premised on the assumption that regulated and certifiable trade is beneficial for all parties, who are expected to respond positively to incentives of generating higher revenues and disincentives against violations that may result in consumer boycotts and unwelcome attention from national regulatory bodies, NGOs, and the news media.

The industry's position that "the problem is controllable" is elegantly summarized by the following statement attributed to Nicky Oppenheimer:

> When you look at the volume of conflict diamonds, which are less than 4 percent of the world production compared to the 96 percent plus that come from good areas, it is obviously in all our interests to drive this percent away. Why should any of us put our business at risk for peanuts like this? That's crazy.[15]

Clearly, it serves Oppenheimer to offer a conservative estimate since it would make the problem relatively small and manageable. The perception of the industry's sincerity, and that of various member countries, is further reinforced through the elaborate structure of the KPCS apparatus. This would avoid greater public inquisitiveness, which may call for greater public accountability of results whether they are measured in terms of reducing the trade in illicit diamonds or measuring the impact of these efforts in the actual reduction in violence and human rights abuses in strife-ridden countries in Africa.

One wonders why such an elaborate system is needed to control the trade in illicit diamonds, which represents an insignificantly small percentage of the total worldwide diamond trade. At the same time, the KPCS devotes far fewer resources and organizational effort to evaluate the effectiveness of its efforts in combating the power of warlords and reducing their sources of income or availability of weapons. Unlike the case of parties that stand to gain from the elimination of trade in conflict diamonds, the KPCS does not address or analyze the issue of the probable reactions and responses of the groups, that is, warlords and other mercenary groups, whose activities would be adversely affected by the success of the KPCS.

A healthy sense of skepticism is in order, however. Illicit diamonds, by their very nature, move through informal and secretive channels, where Oppenheimer at best can claim an educated guess. Estimates by other observers have ranged between 10 and 25 percent of all diamonds mined, and an even higher percentage of diamonds mined in countries where national governments appear to be willing partners in such trade, or that may be unwilling or unable to control it. These greater estimates raise the problems of controlling illicit diamond trade to a significantly higher order of magnitude, with accompanying challenges of controlling their mining and trade.[16]

One should, therefore, legitimately ask how effective or meaningful the entire apparatus of the KPCS is when even by the standards of its organizers there are considerable leakages in the certification process through the entire supply-chain. Moreover, as we shall discuss in a later part of this chapter, the industry has done a very poor job of creating consumer awareness and supply-chain participation at the retail level to slow down, if not eliminate the sale of illicit or conflict diamonds.

Governance Structure of the KPCS

The Kimberley Process Certification Scheme is overseen by an annually appointed Chair representing a state government. The Chair is responsible for supervising the KPCS, the functioning of the working groups and committees, and general administration. There are six working groups that manage the KPCS, each of which is headed by a Chair and has its own organizational structure and members. The first chair assignment went to South Africa in 2003. This appointment has since rotated over the past five years, with Israel being the current chair holder.

Organization Structure and Governance Process of the KPCS

The KPCS has an elaborate organizational structure with various bureaus and sections to manage various aspects of its operations, supply-chain monitoring, certification-process auditing, communication, and public disclosure. These include the Kimberley Process Working Group on Monitoring (WGM), the Kimberley Process Working Group on Statistics (WGS), the Working Group of Diamond Experts (WGDE), the Working Group on Artisanal and Alluvial Production (WGAAP), the Participation Committee (PC), the Rules and Procedures Committee (RP), and the Selection Committee (SC).

The Kimberley Process Working Group on Monitoring (WGM)

The Kimberley Process Working Group on Monitoring (WGM) is in charge of helping members implement the KPCS and deals with issues arising therewith. The WGM is headed by the European Community and is in charge of the peer-review mechanism; co-coordinating review visits in member countries, and studying the participants' annual reports. The WGM is assisted by Israel. It also has a diverse membership base, including two civil society groups: Global Witness and Partnership Africa Canada. Using a checklist prepared by Partnership Africa Canada, the monitoring group undertakes review visits and missions to check for physical evidence of KPCS compliance by the participants.[17]

The Kimberley Process Working Group on Statistics (WGS)

The Kimberley Process Working Group on Statistics (WGS) presents statistical data on the production and trade of rough diamonds. It is chaired by the United States. The group is also in charge of developing and maintaining a website to collect and disseminate export, import, and diamond production information to the working group members and participants. It also offers advice on commodity classification codes of diamonds and develops best practices based on internal consultations.

The Working Group of Diamond Experts (WGDE)

The Working Group of Diamond Experts (WGDE) is the technical arm of the KPCS. It is responsible for identifying and solving technical and practical problems arising from the implementation of the certification. While providing technical assistance to members and making amendments to the certification, WGDE additionally performs the following: proposes changes to the Harmonized System Codes for rough diamonds to the World Customs Organization; classifies diamond powder; harmonizes valuation methodologies; and organizes the international transfer of diamond samples from exploration projects.

The Working Group on Artisanal and Alluvial Production (WGAAP)

The Working Group on Artisanal and Alluvial Production (WGAAP) addresses the challenges of alluvial diamond producers, promotes exchange of best practices, and strengthens internal controls in the implementation of the KPCS. Its objective is to regulate the production of alluvial diamonds and to ensure their traceability from mines to exports. The WGAAP ensures that artisanal diamonds passing through the official export chain are legal and have complied with the rules governing the KPCS. It also encourages diamond-producing countries to draft their own policies and enact legislative reforms to ensure that diamonds contribute to poverty reduction, socioeconomic upliftment, and development of the regions where the diamonds are being mined.[18]

Participation Committee (PC)

The Participation Committee is headed by the Namibia and is tasked with assisting the Chair of the Kimberley Process in admitting new participants, reviewing their eligibility for admission, and monitoring participants' KPCS compliance.

Rules and Procedures Committee (RP)

This committee is in charge of drawing up rules and procedures to be followed in the selection and appointment of office holders in the working groups of the Kimberley Process.

Selection Committee (SC)

Chaired by Israel, the Selection Committee is in charge of reviewing applicants for the position of Vice-Chair of the Kimberley Process. The appointed Vice-Chair becomes Chair the next year.[19] Currently, the Vice Chair is Democratic Republic of Congo.

Participation in the Kimberley Process

As set forth in the Kimberley Process, participation is open on a nondiscriminatory basis to all applicants engaged in the diamond business that are willing to comply with the requirements of the scheme. All prospective participants intending to participate need to notify the current Chair of their interest through diplomatic channels. Upon meeting the minimum criteria set forth in the certification, members are required to identify their mandated institutions for implementing the scheme and inform the same to the Chair and the other participants within a month. Participants are also required to provide details on the laws, regulations, rules, procedures, and other practices they will follow in executing the Kimberley Process. As per requirements, KP participants are allowed to import or export rough diamonds only from other KP members.[20]

Members/Participants and Observers

The number of participants endorsing the Kimberley Process as of February 2011 is forty-nine, representing seventy-five member countries, with the

European Community counted as single participating unit. Participants cover 99.8 percent of the global production of rough diamonds.[21] As of 2009, the following countries requesting membership in the KPCS were under review: Algeria, Bahrain, Burkina Faso, Cameroon, Cape Verde, Chile, Egypt, Gabon, Kenya, Kuwait, Mali, Philippines, Qatar, Swaziland, Tunisia, Mozambique, Uganda, Niger, Panama, and Peru.[22]

The diamond industry's trade body—the World Diamond Council—and civil society groups Global Witness and Partnership Africa Canada are engaged in the creation and the implementation of the Kimberley Process. Further discussions with regard to the involvement of civil society organizations and the diamond industry in the annual reporting process at a national level, reflecting the KP's tripartite (industry, governments, and NGOs) structure are in process.[23]

Implementation of the KPCS

The Kimberley Certificate issued by countries should meet the minimum requirements as prescribed by the KPCS. The certificate should carry the title "Kimberley Process Certificate" and a statement declaring that the diamond handling has followed the provisions listed in the KPCS. Other prerequisites that the certificate should include are country of origin, unique numbering with the Alpha 2 country code, tamper- and forgery-resistant packing, date of issuance, date of expiration, issuing authority, identification of exporter and importer, number of parcels in the shipment, carat weight of the shipment, and the value of the shipment.

The certificate may also comply with the several optional features and procedures included. The scheme mandates that the shipment of rough diamonds can only be exported or imported to and from a co-participant country in the Kimberley Process, and should be accompanied by a government-validated, forge-proof, and uniquely numbered Kimberley Process certificate describing the shipment's contents.

It should be noted here that KPCS compliance varies with the level of participation in the certification process. Consequently, different participants in the diamond-trade channel follow different measures.

Mining Companies and Rough Diamond Buyers (At Source)

Mining companies and rough-diamond buyers must confirm that the countries from which the rough diamonds are being exported or imported are Kimberley Process participants. Furthermore, they must also maintain auditable records verifying the legitimacy of the source and purchase of the diamonds. The mining company and the buyers must instruct the concerned exporting authority to validate the shipment, provide tamper-proof packaging, supply documentation, and include a Kimberley Process certificate. All participants should also comply with the industry's System of Warranties, and warranties must accompany every sale or export of the shipment.

Recipients of Imported Rough Diamonds

The recipients or importers of rough diamonds can only receive shipments from Kimberley Process participants along with a warranty and a Kimberley Process certificate from the exporter. The exporter must confirm receipt of the shipment, and the invoice of every transaction should carry a signed declaration stating that the diamonds have been purchased from conflict-free legitimate sources and are in compliance with the UN resolutions, and that the sellers guarantee that the diamonds are conflict-free.

A similar approach applies to all other participants in the rough-diamond supply-chain. These include rough-diamond dealers trading within a country's borders, rough-diamond dealers in re-exporting, diamond polishers and manufacturers, and diamond jewelry retailers.

Self-Regulation as the Foundation of the KPCS

The entire edifice of the KPCS is designed to facilitate self-regulation on the part of all participants. However, for self-regulation to work it must create systems and procedures that maximize positive incentives for the participants; that is, collective and cooperative action would be beneficial to the self-interest of all participants while at the same time enhancing society's benefits. Such a system should also create negative incentives or disincentives that would discourage participants from exploiting collective action for private good and exacerbating public harm through such actions as free ridership, pressure toward lowering standards of best industry practices, and otherwise exploiting the "commons" through creating negative externalities.

It is, therefore, important to understand that while self-regulation affords maximum opportunity for the participant to establish common principles or standards of conduct, self-regulation cannot be used to allow the participants to determine the extent that each participant would comply with their principles and report its performance in a manner of its own choosing, and without significant effort to independently verify its compliance effort and public disclosure in an orderly manner.

The KPCS and Self-Regulation

The primary purpose of the KPCS is to monitor the chain of custody of diamond shipments through proper documentation, and to account for the source of all diamonds passing through the Kimberley Process. Participants have designated local bodies to oversee the implementation of the KPCS, and the relevant export and import authorities check for KPCS compliance.

The World Diamond Council has initiated a System of Warranties where buyers and traders of rough and polished diamonds are required to maintain auditable warranty invoices for every sale.[24] Furthermore, all invoices exchanged or accompanying diamond shipments are required to carry the following statement:

The diamonds herein invoiced have been purchased from legitimate sources not involved in funding conflict and in compliance with United Nations resolutions. The seller hereby guarantees that these diamonds are conflict free, based on personal knowledge and/or written guarantees provided by the supplier of these diamonds.[25]

Additionally, all industry organizations and their members have adopted rules that require them to

a. trade only with companies that include warranty declarations on their invoices;
b. not buy diamonds from suspect sources or unknown suppliers, or which originate in countries that have not implemented the Kimberley Process Certification Scheme;
c. not buy diamonds from any sources that, after a legally binding due process system, have been found to be uncertified;
d. have violated government regulations restricting the trade in conflict diamonds;
e. not buy diamonds in or from any region that is subject to an advisory by a governmental authority indicating that conflict diamonds are emanating from or available for sale in such region, unless diamonds have been exported from such region in compliance with the Kimberley Process Certification Scheme;
f. not knowingly buy or sell or assist others to buy or sell conflict diamonds; and
g. ensure that all company employees who buy or sell diamonds within the diamond trade are well informed regarding trade resolutions and government regulations restricting the trade in conflict diamonds.[26]

Although participants are responsible for financing their own KPCS, the World Bank offers both financial and technical assistance to the Communities and Artisanal and Small-Scale Mining (CASM) network.[27] These funds are being used for research; grants for monitoring and feedback; technical assistance to guide different stakeholders on legal-, policy-, and technology-related issues; and knowledge development and sharing.

The CASM initiative was launched in March 2001 in response to an urgent plea made persistently at every international meeting on small-scale mining, with the goal of improving coordination between various institutions working in this sector and for better-integrated, multidisciplinary solutions to the complex social and environmental challenges facing small-scale mining communities. CASM has created a knowledge-based community and a strong network of miners, communities, government officials, development agencies, and nonprofit organizations. It also seeks to become a more active promoter and advocate of "good practice" and better-conceived approaches for meeting the poverty challenge and building the basis for more sustainable communities and economies.

Three regional CASM networks have been established in Africa, Asia, and China to provide more direct support to artisanal and small-scale mining communities in these regions.[28]

Internal Controls

All participants in the Kimberley Process are required to establish a system of internal controls to ensure that conflict diamonds are eliminated from the normal supply-chain. Some of the general measures that participants can incorporate while drafting internal controls include appointing official coordinators to deal with KPCS implementation; maintaining information and data for cooperation and transparency among participants; verifying the financial channels of cash purchases of rough diamonds; and informing participants and the chair of individuals and companies involved in KPCS convictions.[29]

Compliance

Trading in uncertified diamonds or exporting certified diamonds to non-KP countries is prohibited. Failure to comply may lead to confiscation or rejection of the diamond shipment or criminal sanctions on the participating members. Members that fail to follow the principles of self-regulation and the System of Warranties initiated by the World Diamond Council may face expulsion from diamond-industry institutions.[30]

All noncompliance and KPCS implementation issues of KP participants are referred to the Chair, who in turn informs all the other member participants and engages in a dialogue to resolve the issue. Review missions are organized by other participants or their representatives to verify KPCS noncompliance, and the results are forwarded to the Chair and the concerned participants while maintaining strict confidentiality.[31]

Accomplishments of the KPCS

The KPCS has been in operation since 2003. It is, therefore, pertinent to ask as to how well the system has accomplished its objective of eliminating illegal or conflict diamonds from the legitimate supply-chain. This is, however, a very difficult task since no one has any control over the groups that mine and trade in illicit diamonds to secure necessary funds to pursue their political and military goals. From our perspective, this is one of most conspicuous omissions in the KPCS. The assumption that success of the KPCS in improving legal trade in diamonds would result in (a) reducing production and trade in illicit diamonds, and (b) limiting, if not eliminating the ability of warring groups to find ways to mine and sell diamonds to buy weapons, is simply unsustainable as a matter of logic, and ignores the reality of the situation as it exists and is apparent to everyone. Therefore, if the ultimate purpose initiative is to reduce violent conflict and human rights abuses, the KPCS must take into consideration the motives and means available to the fighting groups and the price they are willing to pay—engaging in atrocities to maintain their hold on the production and marketing of illicit diamonds.

The official documents of the KPCS describe the accomplishments of the organization's achievements in the following terms:

> *The Kimberley Process Certification Scheme (KPCS) has evolved into an effective mechanism for stemming the trade in conflict diamonds and is recognized as a unique conflict-prevention instrument to promote peace and security. The joint efforts of governments, industry leaders and civil society representatives have enabled the Kimberley Process (KP) to curb successfully the flow of conflict diamonds in a very short period of time. Diamond experts estimate that conflict diamonds now represent a fraction of one percent of the international trade in diamonds, compared to estimates of up to 15% in the 1990s. That has been the KP's most remarkable contribution to a peaceful world, which should be measured not in terms of carats, but by the effects on people's lives.*[32]

The KPCS document, however, does not provide any meaningful information in support of this assertion.

The collaborative nature of the certification for diamond industry is probably its strongest characteristic. From its initiation, nongovernmental organizations have played a major role in the formulation of KPCS goals, processes, and mechanisms of certification. While the initiative is mainly focused on improved government control over diamond production and trading, it was the immediate interest and support, direct involvement, and active participation of all parties—governments, industry representatives, trade organizations, multilateral organizations, and civil society groups—that triggered necessary changes.

The Kimberley Process forbids noncompliant countries' right to trade diamonds with the certified countries. This issue of free trade was one of the initial concerns of the certification scheme in regard to the approval of the Kimberley Process by the World Trade Organization (WTO).[33] But with the overwhelming support of industry members for diamond certification and after petitioning by several member countries, the WTO granted the Kimberley Process a waiver based on the "extraordinary humanitarian nature" of the initiative, which aims to eradicate the illicit diamond trade.[34]

The collaborative nature of the initiative is also seen in the governance and management of the Kimberley Process. All applications for participation in the KPCS are reviewed and evaluated by Participation Committee, which consists of government representatives, industry players, and NGOs. Furthermore, the KPCS system was created to accommodate an ongoing dialogue between all stakeholder groups, which added to constant improvement of the initiative. Annual meetings are held to evaluate progress made by the certification program and to discuss further actions that need to be taken. One of the examples of this process is the Three-Year Review meeting of the KP in 2006, during which several cases of noncompliance on the part of the United States, Venezuela, Brazil, Côte d'Ivoire, Guyana, Togo, and Ghana were presented. All forty-three recommendations for corrective actions that were presented at the meeting were accepted.

The KPCS's official document states that the KP has done more than just stem the flow of conflict diamonds; it has also helped stabilize fragile countries and supported their development. As the KP has made life harder for criminals, it has brought large volumes of diamonds onto the legal market that would not otherwise have made it there. This has increased the revenues of poor governments, and helped them to address their countries' development challenges. For instance, some $125 million worth of diamonds were legally exported from Sierra Leone in 2006, compared to almost none at the end of the 1990s.[35] Data provided by the KPCS suggest starting in late 1990s through early 2000, there was a significant reduction in illicit diamond trade. Angola was the first to introduce the Certificate of Origin requirement for diamond exports, in 1998, followed by Sierra Leone, where between 2000 and 2001 there was a significant increase in diamond trading through official channels.[36]

A proxy measure to assess the effectiveness of the KPCS would be to observe the change in the flow of diamonds in the KPCS supply-chain from all sources, especially from the countries that are suffering from violent conflicts and human rights abuses, and where rough diamonds are the currency of the realm and are used to finance political and military agendas. Unfortunately, an increase in the flow of certified diamonds is a double-edged sword and an unreliable measure. For example:

- An increase in the flow of certified diamonds may result, at least in part, from the phenomenon of "certification capture"; that is, the certification process has been contaminated and thereby allows illicit diamonds to pass through certified channels. The system is akin to money laundering, where money from illegal activities is sanitized by passing it through legitimate channels.
- The success of the certification process may simply result in increasing the risk of trading in illegal diamonds and thereby reducing their price for the producers of those diamonds. Thus, rather than discouraging the production of conflict diamonds and thereby reducing violent conflicts, the system may have the perverse effect of increasing violence and human rights abuses since the warring parties would need to produce more diamonds to generate a similar amount of money to support their military activity.

There is ample historical evidence and contemporary activity to show that no amount of sanctions can completely eliminate trade in illicit products; for example, oil for South Africa sanctions because of its apartheid policies, trade with Iran in violation of sanctions for that country's nuclear power program, and trade in cocaine and other contraband products, provided that there is reward at a higher level of risk. Under these circumstances, it is almost impossible to measure the success of the KPCS in terms of reducing conflict and human rights abuse in war-torn areas of Africa. These conflicts are sustained by a multiplicity of ethnic and religious beliefs, political ambitions of tribal leaders who are unwilling to accept political boundaries that were arbitrarily created by colonial powers, and violence and ethnic hatred, which are immune to rational logic, and where established governments may also have tenuous and suspect claim to power.

In the following section, we present a brief description of leakages in the system and violations of KPCS principles and standards by the very institutions that are solely responsible for creating the certification documents, thoroughly making the system an empty shell where style has superseded substance and process has been substituted for outcome.

Misuse of Documentation

The entire edifice of the KPCS depends on proper documentation and the integrity of various agents in the supply-chain to ensure that all documents are accurate and that information contained in those documents has been verified against the physical properties of the packages containing rough diamonds. Unfortunately, the system has shown persistent failures in the five processes, through either deliberate deception and fraud or lack of trained personnel.

By the nature of its geological formation, diamonds from African alluvial deposits are all similar in their physical characteristics. It is neither possible to differentiate, for instance, Angolan diamonds from Liberian, nor to identify whether diamonds from the same region were excavated prior to, during, or after the conflict period. Therefore, a consistent and reliable system of documentation from the point of extraction of each stone to retail stores' displays is the only feasible way for traders to know if the diamond was legally produced and sold. Any loopholes in the paper trail, therefore, jeopardize the overall effort. Unfortunately, as critics note, these loopholes occur in various stages of the diamond trade. What is most disturbing is that the KPCS lacks effective mechanisms and controls over the certification process, leaving implementation and compliance reporting for certification entirely to local governments and industry participants. These problems have been identified by various NGOs with deep involvement with the KPCS, and also by various UN, U.S., and other governmental bodies in the course of exercising their oversight responsibilities. In this sense, the entire diamond industry, from major producers, diamond processers, and retailers, must also share responsibility for the lackluster effort in promoting and marketing certified diamonds and in consumer education to increase awareness in favor of buying only certified diamonds.[37]

Government Systems for Certifications

Minimum requirements for a country's participation in Kimberley Process Certification Scheme include (a) establishing an internal system of control, and (b) providing a statement of diamond origin certified by a government agent at the border-crossing point. While the KPCS offers some specifics on the physical characteristics of the certification document and what it should include, such as watermarks, a unique number, parcel weight, et cetera, it does not offer any details on the systems the government should employ to guarantee the accuracy of such statements. Countries that join the KPCS are expected to voluntarily create some sort of internal system of control, self-assessment, and reporting of statistical data.

Most of the countries involved in the production of diamonds are characterized by a high level of corruption and general lack of state oversight.[38] This fact raises the issue of credibility of trade companies' compliance with the certification scheme. There is currently no effective monitoring system in place to verify that all state certifications are issued in the legitimate manner.[39] Conflict diamonds from rebel groups can enter a neighboring country and receive a state certificate as originally produced in this country; for example, Revolutionary United Front (RUF) diamonds from Sierra Leon coming to Liberia and being certified as conflict-free Liberian diamonds.[40]

An effective internal control system calls for an effective government that is capable not only of controlling and supervising its mining industry, but also providing adequate infrastructure, protection, and guarantees for efficient mining and trading operations. No African government, including most developed African countries, can currently offer such levels of control.

However, even most developed European and North American countries fail to prove that they have efficient systems in place to control exports and imports of diamonds. In 2006, the U.S. Government Accountability Office released a report investigating state compliance with the Clean Diamond Act and the Kimberley Process Certification Scheme. The investigation revealed significant loopholes in trade documentation and export and import records, and inconsistencies in control and oversight chains.[41]

Supply-Chain Regulation and System of Warranties

The Kimberley Process Certification only applies to international trades; it does not set any specific requirement for internal diamond trades within one country. Diamond trade associations, notably the World Diamond Council, promote a system of warrants to track diamonds through supply and retail chains. However, adoption of this system is voluntary.

In African countries, characterized by predominantly alluvial small-scale diamond production, the supply chain is built on the scheme "digger—middleman—licensed exporter,"[42] Acquiring a license is usually a complex and expensive procedure, and while authorities make an effort to keep track of all middlemen, the number of illegal middlemen is still very high—in 2004 about 3,000 such middlemen were arrested in West Africa.[43] Added to that is governments' poor control of borders and territories occupied by rebels and the spread of black-market operations.

Crossing borders and changing hands from diggers and middlemen to exporters, diamond trading corporations, diamond cutters, laboratories, and reserves, a diamond finally reaches consumers in the retail jewelry market. However, this also seems to be the point where the stream of guarantees dries out. Not only is the claim of conflict-free weakened by multiple transactions and changes of ownership, in many cases it is not even existent. In March 2004, Global Witness conducted a survey of thirty-three U.S. retail stores to verify their compliance with the promises to combat conflict-diamond trade. The survey showed that many of the stores, including international luxury stores, national department stores, and jewelry chains, fail to deliver on this promise. Only 17 percent of the surveyed stores were able to respond in writing about their policies on conflict-free diamonds and warranty system implementation. At the same time, 88 percent of the salespeople, when asked about store policies, were not aware of the conflict-free warranty requirements.[44]

Later same year, the investigation was repeated jointly by Global Witness and Amnesty International. September 18, 2004, was announced as the Day of Action on Conflict Diamonds. A major U.S. jewelry trade association sent out an advisory to its 10,000-plus members warning them to respond promptly to NGO and media inquiries. Nevertheless, despite the public announcement and internal industry advisory, the survey again drew a disappointing picture. Out of eighty-five U.S. and UK companies that were sent management surveys, only thirty-seven (44 percent) responded to the inquiry. Of these, thirty companies (81 percent) did not provide detailed information on warranty system implementation and compliance. In the survey of sales personnel in the 579 stores visited in the United States and the UK, a significantly larger number compared with the March survey (54 percent in the UK, and 27 percent in the United States) were aware of their company's policy on conflict-free diamonds. However, the numbers dropped dramatically when sales personnel was asked to provide copies of the policy, state the specifics of the implementation of the warranty system, and indicate the number of warrants issued to customers. Moreover, even after the trade association advisory, most of the salespeople in the United States (67 percent) simply refused to discuss the issue.[45] This type of survey has been repeated over the years, but the results remain quite upsetting.[46]

Another aspect limiting the credibility of the System of Warrants lies in its written formulation. The system requires issuing invoices stating that the diamonds subjected to the transaction are conflict-free "based on personal knowledge and/or written guarantees provided by the supplier," which opens doors for interpretation.

In the absence of a standardized and enforced system of tracing diamonds through the entire supply and distribution system, there are absolutely no guarantees that the diamonds are conflict-free. "No jeweler can assure their consumers that the diamonds they're buying are clean," says Kristen Patten of NGO One Sky. "Even diamonds advertised as Canadian can't be guaranteed as conflict-free."[47]

Kimberley Process Oversight and Compliance Enforcement

Weak or nonexistent control of the governments over the diamond production, corrupt systems, and absence of a regulatory and legal framework for supply-chain compliance already create a shaky platform for self-regulation. Added to that is a lack of coordination and oversight on the part of the KPCS.

Current interpretation of the KPCS lacks any specifics on the mechanisms and norms of assessment, evaluation, and reporting of countries' self-governance. Some member countries of the KP agreement, such as Russia, which is the second-largest diamond producer in the world, even showed reluctance to disclose diamond trade statistics.[48] The documentation produced by member countries is often delayed and inconsistent. Furthermore, this information is not properly verified. While the KPCS conducts periodic country visits and reviews, the decision to conduct a visit must be approved by all other members and receive full consent from the government officials of the country to be visited. Country visits usually take two to five days, and include (a) meetings with state bodies in charge of export-import operations, customs, and mining-industry and state representatives; (b) visits to customs checkpoints and mining production; (c) review of documentation. The delegations are composed of other member countries' representatives and are therefore in the nature of a peer review.[49] We should also emphasize the fact that the KPCS internal monitoring system is a closed system. In other words, all nonconforming activities by participating actors and the sanctions imposed by the KPCS are held in the strictest confidence and are not made public. The practical impact of this policy is to protect the offending parties and remove public pressure toward better compliance.

It is important to note that almost all of the KPCS country reviews find some room for improvement in countries' compliance with the KPCS. Botswana was repeatedly named the best-performing KPCS member, and its control systems were set as a benchmark for other countries. Nevertheless, activists and watchdogs accused even KPCS's best performer of being in violation of human rights for forcefully displacing indigenous people from traditional land in the mining areas.[50] Moreover, former president of Botswana Festus G. Mogae acknowledged that some of that county's diamonds could be illicit.[51]

Many member countries of the KPCS were repeatedly pointed out by NGOs and media reports to be in violation of the agreement, smuggling diamonds, and abusing human rights.[52] However, KPCS reaction to such allegations is very slow. The process of approval to conduct a review takes a long time since all members have to approve a country visit. Even if the review acknowledges noncompliance, violating countries are not immediately expelled from the member list.[53] Over the seven years that passed since the launch of the KP Certification, three countries have been removed from the member list: Republic of Congo, Côte d'Ivoire, and Venezuela. All of these countries are still listed as voluntary participants of the KPCS, but are not allowed to conduct diamond trade until further notice.

In fact, currently there is no standard procedure for actions to be taken in case of a country's or a company's violation of the KPCS agreement. All in all, the KPCS has neither effective instruments to verify compliance nor a standardized system of addressing various cases of noncompliance.

Perhaps the most notable case showing the inability of the KPCS to provide meaningful oversight of certification compliance and to proactively react to a country's inability to meet the minimum participation requirements is present in the case of the United States. While the United States has the largest share in the import of rough diamonds, the country's internal control systems were found to be for the most part ineffective.[54] These findings were reported not by a civil society group or the mass media, but by an official state entity—the U.S. Government Accountability Office (GAO). The GAO report clearly demonstrated that the United States had failed to provide proof of having an effective internal control system, which is supposed to be a minimum requirement for participation in the KPCS. Nevertheless, the country is still a formal member of the KPCS.

Another example of such negligence is the recent case of Venezuelan diamonds. In a 2007 investigative report, Partnership Africa Canada listed multiple violations of the KPCS agreement on the part of Venezuela and urged the KPCS Chair to expel the country from the list of members.[55] However, no sanctions followed, and Venezuela maintained its KPCS membership status. A year later, Global Witness called for the European Commission -- at that time serving as the Chair of the Kimberley Process—to expel Venezuela for violating the Scheme agreement.[56] During the KPCS Intercessional Meeting in summer 2008, Venezuela announced its temporary "withdrawal" from the agreement, meaning that it would cease all exports and imports of diamonds for two years while it reorganizes its diamond industry. Later same year, two years after PAC's report, the Kimberley Process formed a delegation to conduct the first visit to Venezuela since the KPCS's inception in 2003. The delegation did not include any representatives of civil societies, but nevertheless confirmed all allegations made by PAC in 2006.[57] At the Plenary Session held in Namibia in November 2009, the Participation Committee (PC) requested a report from the other Working Groups on their engagement with Venezuela in assisting the country in developing a plan of action to implement minimum KP standards. The PC has expressed support for providing the necessary assistance to reintegrate Venezuela into the the KPCS.[58]

Another example is Zimbabwe, where a number of human rights atrocities have been reported, along with smuggling and poor records for the country's diamond production and trade.[59] A four-day country visit, conducted in 2007, included representatives of diamond-trade organizations and civil society groups, and revealed that "the overall structure of the implementation of the KP Certification Scheme appears to be working in a satisfactory manner in Zimbabwe, and, in general, meets the minimum requirements of the KPCS." A joint action plan was agreed upon with the government of Zimbabwe to bring the country back into compliance. The action plan provides for a KP-appointed monitor to verify all shipments of diamonds from the Marange diamond fields prior to export. However, the plan does not address the wider context of noncompliance in Zimbabwe's KP system. There is no mention of the central role that the Zimbabwean army continues to play in mining and smuggling, nor does it refer to past and ongoing human rights abuses.[60] While the country remains a member of the KPCS, the accusations of human rights abuses and violations of the Kimberley Process agreement in Zimbabwe continue.[61]

Campaigners for the Kimberley Process Civil Society Coalition, whose members include GW, PAC, and Green Advocates (Liberia), are calling for action in the following areas:

- Governments should introduce explicit provisions that bind KP members to ensure basic human rights in their diamond sectors.
- The consensus-based decision-making process must be reformed to allow swift action and to avoid deadlocks.
- The KP needs an independent statistical analysis, monitoring, and research capacity that sets a high standard of evaluation, avoids conflicts of interest, and ensures follow-up.

- The KP's commitment to diamonds for development must translate into concrete action, particularly in artisanal producing countries.[62]

Cut and Polished Diamonds and Colored Stones

The Kimberley Process Certification Scheme has certain limitations not only in regard to compliance verification and enforcement, but also in its scope of coverage. The Scheme currently calls for export-import certification only of rough diamonds, leaving cut and polished diamonds and colored gems outside of its spectrum.

The largest cutting and polishing facilities are still concentrated in India, where De Beers historically controlled most of the diamond-polishing facilities. In recent years, however, after De Beers lost its monopoly over rough diamonds, diamond-cutting and polishing factories began to expand to more countries, including the African continent, to be closer to production areas. British company Gem Diamonds plans to open facilities in Mauritius, and is considering expansion to Angola, Democratic Republic of Congo, and South Africa.[63] Lev Leviev set up diamond-polishing facilities in several countries, including Russia, Israel, and the African countries of Namibia and Angola.[64]

Inadequate control over diamond-cutting and polishing operations creates an opportunity for illicit conflict diamonds to enter legitimate channels of international trade. This issue has been repeatedly brought to KPCS's attention by its civil society observers.[65] Cases of suspicious trade of polished diamonds were recorded in several nonparticipating countries that also do not have any known cutting and polishing facilities.[66] Countries that are not members of the KPCS or that are prohibited to trade rough diamonds can and in some cases do participate in polished-diamond trading.

It is also very surprising that the Kimberley Process left colored gems out of its certification scheme. Despite their somewhat lower value, colored gems are not much different from diamonds in terms of their production and distribution process and in their potential to fund conflicts. Myanmar, for example, is the source of the majority of the world's rubies. Although the United States stopped official trade with Myanmar to avoid supporting the country's military regime, Burmese rubies still end up on U.S. jewelry retailers' shelves via Thailand and India.[67]

After the discovery of large reserves of rubies, sapphires, and other colored gemstones in the Mozambique Belt, Tanzania, Madagascar, and Mozambique are becoming major players in colored gemstone production and trading. Tanzanite is a recently discovered stone that is more rare than diamonds and therefore is very valuable. It was historically mined by small artisan miners and smuggled into neighboring Kenya to avoid paying taxes.[68] A shocking news story that appeared after World Trade Center attack on September 11, 2001, linked illicit tanzanite trade with Al Qaeda operations.[69] In the early 1990s, local miners were forced off the land, and production is now controlled by the state and the largest local company, TanzaniteOne. However, internal controls over small-scale mining in the vicinity of TanzaniteOne operations are not sufficient to prevent smuggling of the gem.[70]

The KPCS: An Assessment

The aforementioned discussion and analysis leads us to conclude that notwithstanding the seriousness of the problem and the enormity of the challenge, we should expect at best modest results and restrained expectations. We should not build exaggerated hopes of creating a new world order that is both self-sustaining and self-regulating, and that given time and goodwill among participants would lead us to a nirvana here and now rather than in life hereinafter.

The KPCS may eventually lead to some control and reduction in the trade in illicit diamonds, provided the system can improve its enforcement procedures and provide greater transparency and public disclosure of wrongdoers, starting with governments and ending with all segments of the private sector. However, given KPCS performance over the past six-plus years, it does not appear that significant improvements are likely to happen anytime soon. Similarly, for the reasons explained in the previous section, one cannot assume that this would necessarily lead to a reduction in ethnic and sectarian violence in war-torn regions of Africa. It is apparent that for the time being, those who stand to gain from the illicit diamond trade and unstable political regimes are more committed to their cause than their opponents.

Admirers and supporters of the KPCS present it as an "innovative attempt to end conflict by cutting off the ability of combatants to finance war via diamonds." In terms of process, the KPCS is presented as an outstanding example of an inclusive approach involving nation-states, the private sector, NGOs, and international and multilateral organizations. "[The] Kimberley Process is an innovation in global governance that was facilitated by how norms for companies and conflict complemented each other, and fit with the structure and incentive built into diamond markets. Lofty aspirations do not stop here; however, the Kimberley Process is projected to speak to the humanitarian norms that are increasingly a part of global discourse and at the same time builds upon the growing expectation that corporations should behave responsibility."[71]

Unfortunately, when stripped of the usual hype and hyperbole, the KPCS is not an innovative model. Instead it is an overly bureaucratic framework with cumbersome and ever-growing rules and regulations, which are often found to be violated by various parties to such an extent that it makes the entire system suspect. The very institutions that are supposed to certify performance and assure integrity are found to be its worst offenders. Despite the lip service, the diamond industry, from major corporations to retailers, seems to have done very little by way of promoting the sale of certified diamonds or educating consumers to demand such verification.

Appendix 7.1

KIMBERLEY PROCESS CERTIFICATION SCHEME

PREAMBLE

PARTICIPANTS,

RECOGNISING that the trade in conflict diamonds is a matter of serious international concern, which can be directly linked to the fuelling of armed conflict, the activities of rebel movements aimed at undermining or overthrowing legitimate governments, and the illicit traffic in, and proliferation of, armaments, especially small arms and light weapons;

FURTHER RECOGNISING the devastating impact of conflicts fuelled by the trade in conflict diamonds on the peace, safety and security of people in affected countries and the systematic and gross human rights violations that have been perpetrated in such conflicts;

NOTING the negative impact of such conflicts on regional stability and the obligations placed upon states by the United Nations Charter regarding the maintenance of international peace and security;

BEARING IN MIND that urgent international action is imperative to prevent the problem of conflict diamonds from negatively affecting the trade in legitimate diamonds, which makes a critical contribution to the economies of many of the producing, processing, exporting and importing states, especially developing states;

RECALLING all of the relevant resolutions of the United Nations Security Council under Chapter VII of the United Nations Charter, including the relevant provisions of Resolutions 1173 (1998), 1295 (2000), 1306 (2000), and 1343 (2001), and determined to contribute to and support the implementation of the measures provided for in these resolutions;

HIGHLIGHTING the United Nations General Assembly Resolution 55/56 (2000) on the role of the trade in conflict diamonds in fuelling armed conflict, which called on the international community to give urgent and careful consideration to devising effective and pragmatic measures to address this problem;

FURTHER HIGHLIGHTING the recommendation in United Nations General Assembly Resolution 55/56 that the international community develop detailed proposals for a simple and workable international certification scheme for rough diamonds based primarily on national certification schemes and on internationally agreed minimum standards;

RECALLING that the Kimberley Process, which was established to find a solution to the international problem of conflict diamonds, was inclusive of concerned stake holders, namely producing, exporting and importing states, the diamond industry and civil society;

CONVINCED that the opportunity for conflict diamonds to play a role in fuelling armed conflict can be seriously reduced by introducing a certification scheme for rough diamonds designed to exclude conflict diamonds from the legitimate trade;

RECALLING that the Kimberley Process considered that an international certification scheme for rough diamonds, based on national laws and practices and meeting internationally agreed minimum standards, will be the most effective system by which the problem of conflict diamonds could be addressed;

ACKNOWLEDGING the important initiatives already taken to address this problem, in particular by the governments of Angola, the Democratic Republic of Congo, Guinea and Sierra Leone and by other key producing, exporting and importing countries, as well as by the diamond industry, in particular by the World Diamond Council, and by civil society;

WELCOMING voluntary self-regulation initiatives announced by the diamond industry and recognising that a system of such voluntary self-regulation contributes to ensuring an effective internal control system of rough diamonds based upon the international certification scheme for rough diamonds;

RECOGNISING that an international certification scheme for rough diamonds will only be credible if all Participants have established internal systems of control designed to eliminate the presence of conflict diamonds in the chain of producing, exporting and importing rough diamonds within their own territories, while taking into account that differences in production methods and trading practices as well as differences in institutional controls thereof may require different approaches to meet minimum standards;

FURTHER RECOGNISING that the international certification scheme for rough diamonds must be consistent with international law governing international trade;

ACKNOWLEDGING that state sovereignty should be fully respected and the principles of equality, mutual benefits and consensus should be adhered to;

RECOMMEND THE FOLLOWING PROVISIONS:

SECTION I

Definitions

For the purposes of the international certification scheme for rough diamonds (hereinafter referred to as "the Certification Scheme") the following definitions apply:

CONFLICT DIAMONDS means rough diamonds used by rebel movements or their allies to finance conflict aimed at undermining legitimate governments, as described in relevant United Nations Security Council (UNSC) resolutions insofar as they remain in effect, or in other similar UNSC resolutions which may be adopted in the future, and as understood and recognised in United Nations General Assembly (UNGA) Resolution 55/56, or in other similar UNGA resolutions which may be adopted in future;

COUNTRY OF ORIGIN means the country where a shipment of rough diamonds has been mined or extracted;

COUNTRY OF PROVENANCE means the last Participant from where a shipment of rough diamonds was exported, as recorded on import documentation;

DIAMOND means a natural mineral consisting essentially of pure crystallised carbon in the isometric system, with a hardness on the Mohs (scratch) scale of 10, a specific gravity of approximately 3.52 and a refractive index of 2.42;

EXPORT means the physical leaving/taking out of any part of the geographical territory of a Participant;

EXPORTING AUTHORITY means the authority(ies) or body(ies) designated by a Participant from whose territory a shipment of rough diamonds is leaving, and which are authorised to validate the Kimberley Process Certificate;

FREE TRADE ZONE means a part of the territory of a Participant where any goods introduced are generally regarded, insofar as import duties and taxes are

concerned, as being outside the customs territory;

IMPORT means the physical entering/bringing into any part of the geographical territory of a Participant;

IMPORTING AUTHORITY means the authority(ies) or body(ies) designated by a Participant into whose territory a shipment of rough diamonds is imported to conduct all import formalities and particularly the verification of accompanying Kimberley Process Certificates;

KIMBERLEY PROCESS CERTIFICATE means a forgery resistant document with a particular format which identifies a shipment of rough diamonds as being in compliance with the requirements of the Certification Scheme;

OBSERVER means a representative of civil society, the diamond industry, international organisations and non-participating governments invited to take part in Plenary meetings; (*Further consultations to be undertaken by the Chair.*)

PARCEL means one or more diamonds that are packed together and that are not individualised;

PARCEL OF MIXED ORIGIN means a parcel that contains rough diamonds from two or more countries of origin, mixed together;

PARTICIPANT means a state or a regional economic integration organisation for which the Certification Scheme is effective; (*Further consultations to be undertaken by the Chair.*)

REGIONAL ECONOMIC INTEGRATION ORGANISATION means an organisation comprised of sovereign states that have transferred competence to that organisation in respect of matters governed by the Certification Scheme;

ROUGH DIAMONDS means diamonds that are unworked or simply sawn, cleaved or bruted and fall under the Relevant Harmonised Commodity Description and Coding System 7102.10, 7102.21 and 7102.31;

SHIPMENT means one or more parcels that are physically imported or exported;

TRANSIT means the physical passage across the territory of a Participant or a nonParticipant, with or without transhipment, warehousing or change in mode of transport, when such passage is only a portion of a complete journey beginning and terminating beyond the frontier of the Participant or non-Participant across whose territory a shipment passes;

SECTION II

The Kimberley Process Certificate

Each Participant should ensure that:

a. a Kimberley Process Certificate (hereafter referred to as the Certificate) accompanies each shipment of rough diamonds on export;

b. its processes for issuing Certificates meet the minimum standards of the Kimberley Process as set out in Section IV;

c. Certificates meet the minimum requirements set out in Annex I. As long as these requirements are met, Participants may at their discretion establish additional characteristics for their own Certificates, for example their form, additional data or security elements;

d. it notifies all other Participants through the Chair of the features of its Certificate as specified in Annex I, for purposes of validation.

SECTION III

Undertakings in respect of the international trade in rough diamonds

Each Participant should:

a. with regard to shipments of rough diamonds exported to a Participant, require that each such shipment is accompanied by a duly validated Certificate;

b. with regard to shipments of rough diamonds imported from a Participant:
  - require a duly validated Certificate;
  - ensure that confirmation of receipt is sent expeditiously to the relevant Exporting Authority. The confirmation should as a minimum refer to the Certificate number, the number of parcels, the carat weight and the details of the importer and exporter;
  - require that the original of the Certificate be readily accessible for a period of no less than three years;

c. ensure that no shipment of rough diamonds is imported from or exported to a nonParticipant;

d. recognise that Participants through whose territory shipments transit are not required to meet the requirement of paragraphs (a) and (b) above, and of Section II (a) provided that the designated authorities of the Participant through whose territory a shipment passes, ensure that the shipment leaves its territory in an identical state as it entered its territory (i.e. unopened and not tampered with).

SECTION IV

Internal Controls

Undertakings by Participants

Each Participant should:

a. establish a system of internal controls designed to eliminate the presence of conflict diamonds from shipments of rough diamonds imported into and exported from its territory;
b. designate an Importing and an Exporting Authority(ies);
c. ensure that rough diamonds are imported and exported in tamper resistant containers;
d. as required, amend or enact appropriate laws or regulations to implement and enforce the Certification Scheme and to maintain dissuasive and proportional penalties for transgressions;
e. collect and maintain relevant official production, import and export data, and collate and exchange such data in accordance with the provisions of Section V.
f. when establishing a system of internal controls, take into account, where appropriate, the further options and recommendations for internal controls as elaborated in Annex II.

Principles of Industry Self-Regulation

Participants understand that a voluntary system of industry self-regulation, as referred to in the Preamble of this Document, will provide for a system of warranties underpinned through verification by independent auditors of individual companies and supported by internal penalties set by industry, which will help to facilitate the full traceability of rough diamond transactions by government authorities.

SECTION V

Co-operation and Transparency

Participants should:

a. provide to each other through the Chair information identifying their designated authorities or bodies responsible for implementing the provisions of this Certification Scheme. Each Participant should provide to other Participants through the Chair information, preferably in electronic format, on its relevant laws, regulations, rules, procedures and practices, and update that information as required. This should include a synopsis in English of the essential content of this information;
b. compile and make available to all other Participants through the Chair statistical data in line with the principles set out in Annex III;
c. exchange on a regular basis experiences and other relevant information, including on self-assessment, in order to arrive at the best practice in given circumstances;
d. consider favourably requests from other Participants for assistance to improve the functioning of the Certification Scheme within their territories;

e. inform another Participant through the Chair if it considers that the laws, regulations, rules, procedures or practices of that other Participant do not ensure the absence of conflict diamonds in the exports of that other Participant;

f. cooperate with other Participants to attempt to resolve problems which may arise from unintentional circumstances and which could lead to non-fulfilment of the minimum requirements for the issuance or acceptance of the Certificates, and inform all other Participants of the essence of the problems encountered and of solutions found;

g. encourage, through their relevant authorities, closer co-operation between law enforcement agencies and between customs agencies of Participants.

SECTION VI

Administrative Matters

MEETINGS

1. Participants and Observers are to meet in Plenary annually, and on other occasions as Participants may deem necessary, in order to discuss the effectiveness of the Certification Scheme.

2. Participants should adopt Rules of Procedure for such meetings at the first Plenary meeting.

3. Meetings are to be held in the country where the Chair is located, unless a Participant or an international organisation offers to host a meeting and this offer has been accepted. The host country should facilitate entry formalities for those attending such meetings.

4. At the end of each Plenary meeting, a Chair would be elected to preside over all Plenary meetings, *ad hoc* working groups and other subsidiary bodies, which might be formed until the conclusion of the next annual Plenary meeting.

5. Participants are to reach decisions by consensus. In the event that consensus proves to be impossible, the Chair is to conduct consultations.

ADMINISTRATIVE SUPPORT

6. For the effective administration of the Certification Scheme, administrative support will be necessary. The modalities and functions of that support should be discussed at the first Plenary meeting, following endorsement by the UN General Assembly.

7. Administrative support could include the following functions:

   a. to serve as a channel of communication, information sharing and consultation between the Participants with regard to matters provided for in this Document;

   b. to maintain and make available for the use of all Participants a collection of those laws, regulations, rules, procedures, practices and statistics notified pursuant to Section V;

   c. to prepare documents and provide administrative support for Plenary and working group meetings;

   d. to undertake such additional responsibilities as the Plenary meetings, or any working group delegated by Plenary meetings, may instruct.

9 PARTICIPATION

8. Participation in the Certification Scheme is open on a global, non-discriminatory basis to all Applicants willing and able to fulfill the requirements of that Scheme.

9. Any applicant wishing to participate in the Certification Scheme should signify its interest by notifying the Chair through diplomatic channels. This notification should include the information set forth in paragraph (a) of Section V and be circulated to all Participants within one month.

10. Participants intend to invite representatives of civil society, the diamond industry, non-participating governments and international organizations to participate in Plenary meetings as Observers.

PARTICIPANT MEASURES

11. Participants are to prepare, and make available to other Participants, in advance of annual Plenary meetings of the Kimberley Process, information as stipulated in paragraph (a) of Section V outlining how the requirements of the Certification Scheme are being implemented within their respective jurisdictions.

12. The agenda of annual Plenary meetings is to include an item where information as stipulated in paragraph (a) of Section V is reviewed and Participants can provide further details of their respective systems at the request of the Plenary.

13. Where further clarification is needed, Participants at Plenary meetings, upon recommendation by the Chair, can identify and decide on additional verification measures to be undertaken. Such measures are to be implemented in accordance with applicable national and international law. These could include, but need not be limited to measures such as;
    a. requesting additional information and clarification from Participants;
    b. review missions by other Participants or their representatives where there are credible indications of significant non-compliance with the Certification Scheme.

14. Review missions are to be conducted in an analytical, expert and impartial manner with the consent of the Participant concerned. The size, composition, terms of reference and time-frame of these missions should be based on the circumstances and be established by the Chair with the consent of the Participant concerned and in consultation with all Participants.

15. A report on the results of compliance verification measures is to be forwarded to the Chair and to the Participant concerned within three weeks of completion of the mission. Any comments from that Participant as well as the report, are to be posted on the restricted access section of an official Certification Scheme website no later than three weeks after the submission of the report to the Participant concerned. Participants and Observers should make every effort to observe strict confidentiality regarding the issue and the discussions relating to any compliance matter.

COMPLIANCE AND DISPUTE PREVENTION

16. In the event that an issue regarding compliance by a Participant or any other issue regarding the implementation of the Certification Scheme arises, any concerned Participant may so inform the Chair, who is to inform all Participants without delay about the said concern and enter into dialogue on how to address it. Participants and Observers should make every effort to observe strict

confidentiality regarding the issue and the discussions relating to any compliance matter.

MODIFICATIONS

17. This document may be modified by consensus of the Participants.
18. Modifications may be proposed by any Participant. Such proposals should be sent in writing to the Chair, at least ninety days before the next Plenary meeting, unless otherwise agreed.
19. The Chair is to circulate any proposed modification expeditiously to all Participants and Observers and place it on the agenda of the next annual Plenary meeting.

REVIEW MECHANISM

20. Participants intend that the Certification Scheme should be subject to periodic review, to allow Participants to conduct a thorough analysis of all elements contained in the scheme. The review should also include consideration of the continuing requirement for such a scheme, in view of the perception of the Participants, and of international organisations, in particular the United Nations, of the continued threat posed at that time by conflict diamonds. The first such review should take place no later than three years after the effective starting date of the Certification Scheme. The review meeting should normally coincide with the annual Plenary meeting, unless otherwise agreed.

THE START OF THE IMPLEMENTATION OF THE SCHEME

21. The Certification Scheme should be established at the Ministerial Meeting on the Kimberley Process Certification Scheme for Rough Diamonds in Interlaken on 5 November 2002.

22. Annex I

Certificates

A. Minimum requirements for Certificates

A Certificate is to meet the following minimum requirements:

- Each Certificate should bear the title "Kimberley Process Certificate" and the following statement: "The rough diamonds in this shipment have been handled in accordance with the provisions of the Kimberley Process Certification Scheme for rough diamonds"
- Country of origin for shipment of parcels of unmixed (i.e. from the same) origin
- Certificates may be issued in any language, provided that an English translation is incorporated
- Unique numbering with the Alpha 2 country code, according to ISO 3166-1
- Tamper and forgery resistant
- Date of issuance
- Date of expiry
- Issuing authority
- Identification of exporter and importer

- Carat weight/mass
- Value in US$
- Number of parcels in shipment
- Relevant Harmonised Commodity Description and Coding System
- Validation of Certificate by the Exporting Authority

B. *Optional Certificate Elements*

A Certificate may include the following optional features:
- Characteristics of a Certificate (for example as to form, additional data or security elements)
- Quality characteristics of the rough diamonds in the shipment
- A recommended import confirmation part should have the following elements:

> Country of destination
> Identification of importer
> Carat/weight and value in US$
> Relevant Harmonised Commodity Description and Coding System
> Date of receipt by Importing Authority
> Authentication by Importing Authority

C. *Optional Procedures*

Rough diamonds may be shipped in transparent security bags.
The unique Certificate number may be replicated on the container.

Annex II

Recommendations as provided for in Section IV, paragraph (f)

General Recommendations

1. Participants may appoint an official coordinator(s) to deal with the imple-mentation of the Certification Scheme.
2. Participants may consider the utility of complementing and/or enhancing the collection and publication of the statistics identified in Annex III based on the contents of Kimberley Process Certificates.
3. Participants are encouraged to maintain the information and data required by Section V on a computerised database.
4. Participants are encouraged to transmit and receive electronic messages in order to support the Certification Scheme.
5. Participants that produce diamonds and that have rebel groups suspected of mining diamonds within their territories are encouraged to identify the areas of rebel diamond mining activity and provide this information to all other Participants. This information should be updated on a regular basis.
6. Participants are encouraged to make known the names of individuals or companies convicted of activities relevant to the purposes of the Certification Scheme to all other Participants through the Chair.
7. Participants are encouraged to ensure that all cash purchases of rough diamonds are routed through official banking channels, supported by verifiable documentation.

8. Participants that produce diamonds should analyse their diamond production under the following headings:
   - Characteristics of diamonds produced
   - Actual production

Recommendations for Control over Diamond Mines

9. Participants are encouraged to ensure that all diamond mines are licensed and to allow only those mines so licensed to mine diamonds.
10. Participants are encouraged to ensure that prospecting and mining companies maintain effective security standards to ensure that conflict diamonds do not contaminate legitimate production.

Recommendations for Participants with Small-scale Diamond Mining

11. All artisinal and informal diamond miners should be licensed and only those persons so licensed should be allowed to mine diamonds.
12. Licensing records should contain the following minimum information: name, address, nationality and/or residence status and the area of authorised diamond mining activity.

Recommendations for Rough Diamond Buyers, Sellers and Exporters

13. All diamond buyers, sellers, exporters, agents and courier companies involved in carrying rough diamonds should be registered and licensed by each Participant's relevant authorities.
14. Licensing records should contain the following minimum information: name, address and nationality and/or residence status.
15. All rough diamond buyers, sellers and exporters should be required by law to keep for a period of five years daily buying, selling or exporting records listing the names of buying or selling clients, their license number and the amount and value of diamonds sold, exported or purchased.
16. The information in paragraph 14 above should be entered into a computerised database, to facilitate the presentation of detailed information relating to the activities of individual rough diamond buyers and sellers.

Recommendations for Export Processes

17. A exporter should submit a rough diamond shipment to the relevant Exporting Authority.
18. The Exporting Authority is encouraged, prior to validating a Certificate, to require an exporter to provide a declaration that the rough diamonds being exported are not conflict diamonds.
19. Rough diamonds should be sealed in a tamper proof container together with the Certificate or a duly authenticated copy. The Exporting Authority should then transmit a detailed e-mail message to the relevant Importing Authority containing information on the carat weight, value, country of origin or provenance, importer and the serial number of the Certificate.
20. The Exporting Authority should record all details of rough diamond shipments on a computerised database.

Recommendations for Import Processes

21. The Importing Authority should receive an e-mail message either before or upon arrival of a rough diamond shipment. The message should contain details

such as the carat weight, value, country of origin or provenance, exporter and the serial number of the Certificate.

22. The Importing Authority should inspect the shipment of rough diamonds to verify that the seals and the container have not been tampered with and that the export was performed in accordance with the Certification Scheme.

23. The Importing Authority should open and inspect the contents of the shipment to verify the details declared on the Certificate.

24. Where applicable and when requested, the Importing Authority should send the return slip or import confirmation coupon to the relevant Exporting Authority.

25. The Importing Authority should record all details of rough diamond shipments on a computerised database.

Recommendations on Shipments to and from Free Trade Zones

26. Shipments of rough diamonds to and from free trade zones should be processed by the designated authorities.

Annex III

Statistics

Recognising that reliable and comparable data on the production and the international trade in rough diamonds are an essential tool for the effective implementation of the Certification Scheme, and particularly for identifying any irregularities or anomalies which could indicate that conflict diamonds are entering the legitimate trade, Participants strongly support the following principles, taking into account the need to protect commercially sensitive information:

a. to keep and publish within two months of the reference period and in a standardised format, quarterly aggregate statistics on rough diamond exports and imports, as well as the numbers of certificates validated for export, and of imported shipments accompanied by Certificates;

b. to keep and publish statistics on exports and imports, by origin and provenance wherever possible; by carat weight and value; and under the relevant Harmonised Commodity Description and Coding System (HS) classifications 7102.10; 7102.21; 7102.31;

c. to keep and publish on a semi-annual basis and within two months of the reference period statistics on rough diamond production by carat weight and by value. In the event that a Participant is unable to publish these statistics it should notify the Chair immediately;

d. to collect and publish these statistics by relying in the first instance on existing national processes and methodologies;

e. to make these statistics available to an intergovernmental body or to another appropriate mechanism identified by the Participants for (1) compilation and publication on a quarterly basis in respect of exports and imports, and (2) on a semi-annual basis in respect of production. These statistics are to be made available for analysis by interested parties and by the Participants, individually or collectively, according to such terms of reference as may be established by the Participants;

f. to consider statistical information pertaining to the international trade in and production of rough diamonds at annual Plenary meetings, with a view to addressing related issues, and to supporting effective implementation of the Certification Scheme.

Notes

1. Nikos Passas and Kimberly Jones, "Commodities and Terrorist Financing: Focus on Diamonds," *European Journal on Criminal Policy and Research* 12, no. 1 (2006): 1–33.
2. Virginia Haufler, "The Kimberley Process Certification Scheme: An Innovation in Global Governance and Conflict Prevention," *Journal of Business Ethics* 89 Supplement (2009): 403–416.
3. See recent discoveries in Equatorial Guinea, Kazakhstan, Angola, et cetera: O'Brien, 2004; Switzer, 2001; Brown, 2002; Reingold, 2004; Ite, 2004; Giri, 2000; Barrientos, 2000; Newell, 2001; White, 2001; De Matteis, 2004; McGillivray and Pillarisetti, 2004; Klein Haarhuis and Leeuw, 2004; Newbold, 2003; Redclift, 1997; Jenkins, 2004; Goudie, 1999.
4. United Nations General Assembly, "The Role of Diamonds in Fueling Conflict," November 29, 2006, 1–5; http://www.kimberleyprocess.com/background/index_en.html; Global Witness, *Broken Vows: Exposing the "Loupe" Holes in the Diamond Industry's Efforts to Prevent the Trade in Conflict Diamonds*, (London: Global Witness, 2004); Global Witness, *Broken Vows: How Al Qaeda Moved into the Diamond Trade*, (London: Global Witness, 2003); Global Witness, "Rich Man, Poor Man: **Development Diamonds** and **Poverty Diamonds**: The **Potential** for **Change** in the **Artisanal Alluvial Diamond Fields** of Africa," **(2004)**, *www.pacweb.org/Documents/*diamonds*_KP/rich_man-poor_man-eng_(elect)-Oct2004.pdf.*
5. S. Prakash Sethi, "Corporate Codes of Conduct and the Success of Globalization," *Ethics & International Affairs* 16, no. 1 (2002): 89–106; Stiglitz, 2002; Sachs and Warner, 1995; Rodrik, 1997.
6. http://www.diamondfacts.org/pdfs/conflict/Kimberley_Process_Timeline.pdf
7. http://www.kimberleyprocess.com/background/index_en.html
8. http://www.kimberleyprocess.com/background/index_en.html
9. Haufler, op. cit., p. 408.
10. Global Witness and Wexler, 2006, Haufler, op. cit., p. 409.
11. Rapaport Tradewire, "World Diamond Council Calls for International Government Action on Conflict Diamonds," *Rapaport TradeWire*, September 8, 2000; Haufler, op. cit., p. 409
12. http://www.globalpolicy.org/security/issues/diamond/2003/0415back.htmin
13. http://www.globalpolicy.org/security/issues/diamond/2003/0128start.htm
14. http://www.diamondfacts.org/pdfs/conflict/Kimberley_Process_Timeline.pdf
15. Alan Cowell, "Controversy over Diamonds Made into Virtue by De Beers," *New York Times*, August 22, 2000, Section A; Haufler, op. cit., p. 409.
16. Josée Létourneau and Ian Smillie, eds., "Killing Kimberley? Conflict Diamonds and Paper Tigers," *The Diamonds and Human Security Project*, Occasional Paper #15, Partnership Africa Canada, (November 2006), http://www.pacweb.org/Documents/diamonds_KP/15_KillingKimberley_Revised%20Edition_Eng-Nov2006.pdf.
17. 2007 checklist for KPCS review visits and review missions.
18. Kimberley Process Certification Scheme Secretariat—Namibia, "Kimberley Process Plenary Session," November 5, 2009, http://www.kimberleyprocess.com/download/getfile/940.
19. http://www.kimberleyprocess.com/structure/working_group_en.html
20. Official KPCS document, *http://www.kimberleyprocess.com/download/getfile/4.*

21. http://www.kimberleyprocess.com/background/index_en.html
22. Kimberley Process Certification Scheme Secretariat—Namibia, "Kimberley Process Plenary Session," November 5, 2009, http://www.kimberleyprocess.com /download/getfile/940.
23. Ibid.
24. *The Essential Guide to Implementing the Kimberly Process*, http://www.jvclegal.org/ kimberely.pdf.
25. Ibid.
26. Ibid.
27. Kimberley Process Certification Scheme Secretariat—Namibia. "Kimberley Process Plenary Session," November 5, 2009 http://www.kimberleyprocess.com /download/getfile/940
28. "Communities, Artisanal and Small-Scale Mining (CASM)," World Bank, September 2008, http://siteresources.worldbank.org/INTOGMC/Resources /CASMFACTSHEET.pdf.
29. Official KPCS document.
30. *The Essential Guide to Implementing the Kimberly Process*, http://www.jvclegal.org/ kimberely.pdf.
31. Official KPCS document.
32. Retrieved from http://www.kimberleyprocess.com/background/index_en.html.
33. Ian Smillie, "Viewpoint: Conflict Diamonds—Unfinished Business," International Development Research Center, June 7, 2002, http://www.idrc.ca/en/ev-5505–201 –1-DO_TOPIC.html; All Africa, Inc., "Talks Aimed at Stopping 'Blood **Diamonds**' Flow Underway," *Africa News*, April 30, 2003.
34. Rob Bates, "PBS Airs Conflict Diamond Program," *Jewelers Circular Keystone*, May 1, 2003, p. 58.
35. Retrieved from http://www.kimberleyprocess.com/background/index_en.html.
36. Elizabeth J.A. Rodgers, "Conflict Diamonds: Certification and Corruption, a Case Study of Sierra Leone," *Journal of Financial Crime* 13, no. 3, (2006): 267–272.
37. Global Witness, *Conflict Diamonds: U.S. Jewelry Retailers Still Not Doing Enough*, (London: Global Witness, 2007); Global Witness, *The Key to Kimberley Internal Diamond Controls: Seven Case Studies*, (London: Global Witness, 2004); Global Witness, *An Independent Commissioned Review Evaluating the Effectiveness of the Kimberley Process*, (London: Global Witness, 2006); Global Witness, *Déjà Vu: Diamond Industry Still Failing to Deliver on Promises*, (London: Global Witness-Amnesty International, 2004); Global Witness, *Broken Vows: Exposing the "Loupe" Holes in the Diamond Industry's Efforts to Prevent the Trade in Conflict Diamonds*, (London: Global Witness, 2004); Global Witness, *Rough Trade: The Role of Companies and Governments in the Angolan Conflict*, (London: Global Witness, 1998); Global Witness: 1999, A Crude Awakening: The Role of Oil and Banking Industries in Angolan Civil War and the Plunder of State Assets (Global Witness, London); Global Witness, *Déjà Vu*; Global Witness, "Kimberley Process Civil Society Coalition Press Release," (2007), www.globalwitness.org; Global Witness and P. Wexler, *An Independent Commissioned Review Evaluating the Effectiveness of the Kimberley Process*, (London: Global Witness, 2006).
38. "Diamond Industry Annual Review: Sierra Leon 2005," Partnership Africa Canada, February 2005, http://www.pacweb.org/Documents/annual-reviews-diamonds/ SierraLeone_AR_2005-eng.pdf.
39. Rodgers, op. cit., p. 267–272; Partnership Africa Canada and Global Witness, "*The Key to Kimberley: Internal Diamond Controls—Seven Case Studies*," October 2004, *http://www.pacweb.org/Documents/diamonds_KP/key_to_Kimberley-eng -elect_Oct2004.pdf*.
40. Ingrid J. Tamm, "Diamonds in Peace and War: Severing the Conflict Diamond Connection," World Peace Foundation, Report 30, January 2002, p. 64.

41. U.S. Government Accountability Office, "Conflict Diamonds: Agency Actions Needed to Enhance Implementation of the Clean Diamond Trade Act," GAO-06–978, September 2006.
42. Partnership Africa Canada and Global Witness, *The Key to Kimberley: Internal Diamond Controls—Seven Case Studies,*" October 2004, *http://www.pacweb.org/ Documents/diamonds_KP/key_to_Kimberley-eng-elect_Oct2004.pdf.*
43. Ibid.
44. Global Witness, "Broken Vows," March 2004, http://www.globalwitness.org /media_library_detail.php/114 /en/broken_vows.
45. Global Witness and Amnesty International, "Déjà Vu," October 2004, http://www. globalwitness.org/ media _ library_detail.php/124/en/deja_vu.
46. Global Witness and Amnesty International, "Global Witness/Amnesty International U.S. Diamond Retail Survey 2007," February 27, 2007, http://www.globalwitness.org/media_library_detail.php/519/en /global_witness_amnesty_international_us_diamond_re.
47. Rob Bates, "PBS Airs Conflict Diamond Program," *Jewelers Circular Keystone*, May 01, 2003, p. 58.
48. Anonymous, "Controlling Diamonds," *Washington Post*, November 29, 2004, A18.
49. For details, see KPCS Review Visits page: http://www.kimberleyprocess.com/docu- ments/ review_visits_en.html.
50. Ian Taylor and Gladys Mokhawa, "Not Forever: Botswana, Conflict Diamonds, and the Bushmen," *African Affairs* 102, no. 407 (2003): 261–283; "Botswana Bushmen Being Blocked from Going Home," *South Africa News Channel*, January 4, 2007, http://www. news-channel.co.za/Politics/Bushmen.html; Jeff Miller, "Bushmen Living: 'I Chose to Call It Stone Age' Said Tonge," Diamonds.net, March 24, 2006, http://www.diamonds. net/news/NewsItem.aspx?ArticleID=14612.
51. "Press Conference by Botswana President on Diamond Certification Process," United Nations Press Conference, December 4, 2006, http://www.un.org/News /briefings/docs/2006/061204_Botswana .doc.htm.
52. Zoe Eisenstein, "Report Says Security Guards in Angola Abuse Locals," *Reuters South Africa*, September 8, 2006; J. Reed, "Angola Pays Price for Riches Say Reports," *Financial Times*, August 30, 2006, http://www.ft.com/cms/s/0/f55067e2–384b-11db- ae2c-0000779e2340.html?nclick_check=1; "Botswana Bushmen Being Blocked from Going Home," *South Africa News Channel*, January 4, 2007, http://www.news-channel. co.za/Politics/Bushmen.html; Partnership Africa Canada, "Killing Kimberley? Conflict Diamonds and Paper Tigers," November 2006, http://www.pacweb.org/Documents/ diamonds_KP/15_KillingKimberley_Revised%20Edition_Eng-Nov2006.pdf.
53. Partnership Africa Canada and Global Witness, *The Key to Kimberley: Internal Diamond Controls—Seven Case Studies,*" October 2004, *http://www.pacweb.org/ Documents/diamonds_KP/key_to_Kimberley-eng-elect_Oct2004.pdf; All Africa, Inc., "PMMC in Dubious Sale of 'Conflict' Stones?" Africa News: Ghanaian Chronicle, May 21, 2003;* Dino Mahtani, "Conflict Diamonds Smuggled into Ghana, Says UN Report," Financial Times (London), October 7, 2006; Nicol D. Innocenti, "Congo Expelled from Kimberley Code," Financial Times, July 10, 2004.
54. U.S. Government Accountability Office, "Conflict Diamonds: Agency Actions Needed to Enhance Implementation of the Clean Diamond Trade Act," GAO-06–978, September 2006.
55. Partnership Africa Canada, "The Lost World: Diamond Mining and Smuggling in Venezuela," November 2006, http://www.pacweb.org/Documents/diamonds_KP/16_ thelostworld_Eng-Nov2006.pdf.
56. Global Witness, "Kimberley Process Must Expel Venezuela," press release, October 9, 2007, http://www.globalwitness.org/media_library_detail.php/606/en/ kimberley_process_must_expel_venezuela.
57. Partnership Africa Canada, "Venezuela Drops Out," *Other Facets* 29, February 2009, http://www.pacweb.org/Documents/Other-Facets/OF29-eng.pdf.

58. Kimberley Process Certification Scheme Secretariat—Namibia, "Kimberley Process Plenary Session," November 5, 2009, http://www.kimberleyprocess.com/download/getfile/940.

59. Jan Raath, "Mugabe Faces Blacklist over Rogue Diamonds," *Times Online*, June 11, 2007, http://www.timesonline.co.uk/tol/news/world/africa/article1912990.ece.

60. Press release, "Failure to Suspend Zimbabwe from Kimberley Process," *Fatal Transactions*, November 8, 2009, http://www.fataltransactions.org/News/2009.

61. Partnership Africa Canada, "Zimbabwe, Diamonds, and the Wrong Side of History," March 2009, http://www.pacweb.org/Documents/diamonds_KP/18_Zimbabwe-Diamonds_March09-Eng.pdf.

62. Press release, "Campaigners Call for Urgent Action on Zimbabwe Blood Diamonds and Wider Reform of the Kimberley Process to Prevent Abuse," Kimberley Process Civil Society Coalition, October 29, 2009, http://www.pacweb.org/Documents/Press_releases/2009/KP_Plenary-Zimbabwe-2009–10–29-eng.pdf.

63. Allan Seccombe, "Gem Diamonds Sets Up Polishing Business," *MiningMX*, July 23, 2008, http://www.miningmx.com/diamonds/684820.htm; E. Esmarie Swanepoel, "Gem Diamonds Says Plans to Beneficiate in Dubai, Mauritius, on Hold," *Mining Weekly*, May 19, 2009, http://www.miningweekly.com/article/gem-diamonds-plans-to-beneficiate-in-dubai-mauritius-on-hold-2009–05–19.

64. Anonymous, "The Cartel Isn't Forever," *Economist*, July 15, 2004.

65. Global Witness, "Making It Work: Why the Kimberley Process Must Do More to Stop Conflict Diamonds," November 2005, http://www.globalwitness.org /media_library_detail.php/143/en/making   _it_work_why_the_kimberley_process _must_do_m; Amnesty International, "Kimberley Process: An Amnesty International Position Paper," June 21, 2006, http://www.amnestyusa.org/document. php?lang=e&id=ENGPOL300242006; Rory E. Anderson, "Conflict Diamonds: The Problem Persists Despite Progress," Africa Policy Forum, July 5, 2007, http://forums. csis.org/africa/?p=41.

66. Global Witness, "Loopholes in the Kimberley Process: Summary of Trade Statistics Review," October 20, 2007, http://www.globalwitness.org/media_library_detail. php/605/en/loopholes_in_the_kimberley_process_summary_of_trad.

67. Thomas Fuller, "Signs of Slump at Gem Sale in Myanmar," *New York Times*, November 16, 2007; ChannelNewsAsia.com, "Myanmar Auctions Gems, Jade Despite Boycott Calls," *Channel News Asia*, January 20, 2008, http://www.channelnewsasia.com/stories/afp_asiapacific_business/view/ 323717/1/.html.

68. Fiona Symon, "Gem Specialist Puts Ethics on Agenda," *Financial Times*, August 3, 2005.

69. Robert Block and Daniel Pearl, "Bin Laden Is Backed by Rare Blue Gem Called Tanzanite, Much-Smuggled Mineral Is Seen as Source of Support: "Yes, People Here Are Trading for Osman.'" *Wall Street Journal Europe*, November 16, 2001.

70. Fiona Symon, "Gem Specialist Puts Ethics on Agenda," *Financial Times*, August 3, 2005; Richard A. Schroeder, "Tanzanite as Conflict Gem: Certifying a Secure Commodity Chain in Tanzania," *GeoForum* 41, no. 1 (2009): 56–65.

71. Haufler, op. cit., p. 412–413.

8

United Nations Global Compact: An Assessment of Ten Years of Progress, Achievements, and Shortfalls

S. Prakash Sethi and Donald H. Schepers

In June 2010, the United Nations Global Compact (GC) celebrated its tenth anniversary. In summarizing the growth and success of the GC, Georg Kell, its founding director, stated: "What started as a 'small Global Compact Initiative' in 2000, ten years later, the GC stands as the world's largest global corporate responsibility initiative. As of June 1, 2010, over 8,000 signatories—6,000 from business and 2,000 from civil society and other nonbusiness groups— based in more than 135 countries, were committed to implementing the Global Compact principles into business practices and taking actions to advance UN goals, such as the Millennium Development Goals (MDGs)."[1]

Kell's statements are suffused with a lofty vision of the GC's mission and goals, assertions of "self-evident" achievements and the transformational character of the GC's future initiatives that would bring together business, government, and civil society organizations to work in a mutually beneficial manner. Even more important, it would inspire business organizations to conduct their operations in a manner that is congruent with a higher level of corporate social responsibility and accountability.

Unfortunately, Kell's statements are conspicuously silent in areas that matter the most in creating trust in the GC principles and credibility in the claims made by the GC and the signatory companies in implementing those principles. Absent this information, the entire GC enterprise is put under a deliberate cloud of ambiguity regarding what is being claimed and what is being accomplished.

Scope of the Chapter

The primary focus of this chapter is on four issues:

1. Analysis of the antecedents and motives provided by its sponsors as the *raison d'être* for creating the GC, and whether this rationale could be justified

in light of the circumstances existing when the GC was created. This also includes the content of the nine original principles and the tenth principle, which was added to the GC in 2004.

2. An evaluation of the GC's governance structure, sources of funding, policies and procedures, and operational practices, with a view to assessing their capacity for effective implementation of the GC's mandate.

3. An examination of the GC's expansion policies and their potential relevance and impact on the implementation of the GC principles.

4. A determination of the overall progress and effectiveness of the GC during the preceding ten years and its likely progress in the next decade.

Creation of the Global Compact

The United Nations–sponsored Global Compact was the inspiration of UN Secretary General Kofi Annan, who challenged the top leadership of the world-wide business community to enact a global compact between the United Nations and the private sector to promote human rights, improve labor conditions, and protect the environment. He argued that the globalization of markets, as we have known it for the past decade or so, is unsustainable. It will trigger back-lash from large segments of society because the benefits of globalization are distributed too unequally, both within and among countries. Specifically, he asked companies to embrace and enact the nine principles (now ten, with the addition of an anticorruption principle in 2004) their own corporate practices derived from various existing documents by UN agencies and other sources in (exhibit 8.1).

Initial Reaction to the Global Compact

Secretary General Annan suggested that his initiative would provide an over-arching umbrella for various UN agencies, private corporations, and NGOs to work together toward a common goal, as embodied in the GC prin-ciples. However, his actions did not reconcile with his public posture and pronouncements.

1. The GC had limited resources and even fewer professional staff members to manage the launch of the GC and develop an organizational infrastructure to manage the enterprise.

2. Although various UN agencies were given overt recognition as program agen-cies underlying GC principles, they had no direct role or responsibility in GC operations. It was at best a pro forma gesture intended to dampen their criti-cism of the GC structure. The GC organizers were cognizant of the fact that these agencies and the corporate world shared an uneasy relationship, and that an active role for these agencies would be detrimental to the GC's effort to enlist corporate support. The GC organizers did not want their initiative to be viewed by the corporate sector as having "meaningful" input from the UN program agencies.

3. The GC organizers also did not seek or encourage active participation from the relevant members of the NGO community. Consequently, NGO concerns

received even less attention and recognition by the GC than those of the UN program agencies.

From its inception, the GC organizers and their corporate sponsors presented the program as embracing lofty principles and global ambitions.

Exhibit 8.1   The Ten Principles of the UNGC

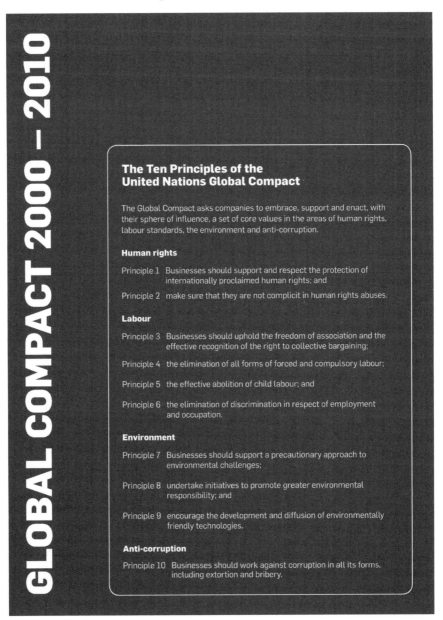

GLOBAL COMPACT 2000–2010

The Ten Principles of the United Nations Global Compact

The Global Compact asks companies to embrace, support and enact, with their sphere of influence, a set of core values in the areas of human rights, labour standards, the environment and anti-corruption.

Human rights

Principle 1   Businesses should support and respect the protection of internationally proclaimed human rights; and

Principle 2   make sure that they are not complicit in human rights abuses.

Labour

Principle 3   Businesses should uphold the freedom of association and the effective recognition of the right to collective bargaining;

Principle 4   the elimination of all forms of forced and compulsory labour;

Principle 5   the effective abolition of child labour; and

Principle 6   the elimination of discrimination in respect of employment and occupation.

Environment

Principle 7   Businesses should support a precautionary approach to environmental challenges;

Principle 8   undertake initiatives to promote greater environmental responsibility; and

Principle 9   encourage the development and diffusion of environmentally friendly technologies.

Anti-corruption

Principle 10   Businesses should work against corruption in all its forms, including extortion and bribery.

Notwithstanding an extensive public relations campaign to build public support for their enterprise, the GC fell like a lead balloon among those NGOs that were the most knowledgeable and most likely to be involved in the activities, and among the UN agencies whose support it sought and whose mission and activities the secretary general was trying to promote through the GC.[2]

Recent Trends Toward Cooperation Between UN Agencies and Private-Sector Corporations

Historically, the United Nations and its various program agencies have had an uneasy relationship. The mandate of various agencies invariably focuses on the global challenges of alleviating poverty, preventing diseases, improving public health and safety, and preventing human rights abuses. Consequently, they often raise significant conflicts where private micro-economic interests could run counter to public policy agendas of these agencies. From the perspective of these agencies, the central issues in the debate on UN–private sector partnership were (a) the choice of corporate partners, and (b) the precise definition of the objectives of such projects. Therefore, the companies most eager to seek the prestige of UN affiliation would likely be the ones that had been criticized for their actions against such issues as human rights, environmental protection, fair labor practices, freedom of speech and association, et cetera. This phenomenon is known as adverse selection.[3]

A case in point is the programs of the World Health Organization (WHO), United Nations Development Programme (UNDP), United Nations Children's Fund (UNICEF), International Labour Organization (ILO), United Nations Environment Programme (UNEP), and United Nations Conference on Trade and Development (UNCTAD). Most of these initiatives, with the exception of humanitarian efforts such as UNICEF, have not fared well and, in some cases, have generated intense hostility and further widened the schism between the UN and the business community.

The UN program agencies were not hesitant in expressing their concern and criticism of the GC's actions. While Kofi Annan had emphasized that the nine principles of the Global Compact derived their lineage from various covenants of UN agencies, these agencies saw the GC as the secretary general's attempt to cozy up to the private sector.[4] More recently, the case of PetroChina and its membership in the UN Global Compact has raised red flags in terms of GC principles and practices. PetroChina joined the GC in 2007, although its parent, CNPC, did not. Moreover, the government of China (the majority owner of both PetroChina and CNPC) and CNPC have assets in Sudan of some $20 billion, where several civil society organizations have accused PetroChina of complicity in human rights abuses.[5]

The GC Board's response to allegations about PetroChina's conduct defies rational logic or a principled stance. After a GC Board meeting to discuss the charges, Georg Kell responded that the board had "decided not to handle this matter as an integrity issue of an individual company, PetroChina." He even found a way to applaud the GC Board's action by stating that PetroChina's step of joining the GC should be "welcomed instead of criticized."[6]

By this logic, any company—regardless of its track record as a violator of the GC principles—would be eagerly welcomed by the GC simply because it has chosen to join the GC. If this is not in itself a convoluted and self-defeating argument, the GC's goal of enhancing corporate conduct on its ten principles is further undermined by the GC's extreme reluctance in removing companies from its roster regardless of their market conduct.

The negative reaction was not confined to the UN agencies. The GC also faced criticism from prominent NGOs, professional groups, and individuals in industrialized and developing countries. These groups faulted the GC on general principles and for its choice of private-sector partners that comprised the initial group of companies joining the Global Compact. For example, Amnesty International noted that some of the companies joining the GC had been notorious for their violations of human rights and benefiting from sweatshop working conditions in developing countries.

> First...we would like to see companies who join the Global Compact make a public statement that they will be open to independent monitoring....Secondly, it has to be reported publicly...all the stakeholders are entitled to have the information resulting from that independent monitoring. And thirdly...a sanctions system has to be envisaged...so that companies who violate these principles cannot continue to benefit from the partnership....We think that those three steps are absolutely essential if this initiative is to be effective, credible and win the trust of human rights organizations.[7]

In a similar vein, a group of prominent international scholars in law, economics, political science, and other professions, and leaders of major international human rights groups advocating the cause of the poor expressed their opposition to the GC in a letter to the secretary general.[8] The group challenged the GC's contention that asking corporations to endorse a vague statement of commitment to human rights, labor, and environmental standards would somehow improve corporate compliance with the ten GC principles, when many of these corporations were repeat offenders of both the law and commonly accepted standards of responsible conduct.

In another letter, a group of legal scholars argued that some of the companies in the partnership were "simply inappropriate for partnerships with the UN and would undermine the organization's integrity." Examples mentioned in the letter made reference to the activities of various companies, including Nike, Shell, BP Amoco, Rio Tinto, and Novartis, to name a few.[9] Similar sentiments were echoed by various groups at the NGO Panel on Corporate Accountability held at the UN on February 15, 2001. James Paul, Executive Director of the Global Policy Forum, commented that the GC embodies "a classically vague statement of principles that does not provide rules for specific situations or complaint procedures of any kind. Nor does it include any form of systematic monitoring." NGO concerns were best summarized by Bruno and Karliner,[10] who identified four fatal flaws in the Global Compact and its partnership programs: wrong companies, wrong relationships, wrong image, and no monitoring or enforcement.

Corporate Support or Lack Thereof for the Global Compact

From its inception, the GC did everything possible to entice corporations to become signatories. It promised the companies "all the prestige" of the UN for the simple act of becoming a signatory with a vague promise to embed the ten GC principles in their operations. Corporate leaders had correctly realized that Kofi Annan did not have strong-enough support from other UN bodies, and thus participation in the GC would not necessarily temper criticism from the UN program agencies. Consequently, they were unwilling to make a mean-ingful commitment to the GC. Maria Livianos Cattui, General Secretary of the International Chamber of Commerce and Industry (ICC), expressed this corporate attitude in a most forthright manner when she stated that "business would look askance at any suggestion involving external assessment of corpo-rate performance, whether by special interest groups or by UN agencies. The Global Compact is a joint commitment to shared values, not a qualification to be met. It must not become a vehicle for governments to burden business with prescriptive regulations."[11]

In the end, there was little left for the GC to do or to say that would mollify its critics. Instead it opted for an alternative track that would ask for patience on the part of its critics. Speaking for the Global Compact, John G. Ruggie, then Assistant Secretary-General and now a professor at the Kennedy School at Harvard University, asserted that the reaction of the business community was favorable. According to Ruggie, the GC is a "learning model, utilizing the powerful tool of transparency. One of the core commitments companies make within the Global Compact is to go public at least once a year, on our Compact website, with concrete steps they have taken to implement the principles of the Compact."[12]

However, as we shall demonstrate in a latter section of this paper, the GC has made little effort toward transparency. It has made no demands on signatory corporations to provide information that is objective and substantial, and that relates to the so-called embeddedness of the GC principles in corporate strategy and operations. The GC documents promoting corporate membership read like the marketing pitches of a salesperson hustling for new business. All the GC asks is that the participating companies annually *issue a clear statement of support for the Global Compact and its nine principles together with publicly advocating it and to provide a concrete example of progress made or a lesson learned in implementing the principles, for posting on The Global Compact's web site*" (emphasis added).[13]

Creation of the Global Compact: A Faustian Bargain

It was apparent to GC organizers that their existence was in serious jeopardy even before they had a chance to get started. Their survival depended on the support of three groups. The first group was the UN program agencies with the financial resources, professional expertise, and on-the-ground experience that could help the GC create realistic programs of private-sector UN partnerships.

The Global Compact deliberately sidelined these groups for fear of alienating their corporate benefactors. The second group included the NGOs that had been toiling in the worst poverty- and conflict-ridden corners of the world. They could not and would not accept vague corporate promises of doing well by doing good. Seeing no viable alternative, the GC chose to enter a Faustian bargain in which it believed that a greater awareness of environmental, social, and governance factors would induce companies (the third group) to voluntarily embed the GC's ten principles into their core business operations. This was a preposterous assumption when all historical evidence and prevailing business practices indicate that voluntary compliance without defining any standards for adequate performance and relevant reporting of facts is doomed to fail. The result of this myopic belief has become all too apparent in the ensuing ten years. Companies have been eagerly exploiting "the commons" of the UN reputation. They have realized that the Global Compact is quite amenable to infinitely stretching the boundaries of the commons by its willingness to offer full dispensation to all sinners, who don't even have to confess their sins or seek redemption from the victims.

Governance Structure and Financial Support

An organization's governance structure plays an important role in determining the influences that shape the organization's mission and evaluate its operational effectiveness and appropriateness of performance-related outcomes, accountability, and transparency. Similarly, the magnitude and sources of financing and the degree to which an organization depends on particular sources for funds exert strong influence on the organization's ability to act independently in its goal-setting, project-selection, and performance-evaluation functions.

In its early stages, the GC's governance structure was rather simple, and was determined by the Secretary-General. From 2002 through 2004, the GC was governed by the Global Compact Advisory Council, a group of twenty individuals from business, government, and civil society organizations who were appointed by the UN Secretary-General to advise him and Georg Kell, the GC's executive head, on developing a long-term strategy for the GC.

In 2004, the Secretary-General called for a review of the GC governance, stating, "To put it in corporate terms, the primary mission of the Global Compact Office should become brand management and quality assurance."[14] The new governance structure, established in 2006, was quite elaborate and complex, befitting an organization with worldwide aspirations. There are now seven bodies that "govern" the GC: the Global Compact Board, the GC Office, the local networks, the Annual Local Networks Forum (ALNF), the Global Compact Leaders Summit, the Inter-Agency Team, and the Global Compact Donor Group. Although all of these groups are listed as part of the governance structure, the real decision making or governance oversight resides with the GC Board and the GC Office. The remaining groups represent activity domains or support event-related operations.

It should be noted here that the current governance structure, the GC Board, does not mention the role, if any, played by the donor countries in GC's policymaking and operations. However, as we shall we see in a latter part of this chapter, this is not a trivial question since country donations account for a majority of the financial support provided to the GC.

The GC Board and the GC Office

The current GC Board is composed of twenty-four members: thirteen from business, two each from international labor and business organizations, four from civil societies, and three ex officio: the Secretary-General as chair, Ban Ki-Moon; executive director of the GC Office, Georg Kell, representing the GC Office and Inter-Agency Team; and Sir Mark Moody-Stuart, chair of the Foundation for the Global Compact.[15] The GC Office operates under the direction of Georg Kell, with eighteen staff members who fill multiple roles.

The composition of the GC Board, and the dominance of business members, raises troubling questions with regard to its independence and objectivity. Of the thirteen business members, six have been on the board since its inception and represent companies from Brazil, Chile, China, France, Denmark, South Africa, and Denmark.[16] In addition, Tata Steel of India has been on the GC Board since 2004. The other business members represent companies from Mexico, the United States, Japan, Spain, Nigeria, and South Korea. To these we must also add the two representatives of international business organizations, bringing the total number of business representatives to fifteen. In contrast, there are only two representatives from the labor organizations. The four civil society organizations represent human rights, anticorruption, and environmental concerns.[17]

The GC Board also reveals a disconcerting level of entrenchment, with very little rotation among the organizations represented by the board members. Of the eight members from international labor and business organizations and civil society, only one has changed in the years of the GC Board, and she replaced her predecessor from the same organization. Of the three ex-officio members, each represents some portion of the UN or GC establishment. Sir Mark Moody-Stuart, the current chair of the Foundation, is also embedded in the business community.[18] Therefore, for all intents and purposes, only six of the twenty-four members belong to other than business-related organizations.

There is also the question of board communication with other elements of the governing structure: the local networks, the ALNF, the Leaders Summit, and the Inter-Agency Team. In particular, the absence of representation from the local networks is inexplicable. As things currently stand, local networks have become the be-all and end-all of GC activities, without which the GC would cease to exist. Currently, much if not all of the communications between the GC Board and these groups filter through the GC Office, giving it tremendous power to influence network structures and thereby reducing the impact of local networks that might be in disagreement with GC Office policies. The challenges of this cumbersome and yet unaccountable governance structure are further exacerbated by what might be called organizational sprawl, that is, the tendency of the GC to expand its organizational structure and operations. During the past ten years, the GC has enlarged its scope of activities to include initiatives such as Caring for Climate, the CEO Water Mandate, the Principles for Responsible Management Education (PRME), and the Principles for Responsible Investment (PRI), among others. And yet, this expansion has not been reflected in changes in the governance structure, raising questions regarding its capabilities and responsiveness to the expanded scope of its activities.

Sources and Magnitude of Financial Support

Financial support for the GC Office has come from two sources: country donations and, since 2006, the Foundation for the Global Compact.[19] We estimate the annual GC Office budget to be between $5 million and $7.5 million.[20] Our analysis conclusively shows that while the entire emphasis of the GC is on private-sector organizations, its funding depends largely on donor countries, without which the Global Compact could not survive.

The case of government-level support also raises troubling questions. Only thirteen of the ninety-three country networks donate to the GC.[21] No information on specific individual amounts is currently available. Our estimate suggests that country-level support represents approximately 60 percent of the GC's total budget.

By any measure, this is minute given the countries involved. It suggests

a. that the amount of funding is much larger than we have estimated, perhaps with some countries making in-kind but unlisted donations;
b. the relatively low importance given to the GC by signatory countries; or
c. that a large part of these funds is contributed by one or two countries, with other nations contributing nominal amounts but with their names added as window dressing.

The implications of assumptions (b) and (c) become ominous with regard to the potential influence of major donor countries (such as China) on the policies and priorities of the GC. It should also be noted the GC held a major conference in China in November 2005, for which China provided the majority of support.[22]

Donor countries are also not pleased with this situation and have called for greater cost sharing on the part of the private sector.[23]

Private-sector fund-raising is managed by the Foundation of the Global Compact. The foundation is governed by four members: two from business, one from an international law firm with strong ties to business, and a university-affiliated academician.[24]

The data for donors and amounts starting in 2008 and summarized in large brackets is available on the foundation's website.[25] An analysis of 2009 donations (using midpoints of the bracketed amounts as estimators) reveals interesting issues. Over 30 percent of the total contributions have come from 2.9 percent of all donors, and 64 percent of all donations have been made by 16.4 percent of all donors. At the other end of the spectrum, 71.3 percent of the donors accounted for a mere 15.2 percent of all donations. This is in sharp contrast with the GC's preferred image of increasing corporate support and adherence. Using the midpoint estimator results in estimated donations of nearly $2.1 million, whereas the GC notes 2009 donations of $1.7

million.[26] This discrepancy suggests many small donations in each bracket surrounding a smattering of large donations.

Local-Network Financial Support

Almost all local networks are expected to raise their own funds to support network activities and network operations, although in rare circumstances, the GC office in New York has provided some support to local networks as seed money for start-up operations. At present, forty-nine of the ninety-three local networks charge some membership fee, ranging from a few dollars to almost $6,000.[27] Of the 4,573 companies reported in the local networks in 2009, only 2,507 (54.8 percent) paid some membership fees to the local network.

Most networks appear to be strained for resources, which seriously limits the scope of their operations. The lack of funding, however, provides an indication to the low value placed upon the GC membership and principles implementation by local participants, and thus highlights the fragility of local networks and all attendant issues.

Companies' reluctance to provide enough support to create vigorous networks reflects their perception of potential gains. Of the some 5,000 firms currently in the GC, only 435 made any donation to the GC in 2009, and 263 have committed to providing financial support to the GC in the first half of 2010. If we assume (and we do) that firms are willing to pay for services or participation in a group that brings them added value, the analysis so far would indicate that the GC has little to offer even to signatory firms. Left to their own devices, most local networks, especially those in developing countries, are unlikely to gain much knowledge based on guidance from the GC office.

At the heart of this paradox is the crucial, and we contend faulty, assertion made by the GC, namely that participation in the GC and use of the GC logo would lend prestige to member companies' posture of enhanced corporate social responsibility and a presumption of compliance with GC principles, thereby adding to corporate goodwill. Our analysis in this chapter effectively repudiates these assertions as untenable, and will remain so given GC's stance regarding meaningful implementation (or lack thereof) of the principles by signatories.

Growth During 2000–2010: More "Said" Than "Done"

Having abandoned any effort to sustain its core mission of embedding the ten GC principles in companies' core business activities, all claims of the GC's reach and growth have been reduced to the lowest possible common denominator: a head count of companies that have agreed to become signatories of the Global Compact. Performance evaluation has been relegated to enumerating activities of the local networks and totting up Communication on Progress (COP) numbers. Starting with fewer than 600 companies in 2,000, the GC has grown to nearly 6,400 participants of various types, excluding companies that have been delisted due to failure to file annual COPs. There are four regions (Africa and the Middle East, the Americas, Asia and Oceania, and Europe and the Commonwealth of Independent States) and ninety-three local networks, either emerging or established, in the GC.[28]

Network design

The UNGC is organized as a non-hierarchical, nested network.[29] The primary role of the GC Office is that of facilitator or information clearing house, with limited subject-matter expertise. Local networks are supposed to assist participating members in the application of GC Principles to local issues and local company operations.

There is an annual meeting of the global network for sharing of best practices on network administration and making governance decisions. Each local network is expected to have one annual meeting, and may also have smaller, more frequent meetings as well. At the local level, there is one network 'focal person' who communicates with the UNGC office and coordinates activities for the local network. All communications between the regional network and the UNGC office go through this focal person.

Flaws in the Network Design

The architecture for local networks is fatally flawed since it violates most of the necessary pre-conditions that would ensure effectiveness in serving members and success in achieving the performance goals of the GC principles.

1. A network is a voluntary collective of members wishing to distinguish themselves from non-member companies to achieve certain values otherwise not available to them. Networks may assume cartel characteristics yielding economic gains for members that would be illegal, i.e., antithetical to society's well-being. Therefore, a network must achieve private gains while simultaneously serving public good.
2. A network, to be socially acceptable, must have the lowest entry barriers that would encourage maximum number of companies to willingly join the group and thereby prevent private gains for the few at the expenses of many.
3. The Membership benefits must be strong enough that companies would make every effort to remain in good standing. At the same time, they would voluntarily pressure the recalcitrant companies to adhere to the network's "rules of the game" or risk exile. Therefore, networks have high exit barriers; i.e., member companies stand to lose considerably by exiting the group, thereby minimizing free riders and preventing entry of companies opposed to network goals.

The GC's utter disregard of these fundamental conditions was previously noted in the response from Georg Kell when he was defending the entry of PetroChina into the Global Compact. PetroChina, a state-owned enterprise, has extensive operations in African countries where there have been widespread incidences of human rights abuses and environmental degradation.

An examination of local network operations reveals trends that are contrary to their survival and growth. Local meetings are organized to do outreach to new members, discuss particular issues, share best practices, and the like. Currently, outreach is still the primary concern of the local networks, and is focused on building networks through increases in head count. This suggests that COP-related activities are relatively low at the global level even though this is one of the primary integrity measures of the GC.[30] Both the GC Office and local Networks are obsessed with outreach, pointing to the fragility of the entire GC enterprise. A declining growth rate, therefore, would be a serious cause for concern to the GC's organizers.

Delisting

The GC identifies itself as an aspirational, not regulatory, framework,—a bone of contention between the GC and its critics. When companies become signatories to the GC, they promise to file annually a Communication on Progress (COP), which is presumed to be a communication between firm and its stakeholders, and not between the company and the GC. There are three basic components to the COP: a CEO statement of support; a report of actions taken since joining or since the last report that either implement the GC principles or support broader UN initiatives; and outcome measurements, indicating metrics used. The choice of principles and the design of metrics are left to the discretion of the corporation.[31]

The GC's policy with regard to the COP has been a work in progress. At present, firms are required to file a COP within one year of acceptance into the GC, which must report on actions taken on two of the four GC principle areas. Within five years, the report is to include actions taken on all four principle areas, though the firm may choose which of the principles in each area it will work on and report. Up until July 1, 2009, firms that had not filed for one year were considered " 'inactive',", and firms that had not filed for two years were considered " 'non-communicating' ", and were then delisted after three years. Prior to March 2010, that procedure had been shortened, and firms that did not file for one year were subsequently and publicly delisted.

In March 2010, the GC Board met to discuss the delisting policy and its current level of implementation. In particular, the GC Board considered this policy to be unduly harsh on firms from non-OECD/G20 countries, where companies were being delisted through lack of capacity or other issues. Consequently, the GC Board issued a moratorium at their March 2010 meeting, suspending the delisting policy and reinstating those firms that had been delisted since 1 January 1, 2010.[32]

The suggestion that a company outside of the OECD/G20 would "lack" resources to prepare a COP—quite a perfunctory report to begin with— stretches credulity. It also flies in the face of statements made by the GC toward enhancing the integrity of corporate compliance with the GC principles. In 2008, the Expert Meeting on the COP issue, convened by the GC Ooffice on the COP issue, stressed that the COP was "essential for upholding the integrity of the UN Global Compact and its participants."[33] The moratorium is meant to be a "…temporary measure to allow for a thorough review of COP preparation and submission procedures to ensure their suitability for all companies. The Board asked the Global Compact Office to present a long-term solution to the COP process at its next meeting in June this year."[34] To date, some three months after that meeting, there have been no further statements.

How does one reconcile all these activities and reporting to the statement made by Prof. John Ruggie and referred to in an earlier part of this paperchapter? To wit, the GC is a learning model utilizing the powerful tool of transparency?. Our analysis suggests that the GC has failed to achieve either of its goals. The dilemma and the solution is are best offered by Humpty Dumpty in Lewis Caroll's book, *Alice's Adventures in Wonderland & Through the Looking-Glass*.

> "When I use a word,", Humpty Dumpty said, "it means just what I choose it to mean—neither more nor less."
>
> "The question is," said Alice, "whether you can make words mean so many different things."
>
> "The question is" said Humpty Dumpty, "which is to be master—that's all."[35]

Expansion Through Diversification: A Solution in Search of Problems

In its strategy of expansion, the GC has sought out opportunities to enlist other organizations by creating new initiatives that would entice them to become part of the GC enterprise. GC initiatives now include, among others, the Principles for Responsible Management (PRME), the Principles for Responsible Investment (PRI), the UN Leadership Forum on Climate Change, the UN-Business Collaboration, and the CEO Water Mandate. For the GC, this was a relatively easy path to growth since the new entities are not expected to do much more than pay lip service to the GC principles and indicate that they are now part of the GC's universal umbrella. Their principles or standards are long on rhetorical promises and short on reporting concrete performance. While they add "numbers" to the GC, they have shown little success either in their self-proclaimed mission or in enhancing the reputation of the GC and its custodianship and shepherding the promotion of its ten principles. Moreover, in keeping with the working model of the GC's core operations, the new entities have no standards of compliance, performance evaluation, or verifiable reporting. Instead, they are asked to provide some sort of "communication on progress," leaving its content entirely at the discretion of the reporting entity.

In this section, we provide a brief analysis and evaluation of two such initiatives that have been heavily promoted by the Global Compact among its major achievements in broadening the application of the GC framework. These are the Principles for Responsible Management Education (PRME) and the CEO Water Mandate.

Principles for Responsible Management Education (PRME)

The GC launched the PRME (pronounced "prime") project in July 2007 at its Leadership Summit in Geneva. It was a collaborative effort by an international task force composed of representatives from some of the world's major universities and business schools, and also included accreditation organizations such as the Association to Advance Collegiate Schools of Business (AACSB) and the European Foundation for Management Development (EFMD), among others.[36] The combined effort of this august group was the creation of a set of voluntary principles (Exhibit 8.2), to which signatory institutions (management schools) would adhere to "inspire and champion responsible management education, research and thought leadership globally" (PRME 2009).[37]

Justification for the program is presented as a two-pronged self-evident truth. One, that market failures and ethical lapses by business corporations around the world that triggered the collapse of investment banking and shook the foundations of the financial industry "strongly augur for a force of change."[38] It also asserts that an increasingly large number of companies have

---

Exhibit 8.2   The Principles of Responsible Management Education

As institutions of higher learning involved in the education of current and future managers we are voluntarily committed to engaging in a continuous process of improvement of the following Principles, reporting on progress to all our stakeholders and exchanging effective practices with other academic institutions:

> Principle 1: *Purpose*: We will develop the capabilities of students to be future generators of sustainable value for business and society at large and to work for an inclusive and sustainable global economy.
>
> Principle 2: *Values*: We will incorporate into our academic activities and curricula the values of global social responsibility as portrayed in international initiatives such as the United Nations Global Compact.
>
> Principle 3: *Method*: We will create educational frameworks, materials, processes and environments that enable effective learning experiences for responsible leadership.
>
> Principle 4: *Research*: We will engage in conceptual and empirical research that advances our understanding about the role, dynamics, and impact of corporations in the creation of sustainable social, environmental and economic value.
>
> Principle 5: *Partnership*: We will interact with managers of business corporations to extend our knowledge of their challenges in meeting social and environmental responsibilities and to explore jointly effective approaches to meeting these challenges.
>
> Principle 6: *Dialogue*: We will facilitate and support dialog and debate among educators, business, government, consumers, media, civil society organizations and other interested groups and stakeholders on critical issues related to global social responsibility and sustainability. We understand that our own organizational practices should serve as example of the values and attitudes we convey to our students.

demonstrated their commitment to enhanced corporate social responsibility "by working to adopt Global Compact Principles and to reform their own activities, such as corruption, in the communities in which they operate."[39] Two, the presumption behind PRME is that management education programs need to take leadership roles to educate future leaders who are capable of coping with the kinds of social, ecological, and governance issues that their organizations will increasingly face in this troubled and resource-constrained world.[40]

When stripped of its hyperbole, the aforementioned assertions are unsustainable both in fact and in claims for the potential of PRME. Capital markets and financial systems have repeatedly gone through bouts of recessions, depressions, fraud, and chicanery over the past century and in different parts of the world. They could not all be blamed on poor management education or ethical lapses in business leadership. The PRME supporters' assertion that businesses are becoming more aware of their corporate social responsibility by becoming GC signatories is not supported by any data.

PRME advocates bemoan the fact that management education has mostly lost the innovative drive of "being in the forefront of creating knowledge," has instead become "merely reactive," and has failed to incorporate these new mandates into their teaching and research programs. They claim that PRME principles will "correct this educational lag by encouraging this new emphasis on corporate social responsibility in business school education."[41] By the measures used by the GC, PRME has achieved remarkable success in the short period of two years, and "now includes over 300 signatories from around the world—with participant numbers increasing nearly 50% in 2009."[42]

Once again, the story of "numbers" is deceptive and misleading. PRME sponsors have made it extremely easy for academic institutions to become signatories. These schools are not even required to prepare or submit any report as to what if anything they plan to do to meet their obligations toward implementing PRME. Notwithstanding, as of May 2009, only 229 institutions have adopted the PRME principles, of which 219 are academic institutions. The significance of this small number becomes even more pronounced in view of the fact that as of May 2009, AACSB—one of the main accrediting body for management schools—had 1,127 member schools, of which 568 were accredited by the organization. Consequently, less than 20 percent of the AACSB member schools have joined PRME.[43] Another important and disconcerting fact to consider is that among the top one hundred Financial Times Global MBA schools, only twenty-four have joined PRME.

One would expect that such a small level of participation, and an even smaller proportion from the top-ranked schools, would provide a cause for self-examination and soul searching by the GC and PRME sponsors. Instead, PRME supporters attribute the unwillingness of the nonsignatory institutions to a lack of vision that must be corrected through greater effort on the part of PRME advocates. In their view, "every business school and management programme *should* [emphasis in the original] adopt these principles."[44]

Inadequacy of the PRME Framework

The PRME framework, as currently structured, suffers from certain fatal flaws that make it highly unlikely that it will ever deliver on its goals without significant changes in its principles, modus operandi, standards of performance, transparency, and outcome-oriented accountability. The first problem with the PRME principles is that they are not really principles. A principle is supposed to provide a rationale for action or its appropriateness thereof.[45] Some GC documents also use the terms "principles" or "standards" interchangeably in describing PRME. However, the term "standard" is also inappropriate in this instance, because PRME does not offer a measure of quality or level of attainment.[46] Devoid of these characteristics, PRME principles are reduced to cajoling their followers to do their best in certain areas of action. The second flaw in justifying the PRME framework lies in its assumption as to the lack of sufficient content in dealing with issues of ethics, corporate social responsibility, and sustainability in the current program offerings at business schools and universities.

There are, however, other explanations for their lack of interest in the PRME.

- Scholars and top-tier business schools consider PRME as a poorly defined framework where participation would not gain them extra knowledge, but rather make them vulnerable to reputational risk because of weak commitment to PRME standards by other signatories.
- Top-tier business schools and universities may have their own well-developed programs dealing with ethics, human rights, and sustainability, with courses offered in different departments of the university and open to business students. The flexibility of these programs and their innovative character is "institution dependent," and is a source of strength for the institutions, which they may be reluctant to expose to the GC type of reporting structure.
- Whereas PRME was endorsed by a large number of business schools and accrediting bodies, these organizations have not used their institutional policies and procedures to support implementation of PRME principles in their member institutions. For example, AACSB has well-defined procedures to introduce such programmatic changes in business school curriculum. AACSB could take initiative by suggesting that at least 15 percent of the course content in a business management degree would be related to the PRME principles. The fact that AACSB and other accrediting bodies have not considered such an option would indicate that they did not expect that such initiative would have any traction from their member schools.

CEO Water Mandate

The CEO Water Mandate was initiated in July 2007. It is designed to "assist companies in the development, implementation, and disclosure of water sustainability policies and practices."[47] The mandate covers six areas of water management (exhibit 8.3).[48] Participation in the CEO Water Mandate is limited to companies only. A company joining the Water Mandate must either be a member of the GC or intend to join within six months following its participation in the Water Mandate.

Exhibit 8.3 CEO Water Mandate[49]

Direct Operations

We pledge to undertake the following actions, where appropriate, over time:

- Conduct a comprehensive water-use assessment to understand the extent to which the company uses water in the direct production of goods and services.
- Set targets for our operations related to water conservation and waste-water treatment, framed in a corporate cleaner production and consumption strategy.
- Seek to invest in and use new technologies to achieve these goals.
- Raise awareness of water sustainability within corporate culture.
- Include water sustainability considerations in business decision-making—e.g., facility-sitting, due diligence, and production processes.

Supply Chain and Watershed Management

- We pledge to undertake the following actions, where appropriate, over time:
- Encourage suppliers to improve their water conservation, quality monitoring, waste-water treatment, and recycling practices.
- Build capacities to analyze and respond to watershed risk.
- Encourage and facilitate suppliers in conducting assessments of water usage and impacts.
- Share water sustainability practices—established and emerging—with suppliers.
- Encourage major suppliers to report regularly on progress achieved related to goals.

Collective Action

We pledge to undertake the following actions, where appropriate, over time:

- Build closer ties with civil society organizations, especially at the regional and local levels.
- Work with national, regional and local governments and public authorities to address water sustainability issues and policies, as well as with relevant international institutions—e.g., the UNEP Global Programme of Action.
- Encourage development and use of new technologies, including efficient irrigation methods, new plant varieties, drought resistance, water efficiency and salt tolerance.
- Be actively involved in the UN Global Compact's Country Networks.
- Support the work of existing water initiatives involving the private sector—e.g., the Global Water Challenge; UNICEF's Water, Environment and Sanitation Program; IFRC Water and Sanitation Program; the World Economic Forum Water Initiative—and collaborate with other relevant UN bodies and intergovernmental organizations—e.g., the World Health Organization, the Organisation for Economic Co-operation and Development, and the World Bank Group.

Public Policy

We pledge to undertake the following actions, where appropriate, over time:

- Contribute inputs and recommendations in the formulation of government regulation and in the creation of market mechanisms in ways that drive the water sustainability agenda.
- Excercise "business statesmanship" by being advocates for water sustainability in global and local policy discussions, clearly presenting the role and responsibility of the private sector in supporting integrated water resource management.
- Partner with governments, businesses, civil society and other stakeholders—for example specialized institutes such as the Stockholm International Water Institute, UNEP Collaborating Centre on Water and Enviornment, and UNESCO's Institute for Water Education—to advance the body of knowledge, intelligence and tools.
- Join and/or support special policy-oriented bodies and associated frameworks—e.g., UNEP's Water Policy and Strategy; UNDP's Water Governance Programme.

Community Engagement

We pledge to undertake the following actions, where appropriate, over time:

- Endeavor to understand the water and sanitation challenges in the communities where we operate and how our businesses impact those challenges.
- Be active members of the local community, and encourage or provide support to local government, groups and initiatives seeking to advance the water and sanitation agendas.
- Undertake water-resource education and awareness campaigns in partnership with local stakeholders.
- Work with public authorities and their agents to support—when appropriate—the development of adequate water infrastructure, including water and sanitation delivery systems.

Transparency

We pledge to undertake the following actions, where appropriate, over time:

- Include a description of actions and investments undertaken in relation to The CEO Water Mandate in our annual Communications on Progress for the UN Global Compact, making reference to relevant performance indicators such as the water indicators found in the Global Reporting Initiative (GRI) Guidelines.
- Publish and share our water strategies (including targets and results as well as areas for improvement) in relevent corporate reports, using—where appropriate—the water indicators found in the GRI Guidelines.
- Be transparent in dealings and conversations with governments and other public authorities on water issues.

It is not clear as to how the mandate fits into the overall scheme of the GC. In one sense, the Water Mandate may be defended as a means to advance the implementation of one or more of the GC principles, such as environment protection and poverty reduction. However, if this were the case, why hasn't the GC chosen to pursue other similar mandates, such as the CEO Human Rights Mandate, the CEO Anti-Sweatshop Mandate, or the CEO Anti-Bribe and Corruption Mandate?

Alternately, one might argue that the CEO Water Mandate is intended to induce corporations to become signatory members of the Global Compact. It is a promotional device, or a carving out of a special purpose, that would appeal to a specific group of companies. Otherwise, why choose to glorify the mandate with the prefix of CEO? It sends a clear and unambiguous message to corporate sponsors that they would influence the mandate's purpose, scope of implementation, measurement of achievement, and public communication thereof. Why are the corporate sponsors the only legitimate owners of the water issue? Is their assessment of how to promote and conserve water use the only legitimate consideration? When examined in these terms, the GC makes a mockery of its mission, debases its claims to high moral authority, and degrades itself as the supplicant of its corporate sponsors.

Governance Structure and Sources of Financial Support

The mandate is governed by a committee of ten corporate members reflecting a cross-section of regional representation. A member of the GC Office represents the rest of the world. Funding for mandate operations (two meetings per year) is done through voluntary contributions and corporate sponsorships.

Progress, Accomplishments, and Failures of the CEO Water Mandate

There are now seventy signatories to the CEO Water Mandate. Requirements for participation in good standing are quite perfunctory and similar to those of the GC. Companies simply send a "letter of intent" from the company's CEO to the GC, and file a yearly report (Communication on Progress—Water) that addresses the six areas outlined in the mandate. The COP-Water is also expected to provide information about the companies' progress on the GC's ten principles.

It appears that even this perfunctory information is a burden for the CEOs and their corporations. Of the seventy current participants, nine are "noncommunicating," indicating that they have not filed the COP-Water as required. This charade of the self-determined "communication on progress" is similar to other initiatives sponsored by the GC, and is just as useful or useless depending on who is viewing the information and for what purpose.

The Water Mandate suffers from a variety of problems that should have been anticipated by the GC if the UN-initiated group was really serious in implementing its ten principles and not making them hostage to corporate sponsors. The Water Mandate has shown little concern for other stakeholders, notably the farmers and villagers whose water use would be constrained by the corporate users of local water. It is a perfect cover that would protect the worst offenders (from the perspective of other water users) by allowing the mandate's corporate sponsors to shape the debate to their own liking without any need to answer irritating questions from groups that hold a different viewpoint. Is this really what the Global Compact is all about?

The Water Mandate does not provide any incentives toward water conservation or disincentives toward water wastage on the part of its corporate sponsors and their supply chains. Water sustainability is completely framed by needs of the firm, and locals are shunted to the side. We would like to emphasize that this lack of concern is intentional and embedded in the mandate's governance structure and sources of financial support, which puts effective constraints on how the scope and magnitude of the water-use issue is defined under the Water Mandate.

First, in a recent report, the Pacific Institute assessed the issues of water policy and reporting in global companies.[50] High priority was given to those companies that were signatories of the Water Mandate.[51] Of the 110 firms studied, only 62 percent displayed conformity with one of the three criteria: describing a systemic materiality assessment process, stakeholder engagement, and using both GRI and AA1000 principles in their reports. Less than half (47 percent) of the companies examined utilized any form of stakeholder engagement and thereby effectively excluded local users of water resources. While the companies were quite interested and able to measure their own water use, "relatively few of them provided information on regional or local water use or any contextual information in which their water uses and/or impacts could be understood."[52]

The Water Mandate allows member companies to frame the debate through creation and dissemination of favorable information. One can usually expect companies to use their competitive advantage in this manner, but should we also expect the GC to become a partner in this exercise?

The plight of local water users is best exemplified by observations made in the Pacific Institute Report. As aquifer levels drop, companies continue to access water and the locals lose out, a phenomenon known as "competitive deepening."[53] The report notes, "Ten percent of the companies described any role they may be playing in 'Water Infrastructure Development.' 'Water Sustainability Advocacy' was by far the criterion with the lowest adherence percentage with only three companies reporting."[54]

A case in point is Coca-Cola, a mandate signatory, in India. Coke's corporate motto on water is "Reduce/Recycle/Reuse." But this belies the real situation in India, where water is the key to the subsistence farming that feeds a majority of people in rural areas. Consumption of Coke products in India has tripled in the past ten years,[55] exerting a major strain on water resources, particularly in rural areas where Coke has sited some facilities. The impact in India's rural areas is telling. In Plachimada, where Coke has sited a plant in the midst of an agricultural area, it has had catastrophic consequences for local farmers. These farmers used to operate their pumps eighteen hours per day to water their fields, but are now limited to four hours per day and the water is brackish.[56] The Energy and Resources Institute (TERI), a nonprofit, university-affiliated research institute located in Delhi, has substantiated overexploitation of the aquifers in a number of areas, as well as the charges regarding pollution.[57]

One wonders why the GC has ignored these issues. If the purpose of the Water Mandate is to make efficient use of water for all parties, why hasn't the GC and its Water Mandate trustees raised these issues in an open forum that would ensure equal participation from all stakeholders, and ensure adequate public disclosure through transparency of deliberations?

The Global Compact: Illusions of Progress or the Lost Decade?

In marking the tenth anniversary of the Global Compact, GC executive Georg Kell spoke eloquently of the progress the GC had made over the previous decade, and outlined a broader and bolder vision for the next decade. Both Kell and Secretary General Moon struck a highly optimistic note as to the GC's achievements to date and its future relevance to the business community and society-at-large. Kell indicated that what started out as a purely aspirational statement of principles has since been transformed into significant achievements.

> In a short period of ten years, "the Global Compact stands as the world's largest, global responsibility initiative. As of 1 June 2010, over 8,000 signatories—6,000 from business and 2,000 from civil society and other non-business groups—based in more than 135 countries were committed to implementing the Global Compact principles into business practices and taking actions to advance UN goals, such as the Millennium Development Goals (MDGs).[58]

> This year marks the 10th anniversary of the UNGC. Our appeal a decade ago for business to "initiate a global compact of shared values and principles" resonates as much, if not more, today....Seen as purely aspirational in the early days, our mission is increasingly achievable—and increasingly called for.[59]

However, Georg Kell's own statements belie his contentions of achievements. For example, in his celebratory note on the GC's ten years of progress, he lists the directional change as from morality to materiality, mainstreaming of the principles, "A" for accountability, changing markets and changing mindsets, and responsible lobbying. He claims that the notion and practice of corporate responsibility—defined as both as implementing universal principles into business practices and taking action to support societal goals—has evolved significantly in the past ten years. As evidence of this comment, he provides a list of achievements (exhibit 8.4).

These aspirational statements sound eerily similar to the tone of the messages in 2000, when the GC principles were first announced. Georg Kell's assertive statement regarding the GC's progress is in keeping with its communication strategy, that is, making optimistic but unsubstantiated statements about progress.

The Global Compact has provided no meaningful information to indicate how and in what manner the signatory companies have improved their conduct over the ten-year period that would reflect a higher level of corporate social responsibility and sustainable business practices. There is, however, little evidence to show that the GC companies, and even those that have been at the

Exhibit 8.4 The First Ten Years

The notion and practice of corporate responsibility – defined as both implementing universal principles into business practices and taking actions to support societal goals – has evolved significantly in the past ten years.

FROM MORALITY TO MATERIALITY. While working towards the common good remains integral to corporate responsibility agenda, it is no longer the only "selling point". Today, environmental, social and governance (ESG) issues – as covered by the Global Compact principles – are understood to be real factors in the long-term viability and success of companies, whether small suppliers or large transnationals.

GONE GLOBAL. Only 47 companies were present at our launch in July 2000. Today, the UN Global Compact is the world's largest voluntary corporate sustainability initiative with over 8,000 business participants and non-business stakeholders from 135 countries. Companies represent nearly every industry and sector, and hail from developed, emerging and developing economies.

GONE LOCAL. Global Compact Local Networks can be found in over 90 countries. Through the networks, participants work individually and collectively to advance understanding and implementation of the ten principles, as well as engage in partnerships around local priority issues.

MAINSTREAMING OF THE PRINCIPLES. The level of awareness of the business relevance of human rights, good governance, and conflict-sensitive practices – as examples – has rapidly grown. So has cooperation among unlikely bedfellows, with unprecedented collaboration occurring between NGOs and companies, and corporate competitors coming together in ways not previously imagined to fight challenges - such as corruption and climate change.

"A" FOR ACCOUNTABILITY. Ten years ago, it was a challenge for companies to simply explain the connection between principles and business, now thousands are communicating annually in public reports on tangible efforts to address ESG issues. Moreover, new efforts to advance disclosure in areas such as human rights, water and anti-corruption are pushing this field to the next level.

CHANGING MARKETS. Until a few years ago there was no framework to mobilize investors around the materiality of ESG issues. Now, through the UN-backed Principles for Responsible Investment (PRI) a network of more than 700 institutional investors, representing roughly $20 trillion in assets, are putting ESG considerations into the heart of investment analysis and decision-making. Importantly, they are using their influence to encourage improvements in sustainability performance by companies.

CHANGING MINDSETS. Through the UN-backed Principles for Responsible Management Education (PRME), there is now a global framework in place for academic institutions to advance corporate responsibility through their curricula and research. There is a long way to go to develop a new generation of business leaders, but with 300 business schools from 50-plus countries signed on to the PRME, a strong movement is afoot.

RESPONSIBLE LOBBYING. Recent collective efforts by CEOs on climate (calling for a global agreement) and anti-corruption (calling for an effective UN Convention against Corruption) are important "firsts", signal-ing the potential impact of responsible business-government relations on global issues. This is a step towards overcoming the disconnect between a company's stated commitment to principles and their, too often, contradictory lobbying efforts.

RISE OF "SOFT" POWER. Ten years ago, the only relationship between policymaking and business was one of regulation. Today, Governments play an increasingly prominent role in promoting responsible business practices, as a complement to regulatory measures, and are taking actions such as raising awareness, building business capacity, developing tools, and providing funding for voluntary initiatives. Also, public-private partnerships have become a mainstay in bringing practical solutions to societal challenges.

forefront of supporting the GC, have in any way demonstrated an enhanced level of respect for the GC principles in their business operations. Instead, the past ten years have been noted for egregious business conduct involving such issues as human rights abuses, child labor and unfair labor practices, product contamination, bribery and corruption, pollution and environmental degradation, and colossal risk to the world's financial system. In most of these cases, many companies involved were also signatory members of the UN Global Compact. It is doubtful that these companies gave any thought to their commitments and responsibilities under the GC. What is equally distressing that the GC did not find such examples as something of concern, or even make public acknowledgement of how far the GC has to go to be taken seriously by either the corporate community or society-at-large.

To the best of our knowledge, neither the GC nor the signatory companies have provided any information that would suggest a higher level of socially responsible conduct when compared with similarly placed non-GC signatory companies in terms of size, industry characteristics, or geographical location. In a recent study, the International Center for Corporate Accountability, Inc., a nonprofit education-research NGO, analyzed corporate social responsibility-sustainability reports (CSR-S) published by 513 corporations from a worldwide database of 1,384 corporations during the period 2009–2010. Of the 513 companies, 221 (41.13 percent) mention some form of involvement in the GC in their CSR-S reports. A detailed content analysis of these reports also showed that among the companies indicating participation in GC, not a single one provided information on how the GC principles were being implemented or embedded in their core business operations; how their performance has changed or improved over the period since their participation began; or what challenges they see in the future with regard to their GC participation. In general, for a large number of companies in this group, the discussion of GC-related activities ranged between twenty-five and seventy-five words. In contrast, the median number of pages for all reports was approximately forty-five, and those that mention the GC had a median length of approximately sixty pages.[60]

A similar situation prevails with regard to the GC's more recent initiatives that bring countries, business schools, city governments, institutional investors, and water users under the GC umbrella of the ten principles. As our analysis in the previous sections has shown, their so-called progress reports, the Communication on Progress (COP), are invariably short on progress and long on rosy forecasts of a promising future.

From the very beginning, the Global Compact has claimed that it is not a monitoring organization and has no regulatory role. There is, however, a major distinction between monitoring for compliance and seeking assurance of accuracy and objectivity of information that is voluntarily provided by the signatory companies regarding their adherence to the GC principles. In the absence of such an assurance, voluntary compliance degenerates into self-proclaimed and unverified assertions of excellent compliance. As such, they must be rejected as self-aggrandizement and unworthy of public trust.

Global Compact: Wither Goes the Future?

What kind of a future should we expect from the Global Compact? As things stand now, all that can be said about the GC is that it is a mile wide and half an inch deep. It is long on promises, short on performance, and mostly silent in terms of transparency and objective reporting. Moreover, everything about the GC's strategy for the future means "more of the same"; that is, its vision of the future reads like a prologue to an unremarkable past and disappointing present. In its current state, the GC is like a thin patina of respectability that provides a temporary protective cover to a mass of tiny swirling particles. There is a buzzing sound but no discernible message; there is a lot of motion, but no direction; and there is a lot of activity, but no measurable outcome. This is an unsustainable situation and will inevitably cause this protective mask to implode and self-destruct.

A major part of the problem lies in the fact that the Global Compact has projected itself as the empyrean of high moral and humanistic values, while in practice it has struggled in the trenches with the lowly mortals—not to save them, but for their patronage to save itself. In this position, it is incapable of either redeeming itself or making discernible progress in its mission. Perhaps the most honorable approach would be for the GC to admit its failure and dissolve itself. Paradoxically, it might even help the GC garner more success in changing corporate behavior. When shorn of the GC's protective umbrella, corporations will have to respond to public pressure for better conduct, responsibility for their actions, and verifiable transparency.

Much as we would like to hope, it is highly unlikely that the Global Compact would contemplate such a course of action. Mission-driven organizations become so passionately involved that a failure to succeed in achieving their goals leads them to blame the external environment and to call for renewed effort. If this were to happen, and we believe it will happen, the GC will continue to become wider and shallower by the day until it runs out of space and depth and becomes a dry bed of sand—not good for itself and not good for anyone else.

Notes

1. United Nations Global Compact Office, *United Nations Global Compact Annual Review—Anniversary Edition*, (New York: United Nations, June 2010), pp. 9–10.
2. Kenny Bruno and Joshua Karliner, "Tangled Up in Blue: Corporate Partnerships at the United Nations," Transnational Resource and Action Group, September 2000, http://s3.amazonaws.com/corpwatch.org/downloads/tangled.pdf, p. 2 For further information, see www.corpwatch.org and www.globalpolicy.org.
3. For a more extensive discussion of adverse selection in the context of the Global Compact, see S.P. Sethi, *Setting Global Standards: Guidelines for Creating Codes of Conduct in Multinational Corporations*, (Hoboken, NJ: John Wiley & Sons, 2003).
4. Bruno and Karliner, op. cit., p. 2.
5. A letter detailing the charges can be found at http://www.unglobalcompact.org/docs/news_events/9.1_news_archives/2009_01_12b/letter_from_CNPC_15Dec2008.pdf.
6. The text of the full letter can be found at http://www.unglobalcompact.org/NewsAndEvents/news_archives/2009_01_12b.html.
7. Excerpts from the statement of Pierre Sane, Amnesty International, June 26, 2000.
8. The number of letters and group voicing their criticism of GC are far too many to be listed here.
9. For details of accusations against these companies, see www.corpwatch.org; Asia-Pacific Human Rights Network, "Associating with the Wrong Company," July 13, 2001; Tim Connor, "Still Waiting for Nike to Respect the Right to Organize," *Global Exchange*, June 28, 2001; Report by Corpwatch, "UN and Corporations Fact Sheet," (under Campaigns: Corporate-Free UN), March 22, 2001. It should be noted that there are many other companies and industry groups seeking affiliation with the Global Compact that were accused of similar misconduct but were not mentioned in the letter. These include, among others, Aventis, Norsk Hydro, Unilever, and the International Chamber of Commerce and Industry (ICC). See www.corpwatch.org, "The Global Compact Corporate Partners," Alliance for a Corporate-Free UN, Sept. 1, 2000, which includes articles such as Elizabeth Neuffer, "UN: Aventis Accused of Breaking Global Compact," *Boston Globe*, June 15, 2001; Nity Annand Jayram, "Norsk Hydro: Global Compact Violator," October 18, 2001; Corporate Europe Observatory, "High Time for UN to Break Partnership with ICC," July 25, 2001; Nity Annand Jayram, "Inconsistencies Galore: A Timeline on Unilever's Mercury Dumping in India," October 4, 2001; information from the Global Policy Forum, which can be found at www.globalpolicy.org; NGO Panel on Corporate Accountability held at the United Nations, February 15, 2001, under the headline "Global Compact with Corporations: 'Civil Society' Responds," www.unglobalcompact.org.
10. Bruno and Karliner, op. cit.
11. Maria Livanos Cattaui, "Yes to Annan's 'Global Compact' If It Isn't a License to Meddle," *International Herald Tribune*, July 26, 2000.
12. Excerpts from a letter written by John G. Ruggie, Assistant Secretary-General, dated July 21, 2000.

13. The Global Compact, published by the Global Compact Office, United Nations, Jan. 2001. See also the Global Compact website, www.unglobalcompact.org.

14. United Nations, *Addressing Business Leaders at Global Compact Summit, Secretary-General Says Experience Shows that Voluntary Initiatives "Can and Do Work,"* United Nations Press Release SG/SM/9387 ECO/71 (2004), at http://www.un.org/News/Press/docs/2004/sgsm9387.doc.htm.

15. Current board members and their affiliations can be found at http://www.unglobalcompact.org/AboutTheGC/The_Global_Compact_Board.html.

16. Jose Sergio Gabrielli de Azavedo, president and CEO, Petrobras, Brazil; Guillermo Carey, senior partner, Carey & Allende Abogados, Chile; Chen Ying, deputy director, China Enterprise Federation, China; Anne Lauvergeon, chair of the executive board, Areva, France; Ntombifuthi Mtoba, chair of the board, Deloitte, South Africa; and Mads Oevlisen, adjunct professor and chair, Lego, Denmark.

17. These are the International Federation of Chemical, Energy, Mine, and General Workers' Unions; the International Organization of Employers; the International Confederation of Free Trade Union; and the International Chamber of Commerce. It should be noted that in 2004 the ICC actively opposed a draft report of the High Commissioner for Human Rights concerning the "Responsibilities of Transnational Corporations and Related Business Enterprises with Regard to Human Rights" as being too dependent on business and not sufficiently dependent on law and regulation, though it is increasingly clear that business is very involved in the devolution of legal structures and regulation under the aegis of globalization. In 2008, the ICC endorsed a revised version of this report that contained stronger language on national law.

18. Jean Rozwadowski, secretary general of the International Chamber of Commerce, replaced her predecessor, Guy Sebban, in 2010. Sir Mark Moody-Stuart is a current director at HSBC Holdings PLC, Accenture Ltd, and Saudi Aramco. Past positions include stints as chair of both Anglo American PLC and Royal Dutch/Shell Group.

19. A full description of the foundation can be found at http://www.globalcompactfoundation.org/.

20. This is based on estimates from the Global Compact Board minutes of November 2007, when it was estimated that the foundation would supply approximately 50 percent of the overall budget, or between $2 million and $3 million per year. We used 8 percent per year as the increase factor for the budget. See http://www.unglobalcompact.org/aboutthegc/the_global_compact_board.html.

21. Over the ten-year history of the GC, donor countries have included Brazil, China, Colombia, Denmark, Finland, France, Germany, Italy, Republic of Korea, Norway, Spain, Sweden, Switzerland, and the United Kingdom. Source: *United Nations Global Compact Annual Review—Anniversary Edition, June 2010.*

22. http://www.unglobalcompact.org/NewsAndEvents/news_archives/2005_12_01a.html

23. Source: http://www.unglobalcompact.org/aboutthegc/the_global_compact_board.html.

24. Sir Mark Moody-Stuart is a current director at HSBC Holdings PLC, Accenture Ltd, and Saudi Aramco. Past positions include stints as chair of both Anglo American PLC and Royal Dutch/Shell Group. James V. Kearney is a senior partner in the international law firm of Latham & Watkins LLP. Caroline L. Williams is president of Grey Seal Capital, LLC. Oliver F. Williams is associate professor and director of the Notre Dame Center for Ethics and Religious Values in Business in the Mendoza College of Business at the University of Notre Dame.

25. These minutes can be found at http://www.unglobalcompact.org/aboutthegc/the_global_compact_board.html.

26. Source: *United Nations Global Compact Annual Review—Anniversary Edition, June 2010*, inside front cover.

27. Based on data supplied by the GC Office.

28. An analysis of local network participants and range of stakeholders for 2009 can be found at http://www.unglobalcompact.org/docs/networks_around_world_doc/Annual_Report_2010/GCLN_2010.pdf, pp. 18 and 25, respectively.

29. Kell, G., & Levin, D. 2003. The Global Compact network: An historic experiment in learning and action. *Business and Society Review*, 108: 151-181; Ruggie, J.G. 2001. Global.governance.net: The Global Compact as learning network. *Global Governance*, 7: 371-378; Ruggie, J. G. 2004. Reconstituting the global public domain – Issues, actors, and practices. *European Journal of International Relations*, 10: 499-531.

30. An analysis of network activities for 2009 can be found at: http://www.unglobalcompact.org/docs/networks_around_world_doc/Annual_Report_2010/GCLN_2010.pdf, pp. 37-40.

31. http://www.unglobalcompact.org/COP/)

32. The press release for this decision can be found at: http://www.unglobalcompact.org/news/20-03-25-2010

33. http://www.unglobalcompact.org/NewsAndEvents/news_archives/2008_05_22.html

34. http://www.unglobalcompact.org/news/20-03-25-2010

35. Lewis Carroll, Alice's Adventures in Wonderland & Through the Looking Glass, (New York: The New American Library, 1960), paperback edition, p. 186.

36. Other affiliated institutions that were part of the project's steering committee included the Aspen Institute's Business and Society Program, the Globally Responsible Leadership Initiative (GRLI), NetImpact (a student organization with more than 11,000 members), and the European Academy of Business in Society (EABIS).

37. Taken from the PRME Mission Statement, found at http://www.unprme.org/index.php.

38. Regina Wentzel Wolfe and Patricia W. Werhane, "Academic Institutions and the United Nations Global Compact: The Principles for Responsible Management Education," in Andreas Rasche and Georg Kell, eds., *The United Nations Global Compact: Achievements, Trends, and Challenges,* (Cambridge: Cambridge University Press, 2010), pp. 149–153, 159–160.

39. Ibid.

40. Ibid, p. 5.

41. Ibid, p. 146.

42. *United Nations Global Compact Annual Review—Anniversary Edition.*

43. Adapted from Wolfe and Werhane, op. cit.

44. Wolfe and Werhane, p. 148.

45. The *Oxford American College Dictionary* (2001) defines "principle" as "a fundamental truth or proposition that serves as the foundation for a system of belief or behavior or for a chain of reasoning."

46. Ibid.

47. http://www.unglobalcompact.org/Issues/Environment/CEO_Water_Mandate/index.html

48. http://www.unglobalcompact.org/docs/news_events/8.1/Ceo_water_mandate.pdf

49. Each section of the mandate has a preamble; the full document can be found at http://www.unglobalcompact.org/docs/news_events/8.1/Ceo_water_mandate.pdf. In the interest of space, we have retained only the actions under each heading.

50. *Water Disclosure 2.0 Assessment of Current and Emerging Practice in Corporate Water Reporting*, study by the Pacific Institute in conjunction with the CEO Water Mandate; found at http://www.unglobalcompact.org/docs/news_events/9.1_news_archives/2009_03_11/Water_Disclosure.pdf.

51. Ibid, p. 12.

52. Ibid, p. 7.

53. http://www.globalpolicy.org/component/content/article/162-general/28046.html

54. *Water Disclosure 2.0*, p. 24.

55. http://www.thecoca-colacompany.com/ourcompany/ar/pdf/2009-operating-group-eurasia-africa.pdf

56. http://www.globalpolicy.org/component/content/article/162-general/28046.html

57. http://www.indiaenvironmentportal.org.in/node/32669

58. *United Nations Global Compact Annual Review, Anniversary Edition, June 2010*, p. 9.

59. Ibid, p. 6.

60. SICCA, "Making Sense of CSR-Sustainability Reports, 2010," www.sicca.ca.org.

Bibliography

About ITTO. *International Tropic Timber Association.* http://www.itto.int/en/ about_itto/.

Abrash, Abigail. "The Amungme, Kamoro & Freeport: How Indigenous Papuans Have Resisted the World's Largest Gold and Copper Mine." *Cultural Survival Quarterly* 25, no. 1, (2001): 38–43.

Alfaro, Laura, and Andres Rodriguez-Clare. "Multinationals and Linkages: An Empirical Investigation." *Economia* 4, no. 2 (2004): 113–156.

Akerlof, George. A. "The Market for 'Lemons': Quality Uncertainty and the Market Mechanism." *Quarterly Journal of Economics* 84, no. 3, (1970): 488–500.

All Africa, Inc. "PMMC in Dubious Sale of 'Conflict' Stones?" *Africa News: Ghanaian Chronicle, May 21, 2003.*

———. "Talks Aimed at Stopping 'Blood Diamonds' Flow Underway." *Africa News*, April 30, 2003.

Allard, Tom. "Nine Slain in 'Inside Job' Attacks on Jakarta Hotels." *Agence France Presse*, July 18, 2009.

Amnesty International. "Kimberley Process: An Amnesty International Position Paper." June, 21, 2006, http://www.amnestyusa.org/document. php?lang=e&id=ENGPOL300242006.

Anderson, Rory E. "Conflict Diamonds: The Problem Persists Despite Progress." Africa Policy Forum, July 5, 2007, http://forums.csis.org/africa/?p=41.

Andreoni, James, and Martin C. McGuire. "Identifying the Free Riders: A Simple Algorithm for Determining Who Will Contribute to a Public Good." *Journal of Public Economics, Amsterdam* 51, no. 3, (1993): 447–455.

Annandale, David, Angus Morrison-Saunders, and George Bouma. "The Impact of Voluntary Environmental Protection Instruments on Company Environmental Performance." *Business Strategy and the Environment* 13, no. 1, (2004): 1–12.

Anonymous. "Controlling Diamonds." *Washington Post*, November 29, 2004, A18.

———. "'Foreign Countries' Could Be Behind Indonesia Mine Attacks: Minister." *Agence France Presse*, July 16, 2009.

———. "Indonesia Sees Need for More Troops in Papua." *Agence France Presse*, March 23. 2010.

———. "Millions Paid for Mine." *Herald Sun*, March 14, 2003, http://www.lexisnexis.com/ us/.

———. "Missing Bullets Mystery." *Herald Sun*, July 14, 2009.

———. "Myanmar's Upstream Sector Hobbled." *Oil & Gas Journal* 98, no. 26 (2000): 24–27.

———. "Six Hurt in Latest Attack on Papua Mine." H*obart Mercury* (Australia), January 25, 2010.

Anonymous. "The Cartel Isn't Forever." *Economist*, July 15, 2004.

Ansley, Greg. "Cleanup for Australian Construction." *New Zealand Herald*, May 7, 2003.

BBC Monitoring Asia Pacific. "Indonesia: Protesters End Blockade of U.S. Mine." *Jakarta Post*, February 26, 2006. Excerpt from article by Tb. Arie Rukmantara, "Stone Fire' Ends Freeport Standoff." *Jakarta Post* website.

BankTrack *Annual Assessment Report.* "Principles, Profits, or PR? Three P investments under the Equator Principles." http://www.banktrack.org/download/going_around_in_circles.

Barboza, David, and Story, Louise. "Toy Making in China, Mattel's Way." *New York Times,* July 26, 2007, http://www.nytimes.com/2007/07/26/business/26toy.html?_r=1.

Barrientos, Stephanie. "Globalization and Ethical Trade: Assessing the Implications for Development." *Journal of International Development,* 12, no. 4, (2000): 559–570.

Bates, Rob Bates. "PBS Airs Conflict Diamond Program." *Jewelers Circular Keystone,* May 1, 2003, p. 58.

Baue, William. "Mining Industry Reports on Its Problems, but Remains Vague on Solutions." *Social Funds* (2002), http://www.socialfunds.com/news/save.cgi?sfArticleId=837.

Beltran, Javier. *Indigenous and Traditional Peoples and Protected Areas: Principles, Guidelines and Case Studies.* (Washington, DC: Island Press, 2000).

Block, Robert, and Daniel Pearl. "Bin Laden Is Backed by Rare Blue Gem Called Tanzanite: Much-Smuggled Mineral Is Seen as Source of Support. 'Yes, People Here Are Trading for Osman.'" *Wall Street Journal Europe,* November 16, 2001.

Bonime-Blanc, Andrea, and Mark Brzezinski. "A New Era in Anti-Corruption: Governments Get Serious About Enforcement." Conference Board Executive Action Report (2010).

Botz, Dan La. "Sewing Alliances: Anti-Sweatshop Activism in the United States: The Race, Poverty Environment." (2007), http://www.urbanhabitat.org/files/RPE14–1_LaBotz-s.pdf.

Brown, Paul. "Oil Money Threatens to Make Killing Fields of Kazakhstan: Wild East Could End the West's Dependence on OPEC but at a Heavy Cost." *Guardian,* December 4, 2002, http://www.lexisnexis.com/us/lnacademic/search/homesubmitForm.do.

Bruno, Kenny, and Joshua Karliner. "Tangled up in Blue: Corporate Partnerships at the United Nations." Transnational Resource and Action Group, September 2000, http://s3.amazonaws.com/corpwatch.org/downloads/tangled.pdf.

Bryce, Robert. "Struck by a Golden Spear." *Guardian* (London), January 17, 1996.

Casey, Nicholas, and Andy Pasztor. "Safety Agency, Mattel Clash over Disclosures." *Wall Street Journal,* September 4, 2007.

Carroll, Lewis. *Alice's Adventures in Wonderland & Through the Looking Glass.* (New York: The New American Library, 1960), 186.

Cattaui, Maria Livanos. "Yes to Annan's 'Global Compact' If It Isn't a License to Meddle." *International Herald Tribune,* July 26, 2000.

60 Minutes. "Cashing in for Profit? Who Cost Taxpayers Billions in Biggest Pentagon Scandal in Decades?" http://www.cbsnews.com/stories/2005/01/04/60II/main664652.shtml.

Cho, Shin. "Agency Costs, Management Stockholding, and Research and Development Expenditures." *Seoul Journal of Economics* 5, no. 2 (1992): 127–152.

Clark, Jeremy. "Fairness in Public Good Provision: An Investigation of Preferences for Equality and Proportionality." *Canadian Journal of Economics* 31, no. 3 (1998): 708–729.

CNNMoney.com. "Mattel CEO to Face Congress, Report Says: Senate and House Panels Set to Have CEO Robert Eckert Testify on the Threat Posed by Toys from China, Company's Reporting Process." (2007), http://money.cnn.com/2007/09/07/news/companies/mattel_congress/ index.htm.

Cockburn, Patrick. "As Much of Georgia Falls Apart, Corruption Stands Firm." *Independent,* November 2003, http://news.independent.co.uk/europe/article79730.ece.

Cockerill, Ian. "Sustainable Development is Good Business Practice." *Miningweb/All Africa Global Media via COMTEX (2002).*

Collingsworth, Terry. "Boundaries in the Field of Human Rights: The Key Human Rights Challenge—Developing Enforcement Mechanisms." *Harvard Human Rights Journal* 15, (2002): 183–203.

Conlon, John R., and Paul Pecorino. "Policy Reform and the Free-Rider Problem." *Public Choice* 120, no. 1–2 (2004): 123–142.

Connor, Tim. "Still Waiting for Nike to Respect the Right to Organize." *Global Exchange,* June 28, 2001.

Conroy, Michael E. *Branded! How the "Certification Revolution" Is Transforming Global Corporations.* (Canada: New Society Publishers, 2007).

Cooper, Cynthia. *Extraordinary Circumstances: The Journey of a Corporate Whistleblower.* (New York: Wiley, 2008).

CorpWatch/Tides Center. "Greenwash + 10: The UN's Global Compact, Corporate Accountability and the Johannesburg Earth Summit." January 2002, http://s3.amazonaws.com/corpwatch.org/downloads/ gw10.pdf.

Cowell, Alan. "Controversy over Diamonds Made into Virtue by De Beers." *New York Times*, August 22, 2000.

Dee, Jonathan. "A Toy Maker's Conscience: How a Business-School Professor and Consultant for Mattel Would Turn 'Made in China' into Something Other Than a Curse." *New York Times Magazine*, December 23, 2007.

Defense Industry Initiative on Business Ethics and Conduct. "Defense Industry Initiatives on Business Ethics and Conduct." (1986), http://www.DII.org.

———. "Origins and Development of the Defense Industry Initiative." (2008), http://www.DII.org.

———. "Public Accountability Report of the Defense Industry Initiative on Business Ethics and Conduct." (2009), http://www.DII.org.

De Matteis, Alessandro. "International Trade and Economic Growth in a Global Environment." *Journal of International Development* 16, no. 4 (2004): 575–588.

Does Certification Make A Difference? (Piracicaba, Brazil: National Union of Book Publishers, 2009), http://www.imaflora.org/arquivos/Does_certification_make_a_ difference.pdf.

Dybvig, Philip H., and Chester S. Spatt. "Adoption Externalities as Public Goods." *Journal of Public Economics* 20, no. 2 (1983): 231–347.

Eisenhardt, Kathleen M. "Agency Theory: An Assessment and Review." *Academy of Management Review* 14, no. 1 (1989): 57–74.

Eisenstein, Zoe. "Report Says Security Guards in Angola Abuse Locals." *Reuters South Africa*, September 8, 2006.

Ellin, Abby. "Suit Says ChevronTexaco Dumped Poisons in Ecuador." *New York Times*, May 8, 2003.

Ethics and Compliance Officer Association Foundation. *The Ethics and Compliance Handbook: A Practical Guide from Leading Organizations.* (Waltham, MA: ECOA Foundation, 2008).

Ethics Resource Center. "Final Report and Recommendations on Voluntary Corporate Policies, Practices, and Procedures Relating to Ethical Business Conduct." Appendix N. President's Blue Ribbon Commission on Defense Management (1986), http://www.DII.org.

Ethics Resource Center, Ethics and Compliance Officer Association, et al. "Leading Corporate Integrity: Defining the Role of the Chief Ethics and Compliance Officer." (2008), http://www.ethics.org/files/u5/CECO_Paper_UPDATED.pdf.

Fabel, Oliver, and Erik. E. Lehmann. "Adverse Selection and the Economic Limits of Market Substitution: An Application to Commerce and Traditional Trade in Used Cars." *Diskussionbeiträge Series I*, no. 301 (2000), http://ssrn.com/abstract=213088.

Fairhall, James. "The Case for the $435 Hammer: Investigation of Pentagon's Procurement." *Washington Monthly*, 1987.

Forest Stewardship Council. "FSC Brings New Prosperity to Legendary Community." (1996), http://www.fsc.org/fileadmin/web-data/public/document_center/publications/case_studies/FSCBringsProsperity_Chico_Mendes_1p.pdf.

———. "Global FSC Certificates: Type and Distribution." (2008), http://www.fsc.org/fileadmin/web-data/public/document_center/powerpoints_graphs/facts_figures/08–12–31_Global_FSC_certificates_-_type_and_distribution_-_FINAL.pdf.

———. *"About FSC: Governance."* http://www.fsc.org/governance.html?&L=0.

Forsyth, Timothy. "Environmental Activism and the Construction Risk: Implications for NGO Alliances." *Journal of International Development* 11, no. 5 (1999): 687–700.

Friends of the Earth. "Behind the Shine: The Real Impact of Shell's Work Around the World." June 2003, http://www.foe.co.uk/resource/reports/behind_shine.pdf.

FSC Chain of Custody Certification, *FSC Rules & Program, Types of FSC Certificates, Chain of Custody.* http://www.fsc.org/134.html?&L=0.

Fuller, Thomas. "Myanmar Auctions Gems, Jade Despite Boycott Calls." *Channel News Asia,* January 20, 2008, http://www.channelnewsasia.com/stories/afp_asiapacific_business/view/ 323717/1/.html.

———. "Signs of Slump at Gem Sale in Myanmar." *New York Times,* November 16, 2007.

Giri, Ananta K. "Rethinking Human Well-Being: A Dialog with Amartya Sen." *Journal of International Development* 12, (2000): 1003–1018.

Global Forest Ownership. *Sustainability.* http://www.internationalpaper.com/US/EN/Company/Sustainability/ForestOwnership.html.

Global Forest Resources Assessment 2005. (Rome: Food & Agriculture Org., 2006), ftp://ftp.fao.org/docrep/fao/008/A0400E/A0400E00.pdf.

Global Forest Resources Assessment 2005: 15 Key Findings. (Rome: Food & Agriculture Org., 2006), http://www.fao.org/forestry/foris/data/fra2005/kf/common/GlobalForestA4-ENsmall.pdf.

Global Witness. "Broken Vows" Exposing the 'Loupe' Holes in the Diamond Industry's Efforts to Prevent the Trade in Conflict Diamonds." March 2004, http://www.globalwitness.org/media_library_detail.php/330/en/broken_vows_diamond_jewellery_retailers_fall_short.

———. *Broken Vows: How Al Qaeda Moved into the Diamond Trade* (London: Global Witness, 2003).

———. *Conflict Diamonds: U.S. Jewelry Retailers Still Not Doing Enough* (London: Global Witness, 2007).

———. *A Crude Awakening: The Role of Oil and Banking Industries in Angolan Civil War and the Plunder of State Assets* (London: Global Witness, 1999).

———. *Déjà Vu: Diamond Industry Still Failing to Deliver on Promises* (London: Global Witness-Amnesty International, 2004).

———. *An Independent Commissioned Review Evaluating the Effectiveness of the Kimberley Process* (London: Global Witness, 2006).

———. *The Key to Kimberley Internal Diamond Controls: Seven Case Studies.* (London: Global Witness, 2004).

———. "Kimberley Process Must Expel Venezuela." Press release, October 9, 2007, http://www.globalwitness.org/media_library_detail.php/606/en/kimberley_process_must_expel_venezuela.

———. "Loopholes in the Kimberley Process: Summary of Trade Statistics Review." October 20, 2007, http://www.globalwitness.org/media_library_detail.php/605/en/loopholes_in_the_kimberley _process_summary_of_trad.

———. "Making It Work: Why the Kimberley Process Must Do More to Stop Conflict Diamonds." (2005), http://www.globalwitness.org/media_library_detail.php/143/en/making_it_work_why_the_kimberley_process_must_do_m.

———. "Rich Man, Poor Man: Development Diamonds and Poverty Diamonds: The Potential for Change in the Artisanal Alluvial Diamond Fields of Africa." 2004, www.pacweb.org/documents/diamonds_KP/rich_man-poor_man-eng_(elect)-Oct2004.pdf.

Global Witness and Amnesty International. "Déjà Vu." October 2004, http://www.global-witness.org/media_library_detail.php/124/en/deja_vu.

———. "Global Witness/Amnesty International U.S. Diamond Retail Survey 2007." February 27, 2007, http://www.globalwitness.org/media_library_detail.php/519/en/global_witness_amnesty_international_us_diamond_re.

Global Witness and Pamela Wexler. "An Independent Commissioned Review Evaluating the Effectiveness of Kimberley Process." (London: Global Witness, 2006), http://www.eldis.org/go/topics/resource-guides/corporate-responsibility/key-issues/extractive-industries/the-diamond-industry/the-kimberley-process&id=22828&type=Document.

Gonzalez, Patrick, et al. "Forest and Woodland Systems." In *Ecosystems and Human Well-Being: Current State and Trends.* (Washington, DC: Island Press, 2005), 585–614. http://www.millenniumassessment.org/documents/document.290.aspx.pdf.

Goudie, Andrew, and Paul Ladd. "Economic Growth, Poverty, and Inequality." *Journal of International Development* 11, no. 2, (1999): 177–195.

Green, George. "Industry Codes of Practice and other Voluntary Initiatives: Their Application to the Mining and Metals Sector." March 2002, http://www.iied.org/pubs/pdfs/ G01042.pdf.

Greenwash Academy Awards Programme. 2002 World Summit. (Johannesburg, South Africa: August 2002), http://www.foe.co.uk/resource/briefings/summit_greenwash_awards.pdf.

Grolin, Jesper. "Corporate Legitimacy in Risk Society: The Case of Brent Spar." *Business Strategy and the Environment* 7, no. 4 (1998): 213–222.

Hamann, Ralph. "Mining Companies' Role in Sustainable Development: The 'Why' and 'How' of Corporate Social Responsibility from Business Perspective." *Development Southern Africa* 20, no. 2 (2003): 237–254.

Harris, Robert G., and James M. Carmen. "Public Regulation of Market Activity: Institutional Typologies of Market Failures." *Journal of Macromarketing*, 3, no. 1 (1983): 49–58.

Haufler, Virginia. "The Kimberley Process Certification Scheme: An Innovation in Global Governance and Conflict Prevention." *Journal of Business Ethics* 89 Supplement (2009): 403–416.

Hays, Constance L. "Mattel Names Kraft Chief to Top Post." *New York Times*, May 18, 2000.

Herrmann, Kristina K. "Corporate Social Responsibility and Sustainable Development: The European Union Initiative as a Case Study." *Indiana Journal of Global Legal Studies* 11, no. 2 (2004): 204–216.

Herve, Moulin. "Uniform Externalities: Two Axioms for Fair Allocation." *Journal of Public Economics* 43, no. 3 (1990): 305–327.

Higman, Sophie et al. *The Sustainable Forestry Handbook*. (London: Earthscan, 2005).

Howard, Jennifer, Jennifer Nash, and John Ehrenfeld. "Industry Codes as Agents of Change: Responsible Care Adoption by U.S. Chemical Companies." *Business Strategy and the Environment* 8, no. 5 (1999): 281–295.

ICCA's 2nd International Conference on Globalization and the Good Corporation, June 26–28, 2007.

Imbun, Benedict Y. "Cannot Manage Without the 'Significant Other.' " *Journal of Business Ethics* 73, no. 2 (2007): 177–192.

Inderst, Roman. "Matching Markets with Adverse Selection." *Journal of Economic Theory* 121, no. 2 (2005): 145–166.

Innocenti, Nicol D. "Congo Expelled from Kimberley Code." *Financial Times,* July 10, 2004.

International Center for Corporate Accountability, Inc., http://www.sicca-ca.org.

International Crisis Group. "Radicalization and Dialogue in Papua." *Asia Report* No. 188–11, March 2010: 18–24.

Ite, Uwem. E. "Multinationals and Corporate Social Responsibility in Developing Countries: A Case Study of Nigeria." *Corporate Social Responsibility and Environmental Management* 11, no. 1 (2004): 1–11.

Jackson, Paul. "The Role of Government in Business Promotion: The Case of Textiles and Garments." *Journal of International Development* 11, no. 5 (1999): 791–796.

Jenkins, Rhys. "Globalization, Production, Employment, and Poverty: Debates and Evidence." *Journal of International Development* 16, no. 1 (2004): 1–12.

Johnson, Justin. P., and Michael Waldman. "Leasing, Lemons, and Buybacks." *Rand Journal of Economics* 34, no. 2 (2003): 247–263.

Johnston, Michael, and Hao Yufan. "China's Surge of Corruption." *Journal of Democracy* 6, no. 4 (1995): 80–94.

Kanninen, Markku et al. *"Do Trees Grow on Money? The Implications of Deforestation Research for Policies to Promote REDD."* (2007), http://www.cifor.cgiar.org/publications/pdf_files/cop/REDD_paper071207.pdf.

Kapelus, Paul. "Mining, Corporate Social Responsibility, and the 'Community': The Case of Rio Tinto, Richard Bay Minerals, and the Mbonambi." *Journal of Business Ethics* 39, no. 3 (2002): 275–296.

Kapstein, Ethan B. "The Corporate Ethics Crusade." *Foreign Affairs*, 80, no. 5 (2001): 105–120.

Karmini, Niniek. "Indonesia to Deploy Special Police Force After Wave of Shootings at Freeport Mine in Papua." *Canadian Press*, July 16, 2009.

Kazmi, Kristina. "Gunmen Attack Bus at Mine in Indonesian Province of Papua." *IHS Global Insight Daily Analysis*, August 17, 2009, http://global.factiva.com.

Kell, Georg, and David Levine. "The Global Compact Network: An historic Experiment in Learning and Action." *Business and Society Review* 108, no. 2 (2003): 151–181.

Kell, Georg, and John Gerard Ruggie, "Global Markets and Social Legitimacy: The Case of 'Global Compact.'" Paper presented at the international conference "Governing the Public Domain beyond the Era of the Washington Consensus? Redrawing the Line Between the State and the Market," York University Toronto, Canada, November 4–6, 1999, p.10. See also Sandra Tesner and Georg Kell, *The United Nations and the Business.* (New York: St. Martin's Press, 2000); United Nations, *The Global Compact.* (New York, 2000).

Kim, Jae-Cheol. "The Market for 'Lemons' Reconsidered: A Model of the Used Car Market with Asymmetric Information." *American Economic Review* 75, no. 4 (1985): 836–843.

Kimberley Process Certification Scheme Secretariat—Namibia. "Kimberley Process Plenary Session." November 5, 2009, http://www.kimberleyprocess.com/download/getfile/940.

King, David, Michael Sainsbury, and John Kerin. "Telstra to Withdraw Staff from Indonesia: Terror Hits Home, the Fear Spreads." *Australian*, October 18, 2002.

Klein Haarhuis, Carolien M., and Frans Leeuw. "Fighting Governmental Corruption: The New World Bank Programme Evaluated." *Journal of International Development* 16, no. 4 (2004): 547–561.

Kolk, Ans. "Trends in Sustainability Reporting by the Fortune Global 250." *Business Strategy and the Environment* 12, no. 5 (2003): 279–291.

Kolk, Ans, and Rob van Tulder. "Setting New Global Rules? TNCs and Codes of Conduct." *Transnational Corporations (United Nations Conference on Trade and Development)* 14, no. 3 (2005): 1–27.

Korn, Leslie. E. "Community Trauma and Development." *Fourth World Journal* 5, no. 1 (2002): 1–9.

Kotarumalos, Ali. "Timika and Freeport Calm, but Tension Still High After Riotings." *Associated Press*, March 16, 1996.

Kraxner, Florian, Catherine Mater, and Toshiaki Owari. "Green Building Drives Construction Market and Forest Certification: Certified Forest Products Markets, 2007–2008." *UNECE/FAO Forest Products Annual Market Review, 2007–2008.* (2008):1–16, http://www.unece.org/timber/docs/certification/2008-cert.pdf.

Lenox, Michael J., and Jennifer Nash. "Industry Self-Regulation and Adverse Selection: A Comparison Across Four Trade Association Programs." *Business Strategy and Environment* 12, no. 6 (2003): 343–356.

Létourneau, Josée, and Ian Smillie, eds. "Killing Kimberley? Conflict Diamonds and Paper Tigers." Diamonds and Human Security Project, Occasional Paper #15, Partnership Africa Canada, November 2006, http://www.pacweb.org/Documents/diamonds_KP/15_KillingKimberley_Revised%20Edition_Eng-.

Levi Strauss & Co. Global Sourcing and Operating Guidelines. http://www.levistrauss.com/Downloads/GSOG.pdf.

MacKay, Scott W., Angela B. Styles, Carl Buzawa, and Douglas E. Perry. "Mandatory Disclosure: A New Reality." (2008), www.dii.org.

Mahtani, Dino. "Conflict Diamonds Smuggled into Ghana, Says UN Report." *Financial Times*, London, October 7, 2006.

Market Opinion Research. *U.S. National Survey: Public Attitudes on Defense Management, Appendix L. A Quest for Excellence: Final Report to the President.* (1986), www.ndu.edu/library/pbrc/36ex2.pdf.

Markon, Jerry, and Renae Merle. "Former Boeing Executive Pleads Guilty." *Washington Post*, 2004.

Matlack, C., G. Smith, and G. Edmondson. "Cracking Down on Corporate Bribery." *Business Week*, December 6, 2004.

New York Times. "Mattel Sets a Conduct Code for Its Suppliers." November 20, 1997, http://www.nytimes.com/1997/11/20/business/mattel-sets-a-conduct-code-for-its-suppliers.html?pagewanted=1.

McGillivray, Mark, and J. Ram Pillarisetti. "International Inequality in Well-Being." *Journal of International Development* 16, (2004): 563–574.

McIvor, Chris. "The Price of Gold." *New African* no. 396, (2001): 26.

McLean, Bethany, and Peter Elkind. *The Smartest Guys in the Room: The Amazing Rise and Scandalous Fall of Enron*. (New York: Portfolio Hardcover, 2003).

Melrose, Rachel. "Big Business is Usually Seen as Being Interested Only in Making Money, but More and More Companies are Realizing that it Pays to Put Something Back into the Community." *Guardian* (London), March 22, 2004.

Miller, G. Wayne. "Manager's Journal: The Rise and Fall of Toyland's Princess." *Wall Street Journal*, February 7, 2000.

Miller, Jeff. "Bushmen Living: 'I Chose to Call It Stone Age' Said Tonge." Diamonds.net, March 24, 2006, http://www.diamonds.net/news/NewsItem.aspx?ArticleID=14612.

Minerals Council of Australia. "Enduring Value: The Australian Minerals Industry Framework for Sustainable Development." (Australia: Minerals Council of Australia, 2005). http://www.minerals.org.au/__data/assets/pdf_file/0006/19833/EV_SummaryBooklet_June2005.pdf.

Miranda, Marta. "Comments on Mining Certification Evaluation Project (MCEP)." World Resources Institute, January 2004, http://www.minerals.csiro.au/sd/Certification/WRI%20Submission.pdf.

Murphy, Dan. "Violence, a U.S. Mining Giant, and Papua Politics." *Christian Science Monitor* 94, no 196, (2002): 1.

Murty, Sushama, and Robert Russell. "Externality Policy Reform: A General Equilibrium Analysis." *Journal of Public Economic Theory* 7, no. 1 (2005): 117–150.

National Bureau of Economic Research. *Moving Up or Moving Out? Anti-Sweatshop Activists and Labor Outcomes*. NBER Working Paper No. 10492 (Cambridge, MA: 2004), Harrison, Ann & Scorse, J., http://www.nber.org/papers/w10492.

National Research Council Division on Earth and Life Studies Board on Environmental Studies and Toxicology and Polar Research Board Committee. *Cumulative Environmental Effects of Oil and Gas Activities on Alaska's North Slope: Activities on Alaska's North Slope*. (Washington, DC: National Academies Press, 2003).

Neale, Alan. "Organizational Learning in Contested Environments: Lessons from Brent Spar." *Business Strategy and the Environment* 6, no. 2 (1997): 93–103.

Newbold, Jane. "Social Consequences of Mining and Present Day Solutions: Region II in Chile Highlighted." *Sustainable Development* 11, no. 2 (2003): 84–90.

Newell, Peter. "Managing Multinationals: The Governance of Investment for the Environment." *Journal of International Development* 13, no. 7 (2001): 907–919.

Nostromo Research for Society of St. Columban. "Sustainable Development Unsustained: A Critique of the MMSD Project." (London), April 17, 2002.

O'Brien, Timothy L. "U.S. Investigates Payments to Equatorial Guinea." *New York Times*, August 6, 2004.

O'Rourke, Dara. "Outsourcing Regulation: Analyzing Nongovernmental Systems of Labor Standards and Monitoring." *Policy Studies Journal* 31, no. 1, (2003): 1–30.

Organization of Economic Cooperation and Development. "Update of Country Descriptions of Tax Legislation on the Tax Treatment of Bribes to Foreign Public Officials." (2009), http://www.oecd.org/dataoecd/58/10/41353070.pdf.

Otterman, Sharon. "Iraq: Oil for Food Scandal." Council on Foreign Relations (2005), http://www.cfr.org/publication/7631/iraq.html.

Paton, Bruce. "Voluntary Environmental Initiatives and Sustainable Industry." *Business Strategy and the Environment* 9, no. 5, (2000): 328–338.

Partnership Africa America. "The Lost World: Diamond Mining and Smuggling in Venezuela." November 2006, http://www.pacweb.org/Documents/diamonds_KP/16_thelostworld_Eng-Nov2006.pdf.

Partnership Africa Canada. "Killing Kimberley? Conflict Diamonds and Paper Tigers." November 2006, http://www.pacweb.org/Documents/diamonds_KP/15_KillingKimberley_Revised%20Edition_Eng-Nov2006.pdf.

———. "Diamond Industry Annual Review: Sierra Leon 2005." February 2005, http://www.pacweb.org/Documents/annual-reviews-diamonds/SierraLeone_AR_2005-eng.pdf.

———. "Venezuela Drops Out." *Other Facets* 29, February 2009, http://www.pacweb.org/documents/other-facets/OF29-eng.pdf.

———. "Zimbabwe, Diamonds, and the Wrong Side of History." March 2009, http://www.pacweb.org/Documents/diamonds_KP/18_Zimbabwe-Diamonds_March09-Eng.pdf.

Partnership Africa Canada and Global Witness. *"The Key to Kimberley: Internal Diamond Controls-Seven Case Studies." October 2004, http://www.pacweb.org/Documents/diamonds_KP/key_to_Kimberley-eng-elect_Oct2004.pdf.*

Passas, Nikos, and Kimberly Jones, "Commodities and Terrorist Financing: Focus on Diamonds." *European Journal on Criminal Policy and Research* 12, no. 1 (2006):1–33.

Pearlman, Jonathan. "Death in Papua: Political Intrigue Clouds Miner's Murder." *Sydney Morning Herald*, November 21, 2009.

Pellow, David N. "Environmental Justice and the Political Process: Movements, Corporations, and the State." *Sociological Quarterly* 42, no. 1, (2001): 47–65.

President's Blue Ribbon Commission on Defense Management. *A Quest for Excellence: Final Report to the President*. (1986), http://www.ndu.edu/library/pbrc/36ex2.pdf.

"Press Conference by Botswana President on Diamond Certification Process." United Nations Press Conference, December 4, 2006, http://www.un.org/news/briefings/docs/2006/061204_botswana.doc.htm.

Press release. "Failure to Suspend Zimbabwe from Kimberley Process." *Fatal Transactions*, November 8, 2009, http://www.fataltransactions.org/News/2009.

Press release. "Campaigners Call for Urgent Action on Zimbabwe Blood Diamonds and Wider Reform of the Kimberley Process to Prevent Abuse." Kimberley Process Civil Society Coalition, October 29, 2009, http://www.pacweb.org/Documents/Press_releases/2009/KP_Plenary-Zimbabwe-2009–10–29-eng.pdf.

PR Newswire Association LLC. "Mattel, Inc., Launches Global Code of Conduct Intended to Improve Workplace, Workers' Standard of Living." (1997), http://www2.prnewswire.com/cgi-bin/stories.pl?ACCT=104&STORY=/www/story/11–20–97/364032&EDATE=.

Raath, Jan. "Mugabe Faces Blacklist over Rogue Diamonds." *Times Online*, June 11, 2007, http://www.timesonline.co.uk/tol/news/world/africa/article1912990.ece.

Rankin, Aidan. "Mind Who You Call Primitive: The West Papuans Holding a Group of Europeans Are Fighting Against Extermination." *Independent* (London), January 17, 2006.

Rapaport Tradewire. "World Diamond Council Calls for International Government Action on Conflict Diamonds." *Rapaport TradeWire*, September 8, 2000.

Redclift, Michael. "Development and Global Environmental Change." *Journal of International Development* 9, no. 3 (1997): 391–401.

Reed, Julia. "Angola Pays Price for Riches Say Reports." *Financial Times*, August 30, 2006, http://www.ft.com/cms/s/0/f55067e2–384b-11db-ae2c-0000779e2340.html?nclick_check=1.

Reingold, Jonathan. "From Angola to Kazakhstan: How to Cure Corruption in Oil Rich States." *Upside Down World* (May 2004), http://www.upsidedownworld.org/ReingoldOil.htm.

Richards, Matt. "Freeport in Indonesia: Reconciling Development and Indigenous Rights." Report on a Public Forum at the Gorman House Arts Centre. Edited by Pat Walsh and Sharmini Sherrard. (Canberra: Australian Council for Overseas Aid, 1996).

Report by Corpwatch. "UN and Corporations Fact Sheet." (Under Campaigns: Corporate-Free UN), March 22, 2001.

Rieffel, Lex. "Indonesia's Quiet Revolution." *Foreign Affairs* 83, no. 5 (2004): 98–110.

Rodgers, Elizabeth J.A. "Conflict Diamonds: Certification and Corruption. A case study of Sierra Leone." *Journal of Financial Crime* 13, no. 3, (2006): 267–272.

Rodrik, Dani. "Has Globalization Gone Too Far?" (Washington, DC: Institute for International Economics, 1997).

Ruggie, John Gerard. "Global.Governance.net: The Global Compact as Learning Network." *Global Governance* 7, no. 4 (2001): 371–378.

———. "Reconstituting the Global Public Domain: Issues, Actors, and Practices." *European Journal of International Relations* 10, no. 4 (2004): 499–531.

Ryan, Missy. "Jungle Energy Project Sparks Controversy in Peru," *Reuters,* December 2002, http://www.planetark.com/dailynewsstory.cfm/newsid/19097/story.htm.

Sach, Jeffery, and Andrew Warner. "Economic Reform and Process of Global Integration." *Brookings Papers on Economic Activity* no. 1 (1995): 1–118.

Schmitt, Christopher H. "U.S. Wages of Sin: Why Lawbreakers Still Win Government Contracts." *U.S. News and World Report*, May 13, 2002.

Schroeder, Richard A. "Tanzanite as Conflict Gem: Certifying a Secure Commodity Chain in Tanzania." *GeoForum*, 41 no. 1 (2009): 56–65.

Schwartz, Mimi, with Sherron Watkins. *Power Failure: The Inside Story of the Collapse of Enron.* (New York: Doubleday, 2003).

Seccombe, Allan. "Gem Diamonds Sets Up Polishing Business." *MiningMX*, July 23, 2008, http://www.miningmx.com/diamonds/684820.htm.

Schoenberger, Karl. 2000. *Levi's Children: Coming to Terms with Human Rights in the Global Marketplace.* http://books.google.com/books?id=Tak28CiEtnoC&pg=PA73&lpg=PA73&dq=levis+code+of+conduct&source=bl&ots=eMZwQ5BXp7&sig=lZ06E5RaIn-ymMVO7Lui62ra7c8&hl=en&ei=W8MrS_bfG5DFlAfO77mbBw&sa=X&oi=book_result&ct=result&resnum=8&ved=0CCUQ6AEwBw#v=onepage&q=&f=false.

Sethi, S. Prakash. "The Effectiveness of Industry-Based Codes in Serving Public Interest: The Case of International Council on Mining and Metals (ICMM)." *Transnational Corporations* 14, no. 3 (2005): 55–99.

———. "Globalization and the Good Corporation: A Need for Proactive Co-existence." *Journal of Business Ethics* 43, Nos. 1–2 (2003a): 21–31.

———. "Globalization and the Good Corporation: A Need for Proactive Co-Existence." *Journal of Business Ethics* 43, nos. 1–2 (2003b): 21–31.

———. *Setting Global Standards: Guidelines for Creating Codes of Conduct in Multinational Corporations.* (New York: John Wiley & Sons, Inc., 2003).

———. "Corporate Codes of Conduct and the Success of Globalization." *Ethics & International Affairs* 16, no. 1 (2002): 89–106.

———. *Multinational Corporations and the Impact of Public Advocacy on Corporate Strategy: Nestle and the Infant Formula Controversy.* (New York: Springer-Verlag, 1994).

———. "A Conceptual Framework for Environment Analysis of Social Issues and Evaluation of Corporate Response Patterns." *Academy of Management Review* 4, no. 1 (1979): 63–74.

Sethi, S. Prakash, and David. B. Lowry. *"Coping with Cultural Conflicts in International Operation."* In *Europe-Asia Dialogue on Business Spirituality*, 67–88. (Antwerpen-Apeldoom: Garant, 2008).

Sethi, S. Prakash, D. B. Lowry, E. Veral, H. J. Shapiro, and O. Emelianova. "Freeport-McMoRan Cooper & Gold, Inc.: An Innovative Voluntary Code of Conduct to Protect Human Rights, Create Employment Opportunities, and Economic Development of the Indigenous People." *Journal of Business Ethics*, forthcoming, 2011.

Sethi, S. Prakash, E. Veral, H. J. Shapiro, and O. Emelianova. "Mattel, Inc. Global Manufacturing Principles (GMP)–A Life-cycle analysis of a company-based code of conduct in the toy industry." *Journal of Business Ethics*, forthcoming, 2011.

Sethi, S. Prakash, Murray L. Weidenbaum, and Paul F. McCleary. "A Case Study of Independent Monitoring of U.S. Overseas Production: Mattel Independent Monitoring

Council For Global Manufacturing Principles (MIMCO)—Audit Report 1999." *Global Focus* 12, no.1 (2000): 137–152.

Sethi, S. Prakash, and Olga Emelianova. "A Failed Strategy of Using Voluntary Codes of Conduct by the Global Mining Industry." *Corporate Governance: The International Journal of Business and Society* 6, no. 3 (2006): 226–238.

Sethi, S. Prakash, and Oliver Williams. *Economic Imperatives and Ethical Values in Global Business: The South African Experience and International Codes Today.* (Boston: Kluwer Academic Publishers, 2000); paperback version (Notre Dame, IN: University Press, 2001).

Sethi, S. Prakash, and Paul Steidlmeier. *Up Against the Corporate Wall: Cases in Business and Society, 6th ed.* (Englewood Cliffs, NJ: Prentice-Hall, 1997).

Sethi, S. Prakash, and Dow Votaw. *The Corporate Dilemma: Traditional Values and Contemporary Problems.* (Englewood Cliffs, NJ: Prentice-Hall, 1973).

SICCA. "Making Sense of CSR-Sustainability Reports, 2010." http://www.sicca-ca.org/scsr_monitor.php.

Simpson, G.R. "Multinational Companies Unite to Fight Bribery." *Wall Street Journal*, January 27, 2005.

Sinclair, Penny, and Julia Walton. "Environmental Reporting Within the Forest and Paper Industry." *Business Strategy and the Environment* 12, no. 5 (2003): 326–337.

Smillie, Ian. "Viewpoint: Conflict Diamonds—Unfinished Business." International Development Research Center, June 7, 2002, http://www.idrc.ca/en/ev-5505-201-1-DO_TOPIC.html.

Smith, Glenn. "Company Codes of Conduct and International Standards: An Analytical Comparison." *World Bank Group*, Part II, March 2004.

South Africa News Channel. "Botswana Bushmen Being Blocked from Going Home." *South Africa News Channel*, January 4, 2007, http://www.news-channel.co.za/Politics/Bushmen.html.

Staff Reporter. "Papuans Demand Closure of U.S. Mine in Indonesia." *Daily Pak Banker*, December 22, 2009.

State of the World's Forests 2007. (Rome: Food & Agriculture Org., 2007), ftp://ftp.fao.org/docrep/fao/009/a0773e/a0773e08.pdf.

Stevenson, Richard W. "Pentagon Disciplines GE for Bribe Scandal." *New York Times*, June 3, 1992.

Stiglitz, Joseph. E. *Globalization and Its Discontents.* (New York: W.W. Norton & Company, 2002).

Story, Louise. "Mattel in Another Recall, Citing Lead in Toys From China." *New York Times*, September 5, 2007, http://query.nytimes.com/gst/fullpage.html?res=9F07E7DF103AF936A3575AC0A9619C8B63.

Story, Louise, and David Barboza. "Mattel Recalls 19 Million Toys Sent from China." *New York Times,* August 15 2007, http://www.nytimes.com/2007/08/15/business/worldbusiness/15imports.html?ex=1344830400&amp;amp;amp;amp;en=18d94724a4755843&ei=5090.

Swanepoel, Esmarie. "Gem Diamonds Says Plans to Beneficiate in Dubai, Mauritius on Hold," *Mining Weekly*, May 19, 2009, http://www.miningweekly.com/article/gem-diamonds-plans-to-beneficiate-in-dubai-mauritius-on-hold-2009–05–19.

Switzer, Jason. "Armed Conflict and Natural Resources: The Case of the Minerals Sector." *Mining, Minerals and Sustainable Development* (MMSD) no. 12 (2001), http://www.iied.org/mmsd/wp/index.html/.

Symon, Fiona. "Gem Specialist Puts Ethics on Agenda." *Financial Times*, August 3, 2005.

Tamm, Ingrid. J. "Diamonds in Peace and War: Severing the Conflict Diamond Connection." World Peace Foundation, Report 30, January 2002, p. 64.

Tapper, Richard. "Voluntary Agreements for Environmental Performance Improvement: Perspectives on the Chemical Industry's Responsible Care Programme." *Business Strategy and the Environment* 6, no. 5 (1997): 287–292.

Tauli-Corpuz, Vicki, and Danny Kennedy. "Native Reluctance to Join Mining Industry Initiatives: An Activist Perspective." *Cultural Survival Quarterly*, Spring 25, no. 1 (2001).

Taylor, Ian, and Gladys Mokhawa. (2003) "Not Forever: Botswana, Conflict Diamonds, and the Bushmen," *African Affairs* 102, no. 407 (2003): 261–283.

Tesner, Sandrine, and Georg Kell. *The United Nations and Business: A Partnership Recovered.* (New York: Palgrave Macmillan, 2000).

The Global Compact. Published by the Global Compact Office, United Nations, January 2001. See also the Global Compact website, http://www.unglobalcompact.org

The Press Trust of India Limited. "Mattel Apologizes to China on Toy Recalls; Four Arrested." (2007), http://www.hindustantimes.com/News-Feed/corporatenews/Mattel-apologises-to-China-on-toy-recalls-four-arrested/Article1-249069.aspx.

Thomas, Evan, Barrett Seaman, and Bruce Van Voorst. "Defensive About Defense." *Time*, March 10, 1986.

Thomas, Gareth. *Fourth Global Environment Outlook Report.* (October 2007), https://www.dfid.gov.uk/Media-Room/Speeches-and-articles/2007-to-do/Speech-by-Gareth-Thomas-Minister-for-Trade-and-Development-at-the-launch-of-the-fourth-Global-Environment-Outlook-report-25-October-2007/.

Thompson, Duane R. "The No-Punch-Back Theory of Regulation." *Journal of Financial Planning* 16, no. 12 (2003): 22–24.

Thompson, Geoff. "Military, Police 'Among Suspects' in Freeport Killings." *Australian Broadcast Corporation*, July 13, 2009, http://www.abc.net.au/news/stories/2009/07/13/2623717 .htm?section=world.

Toeffler, Barbara Ley, and Jennifer Reingold. *Final Accounting: Ambition, Greed and the Fall of Arthur Andersen.* (New York: Currency Doubleday, 2003).

Townsend, Janet G. "Are Non-Governmental Organizations Working in Development a Transnational Community?" *Journal of International Development* 11, no. 4 (1999): 613–623.

Treadgold, Tim. "Stop Worrying and Love Uranium." *Courier Mail (Queensland, Australia)*, June 3, 2005.

United Nations. *Addressing Business Leaders at Global Compact Summit, Secretary-General Says Experience Shows that Voluntary Initiatives 'Can and Do Work'.* United Nations Press Release SG/SM/9387 ECO/71 (2004), http://www.un.org/News/Press/docs/2004/sgsm9387.doc.htm.

United Nations Children's Fund (UNICEF). Statement of UNICEF Executive Director Carol Bellamy to Harvard International Development Conference on Sharing Responsibility: Public, Private, and Civil Society. Cambridge, MA., April 16, 1999, http://www.unicef.org/exspeeches/99esps.htm.

United Nations Department of Public Information, News, and Media Division. "World Population Will Increase by 2.5 Billion by 2050; People over 60 to Increase by More Than 1 Billion." *Press Release POP/952 (2007)*, http://www.un.org/News/Press/docs/2007/pop952.doc.htm.

United Nations General Assembly. "The Role of Diamonds in Fueling Conflict." November 29, 2006, 1–5; http://www.kimberleyprocess.com/background/index_en.html; Global Witness, Broken

United Nations Global Compact Annual Review—Anniversary Edition, United Nations Global Compact Office. United Nations, New York, June 2010, pp. 9–10.

United Nations Press Conference. "Press Conference by Botswana President on Diamond Certification Process." United Nations Press Conference (2006), http://www.un.org/News/briefings/docs/2006/061204_Botswana .doc.htm.

U.S. Consumer Product Safety Commission. "CPSC Announces Hearing on Dangers of Lead Paint." (1976), http://www.cpsc.gov/CPSCPUB/PREREL/prhtml76/76048.html.

United States Department of Labor. "Chronology on Clinton Administration's No Sweat Initiative." (1997), http://actrav.itcilo.org/actrav-english/telearn/global/ilo/guide/apparell.htm.

United States General Accounting Office. "Fraud in Government Programs: How Extensive Is It? How Can It Be Controlled?" GAO/AFMD-81–57 (1981), pp. 28–30.

United States Government Accountability Office. "Conflict Diamonds: Agency Actions Needed to Enhance Implementation of the Clean Diamond Trade Act." GAO-06–978, September 2006.

———. "Defense Contracting Integrity: Opportunities Exist to Improve DOD's Oversight of Contractor Ethics Programs." Report to Congressional Committees (2009.

United States Product Safety Commission. 2009. "Mattel, Fisher-Price to Pay $2.3 Million Civil Penalty for Violating Federal Lead Paint Ban." (2009), http://www.cpsc.gov/cpsc-pub/prerel/prhtml09/09237.html.

van den Bosch, Frans A.J., and Cees B.M. van Riel. "Buffering and Bridging as Environmental Strategies of Firms." *Business Strategy and the Management* 7, no. 1 (1998): 24–31.

van Marrewijk, Marcel. "Concepts and Definitions of CSR and Corporate Sustainability: Between Agency and Communion." *Journal of Business Ethics* 44, no. 2/3 (2003): 95–105.

Vincke, Francois, and Fritz Heimann. "Fighting Corruption: A Corporate Practices Manual." *Transparency International (2003),* http://www.transparency.de/Vincke-Francois-und-Heimann.613.0.html.

Wayne, Leslie. "A Growing Military Contract Scandal." *New York Times*, November 8, 2004.

White, Howard. "Pro-Poor Growth in a Globalized Economy." *Journal of International Development* 13, no. 5 (2001): 549–569.

Wilson, Charles. "The Nature of Equilibrium in Markets with Adverse Selection." *Bell Journal of Economics* 11, no. 1 (1980): 108–130.

Wilson, Forbes. *The Conquest of Copper Mountain* (New York: Atheneum, 1981); Mealey, George. *Grasberg.* (New Orleans: Freeport-McMoRan Copper & Gold, 1996). In addition to the size of the operation, the Grasberg mine is an unbelievably complex engineering venture. The Grasberg deposit is located 13,000 feet above sea level in an area in which about 300 inches of rain falls each year. Building the mine was a remarkable achievement; keeping it running is nearly as daunting.

Wolf, Charles, Jr. "A Theory of Nonmarket Failure: Framework for Implementation Analysis." *Journal of Law and Economics* 22, no. 1, (1979): 107–139.

Wolfe, Regina Wentzel, and Patricia W. Werhane. "Academic Institutions and the United Nations Global Compact: The Principles for Responsible Management Education." In Andreas Rasche and Georg Kell, eds. *The United Nations Global Compact: Achievements, Trends and Challenges.* (Cambridge: Cambridge University Press, 2010), pp. 149–153, 159–160.

Wronunghton, Leslie. "World Bank to Be More Selective in Oil, Gas Loans." *Reuters*, June 18, 2004.

Yerton, Stewart. "And Then the Solders Came." *Times-Picayune*, January 28, 1996.

Yoder, Brandon. "Indigenous People and Oil Production in Ecuador's Oriente." *Fourth World Journal* 5, no. 1 (2002): 80–97.

Young, Scott T. "Leading Environmental Change: The Case of the Global Mining Industry." *Review of Business* 26, no. 1 (2005): 34–38.

Yuspeh, Alan R. "Development of Corporate Compliance Programs: Lessons Learned from the DII Experience." Presentation to the American Corporate Counsel Association, October 24, 1997.

Zaidi, S. Akbar. "NGO Failure and the Need to Bring Back the State." *Journal of International Development* 11, no 2 (1999): 259–271.

Contributors

S. Prakash Sethi is University Distinguished Professor of Management at the Zicklin School of Business, Baruch College, The City University of New York. He is also Forrest Mars, Sr. Visiting Professor of Ethics, Politics and Economics at Yale University, New Haven,CT. Dr. Sethi enjoys international recognition as a pre-eminent researcher and scholar in the areas of corporate strategy, international business, globalization and the multinational corporation, self-regulation and voluntary codes of company and industry conduct, environmental protection and sustainable business, corporate social responsibility and accountability, and ethical norms of business conduct. He has published 25 books and over 140 articles in professional and scholarly journals. He has done pioneering work in creating and implementing international corporate codes of conduct and global supply-chain management. His most recent project involves content analysis of corporate social responsibility-sustainability reports. The most recent report involved 514 corporations from a data base of over 1300 companies from around the world. In addition to his academic responsibilities, Dr. Sethi is the founder and President of Sethi International Center for Corporate Accountability Inc., (SICCA). SICCA is an independent non-profit think tank, which undertakes cutting-edge research and public policy advocacy in the area of enhanced corporate accountability through voluntary corporate codes of conduct in the national and international arena. Under his direction, SICCA has conducted independent external audits of major multinational corporations for compliance verification with the companies' international codes of conduct in a number of countries around the world.

Andrea Bonime-Blanc has served as general counsel, chief ethics and compliance officer, corporate secretary, and risk officer for several global organizations for the past fifteen years. She is chairwoman of the board of directors of the Ethics & Compliance Officer Association. She has authored numerous books and articles on business ethics, compliance, risk management, governance, constitutional change and democratization, and speaks and teaches frequently on these topics. She holds a joint JD and PhD from Columbia University, New York.

Olga Emelianova has been involved in environmental, social and governance (ESG) research and performance monitoring for over 10 years. Currently as a Senior ESG Research Associate at MSCI, inc., she evaluates corporate exposure to regulatory and operational risks related to ESG issues. Until 2010, she was Director of Project Services at the International Center for Corporate Accountability, a not-for-profit monitoring and research group which evaluated corporate and industry-wide social responsibility initiatives. Ms. Emelianova holds an MBA degree from Zicklin School of Business, CUNY.

David Lowry is an Episcopal priest. He is Dean of the Mercer School of Theology (Garden City, New York) and Rector of Christ Church, Manhasset, New York. Previously he served as Director of the Desmond Tutu Center for Peace and Reconciliation at the General Theological Seminary in New York. From 1990 to 2004, Dr. Lowry was a vice president for Freeport-McMoRan Copper & Gold, Inc., where he had responsibility for human resources, community development and human rights compliance, and was President of the Freeport-McMoRan Foundation. Dr. Lowry has degrees in classical languages, theology and history, including a Ph.D from Indiana University.

Donald H. Schepers Dr. Schepers is a Professor in the Department of Management at Baruch College, City University of New York, where he also serves as Director of the Robert Zicklin Center for Corporate Integrity. His field of specialization is corporate social responsibility, and has taught this and business strategy at undergraduate, graduate, and executive education levels. He has published in *Organizational Behavior and Human Decision Processes*, *Business and Society Review*, *Business and Society*, *Journal of Business Ethics*, *Corporate Governance: The International Review of Business in Society*, *Human Resource Management Review*, and *Journal of Behavioral and Applied Management*. He is a member of the Society of Business Ethics, the Academy of Management, the Eastern Academy of Management, the International Society for Business, Economics and Ethics, and the International Association of Business and Society.

Harris Jack Shapiro is Professor and Chairperson Emeritus of Management and former Director of the Center for Management Research, Baruch College, CUNY. He is currently a Senior Research Fellow with SICCA. Before joining the university faculty, was President of Ogden Technology Laboratories, Inc., a subsidary of the Ogden Corporation. Degrees earned are a BME, MBA and Ph.D. (CUNY) and an MS in Management Engineering, (LIU) and he is a Professional Engineer. Co-author and co-editor of three books and over sixty articles published in journals such as Management Science and Academy of Management Journal. He has been a director of several corporations and is the recipient of numerous honors.

Emre Veral is Professor of Operations Management at Baruch College. He currently serves as Deputy Chair of the Management Department, coordinator of the Operations Management programs, and mentor for the Baruch Small Business development center. Professor Veral's academic interests concentrate on operations management with special research focus on improving productivity and efficiency. His contributions to academic research and industry practice include several publications and consulting projects involving scheduling, inventory, forecasting, and capacity management. Professor Veral also serves as Senior Research Fellow at the International Center for Corporate Accountability, and has been involved in corporate code of conduct monitoring of offshore manufacturers.

Tensie Whelan serves as the president of the Rainforest Alliance. She has been involved with the Rainforest Alliance since 1990, first as a board member, and then later as a consultant, becoming the executive director in 2000. Whelan has been working in the environmental field for more than 25 years during which time she served as the vice president of conservation information at the National Audubon Society and executive director of the New York League of Conservation Voters. Whelan also worked as a journalist in Costa Rica, and was the managing editor of Ambio—an international environmental journal based in Stockholm. Prior to joining the Rainforest Alliance as its executive director, Whelan worked as a management consultant to nonprofit organizations such as the Environmental Defense Fund.

Whelan serves on the boards of Social Accountability International, International Institute for Sustainable Development and the sustainable agriculture advisory board for Unilever, and is the co-chair of the steering committee of the Sustainable Food Lab. She holds an M.A. in International Communication from American University's School of International Service and a B.A. in Political Science from New York University.

Index